BUSINESS MANAGEMENT

An Introduction to Business and Industry

COLLEGE OUTLINE SERIES

BUSINESS MANAGEMENT

JOHN A. SHUBIN

BARNES & NOBLE, Inc. • New York

Publishers   •   Booksellers   •   Since 1873

ABOUT THE AUTHOR

JOHN A. SHUBIN is President of
JOHN SHUBIN ECONOMIST, INC.,
a Los Angeles-based consulting firm. He
served the United Nations as a consulting
industrial planner. Formerly, Dr. Shubin
was Professor of Economics at New York
University, where he specialized in the
fields of Industrial and Managerial Economics and in Economic Growth and Development. He received his B.A. degree
from U.C.L.A. and his M.B.A. and Ph.D.
from the University of Southern California. Dr. Shubin has worked as a methods
analyst in industry for a number of years
and has acquired a background that has
proved valuable to his writings in the fields
of business management and industry. He
is the author of *Managerial and Industrial
Economics* (The Ronald Press Co.) and
senior co-author of *Plant Layout* (Prentice-
Hall, Inc.).

Preface

This book endeavors to advance efficient management methods and has been written on the premise that scientific management is best mastered when its principles and techniques are integrated with analytic approaches to all phases of business. It offers step-by-step survey procedures for setting up or improving business functions and systems—for example, it shows how to conduct a promotion study before starting a business, how to select location and equipment, set up the necessary departments (sales, production planning, purchasing), and design a budget system. It incorporates managerial principles and practices at the point in each survey where they are needed and ready for use, thus demonstrating how to apply principles on a practical basis for solving managerial problems.

The book, too, presents methods for dealing with external economic forces that affect business plans and operations. It shows, for instance, how to set or adjust prices, forecast sales, and adapt business operations to seasonal variations. In "wage survey" it shows how to design the company wage structure in relation to both internal and external conditions. In "break-even analysis" it provides a graphic device for appraising alternative business programs and for predicting the effect of cost and price changes on profits.

Business Management covers concisely the subject matter of college Business Organization and Industrial Management courses; but, in addition, it is a guide to working out business problems—one can apply its procedures and prepare survey reports. Thus, it is a useful accompaniment to books on business case problems. In order that the student may gauge his progress, review and discussion questions are offered for each chapter and a final examination (with answers to the questions) is presented at the end of the volume.

The author wishes to acknowledge the suggestions offered by Dr. Samuel Smith and Mrs. Carol Ann Luten of the Barnes and Noble editorial staff which facilitated the preparation of the manuscript for publication.

J.A.S.

vii

Table of Contents

Key Topics in Business Management

(Survey procedures incorporated in * topics)

Key Topics

See index for additional topics and breakdowns.

1: The Rise of Scientific Management

To practice the art of scientific management, the businessman, engineer, or student must acquire managerial insight. He must know how scientific management evolved and must master its analytic methods if he is to make fruitful contributions to business operations and reap commensurate rewards. The scientific management movement evolved during the first half of the twentieth century to meet the challenge of the increasing complexity of modern business enterprise and grew from the recognition of the possibility for more efficient operation.

THE MANAGEMENT MOVEMENT

The growth of the factory system of output created the complex managerial problem of combining and co-ordinating the factors of production (i.e., man, materials, and machines), a problem that was a natural consequence of increased plant size, greater diversity and volume of manufactured products, intricacy of fabrication processes, and specialization of labor. The science of management seriously lagged behind the technical developments of the new industrial era.

The manager in the eighteenth and nineteenth centuries was usually autocratic, forceful, and self-trained. In managing business he relied on intuitive judgment and "rule-of-thumb" practices and procedures. Although specialists in manufacturing techniques were available, there were no specialists trained in management. Managerial functions and practices were frequently improvised to meet problems as they arose. Such improvised methods became fixed managerial practice, and re-examination and reappraisal of them were seldom considered. But the complexities of present-day enterprise demand the attention of specialists in both management and production operations. These specialists provide effective direction and co-ordination of departmentalized functions (finance, engineering, procurement, manufacturing, sales, and personnel). The need for improved business operation can be met by applying the analytic method of scientific management.

Taylor's Pioneer Work. The management movement began around the turn of the century when Frederick W. Taylor critically questioned the practices of tradition-bound management and resorted to scientific analysis for the formulation of better managerial methods. His early conclusions (1880–1890) led eventually to the science of management, of which he is the recognized founder. His ideas took form in the following fundamental principles, which he termed the "duties of management":

> *First.* They [managers] develop a science for each element of a man's work, which [science] replaces the old rule-of-thumb method.
> *Second.* They scientifically select and then train, teach, and develop the workman, whereas in the past he chose his own work and trained himself as best he could.
> *Third.* They heartily co-operate with the men so as to insure all the work being done in accordance with the principles of the science which has been developed.
> *Fourth.* There is an almost equal division of the work and the responsibility between the management and the workmen. The management takes over all work for which they are better fitted than the workmen, while in the past almost all of the work and the greater part of the responsibility were thrown upon the man.[1]

The foregoing principles, and their limited application by Taylor, were only the beginning of a revolutionary approach which challenged traditional business methods. After Taylor's retirement, a gradually expanding group of followers continued to develop the science of management. Although their systems and methods differed from Taylor's in detail, they were fundamentally similar and had the same objectives.

Scientific Management. Present-day scientific management utilizes a body of principles and practices applicable to business operations, such as line-and-staff organization, methods analysis, standardization of procedures, incentive plans, statistical quality control, and budgeting. It employs a scientific approach for solving the problems of business operation and for advancing the development of managerial techniques. Scientific management uses an objective, experimental method

[1] Frederick Winslow Taylor, *The Principles of Scientific Management* (Part 1 of *Scientific Management*) (New York: Harper and Bros., 1947), pp. 36–37.

whereby it begins with a problem or need; collects, classifies, and analyzes data; and formulates a tentative principle or law which it then applies in order to determine its validity and usefulness. In its procedure, scientific management draws upon the findings of such other sciences as economics, statistics, and industrial psychology.

Procedure for a Scientific Managerial Survey. (1) State concisely the business problem, need, or goal (e.g., the setting up of a production-control system or the building of employee morale). (2) Compile all data relevant to the stated purpose; i.e., apply the latest fact-finding and statistical procedures—using financial statements, flow process charts, job analysis, sampling, statistical correlations. (3) Classify and thoroughly analyze the data in order to discover a program of action, a system of practices, or a technique. (4) Formulate carefully the new plan, standard procedure, or technique that is based upon the factual relationships which have been found. (5) Apply the scheme or solution; follow up in order to check on effectiveness in achieving the desired goal; and modify, when necessary, in the light of new findings or changed conditions.

In short, scientific management is not a system with a definitely fixed content and always applicable in all its features; it is rather a system for approaching and solving managerial problems—a system from which grow definite managerial practices suitable for particular situations. The scientific-management approach can be applied to many kinds of surveys: for example, it can be used to formulate procedures for setting up an organization structure, for laying out a new plant, or for designing a wage system. Methods for making these and other special-purpose surveys are outlined in subsequent chapters. In each case the survey procedure derives from the five steps listed above.

"Operations Research"—an Extension of Scientific Management. Through "operations research" management can solve some of its specific tangible problems with greater than ordinary precision. Operations research applies mathematical and experimental techniques (as practiced in physics and biology) to the study of operations, whether business, governmental, or military.[2] Hence, operations research is an extension of the scientific management approach to include advanced mathematical techniques in order to achieve more precise solutions of certain types of business problems.

[2] Operations research was first applied in World War II by teams of scientists engaged by the government to work up recommendations for the improvement of military activities.

Operations research is suitable for problems that have certain characteristics. (1) The problem should not be too broad or indefinite—that is, it should be readily definable so that results can be appraised on the basis of explicit criteria. (2) The problem must consist of tangible, measurable factors so that data can be collected for quantitative study. (3) The problems should offer opportunity for decision between alternative lines of action so that management can choose the one that measures up best in terms of company goals.

Operations research can, therefore, solve such specific problems as deciding how much to spend for maintenance or when to replace equipment; determining the quantity of materials to order in the light of the minimal inventory required for production; and determining when to work the plant overtime or when to subcontract work.

In conducting operations research, analysts [3] generally formulate a model—a simplified representation of the operation which contains the factors of primary importance to the problem. They often set up a model or theory in terms of mathematical equations. The model is usually built up from observed data or experience. The theory describing the operation must always be verifiable experimentally.

Depending on the type of problem, the analyst may apply any number of mathematical techniques. Through a sampling study of scrap volume in previous years, for example, it is possible to determine an allowance for process scrap; or through "statistical quality control," it is possible to reduce scrap (see page 169). Through "linear programming"—the relating of a number of interdependent factors to get the best results—it is possible to schedule job orders on several machines in such manner as to obtain minimum over-all processing time. The analyst, too, can apply such mathematical tools as "quantifying"— the numerical expression of factors that affect the operation; the "Monte Carlo" method—a technique for predicting results through random sampling rather than through mathematical models; and the "game theory"— a specific application of the law of probability.

THE CURRENT PICTURE OF BUSINESS MANAGEMENT

The position of the professional manager evolved with the growth of industry and the trend among large corporations toward the separation of ownership from control. The shifting of control to hired profes-

---

[3] The analyst may be an industrial engineer or a management consultant who has mastered advanced mathematical techniques, or he may be a scientist versed in experimental research.

sional management resulted in wider use of scientific methods of management. Today business management is concerned not only with the initial promotion of enterprise and its internal operation but also with the problem of adapting, expanding, or contracting the firm whenever changing economic conditions and environmental influences require such action.

Functions of Management. Business management is generally divided into two major categories: (1) administration and (2) management proper. Although each has its area of concentration and responsibility, successful enterprise requires close integration of over-all planning and detailed execution.

FUNCTIONS OF ADMINISTRATION. Administration (or "top management") in industry has as its functions the over-all determination of policies and major objectives and the co-ordination of finance, production, and distribution. These functions are assumed by the board of directors and major executives (the president, general managers, and, usually, vice-presidents). Administrators define the intrinsic purpose of the company, establish the primary objectives, formulate the general plan of organization and procedure, inaugurate the broad program, and approve the specific major projects in the program.

FUNCTIONS OF MANAGEMENT PROPER. The execution of the over-all policies and plans determined by administration is the function of management proper—division and department heads, superintendents, foremen, and, sometimes, top executives (often identified as "operating executives"), for company officers frequently serve in an administrative capacity for making over-all policy as well as in a managerial capacity for implementing policy.

FUNCTIONS OF MANAGEMENT CONSULTANTS. The management consultant is an outside expert who specializes in the art of management (or in some phase of it) and sells his services to a firm for the solution of managerial problems and for the achievement of efficient operation. His profession has evolved for two reasons: (1) few small or medium-sized enterprises have a trained group of management specialists who can effectively analyze and appraise the over-all situation and make important recommendations and (2) many executives tied down with managerial responsibilities lack the time to make intensive studies and sometimes lack the detached point of view necessary for an objective appraisal of the results. The consultant surveys methods, practices, and arrangements with a critical attitude that is unhampered by traditional ideas. He attacks each problem from a fresh standpoint and with a

5

background of ideas and experience gained from repeated contact with other organizations. Furthermore, he is comparatively free from the suspicion of prejudice and favoritism which frequently surrounds the recommendations of interested parties within the concern. Ideally, management assigns an inside man to work with the consultant and to follow up new programs and procedures after they have been instituted.

External Influences upon Management. Although business management is concerned primarily with factors internal to the business unit (product design, plant layout, production control, personnel administration), important external factors affect operations and the management of the enterprise as a whole. Top management is not free to formulate policies without regard to these external influences, the more important of which are government regulations (for example, corporation laws, tax levies, decisions of public-utilities commissions, factory laws, and labor legislation), economic fluctuations of the seasonal and business-cycle varieties (changes in market demand and price levels), technological developments, trends in organized labor, and public opinion. Recently there has been more participation by government and organized labor in the management of business enterprises. Management must keep its organization flexible in order to deal effectively with the ever-changing framework of economic, social, and political institutions within which every enterprise operates.[4]

Questions

1. Discuss the factors that have led to the evolution and growth of scientific management.

2. Differentiate between scientific management as a "body of knowledge" and as a "methodology"; illustrate.

3. What are the procedural steps in the "scientific managerial survey"?

4. Explain why scientific management can be applied to the operation of municipalities and government enterprises, hospitals, and farms.

5. (a) What is meant by "operations research"? (b) What kinds of business problems can be solved by operations research?

6. Contrast the functions of "administration" with those of "management proper."

7. What factors in business have led to the growth of the profession of "management consultant"?

8. Discuss the internal and external aspects of modern manufacturing enterprise that make the function of management difficult.

[4] John A. Shubin, *Managerial and Industrial Economics* (New York: Ronald Press, 1961).

2: The Growth of Industry

The most usual means of commercial production before the factory system were the "handicraft" system and the "putting-out," or "cottage," system. The Industrial Revolution gradually displaced these systems of production and ushered in large-scale enterprise. The various forms of business organization, however, developed from the early spread of commerce.

The Early Roots of Business Organization and Management. In England and Western Europe, where production was most advanced during the latter phases of the medieval period, the handicraft system of production preceded the putting-out system. Since there were no clear-cut stages of development, these systems of production, though declining, continued to exist side-by-side with the rise of the factory system in England, on the Continent, and elsewhere.

HANDICRAFT SYSTEM. The business units under the handicraft system were small privately owned shops (sometimes private households) which employed journeymen (workers skilled at given trades) to turn out custom-made products with hand tools. From approximately the fourteenth century until well after the beginning of the factory system in the eighteenth century, consumer goods were produced in this way. Using his own tools, a journeyman carried the fabrication of leather goods, furniture, metalware, or other consumer commodities from the raw-material stage to completion. The designing of the product and the planning of fabrication methods depended upon his own handiwork and ingenuity. Specialization of tasks was not very common. Management was comparatively simple, and the journeyman was left largely to his own initiative.

The business interests and external commercial relations of the handicraft shops were promoted and regulated by *craft guilds*, whose membership included both journeymen and owner-masters in any given vocation (such as carpentry or cobblery). Organized and managed by the members, each association promoted their interests by regulating prices, wages, working conditions, apprenticeships, and the quality of products. Labor relations were simple since the shops were small and little social distinction existed between the journeymen and the masters. Throughout most of the medieval period, *merchant guilds*, representing the traders of a given town, held a monopoly over the town's trade. However, the various craft guilds, in order to avoid the severe regulations of the merchant guilds, began to market their own products and thus gradually brought about the decline of merchant guilds. The craft guilds, during the sixteenth century, eventually gained control over the economic life of the towns.

Putting-out System. The craft guilds were weakened when members, to escape guild regulations, left the towns. The putting-out (or *cottage*) system evolved and was prominent from the sixteenth to about the middle of the eighteenth century. It was marked by the appearance of the middleman-merchant who bought raw materials, "put them out" to workers at their households, and then found a market for the finished products. In some cases the middleman provided hand tools and hand-operated equipment for the craftsman, who thus became gradually separated from the ownership of his tools. Although the putting-out system was time-consuming and the quality of the product difficult to control, it was flexible and it avoided the restrictive practices of the craft guilds. Moreover, business operations were carried out on a broader scale: products were turned out in more variety and in greater volume. The entrepreneur of the putting-out system was the forerunner of the industrialist of the factory system.

Factory System. The factory system made possible the rise of large-scale manufacturing and brought about the managerial problems of co-ordinating and controlling men, materials, and machines in order to attain the desired quantity and quality of goods. These problems gradually led to the development of scientific management and of professional management.

Beginning of the Industrial Revolution. "Industrial Revolution" is the name given to the technological and economic developments that, gathering strength and speed during the eighteenth century and continuing in the nineteenth and twentieth centuries, produced modern large-scale production and business organization. It substituted an essentially self-expanding technology for the relatively static systems of production that had previously existed. Because of a favorable physical and institutional environment, it first evolved in England and then spread to the United States and the Continent. Through a series of inventions (for example, the "spinning jenny," "water frame," "mule," power loom, steam engine, and machine lathe) tools were mechanized and powered. (The steam engine using coal as fuel was the earliest primary source of power.) The more efficient powered machines displaced the hand tools and the skilled labor of the cottage and the handicraft shop. Individuals who possessed or acquired investment funds (industrialists) were able to accumulate these expensive machines, house them in special structures (factories), and profit by the new form of production. Expanding transportation facilities (turnpikes, canals, and railways) broadened the marketing area and linked the sources of coal, iron, and other raw materials with the growing industrial centers.

TREND TOWARD LARGE-SCALE INDUSTRY. The rate of shift from the early manual systems of commercial production to the factory system varied from industry to industry and from region to region. But as it took hold, the Industrial Revolution ran a generally consistent course, at first affecting consumer-goods industries and then capital-goods industries. The textile industry was the first to be affected, then the clothing, metal products, foodstuffs, and transportation industries. Factory output of capital goods (machinery and equipment) and large-scale production of iron and steel have traditionally followed the industrialization of consumer-goods output. It is only in the later stages that mechanized large-scale exploitation spreads to the extractive industries—mining, lumbering, and agriculture. The growth of large-scale industrialization depends not only on the existence of favorable resources, technological development, and savings and investment, but also on the ever-widening scope of the market.

RISE OF AMERICAN INDUSTRY. Because of factors peculiar to America, the industrialization of the United States differed somewhat from that of Europe. The abundance of resources and the comparative scarcity of labor led to the development of machinery, particularly labor-saving, automatic machinery. Relative freedom from feudal traditions allowed industry to seek, largely unhampered, the best and quickest methods. A swiftly growing population in a rich physical environment created a large home market favorable to rapid development of mass-production methods of output, the key to which is the manufacture of standardized interchangeable parts.

PRESENT-DAY INDUSTRIAL TECHNOLOGY. Progress in industrialization has taken new forms. Present-day advances in industrial technology [1]

1 "Industrial technology" may be defined as the application of the analytical methods of science to the industrial arts.

include increasing mechanization; new sources of fuel, new processes, and new materials; new or improved products; and refinement of scientific management. Two or more of these forms of technological progress may be found in almost any industrial innovation. Modern technology and geographic specialization are pushing man toward world-wide integration and interdependence: the tempo of industrialization is being accelerated even in the hitherto underdeveloped areas of the world.

Effects on Production. The rise of the factory system affected production in several ways. (1) Workers were separated from ownership of the tools of production and became dependent on the sale of their labor services to the factory owner. (2) Production became more "roundabout"—machinery and equipment were substituted more and more for labor, thus increasing the proportion of capital and decreasing the proportion of labor required per unit of output. (3) Factory production with its minute division of labor in the fabrication and assembly of standard (interchangeable) parts resulted in a transfer of skill from the worker to the machine, making the quality and quantity of output dependent more upon the machine process than upon the machine operator. (4) Specialization of labor and the transfer of skill to machines decreased the proportion of skilled labor and increased the proportion of semiskilled labor utilized in the output of goods. (5) The complex factory system of production created managerial problems and gradually led to the development of professional and scientific management.

Economic Effects. The economic consequences of industrialization were far-reaching. The most important were these. (1) The more efficient production system led to greater volume output, a higher standard of living, and greater profits which were largely invested in industrial expansion. (2) The joint-stock company and the corporation evolved as the principal means of amassing capital for the exploitation of the new technology. (3) The concentration and urbanization of population in commercial areas created mass markets and facilitated the distribution of goods. (4) The new system of production led to the rise of new economic groups—factory workers and industrialists. (5) By displacing handicraft production, the factory system lowered the status of the skilled craft worker and expanded the labor market to include unskilled male, female, and child labor. (6) The diminished role and the lowered status of the worker in industry were a factor in the growth of trade-unionism, which increased the complexity of labor-management relations. (7) The greater regional specialization and the interdependence of economic activity tended to make economic fluctuations increasingiy severe for both the wage earner and the businessman.

Questions

1. Differentiate between the custom production of early handicraft shops and present-day interchangeable-parts manufacture.

2. Compare and contrast the craft guilds of the handicraft era and present-day trade-unions with respect to membership and functions.

3. Explain why, historically, industrialization took hold first in the consumer-goods industries and only later in the capital-goods industries.

4. Explain how the industrialization of the United States has differed from that of Europe.

5. Illustrate three forms of technological advance present in the development of plastics or synthetic textiles.

6. Explain how mechanization, new sources of power, and widening scope of the market, together with heavy "plow-back" investment, give an industrial economy a dynamic nature (i.e., capability of expansion).

7. Explain the relative ease of present-day industrialization of underdeveloped countries in comparison with industrialization of underdeveloped areas in 1820. In your discussion compare the type of industrial labor required, sources of capital and managerial talent, geographic specialization, size of market (domestic and foreign), etc.

3: Ownership Organization and
Business Combinations

A "firm" is an ownership organization which combines the factors of production in a plant [1] for the purpose of producing goods or services and selling them at a profit. The businessman must carefully compare the relative advantages and disadvantages of various forms of ownership so that he can select the form best suited to his enterprise. The main types of business ownership in the United States are the individual proprietorship, the general partnership, and the corporation.

TYPES OF OWNERSHIP

"Ownership" means the legal title to, and rights in, property, and includes, therefore, the rights of possession and of disposal. The "ownership organization" must be distinguished from the "operating organization" which is set up to administer and manage the business. "Private ownership" exists when individuals exercise the rights and responsibilities of ownership. "Public ownership" exists when political bodies (local, state, or federal governments) create, exercise, and enjoy these rights.[2]

In deciding whether to organize an individual proprietorship, a partnership, or a corporation, the businessman should consider the size and type of the business being started, the amount of capital required, the desired method of distributing earnings and risk, the amount of flexibility and control wanted by management, and the laws and taxes affecting the various forms of ownership. Although in

[1] A "plant" is the physical unit (factory, warehouse, department store) performing productive activities in the output of goods and services.

[2] *Mixed ownership*, which exists when private individuals and public bodies share ownership, is rare in the United States but is not uncommon in Europe.

most cases it is not difficult to decide upon the best form for a particular business, such factors as limited liability must sometimes be balanced against high taxes, or ease of control against the difficulty of raising capital. When a proprietorship or a partnership is no longer suitable or advantageous, there is generally little difficulty in changing to the corporate form of enterprise.

Individual Proprietorship. Under the sole-proprietorship form of ownership a single individual organizes, has title to, and operates the business in his own name.

Advantages. Individual proprietorship is suitable for small businesses (light manufacturing, retailing, farming, etc.) for several reasons. (1) Legal formalities are unnecessary and license fees are low. (2) Centralized control allows flexibility in management, free initiative, quick decisions, and personal satisfaction in achievement. (3) Termination or modification of the business is easy.

Disadvantages. (1) The nature of individual proprietorship usually makes it difficult to raise additional capital, thereby limiting the size of the business and thus reducing the advantages to be derived from mass production. (2) Risk is great since the owner is personally and unlimitedly liable for all debts to creditors. Suits may be brought by or against the proprietor as an individual. (3) The burden of over-all direction and co-ordination may be beyond the proprietor's capacity when the business becomes large. (4) The termination of the business upon the death or serious disability of the owner lends instability to the enterprise.

Partnership. Two or more individuals may form a partnership by making a written or oral agreement that they will jointly assume full responsibility for the conduct of a business.

General Partnership. A partnership agreement may set forth respective rights and obligations, determine the share of ownership each partner is to have, and state how profits or losses are to be distributed. In the absence of such a limiting agreement, the power of control or management is held to be equally divided, and the courts will distribute profits or losses on an equal basis even though the investments of the individual partners may have differed in amount. No partner may transfer his interest without the consent of the other partners.

Advantages. A general partnership has most of the advantages of the individual proprietorship and others of its own. (1) The legal formality for organization is comparatively simple and inexpensive. (2) Because the resources of two or more individuals are combined, a

13

larger amount of capital is usually available, making possible a larger firm than can ordinarily be undertaken by the single proprietor. (3) Credit is more easily available, because all partners are personally liable for the debts of the partnership. The unlimited liability feature gives the general partnership a higher credit standing than a corporation having the same assets. (4) The talents and experience of several individuals may be combined to advantage in the conduct of the business. (5) Changes in the field of business may be effected without the legal formalities that would be necessary under a corporate form.

Disadvantages. (1) In a general partnership each partner is personally and unlimitedly liable for all the debts of the firm. (2) Any partner may bind the firm (that is, all other partners) by his acts in respect to partnership matters. (3) Because control is divided, there may be difficulties and disagreement in management. (4) The size of the firm is limited to the partners' resources, since the sale of securities in the market is not possible as it would be with a corporate ownership. (5) Since death, disability, or withdrawal of a partner terminates the partnership, the general partnership lacks the continuity of existence which makes a business stable.

LIMITED PARTNERSHIP. Many states permit a form of partnership in which one or more of the partners is a general partner and the others are "limited partners" whose liabilities can not exceed their respective investments in the business. Limited partners (generally known as "silent partners") have no authority in the active management. Limited-partnership agreements should be matters of record filed with the proper governmental agency.

Advantages. (1) The limited partnership enables the general partners to obtain additional capital (from the silent partners) without relinquishing managerial control. (2) It allows the firm to continue business by admitting as limited partners the heirs of deceased partners. (3) It enables partners to avoid the heavy taxes imposed by some states on corporations.

Disadvantages. (1) Some additional registration and legal formalities are required—e.g., creditors outside the state must be notified of the limited partnership. (2) In many states there is uncertainty as to what constitutes "participation or nonparticipation" of the limited partners in the management of the business. (3) The validity of the limited partnership is frequently doubtful outside a given state.

Co-operative. The co-operative is a nonprofit organization formed to provide goods and services to members at cost. According to the type of business, these enterprises are classified as "consumer," "producer," or "credit" co-operatives. The business is managed in much the same way as that of other forms of ownership. A board of directors and officers are elected, and periodic shareholders' meetings are held.

From their beginning in Rochdale, England, in 1844, co-operatives have been set up in accordance with certain general principles. (1) Anyone can become a member by purchasing one or more shares of stock, but no member has more than one vote regardless of the number of shares he purchases. (2) Goods are usually offered to the general public at prevailing market prices. (3) Returns on shares of stock are limited to a fixed percentage. (4) The earnings of the business (including interest on stock) are returned to the members (usually as periodic rebates) in proportion to their purchase of goods.

Co-operatives conduct retailing, wholesaling, and manufacturing businesses. So far they have enjoyed an advantage in that their patronage rebates are exempt from income taxes; but even though their influence and scope are growing, they still account for only a small part of the total volume of retailing and wholesaling in this country. Co-operatives for marketing farm products (which have been encouraged by the federal government) have tended to improve the bargaining power of many producers of agricultural products, to enable them to buy more economically, and to eliminate some of the waste in distribution.

The relative insignificance of the co-operative movement in this country when compared to its prominence in Europe can be accounted for by many factors. Most influential among these are the lack of popular interest in co-operatives, the greater mobility of our population, the lack of large-scale efficiencies because of the limited volume of business, the low salaries paid to executives and in some cases the resulting inferior management.

Corporation. The corporate form of enterprise is the most prominent form of organization in all fields of our economy except in farming, small manufacturing, and service and trade businesses.

Private Corporation. To form a corporation the promoters or owners of a business file with the state government an official document known as the "articles of incorporation." The procedure involves the registration of information about the business (name, type of activity) and the payment of initial taxes and filing fees. It also requires compliance with legal formalities regulating the meetings at which specific details of organization must be handled—the election of a board of directors by the shareholders and the appointment of officers by the board. In essence, the granting of a charter by the state creates a corporation, which is composed of a number of shareholders (at least three) who are the legal owners, a board of directors who fix the policies and conduct the business, and officers who actually manage the business. The corporation is created by the state as a *legal entity* ("artificial person"), separate and distinct from the persons owning its stock. It may sue or be sued in its own name, acquire property, and exercise many other rights and privileges that are guaranteed by law to living persons. Frequently corporations are organized in states that have liberal laws, but then, under the rule of "interstate comity" (i.e., courtesy among states), carry on business activity in other states.

Advantages. The reasons for the prominence of corporate ownership lie in certain advantages exclusive with this form of organization. (1) Stability results from (a) the transferability of stock without the assent of all owners; (b) the ease of acquiring new charters to extend the life of the business beyond the usual state limitation of twenty to fifty years; and (c) the fact that neither death nor transfer of interest affects the life of the enterprise. (2) The owners enjoy limited liability: if a corporation fails, the owners are liable only to the extent of their investment. (3) The amassing of large amounts of capital, necessary for large-scale production, is made possible because investors are attracted by the benefits of corporation ownership: availability of small ownership interest,[3] limited liability, and easy transferability of ownership. The resulting large-scale operations increase efficiency.

Disadvantages.[4] (1) Strict adherence to the legal formalities of corporate organization, prescribed by state laws, is necessary. The corporate form does not have the economy and simplicity of organization that are characteristic of the individual proprietorship and the partnership forms. (2) Changes in the line of business, in capital structure, or in other matters pertaining to the corporate charter require a rigid observation of additional legal formalities. This handicap may be partially offset by acquisition of a very broad charter.

[3] The fact that investment in securities can be small attracts many little investors and enables big investors to diversify their holdings, thereby reducing investment risk.

[4] A social disadvantage frequently cited is the tendency toward the separation of ownership from control in large corporations. Because of the issuance of a small proportion of voting stock, management's use of the proxy device, and the growth of holding companies, many stockholders have little or no voice in the management of the business.

PUBLIC CORPORATION. Federal, state, and local governments carry on a number of enterprises. Many of these are organized into government-owned corporations (for example, the Reconstruction Finance Corporation, the Federal Deposit Insurance Corporation, the Commodity Credit Corporation, the Tennessee Valley Authority, and the Atomic Energy Commission). Often they operate much like private enterprises, and some expect to realize a profit. In their "pure" form and after they are established, they are characterized by political, administrative, and financial autonomy.

Public corporations are organized for various purposes under special acts of Congress or are incorporated under the laws of states. For each public corporation (federal, state, or local) a legislative act determines the scope of activity and the broad policies, outlines the organization, and formulates the financial structure and other basic features. The operating funds come from the public treasury (through legislative appropriation), from authorized public loans and bank credit, and from profits.

BUSINESS COMBINATIONS

In many industries during the past eighty years the size of the business unit has tended to increase and the number of firms to decrease. Many factors have contributed to the combining of business firms. Among them are the possibility of reducing "wasteful competition" and of securing larger profits, the desire for prestige and power on the part of top management, and the *economies obtainable from large-scale operations:* [5] mass-production methods and specialized machinery (through increased speed in production) lower labor and capital cost per unit of output; bargaining power in quantity (discount) buying and by-product output lower material costs and achieve more complete use of materials, including wastes; full-time use of managerial and technical specialists increases operating efficiency; volume distribution lowers marketing and promotion cost per unit of sale; large research laboratories achieve technological advance; and better credit standing and flotation of large security issues lower financing costs.

[5] When a business firm is too large, it may become unwieldy and inefficient because of the managerial difficulty of co-ordinating diverse functions—that is, the firm is subject to the law of diminishing returns. In actual practice, however, as a firm grows, top management can revise and simplify the structural organization (thereby partially offsetting the law of diminishing returns) by splitting up the operating units into logical divisions and branch plants, each under a separate works manager or plant manager. (See Ch. 6 for discussion.)

The various types of business co-operation and combination are outlined below.

Informal Methods of Combination. Pools, interlocking directorates, "gentlemen's agreements," patents, and similar devices have been employed by groups of companies to enable them to act in unison on certain phases of their operations or to supply the means by which one company can control the others. Companies which enter into such agreements retain their independent identities but set up working arrangements for various purposes: for example, to share markets, eliminate competitors, restrict production, control prices, or pursue common labor policies. These loose combinations have in some instances been short-lived because there has been no way to hold reluctant members to the terms of the agreement. At other times these arrangements have been deemed monopolistic ("in restraint of trade"), and the government has acted to impede or prevent their functioning.

Trust. The desire to overcome the weaknesses of informal combinations led in the third quarter of the nineteenth century to the development of a more formal device, the trust. Under this arrangement, enough shares of stock to control the voting power in several corporations were transferred to a board of trustees. The original shareholders received in turn trust certificates giving them proportionate shares in the earnings of the stock held in trust. Controlling several companies in this manner, the trustees elected boards of directors and officers to carry out the purposes for which the trust had been organized. The objectives were to establish uniform policies, to increase profits, to eliminate competition, to control prices, and to obtain the economies of large-scale operations. Because of their monopolistic features, trusts were prohibited and many were dissolved by the federal government through the "trust-busting" power granted by the Sherman Act of 1890 and the Clayton Act of 1914.

Merger. Because of the illegality of the trust, merging—a more direct and legal method—is now employed to form combinations. A *merger* occurs when a single company acquires all the assets of one or more other companies and either absorbs them into its existing organization or forms a new corporation of the several formerly independent companies. Through mergers many individual proprietorships and partnerships have lost their identity.

Holding Company. In the past fifty years the holding company has been the chief means of building huge combinations. Since the holding company is formed through securities manipulation and the combining companies retain their identities, it avoids some of the problems associated with the merger. Such a combination is formed by organizing a corporation (the holding company) with sufficient capital to secure the controlling stock of the corporations that are to be combined. The holding company may exchange its own stock for the original shares of the owners, or it may purchase the required shares for cash. Gigantic combinations are formed when holding companies are pyramided; i.e., when a number of operating companies are grouped under one holding company, several holding companies grouped under a superholding company, and so on. Through such pyramiding, the top holding company with comparatively little capital can control an industrial empire. The holding company has, on the whole, successfully evaded prosecution as a monopoly. Low-cost production and other economies of large-scale enterprises have been a strong argument for holding companies, and this fact undoubtedly has restrained the courts from acting too severely in antitrust suits against them.

Trade Association. Co-operation and joint action by companies are not illegal per se. Trade associations have been legitimately formed by members of the same industry to publish trade journals, carry out market surveys, promote joint advertising, develop common accounting practices, exchange technical information, pursue common labor relations policies, and represent business interests before legislative bodies. Over two thousand such organizations are nationwide in scope.

Structural Types of Combination. Multiple-plant operation (in which a "central office" is the directing unit) exists when two or more plants are controlled or operated by one managing interest, such as a holding company. Central-office units in 1947 controlled 35,213 establishments and employed 56 per cent of the factory wage earners. Structurally, multiple-plant enterprises are organized as horizontal, vertical, or complex combinations.

HORIZONTAL COMBINATIONS. A horizontal combination exists when two or more plants engaged in the same or similar business are under one management—for example, a chain of bread-baking companies, a group of canneries, or meat-packing plants. These multiple-plant enterprises benefit from such advantages as quantity discounts on purchases, lower selling and advertising costs, specialization of managerial functions, and the full-time operation of several plants during slack periods while one or more plants are shut down.

VERTICAL COMBINATION. A vertical combination exists when each plant in the combination performs given processes in the successive stages that make up the complete cycle of production from primary raw materials to final product. In the textile industry, for example, management may integrate the plants engaged in the following successive stages of production: the processing of wools into yarn, the weaving of the yarn into cloth, and finally the manufacturing of the cloth into suits. Another example is found in the steel industry, where management attains vertical integration by engaging in mining operations (coal, iron, limestone), running a coking plant, producing pig iron in blast-furnaces, turning pig iron into steel ingots in the converting mill, and, finally, fabricating various finished products in the rolling mill. Vertical combinations attain low-cost production through specialization and standardization, elimination of some operations, reductions in inventories, reliable delivery of uniform quality materials, elimination of selling costs for materials, and specialization of managerial functions.

COMPLEX COMBINATION. A complex combination may include plants that are both vertically and horizontally combined as well as plants that produce a variety of products that may be complementary or unrelated to the main line of the business. Many large corporations are, to some degree, combinations of the complex type. General Motors, for instance, is a horizontal combination of automobile plants with some vertical integration, but it also owns plants that turn out refrigerators and other unrelated products.

Questions

1. Explain the advantages of the corporation over the individual proprietorship and the partnership and the resulting prominence of the corporation as a form of ownership in large-scale enterprise.

2. Discuss the features of the corporation which facilitate the selling of securities (financing) and thus enable the amassing of a large quantity of capital.

3. Explain the underlying purposes of co-operatives and illustrate the types that may be organized.

4. Explain why manufacturing firms have been increasing in size during the past eighty years.

5. Discuss and illustrate current methods for forming combinations.

6. Explain and illustrate the pyramiding practice of holding companies.

7. Discuss the beneficial service functions performed by trade associations for their members.

8. (a) Differentiate between the horizontal and the vertical combination. (b) What are the special economies that accrue when plants are vertically integrated?

4: Financing Business Enterprise

The financing of business involves accumulation of capital through "investment," the laying out of savings by individuals and organizations for an expected profit. Each enterprise must determine the amount and kind of capital it needs and then must plan its financial structure, provide for expansion, and, if it is a corporation, sell its securities and avoid undue overcapitalization or undercapitalization.

INVESTMENT CAPITAL

"Capital" in business practice consists of the money and credit needed to start and operate an enterprise. It includes also the physical assets and the intangible assets—securities, good will, patent rights, accounts receivable, and other claims to wealth held by the firm.

Savings and Capital Markets. Funds for investment come from various types of "savings." Individuals save directly when they set aside unexpended earnings and save indirectly when they pay life-insurance premiums or purchase annuities. Business firms save when they retain profits for investment in the enterprise, for purchase of securities, or for other purposes. Federal and state governments bring about "forced savings" in the economy when they expend funds (acquired through taxation and borrowing) on defense plants, atomic-energy plants, irrigation and hydroelectric projects, highways, and other public works.

Individual and business savings flow into *capital markets* which serve various areas and provide different kinds of investment funds and loans for borrowers. Investment banks and finance companies acquire funds which they make available for investment and loans. Insurance companies, foundations, and other endowed institutions accumulate funds which they invest directly or use to purchase securities from investment banks, the issuing firms, stockbrokers, or the government. The accumulated funds of commercial banks are held as reserves against which the banks make short- and long-term loans. Heavy government expenditures for defense and other purposes (particularly those based on borrowings from commercial banks and from federal reserve banks) increase the flow of purchasing power. Part of this money becomes investment funds in the form of retained profits of companies and of bank deposits made by individuals and business firms.

Types of Capital Needed by Business Firms. Capital funds for investment and credit are generally classified, according to the period for which they are used, as "long-term," "intermediate," and "short-term." These classifications are useful in that they show the different financial needs of a business and the sources and methods of financing.

LONG-TERM CAPITAL. Long-term capital (funds from the sale of stocks and from ten-, twenty-, and thirty-year loans) is needed for the purchase and improvement of land, the erection of buildings, the purchase of heavy equipment, the acquisition of intangible assets, and the promotion and operation of business. Such capital comes from a number of sources. Investment-banking houses supply long-term capital when they underwrite securities—i.e., accept new issues of stocks and bonds. They buy the new securities of the issuing companies at "wholesale" prices and, in turn, sell them at higher prices to individual investors, business firms, insurance companies, endowed institutions, and trust funds. Individuals, institutions, and endowed foundations supply long-term capital funds when they purchase securities from the issuing firms or from stockbrokers. Commercial banks supply such capital when they seek outlets for their funds in fixed-term loans of from ten to twenty years' maturity. Large corporations increasingly rely on *internal finance* (retained profits) for funds.

INTERMEDIATE CAPITAL. Intermediate capital (usually two- to three-year loans) is borrowed (primarily as trade credit) for tools and light equipment having a life of only several years.

SHORT-TERM CAPITAL. Short-term capital (usually thirty-, sixty-, or ninety-day loans) is borrowed for the needs of current operation (materials, labor) or to meet the seasonal upswing of business. Regular commercial banks, mortgage and finance companies, and trade credit are the primary sources of short-term capital. In the small-loan field such funds are obtained from personal-loan companies, personal-loan departments of banks, credit unions, and private lenders.

COMPANY FINANCING

The capital structure and the financing of a new enterprise must be planned; they can not be left to chance. The *goals* of sound financial planning are accumulation of adequate funds at low cost and provision for future capital needs. Sound financing keeps expenses (interest and carrying charges, losses through bad debts, obligations to pay dividends on preferred stock) at a minimum and maintains sufficient liquidity and reserves to meet emergencies.

Procedure for Financing a New Enterprise. (1) Determine the immediate and future financial needs, (2) classify the stock to be issued (thus designating the sources of funds), and (3) acquire funds through the sale of securities.

Determination of Financial Needs. Financial requirements are determined by calculating the total amount necessary for fixed capital, working capital, and costs of organizing and promoting a business. The total of the immediate requirement plus an estimate of financial needs for future expansion determines the "authorized stock" [1] to be requested in the application for a corporate charter.

NEEDS FOR FIXED CAPITAL. "Fixed capital" is the funds required for the acquisition of those assets that are to be used over and over for a long period—such assets as land and improvements, buildings, machinery, equipment, and tools. The term also applies to the assets themselves. Funds necessary to acquire fixed assets can be estimated from the purchase price of business sites, the cost of erecting buildings, and the cost of equipment and installation. [2]

NEEDS FOR WORKING CAPITAL. "Working capital" is the amount of funds necessary to cover the cost of operating the enterprise. The amount needed is based on a number of calculations: (1) the cost of inventory, including the estimated stock of raw materials, purchased parts, supplies, work in process, and finished goods; (2) wage-and-salary bill (costs of direct labor, indirect labor, clerical staff, and managerial and supervisory staffs), (3) overhead costs (other than salaries and wages of indirect labor), including those of maintenance and service activities, utilities and fuel, property taxes, and insurance; (4) costs of sales activities such as advertising, promotion, shipping services, and credit extension to customers.

In general, funds for working capital should be sufficient to meet the current liabilities and the peak requirements of seasonal variations and to enable the firm to take advantage of the special purchasing oppor-

---

[1] "Authorized stock" is the amount of stock, both common and preferred, which the state allows a corporation to issue.

[2] The value of such intangible assets as trade-marks, secret processes, good will, and oftentimes patents are established only by operational experience over a period of time.

tunities that occur from time to time. Working capital in a going concern is a "revolving fund": it consists of cash receipts from sales which are used to cover the cost of current operations. The shorter the time cycle of production and the more rapid the turnover in the sale of goods, the smaller the needs for working capital.

NEEDS FOR PROMOTIONAL EXPENSE. In addition to making provision for fixed and working capital, the calculation should include the funds necessary to cover the promotional costs that will be incurred prior to actual operation and the possible losses before the business becomes a paying concern. Promotional expenses include the initial fees, taxes, engineering and development costs and outlays for advertising.

Classification of Stock. Drawing up a plan for the financing of a corporation requires determination of the capital structure—that is, primarily, the classification of stock into categories such as common and preferred shares. Stock certificates are the evidence of ownership of corporation capital; the particular class of stock held by a shareholder establishes his relationship to the corporation and to the holders of other types of stocks—in short, his rights and limitations.

Various types of common and preferred classes may be set up. Holders of *common stock* usually exercise control over a business through the voting power of their shares and have residual rights to earnings and assets. Holders of *preferred stock* generally have no voting rights, but they enjoy certain preferences—for example, the rights of priority with respect to net assets upon the liquidation of the corporation or to dividends at a stipulated rate or both. Prior rights to dividends may be cumulative or noncumulative. On *cumulative shares* of stock, dividends not paid in a given year are paid in a following year, if and when they are declared; on *noncumulative shares*, dividends not paid in a given year may never be paid. *Participating preferred stock* sometimes pays a higher dividend than the stated rate—i.e., a dividend as high as that paid on common stock. A nominal value may be assigned to the shares (*par-value stock*); or no nominal value may be designated (*no-par stock*).[3]

Stock classifications are determined partly with an eye toward the immediate need for capital funds and partly with an eye on the needs for future expansion. For example, stock with preference as to dividends may be issued to attract those investors who seek only a fair, assured return and who do not wish to incur the risks of heavy losses in the

[3] "Par," which refers only to the stated value of the stock, is used mainly as an evaluation for tax purposes. The market value of securities depends upon many factors and generally shows little relationship to the par values after the date of issue.

hope of large gains, as do some common-stock holders. The various advantages and disadvantages to the firm must be considered by those who determine the classification of stock—e.g., the creation of demand in the securities market for the shares, control over the enterprise, burden on the company of a preferred dividend "obligation," legal advantages, and tax advantages.

Sale of Securities. When promoters launch a large incorporated enterprise, the securities are usually marketed through investment-banking houses, but promoters are sometimes able to sell new issues of securities directly to investors. Large corporations can usually sell new issues of securities directly to their present stockholders, outside individual investors, and institutions. Small enterprises, not having the services of investment-banking houses available to them, frequently have difficulty in selling securities. Such firms must find interested parties who will advance the funds. Fixed capital is sometimes acquired in "direct form" when the organizers and stockholders of the enterprise exchange land, buildings, or machinery for stock.

In the individual proprietorship and the general partnership, owners usually rely on their own savings as the primary source of long-term investment capital. In the limited partnership, the silent partners often furnish funds. Small enterprises usually secure growth funds by "plowing back" the profits and by borrowing.

Acquisition of Capital for Expansion. Well-managed corporations can ordinarily accumulate capital for expansion through normal business operations—that is, through the investment of retained profits. The financing of expansion is, in addition, accomplished through the sale of unissued stock to present stockholders, outside individual investors, investment banks, or agencies dealing in long-term financing.

A "loan" represents an opportunity to improve the enterprise and increase its earning power, but it is also potentially very risky. The net value, or the equity, of the business is used as collateral in borrowing funds.[4] Loan funds (i.e., equity capital) may be borrowed from commercial banks or acquired through the sale of bonds. "Bonds," usually backed by a mortgage on part or all of the company's property, are the firm's promise to repay a loan.

Borrowing money is advisable only when there is a good working margin between the interest rate on the borrowed capital and the ex-

---

[4] "Equity" is the net value of property determined by subtracting from its total value all debts and liens charged against it. The equity of the firm can be used as security to guarantee the payment of a loan.

25

pected level of earnings from the use of that capital. Such borrowing is generally identified as "trading on the equity." Firms often borrow money to secure additional working capital to meet seasonal needs.

Avoidance of Overcapitalization and Undercapitalization. Sound planning of the financial structure avoids excessive overcapitalization or undercapitalization. *Overcapitalization* exists when the book value of a firm's outstanding (i.e., issued) capital stock is higher than the market value of its net assets or is greater than is warranted by the potential profits of the firm. Such "watered stock" burdens the firm with large annual franchise and capital stock taxes, understates the real earning capacity, and may lead to charges of fraud in the financing of the firm. *Undercapitalization,* on the other hand, exists when the book value of the firm's outstanding stock is less than the market value of the net assets and is small relative to the earning power of the firm.[5] Such capitalization overstates the earning power of the firm, entices new producers to enter the field, and results in a clamor for greater dividend declarations and demands for higher wages.

Questions

1. Compare the sources and uses of long-term capital with those of intermediate and short-term capital. Explain why it is unwise to attempt to satisfy long-term capital needs with short-term capital.

2. Explain and illustrate the goals of sound business financing.

3. Outline and briefly discuss the procedure for financing a large corporation.

4. Compare and illustrate fixed capital and working capital.

5. Discuss the factors that would influence the classification of securities issued by a large corporation.

6. Explain the advantages which a large, well-known corporation has over a small corporation in the initial sale of securities and in borrowing.

7. Explain and illustrate "trading on the equity." When is it more likely to occur—during a depression or during a period of prosperity?

8. Explain under- and overcapitalization and indicate how either may occur during a period of depression or of prosperity.

---

[5] For example, the book value of physical assets may be lower than the market value if the plant and equipment were cheaply purchased when the government was rapidly selling its "war surplus plants."

5: Organization: Structural Types and Principles

The top management (or administration) of a modern business formulates the policies, decides upon the organization structure, and co-ordinates finance, production, and distribution. Management proper carries out the objectives and policies which have been determined by the administration. "Internal organization" is the division of activities into definite functions and assignments for executives, departments, and groups of employees—it is the mechanism by which operating management achieves the ends determined by the administration.

TYPES OF ORGANIZATION

The basic principles of organization can be illustrated by outlining three types of structure. *Line organization* is the earliest and simplest type; it is still found in many small businesses. *Functional organization* is an ideal or theoretical type which has never been widely adopted, but which has influenced practical organization structure. *Line-and-staff organization* is a combination of features of the first two types, and some form of it is now generally used by medium- and large-sized business establishments.

Line (Scalar, or Military) Organization. Authority is passed down directly from the general manager or boss to the various subordinate executives in charge of particular activities and from them to lower-level supervisors who in turn direct the workers. The flow of authority and instruction can be traced in an unbroken line from the manager to the worker (see Fig. 1).

Each section or department on the same level of authority is a complete, independent, self-contained unit. The head of each section is supreme in his own field and is responsible only to the man directly above him. Contact between the various shops or departments is es-

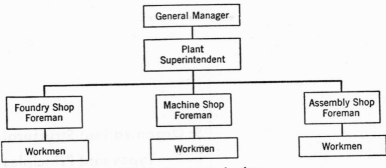

Fig. 1. Line organization.

tablished through the superintendent. Each foreman or supervisor is responsible for all the activities in his department (planning and routing work, inspection, maintenance, personnel). The workmen in his shop are responsible directly to him.

Advantages. (1) A clear-cut division of authority and responsibility makes performance or nonperformance of duties readily traceable. (2) Owing to the simplicity of line organization, discipline and control are easily achieved. (3) Quick action, with a minimum of red tape, is possible.

Disadvantages. (1) There is a lack of specialization, with resulting inefficiency because each supervisor is responsible for a variety of duties in not all of which can he be an expert. (2) Supervisors are usually overladen with matters which require personal attention. (3) It is difficult to secure foremen with the necessary all-round ability and knowledge. (4) So much reliance is placed on foremen that their absence disrupts or cripples the organization. (5) There is an undue reliance upon the skill and knowledge of the workmen.

In its "pure" form, line organization is found only in the small shop or business; because of its limitations, it is inadequate for large business operations. However, features of line organization are found in every modern organization structure.

Functional Organization. Near the turn of the century, Frederick W. Taylor developed "functional organization" to help overcome the difficulty of finding supervisors who could successfully carry out all the diverse duties of the foreman's position in line organization. Functional organization divides managerial activities so that each head, from the assistant superintendent down, has as few functions as possible to perform and is able to become a specialist in these. Authority from top down is delegated according to the functions. Taylor divided the responsibility of shop supervision among several foremen, each specially qualified and in charge of a certain aspect of the work. The workers were to take orders from more than one superior, but only in regard to the particular function over which each had control (see Fig. 2).

In functional organization, the general planning and clerical activities are placed in the hands of four office specialists—route clerk, instruction clerk, time and cost clerk, and shop disciplinarian. Four shop foremen (gang boss, speed boss, inspection boss, and repair boss) supervise and help the workers, each foreman assisting only in his particular function. The gang foreman directs the setting up of tools into the machines (for example, the installation of jigs and fixtures) and the efficient movement of materials from machine to machine. The speed foreman instructs workers in the proper use of cutting tools and machine operations so that they may reach a specified rate of output. The inspection foreman regulates the quality of the work. The repair foreman supervises machine upkeep and maintenance.

Advantages. (1) Specialization in supervision makes efficiency possible. (2) Men of required supervisory talent are readily found and easily trained for particular duties. (3) Specialized and skilled supervisory attention is given the workmen.

Disadvantages. (1) Discipline, control, and co-ordination of func-

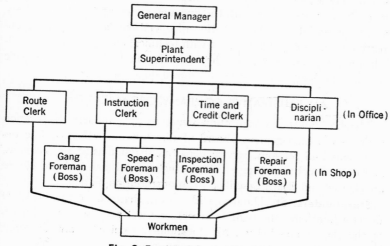

Fig. 2. Functional organization.

tions are difficult to attain: men cannot work effectively under two or more foremen at the same time. (2) The spheres of authority tend to overlap and give rise to friction. (3) The difficulty of locating and fixing responsibility for poor performance (because of ease of "buck passing") lowers morale.

Because of these disadvantages, "pure" functional organization has never been generally adopted. Nevertheless, modern organization structure uses the principle of functional specialization when it establishes staff or functionalized service departments.

Line-and-Staff Organization. When properly designed, the line-and-staff organization combines the best features of the line type and of the functional type of organization. Its strength lies in the fact that it can attain control through the clear-cut and undivided delegation of authority and responsibility and can achieve operating efficiency through specialization (see Fig. 3). The principle of undivided responsibility is maintained by the direct flow of authority from top to bottom. Each line supervisor directly controls the man under him and is held responsible for production activities. He does not, however, carry the same load of duties that he would under the line organization. Functionalized service departments and staff-assistant positions (governing personnel, accounting, maintenance, production-planning, inspection) are set up to advise, serve, and work through the line foremen as well as through the organization as a whole. The experts of the service departments do not give orders directly to the workers. In short, the line men are delegated the authority and responsibility for the execution of operations; and the service departments are appointed to assist with technical and specialized knowledge, analysis, and research. The internal structure of a given service department, however, is usually organized on a line basis.

AN ILLUSTRATIVE COMPANY ORGANIZATION

The line-and-staff organization structure of a modern corporation includes top management (board of directors and officers), line departments and sections, service departments, staff-assistant positions, and committees (see Fig. 3). The structure and standard procedures are charted and clearly described in an organization manual.

Stockholders. Stockholders with voting shares elect the board of directors and have the right to accept or reject proposed amendments to the charter and bylaws. All stockholders receive an annual report on the condition and progress of the company.

Board of Directors. The main function of the board is to determine company objectives, general policies, and plans. Acting as a body, the board has ultimate control; it keeps check upon company affairs to insure that the general policies are being observed and that the objectives are being achieved. The board usually selects from its membership an executive committee to handle affairs between meetings and appoints the chairman of the board to preside over the committee. It may appoint a financial committee to handle fiscal matters—subject to board approval. It may also form an auditing committee, which will hire public accountants to examine the books and certify the financial statements.

The board selects the president, general manager, vice-president, and perhaps other principal officers and lays down the over-all plans for them to follow. The president and other principal officers are themselves frequently members of the board of directors.

President. The president derives his authority from the board for the direction of the business and the implementation of the company policies. He selects, usually with the aid of the general manager, executives for major departments or divisions and appoints staff assistants (administrative, public-relations, legal) who report to him. He presides over the operating executive committee, whereby he co-ordinates the main functions (manufacturing, engineering, sales, finance, and personnel) and formulates key departmental policies within the scope of the general policies laid down by the board of directors.

General Manager. The general manager assumes the immediate functions of directing, co-ordinating, and controlling the operating phase of the business so that the various departments work together as a team. He may serve as vice-president.

Secretary. The secretary takes custody of important documents and corporation books, submits reports and statements to the state and federal governments, is in charge of the transfer of corporate stock, and keeps the minutes of stockholders' meetings.

Treasurer. The treasurer formulates financial policies, subject to the approval of the president and the committee of the board which reviews such affairs. He controls investment funds and securities, is in charge of financial reports, and manages other related matters. In a small firm his functions may be combined with those of the controller, who deals with the internal phase of the same problem.

Major Departments. According to the character and needs of the business, the activities of the firm are segregated into major functions.

31

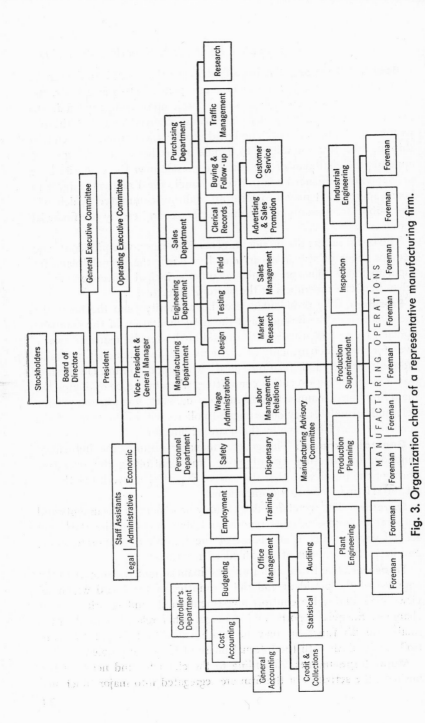

Fig. 3. Organization chart of a representative manufacturing firm.

The company is then so organized that a department is set up to perform each function. Each department, in turn, is broken down into subdivisions, which execute phases of the functions.

ENGINEERING DEPARTMENT. The engineering department has charge of product research and development, the design of products, the preparation of drawings and other specifications for production, the selection of equipment and methods (usually in collaboration with the process-engineering or industrial-engineering section), and the preparation of data necessary for manufacturing and production control.

MANUFACTURING DEPARTMENT. The manufacturing department has charge of the subfunctions of production operations and of service activities.

Production-Operation Sections. Directly under the manufacturing, or "works," manager is the superintendent of production operations, who supervises the activities of the foremen of the various plant-operating departments. (Foremen usually have assistant foremen who direct the workers in various sections of their departments.)

Service Sections. Generally four service subdivisions facilitate the work of production operations: (1) production-planning and control, (2) inspection, (3) plant engineering and maintenance, and (4) industrial engineering. The production-planning-and-control section prepares and releases to the plant production orders (based on sales requirements). The inspection section checks materials and the quality of work against the specifications made by the engineering department. The plant-engineering-and-maintenance section is in charge of upkeep and repair of the plant and its equipment. The industrial-engineering section undertakes managerial and cost-reduction programs (e.g., reappraisal of organization structure, work simplification, and modernization of plant). The recommendations they make as a result of the studies are, when approved, put into effect.[1]

PURCHASING DEPARTMENT. The purchasing department is in charge of procurement of materials, component parts, supplies, tools, machinery, and office equipment. In addition, it seeks out new types of materials as a service to the engineering department, and it sells obsolete materials and scrap. When procurement activities are comparatively simple, the purchasing function should be placed under manufacturing.

---

[1] Industrial engineering is usually placed under manufacturing because much of the work of the department is associated with manufacturing; however, it is not uncommon for industrial engineering to be placed under the general manager and on the same level with manufacturing.

SALES DEPARTMENT. The sales department is in charge of merchandising and distribution. This includes the development of channels of outlet, the opening up of new markets, sales forecasting, actual sales, and sometimes the servicing of goods which have been sold. The department is likewise responsible for making specific recommendations for improving company products and for suggesting new products.

CONTROLLER'S DEPARTMENT. The controller's department maintains records, manages and controls internal finance, and provides general office services for the company. The departmental functions include accounting (general, cost, and tax); preparation of financial reports, payrolls, and statistical reports; budgeting; supervision of credit and collections; and the provision of stenographic, filing, duplicating, and mailing services.

PERSONNEL DEPARTMENT. The function of the "industrial-relations" department includes all the activities necessary to secure and maintain an efficient working force. In a large organization, the industrial-relations director reports to a major executive and has jurisdiction over all matters pertaining to the company personnel. The personnel function includes recruitment, placement, and retirement of employees; training; participation in wage administration (job evaluation, incentives); transfer and promotion; health and safety measures; and labor-management relations. Frequently the personnel director reports to the head of the manufacturing department since that department has the largest payroll and, therefore, the largest amount of personnel work.

Questions

1. Distinguish between ownership organization and internal organization; and between line organization and functional organization.

2. "The line-and-staff organization combines the best features of the line type and of the functional type of organization." Discuss the "best features" that are combined in the line-and-staff organization.

3. Differentiate between the functions of the board of directors and the functions of the president.

4. Compare the functions of the treasurer with those of the controller.

5. Identify three major engineering functions in a typical manufacturing firm (see Fig. 3) and explain the duties under each.

6. Study Fig. 3 and draw up an organization chart for a small furniture-manufacturing firm with 100 employees.

6: Organization Development and Improvement

A well-designed organization structure with qualified personnel in all key positions achieves effective execution, co-ordination, and control of the policies and functions of the firm. Although a line-and-staff type of organization is now generally used by medium- and large-sized firms, it has many variations even among companies engaged in the same field of business. When an enterprise is started, the organization structure should be designed to suit the size of the company, the scope of its business operations (including the kinds of products and processes), the channels of distribution, and the plans for future development. As the company grows and as business conditions change, the structure must be modified and kept up-to-date through periodic re-examination.

DEVELOPMENT OF AN ORGANIZATION STRUCTURE

Procedure for Designing an Organization Structure. (1) State the objectives and scope of business operations; (2) separate the activities logically and set up distinct functional divisions; (3) delegate formal authority and responsibility; (4) assign specific duties to departments and their subdivisions; (5) establish the required staff-assistant positions; (6) set up the required committees; (7) develop systems of standard procedures and instructions for all routine activities; (8) prepare a policy manual and an organization chart and manual; (9) select qualified personnel.

Statement of Policies and Scope. Since company policies are reflected and carried out through the organization structure, a clear and complete statement of the firm's objectives and scope of operations must be formulated before the structure is developed. "Policies" may be defined as the general rules or guiding principles by which managerial decisions, programs, and procedures are determined. For example, policies may stipulate an emphasis on industrial research, a financing of expansion from retained profits, a growth based on regional dispersal of plants, an output of quality products, and a progressive personnel-relations program. Policy statements must be written in clear and concise terms; they must cover the scope of business activities and the general conditions to be anticipated; they must have a permanent yet flexible character; and they must be practicable.

Logical Separation of Activities. Large multiple-plant companies turning out many products may set up branch plants along product lines, along territorial lines, or both. For example, a corporation selling products nationally may concentrate all its plants in one area, each plant manufacturing a separate product; it may have plants in several areas of the country, each manufacturing all the products marketed in a given area; or it may have some combination of these.[1]

To attain benefits of specialization and division of labor, every company, whether single- or multiple-plant, will separate its activities on the basis of primary functions—finance, engineering, purchasing, production, sales, and industrial relations. A small firm will have few divisions; a larger firm may have many. A firm with geographically scattered plants may concentrate many of its nonmanufacturing activities (procurement, sales forecasting and promotion, product engineering) at the home office or distribute them to each branch for local direction. The degree of home-office centralization of control should be determined by the importance or difficulty of the decisions to be made. All such decisions depend upon the nature and scope of the business and upon the outlook and attitudes of top management. Company policies should cover these basic organizational problems.

SIMPLICITY. The separation of functions and their logical subdivision should be definite and avoid overlapping. Each of the main functions will serve as a basis for a department if the proper breakdown and charting technique are employed.

HOMOGENEITY. The functions and their subdivisions should be based on the principle of homogeneity—that is, groupings should bring together activities that are similar or directly related. For example, the manufacturing function (and the department handling it) may be logically subdivided according to products, processes, or classes of equipment; and the selling function may be subdivided according to territory, type of product, or class of customer.

[1] Geographic dispersal of plants and other company establishments is discussed in Ch. 8.

The organization structure should be built around the main functions rather than around an individual executive. An organization which is built around an individual, however competent, lacks permanence and strength: the organization may be disrupted if the executive is incapacitated. On the other hand, the abilities and limitations of individuals (the personal equation) must be taken into account. Sometimes it is necessary to consider the man who is available and then to draw the outlines of the job to fit his capacities.

Delegation of Formal Authority and Responsibility. Effective managerial control necessitates a clear flow of formal authority and responsibility [2] from the top to the bottom of the organization. Authority should be delegated as far down in the organization structure as practicable. The limits on the sphere of authority must be carefully determined so that there will be no activities which are not covered and no overlapping of assignments. Responsibility must always be accompanied by the authority necessary to control the activities or to perform the work.

DETERMINATION OF SPAN OF EXECUTIVE CONTROL. In allocating functions and duties one must determine the span of executive control in order to avoid overburdening the officers. A single executive or department head can successfully direct only a limited number of subordinate executives or supervisors, generally no more than five or six in an average firm; when activities are routine, or closely related, however, he can direct a larger number.

ESTABLISHMENT OF LEVELS OF AUTHORITY. The hierarchy, or vertical subdivisions—that is, the relative rank of each position with respect to other positions throughout the organization—must be determined. This is accomplished by setting up three or more parallel levels in the various departments under which respective positions will be grouped. For example, the ranks of authority from top to bottom may be the president, managers, department heads, supervisors and foremen, group leaders, and workers. The individual in charge at each level is limited by his predetermined sphere of control and is subject to higher authority. A superior, however, should always be held accountable for the acts of his subordinates.

[2] "Authority" in the organization structure may be defined as the right of one person to require another to fulfill specific duties. "Duties" are the activities an individual is required to perform because of the rank and position he occupies in the organization. "Responsibility" may be described as the obligation and accountability for the performance of delegated duties.

Assignment of Specific Duties to Departments. Duties are assigned to the various departments and their subdivisions on the basis of the functionalized breakdown of operations and activities. The duties of every individual should be confined to a single leading activity wherever this is economical. (Small firms will find it necessary to group under one head two or more related functions such as sales and purchasing.)

As the organization structure is developed, it must be properly charted, titles of positions at each level of authority must be standardized, and specific duties must be assigned to each position. The duties that service departments and their subdivisions (personnel, controllership, procurement, plant maintenance) perform for line departments (such as manufacturing) must be clearly designated. Assignment and standard instruction sheets should be drawn up to show the scope and lines of authority within the organization.

Establishment of Staff-Assistant Positions. Staff-assistant positions should be created to increase the effectiveness of line executives. The staff assistant is an expert (corporation attorney, economist, statistician, administrative secretary) in some phase of business operation. He should be given definite assignments, but should not take over the executive's authority or line duties. His work may include information-gathering, drawing up recommendations and advising on such matters as business trends and labor relations, and aiding in the formulation of decisions and instructions.

Establishment of Committees. Although the segregation of activities into functional divisions and subdivisions secures the benefits of specialization, it increases the need for co-ordinating the work of specialists and having them look beyond their individual fields to the aims of the company as a whole. An important function of each executive is to achieve teamwork—that is, to reunite subdivided work and to time activities. The larger the firm, the greater the need for co-ordination of the various units into an integrated working whole, and hence the establishment of committees.

BENEFITS OF COMMITTEES. Committees foster the spirit of co-operation; provide a pool of ability, experience, and judgment; furnish a clearinghouse for common problems; secure a meeting of minds to appraise results of operations; help avoid costly errors; broaden the viewpoint of members; and develop new leadership.

KINDS OF COMMITTEES. An adequate number of standing committees should be established in the organization structure, usually one committee for each level of authority. An executive committee at the top management level is ordinarily necessary to assist the president in formulating and revising company policies, in planning the course of the business, in considering the major projects and programs, and in dealing with emergency problems that affect the company as a whole. Committees at the lower levels (e.g., shop conferences of foremen) are needed to solve problems of operation and to co-ordinate activities. Temporary committees may be established from time to time to deal with special projects, to investigate problems, and to disseminate information.

STANDARDS FOR SETTING UP AND CONTROLLING COMMITTEES. (1) All committees should have enough members for adequate representation but not so many as to become unwieldy. (2) The individuals selected for membership must be among those directly concerned with the purpose of the committee though others who can make special contributions may be included. (3) Committee work must be planned, and prior notice of the agenda should be provided so that members can study the problems in advance and be prepared to offer solutions. (4) The frequency and duration of the conferences should be such as to get practical results, but not so time-consuming as to interfere with the members' regular duties.

Development of Standard Procedures for Routine Activities. Unless standard procedures are developed for the routine contacts and activities between and within departments, these contacts must be made through time-consuming, formal channels of authority; i.e., referred to superiors, who in turn refer them to the appropriate subordinate. Thus, in the absence of procedures for recurring activities, executives are overburdened with detail and do not have time to deal with the broader problems of the business.

SYSTEMATIC MANAGEMENT. Standard procedures and instructions are designed not only to relieve executives of routine duties but also to provide a means for systematic management and control. "Systems" are introduced to cover such activities as routine contacts between sales and production planning, engineering and manufacturing, and the employment office and shop foremen. Once standard procedures have been developed and authorized by management, common activities do not come to the executives' attention again until a procedural change is necessary. This arrangement, known as the *principle of exceptions,* increases managerial efficiency by allowing executives to concentrate solely on matters of policy and on variations from the standard plan of activities.

In essence, standard procedures are carefully thought-out instructions which include statements of purpose, written step-by-step rules, specially designed forms, designation of the individuals involved, and specification of the time of execution. Although procedural systems are an integral part of the organization structure, they should not be developed until there is sufficient need for them. Care must be taken to see that systems do not become an end in themselves or the "trappings of bureaucracy."

PRINCIPLES FOR STANDARD PROCEDURES. The development of systems should be centrally controlled so that they can be designed to implement the purposes and the policies of the firm. (1) Systems should be so drawn up as to avoid friction and duplication of effort. (2) They must achieve definite, useful ends and cover only recurring needs. (3) They must be simple and easy to understand. (4) They should fix responsibility for mistakes. (5) They should be economical: a system should cost no more than it is worth. (6) They should be periodically appraised for their effectiveness and economy: obsolescent systems and forms should be weeded out.

BENEFITS OF STANDARD PROCEDURES. When properly designed, systems achieve certain advantages. (1) By applying the principle of exceptions, they free executives from trifling concern with recurring detail. (2) By introducing method and order, they reduce costs, improve control, and help fix responsibility. (3) As a means of managerial direction, they are clear and easy to remember. (4) They provide a ready-reference file of current executive instructions and decisions.

Preparation of Manuals and Organization Charts. Effective managerial direction and control are facilitated by policy manuals, organization charts, and organization manuals. These enable executives and subordinates to have a thorough understanding of their respective roles in the whole management picture: they encourage full devotion of energies to the effective discharge of proper functions, and they preclude duplication of effort, friction, and working at cross-purposes.

POLICY MANUAL. Company objectives are best summarized in a policy manual which clearly states general and departmental policies.

ORGANIZATION CHARTS. As an organization is being constructed, it should be graphically outlined on charts showing the over-all breakdown into departments, sections, and units (or groups) and defining the positions of staff assistants and committees. These charts should also indicate the span of executive control, the levels of authority, and the functional relationships among the divisions (see Fig. 3). Generally there are one chart for the company as a whole and auxiliary charts for each department.

ORGANIZATION MANUAL. Although organization charts present a graphic structural breakdown of the company, they do not specifically stipulate how each unit of the organization should function. They need, therefore, to be supplemented by an organization manual containing written specifications for each executive office, department, committee, and key job. Such specifications should cover objectives, functions, jurisdiction, responsibilities, relationships, and limits of authority. The organization manual should also include *department write-ups*, containing the name of each department, its function in the organization, its duties (including services to other departments) and those of its individual sections, and the title of the department head with a listing of his special duties. The manual should clearly indicate which parts of the organization are to provide services to line functions.

Selection of Qualified Personnel. The best means of selecting personnel is to analyze the requirements of each position and then to find a man whose qualifications measure up to the requirements. Executives should be men of sound judgment with well-balanced training and qualities of *leadership*. Effective, dynamic leadership depends upon the leader's capacity to plan and direct operations and his ability to win confidence and enthusiastic participation. Executive ability can be effectively utilized only when definite plans have been made and standards of performance set up and when executives have been relieved of routine activity by systems of procedures which enable them to concentrate on long-range planning, over-all direction, co-ordination and control, and current problems and matters which cannot be covered by standard instructions.

RE-EXAMINATION OF AN ORGANIZATION STRUCTURE

A company organization may need to be re-examined for any one of several reasons: it may have been improperly set up in the beginning; it may have become inadequate because of the growth of the firm; it may have become obsolete because of changes in the character or needs of the business; temporary and improvised arrangements may at one time have been made in the assignment of new departmental functions and responsibilities but have become more or less permanent, so that the structure is illogical and unwieldy and control difficult to maintain.

It is therefore important that management periodically survey and reappraise the adequacy of its organization structure.

Before making a reorganization study, however, top management must impress upon all key executives the need for such a survey and the contribution of a streamlined internal structure to competitive efficiency. The realization of this need is paramount in getting the co-operation of department heads, without which no reorganization can be successful.

The Choice of an Analyst. The survey of the organization may be assigned to a competent staff officer, to a committee, or to the industrial-engineering department. When drastic revisions are likely to be needed, however, it is usually wiser to hire a management consultant to do the job; a competent outside analyst is more likely to have the unbiased point of view necessary for his recommendations to be received with confidence. Top management must be aware of the effect of the reorganization study on the morale of personnel.

Procedure for Improving an Obsolescent Organization. (1) Review company policies, (2) collect pertinent data, and (3) analyze the existing organization structure for profitable revamping. Finally, make revisions and improvements and provide for orderly transition so that current operations will not be disrupted.

Review and Restatement of Company Policies. A review of company policies should precede detailed analysis of the organization structure, since the organization must be the expression of, as well as the means of achieving, the goals outlined by the policies. Top management may have failed at the outset to formulate policies covering every important phase and aspect of the business; the original policies may simply have become defunct. In any case, top management must now formulate comprehensive current policies and revise old ones.

Collection of Data. The analyst should begin by preparing organization charts and duty sheets that portray current conditions. These will enable him to visualize company operations as a whole and to judge the soundness of the actual organization. He will realize that any practices which cannot readily be charted are likely to be illogical and confusing to employees.

In collecting his data, he should consult the existing charts and manuals; but he should not rely upon them for they may be inadequate or out-of-date. He should visit the heads of all departments and sections and obtain complete statements of their functions, scopes of authority, responsibilities, and relationships with other executives—

42

that is, he must find out what they understand their individual duties to be.

Analysis of Organization Structure. As the analyst collects data, he studies the current organization structure to determine shortcomings. A comprehensive analysis will produce improved organization charts and an improved manual which will eliminate weaknesses and set forth sound principles of organization based on the needs of the firm. The organization analyst must be realistic, use good judgment, and consider the human equation. His recommendations for revising the organization structure may include reallocation of functions and combinations of duties; elimination of some departments, sections, positions, and committees or creation of others. He must show how his recommendations will increase efficiency and reduce costs.

CHECKLIST OF TYPICAL FLAWS. The following paragraphs summarize typical flaws the analyst may uncover.

1. *Vagueness in Assignment of Duties.* Top management may have failed to establish clear-cut policies concerning important phases of the business. Hence, heads of departments may not clearly understand their own functions and spheres of activity. There may be overlapping of authority: executives may cut across organizational lines in issuing orders, and there may be confusion between line duties and staff duties with staff officers giving orders to subordinates of line officers.

2. *Responsibility without Delegation of Authority.* The firm may have failed to delegate adequate authority to its executives: if duties are to be discharged, they must be accompanied by authority.

3. *Overburdening of Executives.* The span of executive control in some cases may be excessive (that is, too many diverse activities may have been placed under one head), necessary staff assistants may be lacking, adequate standard procedures for routine activity may not have been set up, or executives themselves simply may not know how to delegate authority to subordinates.

4. *Lack of Co-ordination among Departments.* Absence of the unifying force of an effective executive committee may have led to working at cross-purposes, friction, and inefficiency.

5. *Illogical Assignment of Duties.* Duties that should logically be assigned to one department may have been assigned to an-

other. Illogical arrangement exists, for instance, when matters of credit and collections are assigned to the sales department instead of to the controller's department or when the authority to specify quality standards is assigned to the inspection department rather than to the engineering department.

6. *Assignment of Unrelated Duties to a Single Executive.* A small company may need to assign unrelated functions to an executive. As the company grows, he may retain these functions though efficient organizational structure would call for a change.

7. *Splitting of Functions among Departments.* Functions may be needlessly split among departments; for example, changes in the design of a product may be made independently by various members of a firm instead of by the engineering department. Ideally, each function should be centralized in a single department.

8. *Duplication of Functions.* Sometimes several departments perform the same tasks; for instance, various sections of an organization may maintain files of the same kinds of records.

9. *Neglect of Important Functions and Undue Stress upon Secondary Functions.* A company may ignore effective control of materials while it emphasizes stockroom classification of materials; or it may ignore the matter of preventing defective work while it emphasizes the salvaging of defective products.

10. *Improper Selection of Executives.* Men of high ability may be kept in subordinate positions while men of mediocre ability—because of "pull," nepotism, chance, or the rapid growth of the company—hold important posts. If this situation is unremedied, the company will lose some of its best talent.

11. *Poor Ranking and Lack of Standard Nomenclature.* Levels of authority among departments may not be parallel. The titles for subdivisions and positions of comparable rank may not be uniform: for example, one subordinate executive may be identified as a "section head," another as a "supervisor," and a third as a "superintendent."

Recommendation of Orderly Transition. The analyst should propose a plan for orderly transition from the old to the new organization structure. The transition must avoid damaging the morale of the personnel and avoid disrupting current operations. Some changes may be made immediately; others may take longer, for the management may want to ease transitions by waiting for an anticipated expansion of business or for the retirement of certain executives and supervisors. Displaced supervisory personnel, with long company service or knowledge of the business, may be appointed heads of new sections or placed in staff-assistant positions where they can make a pertinent contribution to the firm.

Questions

1. Outline the procedural steps for the design of an organization structure.

2. Explain and illustrate the meaning of "homogeneity," "authority," "responsibility," "span of executive control," and "levels of authority."

3. Explain and illustrate how top management can achieve teamwork and co-ordination through a clear definition of policies and an effective use of committees.

4. Explain and illustrate how the effectiveness of an executive can be increased (or how his burden may be reduced) through the use of staff assistants and the application of the principle of exceptions.

5. Draw up an organization chart for a corporation operating a chain of eight drugstores or food markets in a given city. In the structure show which of the firm's "service functions" you would place in the central office.

6. Design an organization structure for a large liberal-arts college. In developing the structure, get information from a school bulletin, observe the procedure on page 35, and include typical procedures and committees.

7. Why must organization structures be periodically re-examined? Outline the procedural steps for re-examining an organization structure for improvement.

8. Illustrate the typical organizational weaknesses you may find in a rapidly growing corporation. Explain how "morale" is adversely affected by a poor organization structure.

9. A light manufacturer (producer of furniture, automobile accessories, men's suits, etc.) with one thousand employees has bought out, and is to absorb, two firms in the same line of production with about five hundred employees each. Outline the procedural steps you would follow for setting up a new organization and draw up an illustrative chart for the completed merger. (Assume the existence of three separate plants in the enterprise.)

7: Business Promotion, Planning, and Risks

Before a new firm or branch is started, its promoters should conduct a thorough survey to determine whether it will be sufficiently profitable to justify the investment and time needed for its establishment; and they should plan and organize the new enterprise so as to minimize anticipated risks and to assure sound future growth.

THE SURVEY FOR PROMOTING A BUSINESS

Procedure for Starting a Business. (1) Analyze the proposed products and the market; (2) analyze and forecast the economic prospects for the venture; (3) determine the major goals and the scope of operations; (4) design the products for maximum marketability and low-cost output; (5) determine the size of establishment that will be initially needed; (6) select a proper initial location for the business; (7) determine which parts to make and which to buy; (8) select and lay out the process, equipment, and buildings; (9) determine the amount of funds needed and the anticipated profits, and select a plan for financing; (10) set up the organization structure and choose personnel; (11) launch the business—acquire land, start construction, buy equipment.

These interrelated steps, which include all the considerations from the inception to the actual manufacture and sale of a product, are summarized briefly in this chapter and are more fully discussed in later chapters.

Obviously, not every survey calls for all of the steps. The survey for a hotel or television and radio repair company, for example, will not be concerned with product engineering (step 4) or with the decision to buy or make parts (step 7); and the survey for the establishment of a branch plant for furniture manufacture, for fabrication of automobile parts, for meat packing, or for the handling of other commercially established products can obviously draw upon much detailed information that is already available.

Product and Market Analysis. An over-all product and market research study is made when the development of a product or an idea has reached the stage where it is ready for commercial exploitation.[1] This study involves detailed analyses of the utility and the marketability of the product, the character of the demand (whether steady or fluctuating), the potential extent of demand, the anticipated competition, and the possible marketing outlets.

PRODUCT. So that each item may be designed for maximum salability in a chosen price field, the product analysis must be made from the viewpoint of the prospective consumers. For such items as cameras, portable radios, powered lawn mowers, or house trailers, for example, the analyst will note that consumers are interested in performance, size, weight, durability, and form or styling at a given price. The analyst should also consider the advisability of offering more than one model or size. Data on consumer preferences and other marketing problems may be compiled from well-planned questions presented to a selected consumer panel, from a sample trial of the product, and from a survey to determine to what degree existing products meet buyers' needs. After the consumer's reaction has been obtained through such market tests, the salability of the product at a given price range can be appraised.

CURRENT DEMAND. The nature of the demand for the product or service must also be investigated. The demand for a repeat-sales article (such as a light bulb or a toothbrush), for instance, may be greater than the demand for an item which can last for years (such as a wrist watch or fountain pen). If the product is a necessity (for example, a basic food, a razor blade, or a medicine), the demand is likely to be comparatively steady—i.e., somewhat "inelastic"; if a luxury (for instance, leather dress gloves, jewelry, or brandy), the demand will probably be more "elastic." [2] If the item is a durable good (such as a refrigerator, typewriter, piano, or other commodity that has a continuous use over a period of time), then the demand may fluctuate widely over the various phases of the business cycle.

POTENTIAL DEMAND. The size of the market, the number of consumers and their purchasing power and buying habits, and the trend

[1] The industrial research, development engineering, and product evaluation carried on prior to this time are discussed in Ch. 9.

[2] An "inelastic demand" is one which decreases or increases in relatively small volume as prices rise or fall; an "elastic demand" is one which decreases or increases in relatively large volume as prices rise or fall.

of consumption make up the potential demand for a given product. The size of the market (local, national, or international) is limited by the ease and cost of shipment, the uniqueness and patent protection of the item, and trade barriers. A bulky inexpensive product, such as bread, may have only a local market; whereas high-priced cosmetics, surgical instruments, or recently patented drugs may have an international market.

When the item under survey is a consumer good (e.g., clocks, liquor, or other products that directly satisfy desire), the study should determine the number of possible consumers and their buying preferences—that is, "who" will buy the item and "when," "where," and "how" it will be purchased. When the item is an industrial product (e.g., a newly developed packaging machine or an automatic gauging instrument), the study should ascertain what industries can use it, how many consuming firms are in the market, and what substitutes, if any, are available. The trend of consumption of the same or similar products may be a prime factor in ascertaining potential demand. If the trend has been downward over a period of years, the signs are in the main unfavorable. If, however, the trend has been upward, the chances for success are greater.

COMPETITION. The extent and kind of competition should be carefully appraised before an attempt is made to penetrate the market. If the product is an everyday article such as a watch, china, or cutlery, it may prove advantageous to design the item for low-cost output in order to do business in large volume at a small profit margin; if, however, it is unique, it may be wiser to design a high-grade commodity (for example, an expensive cosmetic) to be sold at a large profit margin. If the market to be invaded is one with relatively few producers, the monopolistic pricing practices of the industry should be considered before a tentative price is set. If the market is highly competitive, however, the product will have to be sold at the going market price. In order to secure the best competitive advantage, products and services should be made as distinctive as is economically possible. They may be made so not only through special design features, but also through convenient and novel packaging, informative labeling, instruction sheets, and impressive trade-marks such as "Cat's Paw," "Nabisco," and "Kodak." [3]

---

[3] A "trade-mark" is a distinctive name, symbol, or design placed upon products and used to identify a specific seller or producer. It is acquired by the first to apply the mark to products, and it may be registered with the Patent Office in the United States.

If the item is to be protected by a patent,[4] it is best to get a *basic patent*, one that has scope sufficient to cover the fundamental features of the innovation—be it product, material, or process. Such a patent will secure the right to exclusive commercial exploitation and will enable the manufacturer to dominate a large part of the field. Efforts should be made to fortify the patent position and to acquire additional patents which cover related or future applications of the innovation as well as any minor structural changes in the original invention.

MARKETING OUTLETS. The sales promotion plan and the channels of distribution should be appropriate to the product and the market.[5] Consumer buying habits and commercial custom in the particular field are factors to be considered in the selection of outlets. Potential distributors may include retailers, wholesalers and jobbers, industrial dealers and distributors, and manufacturers' agents. A tentative plan for consumer credit and financing and for sales allowances and discounts should be formulated on the basis of the marketing channels selected.

Economic Analysis and Forecast. All facts about the current business and economic situation and about future trends, insofar as they bear on the given venture, should be analyzed and appraised. Among those that pertain to the promotion, organization, time of launching, and probable success of a given business enterprise are: the secular trend (long-term changes), the business cycle, seasonal variations, and special economic problems such as those which occur in a wartime economy. The interaction of the secular, cyclical, seasonal, and special factors creates the economic environment to which a promotional plan must be adapted and in which a business must be launched and operated.

SECULAR FACTOR. Basic changes in consumer wants and tastes, the rate of population growth in various areas, fundamental technological developments, and increase or depletion of natural resources make up the secular trend whose effects on a given venture must be evaluated.

Examples of changes in consumer tastes are the increasing consumption of domestic wine and the declining popularity of hats for

---

[4] A "patent" is the right to exclusive ownership of an invention and is granted by a government to an individual or organization for a term of years. The law awarding "the exclusive right to prevent all other persons from making, using, or selling specimens of the invention" may be enforced through the courts. Patents, in the United States, are issued for any new and useful art, substance, machine, or process for a term of seventeen years.

[5] Marketing and channels of distribution are discussed in Ch. 22.

49

men. The importance of population growth can be seen in the mushrooming of new enterprises (e.g., in building supplies and in furniture) on the Pacific Coast, particularly in Southern California. The impact of technology is illustrated by the rapid growth of television and the comparative decline of the motion-picture industry. The importance of rich resources is exemplified by the continued growth of oil refineries and chemical plants along the Gulf Coast; whereas the comparatively limited resources of New England partly account for its slow business expansion.

CYCLICAL FACTOR. The *time of entry* into business must be selected with regard to primary cyclical influences (prosperity, recession, depression, and recovery) which effect changes in employment, in national income (purchasing power and demand), in availability of investment funds, in price levels, and in consumer attitudes of optimism or pessimism. Because of cyclical influences, wide fluctuations usually occur in consumer demand for luxury services (e.g., those provided by tourist resorts and restaurant businesses) and durable commodities (e.g., automobiles), whereas the demand for necessities (e.g., milk, cooking oil, laundry soap) is comparatively stable. Unless the long-run business prospects are very favorable, an enterprise which requires a large investment in land and physical facilities should avoid entering business during a peak-prosperity period when the cost of such fixed assets is high. Enterprises that can be established on a moderately profitable basis during depression and recovery periods reap advantages in terms of low-cost land, buildings, and equipment and thus enjoy low initial overhead costs which may mean high profits during prosperity.

SEASONAL FACTOR. If the business is one with marked seasonal variations in the volume of production (e.g., fruit canning), allowances and adjustments must be made. The survey should take into account the possibility of manufacturing complementary products during the slow period. For example, a firm manufacturing air-conditioning units for summer sale may use the same facilities to turn out heating appliances for winter sale; and a firm producing bathing suits for summer sale may turn out corsets and brassières for winter sale.[6]

SPECIAL FACTORS. In addition to forecasting the cumulative influence of the secular, cyclical, and seasonal factors affecting a given business, the survey must appraise such special economic problems as the securing of defense contracts during a wartime economy; the material and equipment shortages that will occur during a postwar period; gov-

---

[6] The problem of stabilizing production is discussed in Ch. 21.

ernment policy with respect to taxes and expenditures, bank credit and interest rates, tariff changes, and stockpiling of raw materials. The survey should also analyze *business mortality*—the number of business failures in a particular field. Economic and business data relating to a given industry or area can be secured from the Department of Commerce, industrial departments of state governments, the Committee for Economic Development (CED), chambers of commerce, and trade associations and from such publications as the *Federal Reserve Bulletin, Survey of Current Business,* financial journals, and crop reports.

Objectives and Scope. When market research and an economic analysis of a business venture have been completed, the major objectives and the scope of operations should be outlined in an *over-all plan* and in *policies.* The over-all plan will guide the development of the firm with respect to manufacturing and marketing activities, expansion and degree of integration, and business adaptability and stability.

Promoters initially outline the scope of business through *product planning:* the number and size or models in the line; additional manufacturing or service fields into which the business might expand; the quality and price range in which the firm will compete; a decision as to whether or not consumers will be serviced; and methods whereby products will be marketed—e.g., by selling either directly to consumers or through outside distributors.

The promoters should decide how extensive the projected firm is to be: how many divisions (plants, warehouses, sales establishments) would be economical and whether the firm should concentrate in one location or branch out. Their decision may be to concentrate initially at a single spot and later to expand on a decentralized basis. The amount of possible and desirable flexibility in production facilities must also be determined. In appraising need for flexibility, promoters should take into account the nature of the product and market (fixity of product design and possible changes in style, consumer tastes, and demand), as well as the best methods of achieving stability of operation in the face of seasonal and cyclical fluctuations.

Design of Products. Good design assures the proper functioning, performance, and styling of products for maximum consumer utility and marketability. Products must be designed for economical manufacture as well as for appeal to consumers at a given price range. The completed design is presented in drawings, bills of materials, chemical formulas, description sheets, and other types of specifications.

The various models or sizes in the line should be planned so as to achieve maximum interchangeability of parts and subassemblies and yet maintain the required distinctiveness among products. Interchangeability reduces investment in plant facilities and makes for continuous use and flexibility of production equipment since the same machinery can be employed in the output of parts going into various final products. (Product engineering is discussed in Ch. 9.)

Size of Establishment. The initial size of the establishment must be based on judicious sales estimates. The previous market analysis will have determined only the potential demand; an intensive market analysis must now be undertaken to determine the best promotional methods for converting potential demand into actual sales and to forecast short-term and long-term sales. With accurate sales estimates, the firm through "break-even" analysis [7] can avoid investing in an establishment that is too large and expensive to be profitable at the outset—but can select a size sufficiently large to take care of the initial sales and their expected increase during the years immediately ahead.

Location. The general location and the specific site are chosen on the basis of proximity to markets, access to low-cost materials, availability of labor, ease and cost of shipping, and other needs of the given enterprise. The more important of the foregoing factors (which depend on the specific enterprise) should be favored during the selection if the location is to permit the lowest cost in producing and distributing the commodity or service. In view of the large financial commitments involved in the acquisition of a business site and the seriousness of the handicap of a poor location, careful analysis and a comparison of total operating costs between suitable locations should be made before a permanent site is chosen. (The procedure for selecting a business location is discussed in Ch. 8.)

Determination of Which Parts to Make and Which to Buy. Few firms manufacture all the parts and materials needed for their final products or services. The decision whether to make or buy a given part, subassembly, or material involves a comparison between the cost of producing the item and the cost of buying it. An item is purchased when it can more cheaply be procured from a vendor (with assurance of reliable quality and delivery) than produced by the firm. Standard supply items, parts, and materials consumed in comparatively small quantities are usually more economical to buy than to fabricate. The extent

---

[7] See Ch. 26 for discussion.

to which a firm will engage in turning out items that go into its finished goods partly depends upon the degree to which vertical integration of production is profitable.[8]

Selection of Process, Equipment, and Plant Layout. Physical facilities must be selected and a layout plan developed for economical output of the required volume of products or services, for desired flexibility in production, for ease of future expansion of output, and for other goals determined by the survey.

PROCESS AND EQUIPMENT. The selection of the process and equipment is based largely on the design specifications and bill of materials (which determine how the parts and product can be manufactured) and on the required volume of output. The larger the volume to be produced, the more specialized and efficient the equipment can be. When alternative equipment and processes are practicable, the cost and efficiency of each should be compared before a choice is made. The desirability of leasing production facilities should be considered, particularly when corporate profit tax rates are high or when the probability of success in the venture is not very definite. In general, equipment and buildings can be effectively selected only in conjunction with the development of the layout plan for the establishment.

LAYOUT. The aim of layout engineering is to organize the physical facilities (including the arrangement of equipment and buildings and the allocation of space for each activity) so as to insure an efficient output of products or services. The kind of building to be selected and designed is that which best fits the over-all needs of the *layout plan* and the chosen business site—metropolitan, suburban, or rural. (The procedure for the layout of a business establishment is discussed in Ch. 17.)

Funds, Profitability, and Financial Plan. At this point, the prospects for profitability must be determined and the financing of the proposed enterprise must be planned. The profitability of the projected firm can be estimated only after the total investment requirements are computed and sales receipts estimated.

FINANCIAL NEEDS. The amount of funds required for the enterprise can be computed when the scope of business operations has been clearly outlined; when a detailed layout plan and equipment lists have been prepared; and when figures on the cost of land, equipment, buildings, inventory, and operational needs have been compiled. (These cost data can be acquired from such sources as equipment manufac-

---

[8] See Ch. 3 for discussion of vertical integration.

turers, building contractors, those who have the facilities to lease, and suppliers.) It is not the current costs that are relevant but the esti-mated future costs—that is, when the firm will be requiring facilities and conducting business. Obviously, the more thorough the survey, the more accurate the data. Funds must be sufficient to meet fixed-capital, working-capital, and promotional needs. (The procedure for computing investment requirements is discussed on pp. 23–26.)

PROFITABILITY. After the total investment has been calculated and the sales receipts estimated, anticipated profits can be computed. The annual net profits can be estimated from a projected profit-and-loss statement—that is, from a consideration of gross sales receipts minus cost of production, distribution, and administration.

The estimated annual net profits should be expressed as a *percentage of investment*—e.g., $50,000 net profit on an investment of $500,000 is a return of 10 per cent. Whether a given rate of return on the in-vestment is considered sufficiently high to justify starting a new enter-prise depends upon the return possible in other fields of enterprise, the kind and magnitude of risk involved in the business, the flexibility of operations, the ease of withdrawing the investment from the enterprise, the phase of the business cycle,[9] and other economic prospects—e.g., the rate and trend in profit tax, excise tax, and tariffs.

It is customary to express profits as a *percentage of net sales receipts;* for instance, $10,000 net profit on $200,000 net sales receipts is a return of 5 per cent. This expression of profits is not a true measure of profita-bility, however, since it ignores the amount of the total investment in a business and the annual turnover in sales. The calculation of profits as a percentage of the investment in a new enterprise provides a truer measure of profitability.

The computation of the annual rate of return on the investment of a firm that has been in business for many years is complicated by the problem of determining its *real financial value*. Then again, the earn-ing capacity of the business affects the value of the firm, since the value is generally determined by capitalizing the average annual income from the business.[10] Thus, even though the original investment in a firm may have been only $30,000, the company might be able to

[9] A return of 11 per cent on initial investment in a depression period may be considered sufficient to justify entry into business; the same return during a prosperity period may be considered inadequate and risky.

[10] A capitalization based upon $15,000 annual income at 15 per cent $\left(.15 \overline{)15,000.00} ^{100,000} \right)$, for instance, is $100,000—the "market" value of the business.

sell its business for as much as $100,000 if its annual net profits average $15,000, which is a 50-per-cent return on the initial investment.

Organization Structure and Personnel. When the decision to launch the enterprise has been made, an internal organization structure is set up. The major functions of the business (e.g., engineering, manufacturing, and sales) are arranged as logical divisions, established as departments, and subdivided into sections. The structure is outlined in an organization chart; and the duties of top officers, department heads, section chiefs, supervisors, committees, and staff assistants are stipulated in an organization manual. Qualified men are selected for all key positions. Top management—through its policies, directives, committees, and standard procedures—guides and co-ordinates the operations of the firm. (The procedure for developing an organization structure is discussed in Ch. 6.)

Launching of the Enterprise. The firm is launched by assembling and organizing the physical facilities, developing operation and production processes, advertising its products and initiating a sales-promotion campaign, recruiting labor, and accumulating inventories. This involves purchasing an appropriate business site, contracting for the erection of the building, and purchasing and installing machinery, equipment, and fixtures according to the layout plan. Operation and production processes are further developed through work-routing sheets, instruction cards, and systems of standard procedures. The more complex operations should be tested by pilot runs before final standardization. Each of these various activities is discussed in detail in subsequent chapters.

CONTINUOUS BUSINESS PLANNING: REDUCTION OF RISKS

Once the enterprise is launched, the initial program does not remain unchanged: management, if it is to maintain solvency and long-run profitability, must periodically reappraise its business situation and plan its over-all program to fit the economic environment and business trends. Therefore, depending on its analysis and forecast of external forces and trends, farsighted management formulates such *company plans* as (1) an expansion program for the upswing phase of the business cycle, or a suitable cutback or contraction program for the recession phase; (2) a product program for the introduction of new items or models to meet competition and shifts in market demand; (3) a comprehensive modernization program to keep its facilities technologically up-to-date; (4) a business merger program; or (5) the best combination of the foregoing types of programs. Such program plans usually modify a firm's scope of operations, facilities, and manpower and material requirements.

Because of the changing economic environment and uncertainty of business and the unpredictability of human behavior and of natural forces, risks are inherent in business operation. Management must, therefore, set up and maintain a program for minimizing risks and losses. A knowledge of the nature and main sources of risks is the first step in the planning of a program for their prevention or reduction.

Sources of Risks. Risks and losses may arise from economic fluctuations, wars, technological change, new laws affecting business, hazards to company personnel and property, and hazards and loss to outsiders for which the company is liable. Shortsighted planning and mismanagement are also causes of financial loss.

ECONOMIC FLUCTUATIONS. Rapid changes in style or shifts in consumer tastes adversely affect a firm that is overstocked with slow-moving goods. Because of overspecialization a firm may find it costly to adjust to such unanticipated turns in the market. Similarly, if the price of finished goods in a highly competitive industry takes a temporary dip, a company that has purchased raw materials at high prices suffers losses. For business as a whole, moreover, certain phases of the business cycle bring widespread losses and many bankruptcies. The excessive optimism associated with the "boom" of the prosperity phase of a cycle tends to promote overexpansion of capacity during a period when construction and equipment costs are high. When a recession sets in, demand declines, prices fall, and sales receipts dwindle; meanwhile, the cost per unit of product remains high owing to heavy overhead charges stemming from idle capacity.

WARTIME DISRUPTION. Although firms engaged in military production or the output of "essential commodities" do a profitable business in wartime, firms in "nonessential" fields of business (particularly those with facilities not easily convertible to military output) operate at low levels or are shut down because of shortages of materials, equipment, and labor. Export firms, owing to the difficulty of maintaining foreign sales, are also adversely affected.

TECHNOLOGICAL CHANGE. Technology may cause losses by rendering obsolete the facilities and products of a given firm when a rival firm adopts newly patented processes and materials. A firm, too, may be hampered by a poor location if economical methods of extracting raw materials are developed in distant areas whereby competing firms will be favored because of their locations.

New Laws Affecting Business. The levying of new excise taxes and the reduction of tariffs, though perhaps socially desirable, tend to reduce the sales revenue of affected firms. New zoning ordinances, laws to control noxious fumes, and increased property taxes may raise the cost of operations and may thus adversely affect the competitive position of urban firms that can not economically abandon their location in a high-cost metropolitan area.

Hazards to Personnel and Property. The untimely death of a key executive may seriously disrupt some phase of business operations. Moreover, under workmen's compensation laws, the employer must contribute to compensation for injuries caused by accidents or disease occurring while the employee is on the job, even though the worker is at fault. Damage and destruction to company property and interruption of business may result from storm, flood, explosion, fire, accidents during processing, or improper storage of materials.

Company Liability for Loss to Public. A firm may be liable for injuries suffered by customers while they are receiving services or visiting the business establishment; it may be liable for commodities harmful to health or dangerous in use; and it may be liable for damage caused by company vehicles to the property of outsiders.

Program for Minimizing Risks and Losses. To minimize risks and losses, management should not only emphasize thoroughness in its initial promotional survey, but it should also plan and adopt an overall program which includes a minimum-investment policy, maximum business adaptability and accurate forecasting, a risk survey, a safety program, and insurance.

Comprehensive Survey. Many risks can be avoided if businessmen conduct a thorough study to determine the probable success of an enterprise before they decide to float it. The results of the survey should be accurately appraised; and, in cases of doubt, aid should be obtained from bankers, business consultants, government agencies, and economists. High-caliber executives should be sought early in the initiation of the new firm.

Minimum-Investment Policy. Financial risk in the ownership of property can be reduced through adoption of a minimum-investment policy. If the future is uncertain, light manufacturing enterprises that would be easy to expand (e.g., those manufacturing small instruments, sporting goods, or apparel) should start on a modest scale. Enterprises requiring a substantial commitment of capital can often avoid investing funds in fixed assets by leasing buildings and other facilities, buying fabricated parts and subassemblies from subcontractors, and selling through outside distributors. Once success is assured, management can erect its own building, acquire more equipment for the manufacture of parts and subassemblies, and sell through its own channels of distribution.

BUSINESS FORECASTING AND ADAPTABILITY. Business firms in industries characterized by shifts in demand and in consumer tastes and confronted by rapid technological change (e.g., radio, television, and phonograph records) should not only emphasize a minimum-investment approach, but should also stress maximum flexibility (consistent, however, with low operating costs) in production facilities, in organization structure, and in procurement methods. By "hedging" they can minimize losses caused by fluctuations in the price of raw materials (see page 175).

Effective adaptability of business operations to external change (i.e., turns in the business cycle, technological advances, governmental policies and laws, and labor-union programs) can be increased through foresight, comprehensive forecasting, and research. Executives can anticipate business trends by studying economic indices and such barometers as national income figures, employment figures, and trends in price levels and interest rates. Keeping abreast of technological advance and avoiding obsolescence call for a progressive industrial-research program. Small firms unable to afford the expense of costly research may engage the services of commercial laboratories. Current governmental policies and pending legislation must be reviewed, and union policies and the pattern of labor's demands in collective bargaining must be constantly studied.

RISK SURVEY. The scope of business activities should be reviewed to discover where financial losses may occur and what preventive measures can be taken—that is, risks should be attacked at the point of prevention rather than at the point of loss. In each case, the expense of eliminating risk should be balanced against the possible losses. As protection against the loss of key men, understudies should be thoroughly trained. An adequate system of records to cover important phases of the business should be maintained. The title to the company's real estate should be checked. Sound credit policies, the accumulation of financial reserves for contingencies, and other methods for the maintenance of liquidity should be stressed.

SAFETY PROGRAM. Losses caused by injuries and accidents may assume large proportions unless controlled by a progressive safety program directed by a competent safety engineer or an aggressive safety committee. Well-organized safety programs can improve morale and eliminate losses through the reduction of hazards both to physical property and to the employee's health and safety.[11]

INSURANCE. Insurance is available for almost all calculable risks— credit losses, dishonesty of employees, theft, fire, explosion, windstorm, and public liability. Insurance is the final recourse for the residue of risk which remains without possibility of elimination. Insurance companies, on the basis of past experience and the *law of large numbers,* calculate the probability of a given type of loss and adjust the premiums to cover the total sum. Thus, the individual firm through insurance coverage can substitute small losses (premiums which it includes as a cost of current business) for a potential loss uncertain in amount and time.

Questions

1. Explain why a promotion study to launch a branch establishment for the output of a commercially established product can be more accurate than a promotion study to launch a business for the output of a newly developed product.

2. Why is the decision to buy or make given parts often influenced by the location of the firm?

3. Why will the demand for a durable consumer good generally fluctuate more widely throughout the various phases of the business cycle than the demand for a nondurable consumer good? Explain.

4. Illustrate how regional secular trends affect the long-run prospect of a business.

5. What factors determine the potential demand and the territorial size of the market for a given product?

6. How can data on consumer preferences in products be compiled?

7. (a) How can distinctiveness in products and servicing be achieved? (b) How does such distinctiveness affect the firm's "competitive" standing?

8. Can the amount of funds needed to start a business and the firm's profitability be realistically estimated before the required processes, equipment, and location are selected?

9. How can the break-even chart aid in selecting the best initial size of the establishment?

10. Why should business mortality figures, broken down regionally, be studied before a given type of business is started?

[11] The procedure for developing a safety program is discussed at the end of Ch. 23.

11. (a) Compare and evaluate "percentage of net sales receipts" and "percentage of return on investment" as a basis for measuring the profitability of a newly established firm. (b) What is the validity of "percentage of return on investment" as a measure of profitability for a firm that has been in business for many years?

12. What factors determine whether a given rate of return on investment is sufficiently profitable to justify starting a new business?

13. Why should promoters of a firm requiring heavy investment in fixed capital generally avoid going into business during the peak of prosperity?

14. Discuss the advisability of starting a business during a depression period when it promises a moderate return, say, 8 per cent.

15. What are the primary causes of business risk?

16. (a) How does the minimum-investment approach minimize risk? (b) What are some offsetting disadvantages of such a policy?

17. Why is it prudent to carry wider insurance coverage during periods of a high profits tax than during periods of a low profits tax?

8: Location of Business

The need for selecting a business location arises when a new enter- prise or branch is to be established, when a firm must move because it has outgrown its facilities or can not obtain a new lease, or when an undesirable location is to be abandoned. The *ideal location* is one that permits the lowest unit cost in the production and distribution of a product or service. Selection of a poor location usually results in some permanent handicap (for example, lack of space for storage or ex- pansion, depletion of local raw-material resources, or higher taxes than anticipated). Since locating a business involves a large, relatively per- manent investment, a mistake in selection can not be corrected without large losses.

Factors Influencing the Choice of the General Location. In select- ing a general location for its establishment, management must investi- gate the present and probable future adequacy of markets for the product, sources of raw materials, labor supply, transportation, power and fuel supply, and proximity both to allied and to necessary service industries. In addition, it must consider the climate of the locality, the character of the community, local and state tax rates, the possible ex- istence of hampering laws and regulations, and the advantages of de- centralization (geographic dispersion of company establishments).

Since the relative importance of the considerations varies from in- dustry to industry, *a location survey must be based on the specific re- quirements of a given enterprise*, and must therefore determine whether or not the location meets first the primary, and then the secondary, requirements. For example, firms dealing in retail and service activities (such as automobile sales and repair, laundering, or cleaning and dye- ing) will place primary emphasis on the availability and size of the

61

local market and on the cost of land and building or the cost of rent; but firms engaged in heavy manufacturing (such as production of steel and nonferrous metals, of cement, or of glass products) will place primary emphasis on the availability and adequacy of raw materials, fuel and power, transportation, and labor.

PROXIMITY TO DESIRED MARKETS. A business must have easy access to a growing market. Nearness to market will be emphasized by producers who sell bulky commodities which are costly to ship (e.g., brick and clay products), by producers who cater to a large local market that sets the pattern for style changes and indicates shifts in demand (such as producers of women's apparel), and by those who provide technical advice and servicing (such as tool-and-die companies).

PROXIMITY TO SUPPLY OF RAW MATERIALS. Nearness to raw materials is a primary locating factor if the materials are perishable, if they are of such bulk that they are expensive to transport, or if their weight can be substantially reduced by processing. This is well illustrated by fruit and vegetable canneries and sugar refineries, which must locate in food-growing areas.

AVAILABILITY OF LABOR. The adequacy of the labor supply in a given area must be considered in terms of the types of skilled labor required by the business. Firms requiring a variety of skilled labor can usually recruit the needed personnel by locating near large urban areas such as Chicago, Detroit, Birmingham, or New York City. It is generally unwise for a manufacturing firm to overemphasize "cheap labor" as a locating factor because—owing to minimum-wage laws, the increasing mobility of labor, and increasing unionization—wage rates are tending to become equalized and the apparent advantage of low wage rates in a given area is likely to prove short-lived.[1]

ADEQUACY AND COST OF TRANSPORTATION. In general, industries that use bulky materials and ship finished commodities tend to locate in areas where the cost of transportation is at a minimum. When other considerations permit, for instance, such establishments as oil refineries, cement mills, and automobile assembly plants producing for export choose areas where low-cost water transportation is available.

ADEQUACY AND COST OF POWER AND FUEL. Proximity to cheap power and fuel (coal, oil, natural gas) is important in the location of electrochemical, iron-and-steel, aluminum, glass, pulp-and-paper, and other

[1] In recent years, geographic wage differentials have been reduced through industry-wide collective bargaining and increased industrialization of formerly less developed areas.

industries using large amounts of these elements. The reliability of the supply, as well as its cheapness, must be investigated. The development of long-distance transmission of electricity has somewhat tended to minimize the importance of proximity to power in the location of many light manufacturing industries.

PROXIMITY TO FIRMS IN SIMILAR FIELDS. A location near other firms engaged in the same or similar lines of business is often advantageous because buyers are already attracted to the area; transportation facilities are usually good; many waste materials are easily disposed of (sometimes at a profit); financing is easier; and skilled labor, a variety of materials, and service and supply industries are available.

But there may be disadvantages to locating in specialized areas, too. A region may be rendered less desirable by the influence of outmoded business methods and restrictive union practices. Economic and technological changes, such as a shift in population and market and the development of new and cheaper sources of materials, may have eliminated some former location advantages.

SUITABILITY OF CLIMATE. Although modern systems of heating and air conditioning can control indoor temperature and humidity, the climate of a region nevertheless affects the vigor and alertness of human beings: variability of climate within moderate limits contributes to personal efficiency. Moreover, climate partly determines the cost of erecting suitable buildings and providing heat and air conditioning.

CHARACTER OF THE COMMUNITY AND SPECIAL INDUCEMENTS. Progressive regions provide good government, aid in location studies, and afford low-cost financing and specialized banking services. Some communities offer free or inexpensive land, power, and other benefits. Some have low-priced buildings (e.g., surplus defense plants) which should not be overlooked when choice of location is being considered.

REASONABLENESS OF STATE AND LOCAL TAXES. Tax rates on business income, property, and sales—as well as employee accident-insurance premiums—must be considered, for they vary in each area. Similarly, building codes and zoning laws, established to fit community needs, vary with respect to such requirements as control of fumes, disposal of waste products, and fire-resistant construction.

SUITABILITY TO DECENTRALIZATION. Decentralization occurs when there is a transfer of production to newly constructed plants in outlying areas where resources are favorable and the population is increasing; it is prompted by such advantages as nearness to growing regional markets, more favorable labor relations, and ease of future expansion.[2] Industries not requiring a heavy investment to achieve the benefits of mass production (e.g., those dealing in household appliances or food) can operate economically on a decentralized basis by establishing small-scale plants. However, some enterprises because of their enormous size can feasibly establish branch plants in widely scattered areas (for example, rubber tire and auto assembly factories).

Factors Influencing the Choice of the Local Site. After a general location has been chosen, the advantages and disadvantages of a particular location—metropolitan, rural, or suburban—should be carefully investigated; and the benefits offered by the "manufacturing district" should be appraised.

TYPE OF COMMUNITY. In general, the big city offers particular benefits to the small enterprise, the town offers advantages to the large manufacturing firm, and the suburb often best suits the medium-sized establishment.

City. An urban location has the advantages of a local market, an ample and diversified labor supply, proximity to allied industries, public-utility services, good shipping services, and educational and social facilities. The foregoing benefits must be weighed against the higher cost of land, higher taxes, greater building restrictions, and usually more complicated labor relations than would be found in small communities.

Town. Rural or small-town locations offer the advantages of cheap land, room for expansion, low taxes, few costly building and operating restrictions, and comparatively simple labor relations. Counterbalancing these advantages are the typical absence of allied industries, less adequate shipping and public-utility services, fewer educational and social facilities, smaller labor market, and frequently less adequate housing. A large corporation often can assist in providing housing, and usually it can overcome the problem of labor shortage, since it can attract, recruit, and train an adequate labor force.

Suburb. A suburban location offers a compromise between rural and city locations. In many cases it can provide both the advantages of a city (chiefly an available labor supply and market) and a town (primarily cheaper land and lower tax rates) with few of the disadvantages.

---

[2] By granting rapid tax-write-off benefits on plant expansion to firms doing defense work, the federal government has promoted plant dispersal. It has generally stipulated that new defense plants be located at least ten miles outside of metropolitan centers and other target zones.

However, possible changes in zoning laws, increased tax rates, and congestion should be anticipated.

AVAILABILITY OF MANUFACTURING DISTRICTS. Privately developed manufacturing districts (such as the Central Manufacturing District in Chicago, the Southeastern Industrial District in Atlanta, and the Bush Terminal in New York City) offer many useful benefits which should be considered in choosing a site. These districts provide financial assistance, construction aid, and dependable services (power, water, transportation facilities, plant protection) at low cost or on a co-operative basis. Low tax rates are frequently an additional benefit.

Procedure for Selecting the Location of a Specific Enterprise. Since the factors to be considered in locating a firm are not of equal importance, a survey should be made to determine the most pertinent in a given case. In general the relative importance of the factors can be determined on the basis of their proportionate share in the unit cost of production and distribution—e.g., direct labor may account for 40 per cent of the cost per unit of product, materials for 20 per cent, and overhead for 40 per cent. After the various factors have been weighed, favorable regions can be selected.

Consideration of the General Factors. For each of the likely areas the following types of data (depending on the particular enterprise) must be compiled: (1) the size of the local market and the cost of shipping to central markets; (2) materials—the cost of delivered raw materials, fuel, and power; (3) labor—the availability and wage rates of the required types of employees; (4) land—the availability and cost of sites; (5) the availability of suitable buildings; (6) the availability of needed service industries; (7) the character of the community with respect to taxes, restrictive laws, public services, and financial and educational facilities.

Computation of Investment and Cost of Production and Distribution. Next the required capital investment and the unit cost of production and distribution for a given volume of output should be computed for each prospective location. The table on the following page illustrates such a computation.

The location that offers the lowest costs of production and distribution will be given prime consideration. If the unit costs of production in the various locations are somewhat comparable, the location that requires the least capital outlay for fixed investment will be preferred. The final selection will depend not only upon the immediate investment and cost of production, but also upon the possible future trends:

Fixed Capital Requirements

LOCATION	A. NEW YORK	B. PHOENIX	C. LAS VEGAS
Land	$	$	$
Building			
Improvements			
Equipment			
Total	$	$	$

Unit Cost of Production and Distribution

LOCATION	A. NEW YORK	B. PHOENIX	C. LAS VEGAS
Materials	$	$	$
Direct labor			
Overhead			
Insurance			
Salaries			
Utilities			
Taxes			
Depreciation, etc.			
Distribution			
Total	$	$	$

the need for expansion of plant facilities; market changes; economic growth; wage rates; technology; taxes; and government programs for development of transportation, power, etc. The choice should be re-checked against detailed information obtained from local firms, banks, and government agencies.

Questions

1. Discuss the factors that have prompted the migration of the textile industry from New England to the South during the past fifty years.

2. Explain how climate influenced the establishment of the motion-picture and aircraft industries in Southern California.

3. Indicate in the order of importance three factors that would be considered before locating a firm (a) that manufactures low-priced toys, (b) that produces condensed milk, and (c) that produces bottled soft drinks.

4. Discuss the advantages of locating branch department stores in suburban areas of large cities.

5. Explain why the Ford Motor Company has widely scattered assembly plants, whereas it fabricates many parts and produces most of its subassemblies in Detroit.

6. Explain why a medium-sized plant manufacturing furniture and fixtures would find it more advantageous to locate in a suburb than in a city.

7. List the factors that would be important and outline the procedure for locating a large brewery.

8. What kind of businesses now located in the New York City area will be affected by the St. Lawrence Seaway Project, which promises cheap power and low-cost water transportation?

9: Research and Product Engineering

The growing productiveness of industry stems from technological advances made possible by research.[1] Utilizing the scientific method, research manipulates concepts and materials for the purpose of extending, refining, or verifying knowledge; the knowledge so gained may aid in the formulation of a theory or it may facilitate the scientific practice of an industrial art.

FUNCTION AND ORGANIZATION OF RESEARCH

Whereas pure research [2] deals with the basic sciences (mathematics, physics, *et al.*) and is engaged in principally for the sake of knowledge itself, applied *industrial research* has as its purpose the translation of the findings of pure research into new or improved processes, materials, and products. In recent decades applied research has become a necessary part of progressive management. (Post-World War II expenditures for private industrial research approximated one billion dollars annually.)

Typical Achievements of Applied Research. Although the various kinds of technological progress in industry are interdependent, a number of characteristic *forms* can be identified—developments in energy and fuel, in processes, in materials, in products, and in scientific management. A new, or improved, product can therefore be the result of a newly developed fuel, process, or material, or a new combination in the existing technology.

[1] The achievement of long-term gain in industrial productivity also calls for an increase in savings and capital investment, discovery and exploitation of resources, and a larger supply of skilled labor.

[2] Pure research is concerned with exploring the unknown to extend the boundaries of knowledge, to discover new facts, and to learn more accurately the characteristics of known facts, without any particular thought as to immediate practical utility.

9: Research and Product Engineering

DEVELOPMENTS IN ENERGY AND FUEL. Beginning in the Industrial Revolution with water power and coal, research has expanded the sources of energy to include oil, natural and artificial gas, and atomic power. Constant progress is being made in the development of new sources of energy and in the more economical use of existing fuel. Automatic stoking and improved boiler construction, for example, have decreased the amount of coal required to turn out power.

DEVELOPMENTS IN PROCESSES. Both mechanical and nonmechanical processes are being made more efficient. Not only are automatic machines replacing hand-controlled equipment, but large machines which consolidate many operations are replacing groups of small machines. In the manufacture of automobiles, for instance, huge presses turn out large "one-piece" sections (e.g., chassis and body roofs) which are used instead of sections built up from small parts that require time-consuming fabrication and assembly. Nonmechanical processes include those having to do with electricity, chemical reaction, and electro-chemical action. The substitution of spot and seam welding for riveting illustrates how an electrical process can lessen manual work.

DEVELOPMENTS IN MATERIALS. Rapid progress is being made in the development of new materials (e.g., plastics and synthetic textiles), in the improvement of existing materials (e.g., glass and steel alloys), in the adoption of cheaper substitute materials, and in the more efficient use of raw materials (e.g., the introduction of the "flotation process," which has extended copper reserves by making possible the commercial exploitation of low-grade ores).

DEVELOPMENTS IN PRODUCTS. New products (and by-products) and the improvement of existing commodities for utility and economy in output are characteristic of technological progress. Thus, television and three-dimensional motion pictures are innovations intended to increase consumer satisfaction. Examples of products improved in quality and durability are long-playing records, home refrigerators, and homogenized milk. Finally, useful commodities derived from waste materials result in conservation as well as cost reduction.

DEVELOPMENTS IN SCIENTIFIC MANAGEMENT. Research is broadening the scope and refining the techniques of scientific management. The use of production-control charts, break-even charts, statistical quality control, job evaluation, and industrial psychology are recent developments. Moreover, scientific management is spreading to farming, hospitals, governmental units (e.g., "city manager" plans), and other nonbusiness organizations. (Advances in scientific management

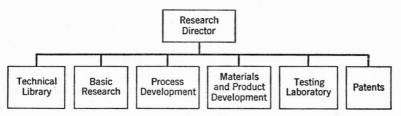

Fig. 4. A centralized industrial research department.

were discussed in Ch. 1. Market research, which is a special phase of scientific management closely related to product development, is discussed in Ch. 22.)

Types of Research Organization. The research function may be organized on a centralized, decentralized, or combination basis; or it may be assigned to an outside agency. Management must select the organizational plan for research that best fits the firm's scope of operations and need for technology and growth.

CENTRALIZED PLAN. In the centralized plan, research is set up as an independent division under a research director who is frequently given the status of a vice-president (see Fig. 4). The staff may be subdivided according to project programs or it may be broken down into special fields such as chemical, electrical, mechanical, and metallurgical. Centralized control of research can effectively focus scientific talent on well-defined company-wide objectives. When centralization is carried to excess, however, the research division may neglect problems in manufacturing and thus fail to make improvements whose cumulative effect over a period of years would be spectacular. The centralized plan of research is generally adopted by the large corporation. It is employed by many medium-sized firms when they concentrate the research function in a section of the engineering department; or, conversely, when they make engineering a section of the research department. The responsibility for research and product design may, in a small firm, be delegated to an operating executive.

DECENTRALIZED PLAN. A number of small research staffs may be set up—one for each branch, plant unit, or manufacturing department of a company. Under such a plan, research can be closely geared to the requirements of the various divisions of the company. The dispersal of research personnel and laboratory facilities, however, may result not only in duplication but also in making difficult the marshaling of research talent for company-wide technological goals. The development of new products and processes may thus be sacrificed for mere refinement of current production techniques. Nevertheless, the decentralized plan of research, despite these disadvantages, may be the most suitable for firms with plants in diverse fields of manufacture.

COMBINED CENTRALIZED AND DECENTRALIZED PLAN. Features of both centralization and decentralization may be combined in one plan to achieve considerable flexibility. Such a "combination plan" can enable a large corporation in diverse fields of manufacture to enjoy the advantages of a broad research program and to attain balanced technological gains for the company.

OUTSIDE AGENCIES. A number of outside organizations perform industrial research. (1) Technological research institutes (commercial laboratories) sell their services usually to small and medium-sized companies that lack the facilities needed for specific projects. (2) Some educational institutions undertake confidential research for private concerns on a business basis. (3) Trade associations and special industrial groups frequently engage in market- and product-research surveys of common interest. These surveys are restricted to types which do not affect the competitive standing of the member companies. (4) Government agencies perform both generalized and specialized research that may aid business as a whole.

THE DIRECTION OF RESEARCH AND PRODUCT ENGINEERING

Over-All Procedure for Industrial Research and Engineering. (1) Formulate the research program and budget on the basis of the firm's financial and competitive position and the potential fields for profitable research and their technological feasibility; (2) set up the goals (criteria) for the selection of research development projects (new or improved products and processes) that can be profitably utilized; (3) through a competent research director assure effective research practice and implementation and evaluation of research developments; and (4) through proper engineering organization and practice assure effective translation and preparation of research results for plant application (product design and processing).

The Research Program. Management can direct its industrial research by the type of organization plan it selects for the research function, the types of objectives (new or improved products, process development, cost-reduction) it emphasizes in its research program, and the amount of funds it appropriates for the various research projects. Management may determine the size of its research expenditure on the basis of sales volume, proportional to the firm's profits, or on a combination of both sales and profits. The outlay for technology must take into account not only what the firm can afford but also the research results needed.

Primary aims emphasized in research are to preserve the profitability of the firm's current investment, to ward off technological obsolescence, to maintain the firm's competitive position, and to insure success in the firm's primary fields of business. To be effective, research must be guided; it must not follow a hit-or-miss procedure. If unrestricted, it might produce such a diversity of techniques and items to manufacture as to go beyond the capacity of a company with limited capital and marketing outlets. Research, therefore, should be conducted in those fields of science and technology that are fairly directly related to the commercial interests of the firm; and the program must provide for the proper balance between exploratory research and development projects for early application. The company should select research projects and proposals (suggested by the research staff and various departments) on the basis of cost and time needed for solving the problems, the value to the firm of the results anticipated, and the technological feasibility of attaining solutions.

The research director ordinarily draws up the initial research program (budget) and submits it to the "research and development committee" comprised of the general manager and the departments of manufacturing, engineering, sales, and research. (The director should, therefore, be intimately familiar with the firm's policies, aims, and problems in order to anticipate its technological needs.) The committee analyzes and appraises each project and presents the results to top management for approval or rejection in the final research budget. The committee also periodically reappraises the research program for progress and proper emphasis and balance.

Goals in Product Development. Management, in its appraisal of a new product or an idea for a product, considers these points: How will the public accept this product? How will this new product affect the sale of the company's established line of goods? What is the anticipated sales volume and can the market be protected? How economically can the product be developed and manufactured?

CONSUMER ACCEPTANCE. To gain acceptance, products must be developed in the proper models and sizes for convenient and effective performance, for durability, and for appearance and styling; moreover, they must be designed for economy in factory production to insure a suitable price. Effective market analysis will define the quality and price that should satisfy consumers, whereas research and engineering will develop low-cost design which will embody the results of the market study.

MAINTENANCE OF A BALANCED LINE OF PRODUCTS. The new item might properly fill out an established line of products, but it could also adversely compete with some existing item. Again, it might deserve special consideration as a cheaply producible by-product.

ANTICIPATED OUTPUT AND MARKET PROTECTION. Estimated output depends largely upon market analysis and forecasting, for the anticipated volume of sales is a prime factor in determining whether a product should be developed, how the product should be designed, whether certain parts should be manufactured or purchased, what methods of manufacture should be employed (e.g., to what extent mass-production techniques would prove feasible), and what the size and location of the plant should be. Expected output depends also upon the amount of market protection which can be obtained through patents and secret processes (see Ch. 7).

ECONOMICAL MANUFACTURE. Research and engineering expenses and manufacturing costs (including the investment in facilities) should be closely estimated to determine how economical production can be and how big a return on investment can be expected. Simplified design and the use of standard materials, parts, and subassemblies should be emphasized so that savings may be effected through maximum adaptation to low-cost mass-production methods of manufacture. Company production and distribution facilities should be studied to determine whether idle capacity, or capacity not used during "slack" seasons, can be employed for the newly-developed product or complementary item and whether waste materials can be turned to gain.

Research Practice. An invention [3] of a research laboratory undergoes elaborate testing, development, and evaluation before it is taken over by an engineering department for plant application.

THE INITIAL IDEA. Although many inventions result from exploration and discovery, research must, nonetheless, be directed by company policies and budgetary appropriations toward company technological

---

[3] "Invention" is the act of going through the steps necessary to make an item or process patentable—that is, thinking up an idea and then putting it into some physical form, such as a drawing or a model.

problems and goals. A commercial idea for a research project may, however, originate anywhere in the organization.

PREPARATION OF A CRUDE MODEL OR PROCESS. The scientist learns all that he can about the new idea, its possibilities, and its limitations. He calls for data from the scientific library and consults with the firm's patent attorney to make certain that a prior patent has not been granted. He then plans a program for further investigation. If the idea is tentatively accepted by his supervisor for preliminary development, the first experiment is usually a simple test of the product or process or the construction of a crude working model. After he creates a successful working model, he prepares a written report summarizing all that is known of the model's utility, potentialities, and limitations. He submits the report, together with a plan outlining proposed future action, to the research director for approval.

COMMERCIAL EVALUATION. The research director critically appraises the idea from the point of view of company policy, of scientific and economic practicality, and of possible patent infringement. If the idea has to do with a new product, the market-research group evaluates its marketability. Finally, the research and development committee approves or rejects the project on the basis of its value to the firm.

ESTABLISHMENT OF A DEVELOPMENT PROJECT. After a project has been authorized, the director outlines the aims and scope of the project, assigns the various phases to specialists, establishes a tentative timetable, and allocates funds.

EVALUATION OF A WORKING MODEL OR PROCESS. The research staff subjects the working model to laboratory investigations and studies for the development of an improved model. It tests the model as a unit and each part separately. It considers variations in design, materials, and possible methods of manufacture. If the invention is a process, every step is tested separately. Periodically the director reviews the project to clarify or redefine its aims or perhaps to decide whether or not it is worth continuing. Upon completion of the research task, the director knows how the new device works, what it will do, how to make it, what material it requires, and what its production is likely to cost. From the foregoing critical analysis, the research staff recommends a final design to the engineering department. The idea, having reached a practical stage in the laboratory, is now ready for top management's approval and commercial exploitation. The new product or process is launched after the engineering department has conducted a test run in the plant preparatory to full-scale operation.

Engineering Organization and Practice. The chief engineer, who usually reports to the general manager, directs the departmental function.

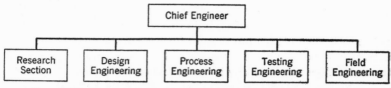

Fig. 5. An engineering department of a manufacturing firm.

Low-cost output of standardized products calls for *engineering preparation* involving eight steps. It is these that the chief engineer directs: (1) development of an efficient product design; (2) preparation of materials specification, parts lists, and drawings of parts, subassemblies, and final assemblies (Figs. 6 and 39); (3) determination of which parts to make and which to buy; (4) selection of methods of manufacturing and equipment for the required rate of output; (5) layout of equipment and machinery; (6) preparation of tools, jigs, fixtures, and gauges (Fig. 7); (7) preparation of operation sheets for the routing of work; and (8) trial runs before the final standardization of product and process (Fig. 8).

DESIGN ENGINEERING. Design engineering covers three major fields: (1) design of new products for the firm's regular line or for a supplementary line, (2) redesign of existing products for lower production costs and for new and wider uses and appeal, and (3) improvement in packaging for more salable sizes, greater appeal to the market, and convenience to consumers.

Design of New Products. The design group takes the findings of the research department or the research section (if it is subordinated to engineering) for further development and adaptation to factory use. It makes studies and tests to determine the best and cheapest materials, to eliminate unnecessary parts, and to attain maximum interchangeability of the remaining parts—all with the view to achieving efficient product design. Efficient designs are those which promise low-cost output and mass sales within a given price range. The product engineers prepare and present their final results to the process-engineering, manufacturing, and other departments in the form of detailed drawings, parts lists including part names and numbers, and specifications of materials.

74

Product Design

Changes in the Design of Products and Packaging. Products and packaging are redesigned (1) to keep abreast of style changes, maintain sales, and meet competition; (2) to improve design and correct weaknesses; (3) to cut costs of production by simplifying the design, adopting cheaper materials, using lower-cost methods, and reducing scrap and waste; and (4) to meet foreign specifications.

Although any department may suggest a design change, final decision

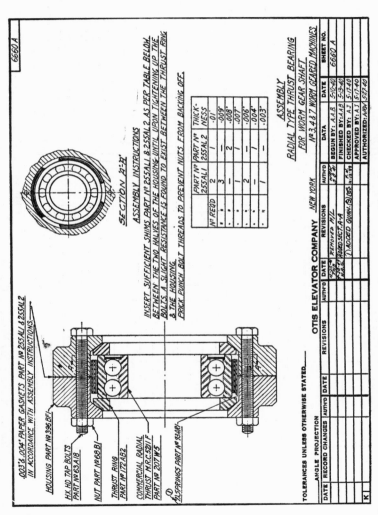

Fig. 6. An assembly drawing and instructions. (Courtesy Otis Elevator Co.)

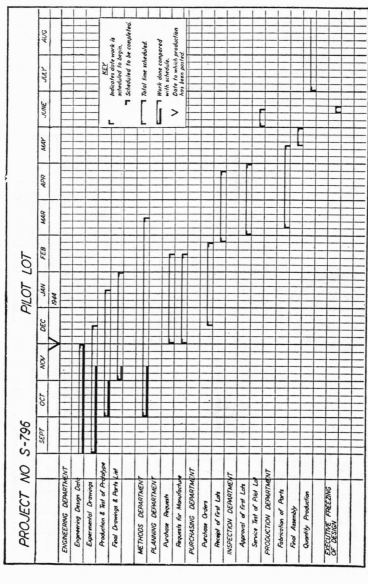

Fig. 8. The schedule of a pilot lot from the engineering stage to quantity production—an application of the Gantt chart. (By Wallace Clark)

and control should rest in the engineering department. It is wise to set up a standard procedure for the proper analysis, timing, and implementation of design changes. Since design changes are expensive, it is advisable to compute and weigh the cost of making a change against the benefits to be derived. The cost may involve the scrapping of existing tools, parts, and materials; the preparation of new drawings, tooling, and operation sheets; and losses from the interruption of production schedules.

PROCESS ENGINEERING. Through the analysis of the completed design (drawings and materials specifications) and of the volume to be produced, process engineering develops and specifies the most appropriate and cheapest methods of fabrication, processing, and assembly. In set-

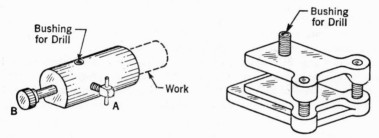

Fig. 7. Tools—typical drill jigs. Left, screw A holds work, plunger B ejects it.

ting up production for a new item, process engineers select machinery, develop and design equipment and tooling, aid in the layout of plant facilities, and develop operation sheets and production standards. When all is complete, they make a test run in the plant preparatory to full-scale operation. If, however, owing to its complexity, a product or a process can not economically be put on a production basis, it is put through a "pilot-plant" stage for further improvement. In the pilot-plant phase of development, the product (i.e., its design and materials specifications) or the process is improved and refined to the point where regular plant personnel can turn out production in the factory without prohibitive waste and interruption.

TESTING ENGINEERING. The testing laboratory performs metallurgical, chemical, electrical, and other tests and experiments for the engineering department. It is periodically called upon to run tests of proposed materials, improved designs, and completed products. In some firms the engineering laboratory also tests samples of purchased materials, work in process, and completed goods and transmits the results to the inspection department. It sets up appropriate routines for expeditious performance of these tasks.

FIELD ENGINEERING. Field engineers install the products for customers, provide instruction for their operation and use, and sometimes handle customer complaints with respect to performance or failure. Because of their familiarity with the way consumers use the product and the difficulties that are encountered, field engineers frequently offer valuable suggestions for product improvement.

Questions

1. What are the primary factors that give rise to long-term growth in industrial output capacity?

2. Distinguish between pure research and applied research.

3. Enumerate five characteristic forms of technological progress that stem from industrial research and illustrate their interdependence.

4. Does a large holding company have an advantage over the medium-sized firm in the development and availability of technological progress? If so, why?

5. On the basis of its capability in industrial research, can a medium-sized firm producing and selling an item nationally (e.g., quality chemicals or electrical products inexpensive to ship) continually maintain its competitive position against a giant corporation? Explain.

6. (a) Through what "outside" research agencies can a small firm increase its research potential? (b) Indicate the nature or type of research for which "outside" research agencies are best suited.

7. How can top management direct and guide industrial research and technological advance?

8. Illustrate in detail how the following would enter into the appraisal of a new product for manufacture: (a) consumer wants and acceptance, (b) effect on line of products, (c) anticipated volume of sales, (d) estimated cost to develop, (e) possible economical manufacture.

9. What are the usual steps in research procedure from the initial invention of a product to the engineering stages?

10. Distinguish among product engineering, process engineering, plant engineering, and industrial engineering.

11. Discuss the steps involved in the over-all engineering of a mechanical product (e.g., cash register or motor cycle) preparatory to large-scale output.

12. What are the various reasons or purposes for which products and packaging may be redesigned?

13. What procedure would you establish to achieve centralized control over the redesign of products and packaging?

10: Standardization, Diversification, and Simplification

Successful managers apply the priniciples of standardization, diversification, and simplification to direct and develop business enterprise. Through *standardization* they establish rational specifications for type of products, measurements, quality, processes, and practices. Through *diversification* they increase sales and stabilize business by adding new lines of products, sizes, models and styles, and services. Through *simplification* they decrease the cost and complexity of business by reducing the variety of products and services through the elimination of nonessential differences, superfluous types (sizes, models, or styles), and types which bring only a marginal profit.

Standardization. The role of standardization in industry grew with the rise of modern business, and its importance was enhanced by the spread of scientific management. During World Wars I and II the federal government contributed to the standardization movement when its procurement agencies specified rational standards for the commodities and materials to be purchased. These standards were designed to conserve materials, plant capacity, and manpower. The movement toward standardization has continued to spread in industry and to receive organized national and international attention. Trade associations and technical societies, through the participation of the members, have established many of the standards used in industry. One important body in the standardization movement is the National Bureau of Standards, which, at the request of private industry, tests and establishes working standards for any item, maintains the standards of weights and measures, and develops testing methods and apparatus. Another is the American Standards Association, which is composed of a number of engineering societies, industrial trade associations, and government departments. It co-ordinates the work of committees representing member groups, approves and publishes industrial and engineering standards and safety codes, and represents American industry in its attempts at international standardization.

POSSIBLE ADVANTAGES. Standardization is an important function of management because it makes possible the control of manufacturing, purchasing, accounting, and other activities at a definite level of performance and quality. Business operation improves and costs decline when materials, procedures, and products are predetermined so that future practices will conform and be appraisable. The primary fields in which standards can beneficially be established include products, materials, processes, equipment, and procedures.

Product or Services. Standardization, when applied to product design, determines the specific performance, form, size, dimensions, and quality of a product or group of products; when applied to services (e.g., insurance and banking), it specifies the particular activities to be included and the level of their performance. Economies of mass production and uniform quality are achieved through the stipulation of definite specifications (which include tolerances or allowable variations) for component parts and subassemblies that go into a product or group of related items to be manufactured in volume (e.g., television sets and prefabricated houses). In designing products or specifying services, there may be a need for compromise between the desire of consumers and the goal of economy in output.

Good design engineers create diverse-appearing products from standardized materials, parts, subassemblies, and processes. Such items as gears, fittings, frames, and subassemblies can be contrived to suit several different finished products. Drawings and specifications of standardized parts and subassemblies can be catalogued and used when there is a need for the same or similar items in the design of new products.

Materials. Standardization and careful specification of the raw materials going into a designed product are prerequisite to mass production and effective control of production processes and of quality. If raw cotton fibre, for example, is not comparatively uniform in length and quality, processing in the mill may be difficult and the cloth will not be of the required grade. Material standards are required not only for economical production but also for effective procurement, work simplification and time study, production planning, and inspection.

Processes, Equipment, and Tools. The standardization of the product, and its component parts and materials, makes possible the standardization of processes, equipment, and tools. Automatic machinery and maximum division of labor can thereafter be introduced for production processes. Each job can be standardized and each worker can be trained for a specialized task. Efficiency can be gauged by comparing the actual results of operations with predetermined standards.

Managerial Procedures. The development of a good organization structure requires careful formulation and standardization of managerial practices, including departmental and interdepartmental procedures, terminology, and nomenclature, which can then be compiled in a manual of "standard practice instructions." Such standardization contributes to efficiency, accountability, and control.

Performance and quantity-control standards can be established in terms of rates of output for workers, machines, and processes; in terms of amounts of inventory in storage (as "goods in process" and as "finished stock"); and in terms of sales and consumer credit.

POSSIBLE DISADVANTAGES. When standardization is excessive, with specifications covering too many aspects of business operations and with extreme standards, the resulting specialization makes business operations rigid and costly. The lack of sufficient flexibility in the use of men, materials, and machines and in the performance of office work, purchasing, sales, and other activities makes a firm vulnerable to obsolescence and to dislocations when external factors (e.g., market shifts, fluctuations in demand, technology) make changes necessary. Furthermore, excessively standardized operations and procedures make work irksome for employees, result in red tape, and lessen individual initiative and expression. Moreover, unless over-all company standards are determined in a comprehensive manner by a central agency, rather than determined independently by various departments, conflicting standards will defeat the primary purpose.

Diversification. Diversification may be accomplished by adding new products to the regular line or by introducing established products into new fields. The demands of consumers for distinctive products and the need for greater sales are the primary reasons for diversification.

POSSIBLE ADVANTAGES. Diversification offers the following benefits: (1) it increases the volume of business through sales of new products and distinctive varieties; (2) it makes possible a balanced line of products; (3) it can put idle plant capacity and distribution channels to profitable use; (4) it utilizes waste materials for by-products; (5) it may eliminate seasonal slumps and keep distributors busy the year round; and (6) it tends to stabilize business by avoiding dependence on the sale of a few products.

POSSIBLE DISADVANTAGES. When diversification is carried to the extreme or when the foregoing aims are not effectively achieved, the consequences may be a more complex manufacturing process, larger and more varied inventories, shorter production runs, and difficulty in planning and controlling production.

Simplification. Simplification reduces excess and undesirable variety in products in order to eliminate waste and to attain economy.

POSSIBLE ADVANTAGES. Simplification offers the following benefits: (1) it reduces the amount of machinery and tools needed; (2) it lessens labor costs through increased specialization of tasks and through ease in hiring and training; (3) it reduces the required amount of raw materials, goods in process, and finished inventory; (4) it increases utilization of equipment through longer production runs and fewer machine setups; (5) it steps up the turnover of inventory and makes prompt delivery possible; and (6) it improves quality and lowers unit costs and prices, thus making possible an increase in sales.

POSSIBLE DISADVANTAGES. Simplification may make the line of products too narrow and lessen the company's ability to cater to the needs of the market. Moreover, the anticipated economies from simplification—i.e., reduced working- and-fixed-capital needs—can be only roughly measured. The gains from decreased fixed-capital (equipment) needs may be only theoretical since financial outlays for existing facilities have already been made. And again, the benefits of simplification may not always be realized in the short run unless the company spends additional funds for some required specialized facilities.

Development of Programs for Standardization, Diversification, and Simplification. Company standards, though they may have been the best for the conditions prevailing when they were set up, must be periodically re-examined for suitability to current needs. To examine and evaluate current needs, management should establish a "standards division" or a regular committee composed of representatives from the sales, the engineering, the manufacturing, and the purchasing departments.

STANDARDIZATION PROGRAM. The standards division accepts or rejects proposed standards and generally advances the program of the firm. In its analysis it evaluates the impact of such factors as increased or revised output capacity and technological advance (i.e., new production methods, materials, and managerial techniques) on the effectiveness of current standards in product design, materials, and processing methods. For example, an improved machine or an improved metal alloy may

Diversification and Simplification Program

lead to higher quality and workmanship than have been possible in the past. (See Ch. 18 for "establishment of standards.")

DIVERSIFICATION AND SIMPLIFICATION PROGRAM. In appraising the opportunity for profitable diversification in products and services, the standards group can review the completeness of its line of products, the need for eliminating seasonal slumps, possible uses of waste materials, available production and distribution capacity, and managerial and engineering talent. The sales department generally prefers a wide variety of products priced to meet the purchasing power of a large number of consumers since this facilitates marketing. On the other hand, engineering, manufacturing, and purchasing departments generally favor a reduction in the variety of products since this reduces the complexity of their respective problems. Actually, simplification may be beneficial even to sales departments: it may lower prices, produce better goods, and make possible a quicker sales turnover.

A simplification program calls for careful analysis and evaluation of (1) the number of products and models and current sales and future marketing possibilities of each item, (2) the contribution of each item to profit and the share of overhead expense it carries, and (3) the degree of standardization and interchangeability of parts.

Each item should be carefully reviewed for possible elimination or for redesigning to increase the interchangeability of parts and reduce superfluous varieties, sizes, and differences. The results of the program should be appraised on the basis of gain in sales and profits.

Questions

1. Explain how the growth of the standardization movement aids the exchange of commercial technical information and facilitates trade.

2. Explain why the product and its component parts must be standardized before processes, machines, tools, and tasks can be standardized.

3. What are the effects of frequent product design changes on plant facilities, processes, and inventories?

4. Distinguish among standardization, diversification, and simplification.

5. Explain how a product-simplification survey can reduce the amount of working capital and fixed capital required for business operations.

6. If you were to undertake a company diversification and simplification program, (a) what would be your goals (i.e., the advantages to be gained), (b) what possible disadvantages would you guard against, (c) what factors would you study and evaluate, and (d) how would you appraise the final results?

11: Plant Equipment and Handling
of Materials

The modern manufacturing plant is, in essence, a giant machine made up of synchronized pieces of equipment which include production devices (lathes and grinders), handling devices (roller conveyors and pneumatic tubes), and service devices (power plant and tool cribs), all sheltered by an appropriately designed building.

Executives outline the scope of business operations by setting policies stipulating products to be manufactured, the size of the plant, the degree of vertical integration and flexibility, and anticipated future expansion. In this way they guide the selection and organization of plant facilities for the most productive combination of equipment and labor. Practical selection of facilities depends upon an accurate appraisal of equipment with respect to its suitability for given work, rate of output, reliability and adaptability, and purchase price and economy in operation.

PLANT EQUIPMENT

Progress in industrial technology has led increasingly to "extensive mechanization" (displacement of manual methods by mechanical ones), to "intensive mechanization" (displacement of hand-manipulated machines by automatic ones), and to the use of "multioperation" machines (machines which can perform a number of different operations on a single piece of work or which can perform similar operations on many pieces). These developments have been accompanied by innovations in processes (chemical or electrical, for example). Consequently, a given investment now produces more goods than it could have produced at any time in the past and, furthermore, the purchase of new machines and devices to replace old units effects "capital savings"—that is, more goods can be produced per dollar of investment.

Special-Purpose vs. General-Purpose Machines. A "special-pur-pose" machine can perform identical work at high speed (e.g., the multiple-drilling machine specially designed for boring all the holes in Ford V-8 engine blocks), whereas a "general-purpose" machine can perform a variety of operations on different sizes of materials or on different kinds of parts (e.g., a radial drill adaptable for boring holes in various sizes of boiler plates, machine bases, or engine blocks).

Management is frequently confronted with the problem of choosing between special-purpose and general-purpose equipment (Fig. 9).

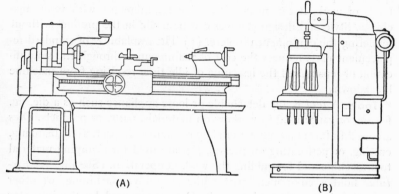

(A)   (B)

Fig. 9. (A) General-purpose machine—a lathe adaptable for drilling, boring, milling, and threading operations. (B) Special-purpose machine —a multiple-spindle drilling machine for drilling several holes simul-taneously on interchangeable parts.

Sometimes it can attain the benefits of both by adapting general-purpose machines to special uses—for example, by installing attachments (automatic feeding devices, or timing and conveying devices) to a series of general-purpose machines.

Special-purpose equipment can be economically employed when a large volume of highly standardized products is to be turned out. The volume of output must be sufficient to absorb the high overhead charges and the heavy investment that specialized facilities involve. Because of the comparative inflexibility of special-purpose equipment, important changes in the design of the product or in methods of production make such equipment susceptible to rapid obsolescence. Moreover, strong seasonal and cyclical fluctuations can result in idle plant capacity.

ADVANTAGES OF SPECIAL-PURPOSE EQUIPMENT. (1) Specialized facilities make possible high output with low labor cost and investment per unit. (2) They permit the use of semiskilled labor (general-purpose equipment requires trained and experienced men for setting up and putting out the work). (3) They make possible close uniformity in the quality of the product so that there is less need for inspection.

ADVANTAGES OF GENERAL-PURPOSE EQUIPMENT. (1) Because of its comparative standardization, general-purpose equipment is available at lower prices (and hence requires less investment) than custom-made, special-purpose equipment. (2) Because of its adaptability to various kinds of work, it can meet production requirements with fewer machines. Style and design changes can be made in the product without rendering the equipment obsolete. (3) The availability of standard replacement parts reduces the cost of maintenance through the simplification of repairs and the lessening of idle time resulting from machine breakdowns.

Tools. A *tool* is any detachable or loose appliance such as a die, jig, fixture, or gauge used in working on materials, parts, or products. *Dies* are used to form or work material by pressure or impact, as by blanking, cutting, or perforating on presses. *Jigs* are used for clamping material to a machine and for guiding the work in operation. (See Fig. 7.) *Fixtures* hold a component part while assembly, machining, or other operations are performed upon it. *Gauges* are used by the inspector or operator as a standard with which to measure or check the accuracy of the work and of machine setups.

A plant is "tooled up" when the required dies, jigs, fixtures, and gauges are ready for use with specific machines and operations. "Retooling" is necessary when a product is redesigned or when new models of the product are to be introduced.

Control over Plant Equipment. Management, particularly in growing industries (electronics and pharmaceuticals, for example), generally outlines two or more goals in the plant and equipment budgets—for example, the setting up of a new plant or service establishment; the expansion, replacement, or modernization of an existing plant; or the revision of a plant for putting out improved models or new products.[1]

---

[1] (a) See Ch. 26 for a discussion of the plant and equipment budget.

(b) Conversion of a plant (e.g., automobile or aircraft) to military production and its reconversion to consumers'-goods output is a special phase of "plant revision for the output of new products." The tooling-up phase of conversion to the output of military goods and of reconversion to output of consumer products has been a serious bottleneck in production because of the

New equipment and products are generally adopted by industry at a rate slow enough to allow for revision, modernization, and orderly expansion through the use of replacement funds [2] and without too great a need for new investment. Technological advance is thus directly reflected in the purchase of equipment. Firms buy equipment for replacement purposes when the increased efficiency derived from the new facilities enables the equipment to pay for itself in approximately three years. Equipment is best selected in conjunction with the development of plant layout plans. (See Ch. 17 for plant layout procedure.)

Procedure for Selecting Equipment. (1) Observe logical priority in selection—first, production machines; then, service equipment; finally, an appropriate building; (2) appraise the performance of equipment as to quality of work and rate of output, efficiency in the use of fuel and power, reliability in operation, and ease of adjustment and maintenance; (3) choose the most economical equipment on the basis of the following factors: kind of operations and quality of work needed, volume of production to be attained, amount of flexibility desired, proper integration with machinery on hand, and number of machines needed at each successive operation for uniform flow of work in process.

PRIORITY IN SELECTION OF VARIOUS CLASSES OF EQUIPMENT. In the establishment of a new plant or in a big expansion program, the production machines selected (e.g., steam forging hammers, pneumatic devices, or electric oven) will largely determine the kind and amount of service and other facilities needed (e.g., steam boiler, air-compressor unit, or power plant). Therefore, to achieve an effective combination, integration, and balance in operating capacity, the problem of equipment selection must be viewed in its entirety and approached in a logical way. (1) Production machinery—machinery which is used at specific work centers to process the materials or products—should be

---

considerable time required for designing, fabricating, and testing tools. Tooling-up for new production is not a serious impediment during normal peacetime business since all firms do not tool up at the same time and such excessive demands are not placed on the tool-and-die companies as in wartime.

[2] "Replacement funds" are retained costs stemming from accruals to depreciation reserves. "Depreciation" is a reasonable allowance for exhaustion, wear and tear, or obsolescence of physical property used in business (see Ch. 25 for discussion). From 1945 through 1951 corporate businesses used replacement funds totaling 40 billion dollars to cover more than 20 per cent of their over-all capital expenditures; they used retained profits totaling 60 billion dollars to cover 35 per cent; and they acquired funds from external sources to cover the balance of their capital needs (U.S. Department of Commerce, *Survey of Current Business*, April, 1952, page 4).

selected first. (2) Service equipment necessary to facilitate the operation of production machinery should be selected next. This class of equipment includes materials-handling devices; the power plant; inspection, storage, and maintenance facilities; and lockers and showers for employees. (3) The type of building design best suited to the needs of the layout and process [3] should be selected last.

In limited plant-expansion or revision programs, existing large service equipment (such as overhead bridge cranes, expensive refrigeration rooms, or power plants—all of which may have been initially acquired with extra capacity for future needs) determines the kind and number of production-machine units that can be installed without additional outlay for expensive service equipment.

APPRAISAL OF EQUIPMENT PERFORMANCE. Facilities to be selected—whether for a manufacturing plant, for a service establishment such as a large cafeteria or a cleaning and dyeing plant, or even for an individual consumer (for example, a housewife purchasing a vacuum cleaner)—must be appraised on the basis of performance. (1) Each machine selected should perform at the necessary level of quality and output. (2) Each machine should combine high efficiency and low fuel and power cost with the least possible investment. (The efficiency of a machine is measured by the ratio of the input of energy [fuel and power] to the output of work or power.) Special installation requirements and other utility needs of equipment should be reviewed. (3) Each machine should be checked for durability and for reliability of performance. (4) Each machine should be studied for ease of servicing and repair, and machines that require frequent adjustment and rely on costly maintenance should be avoided. Furthermore, inquiry should be made to determine whether replacements parts can be quickly procured.

FACTORS IN SELECTION OF EQUIPMENT. The ultimate goal in selecting facilities is to acquire equipment that will insure economical output of the required products in the desired quantity. This means low initial investment in equipment (i.e., low purchase price and installation cost), low machine operating expense, and low processing cost in terms of labor and material input. Before the goal can be achieved, management must provide the following data to guide selection: the immediate rate of output and the future rate to be attained; the length of the work week and number of shifts (single, double, or triple) the plant will operate; the kind and amount of adaptability in facilities

[3] For discussion see Ch. 12.

desired; and the kind and amount of existing equipment (if any) with which new facilities are to be combined.

Engineers can then select equipment by analyzing and appraising specific factors.

(1) Engineers study product specifications (blueprints and bill of materials) and prepare process charts [4] (summaries of required sequences of operations) on the basis of which they determine the kinds of production machines needed; for instance, whether shear presses, power saws, or blow torches are best suited for cutting the specified metals.

(2) They take into account the projected volume of output to determine the extent to which mass production is economically feasible and where special-purpose equipment should be used.

(3) They appraise the probable changes in products, and the types of products that may be adopted, in order to determine the amount of adaptability required and where general-purpose machines should be used.

(4) They investigate the capacities of machines and compute the number of machine units required to achieve the desired rate of output and a uniform flow of work. (In computing the required machine capacity they provide time for machine setups and normal delays caused by repair crews, inspectors, movemen, etc.)

(5) They combine best-suited equipment to achieve over-all "balanced capacity," avoiding acquisition of unusable idle capacity and avoiding bottlenecks that hold up production. When they combine facilities, they provide for ease of expansion and for extra plant output capacity [5] to meet the estimated increase in business volume in the years immediately ahead.

HANDLING OF MATERIALS

Handling of materials is an integral part of the production process. It involves piling, loading, unloading, and transporting parts or raw materials from the time of receiving to the time of shipping the manufactured products. It includes movement from machine to machine and movement among the various departments and buildings of the

[4] See Ch. 15 for discussion.
[5] See Ch. 26 for a discussion of how break-even charts can be used for control of output capacity.

Breakdown Of A Typical Product Cost

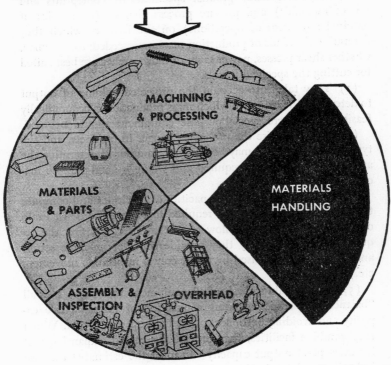

Fig. 10. Typical materials handling costs that enter into the final cost of a manufactured product. (Courtesy *Mill & Factory*, January, 1947)

MATERIALS CONVEYED TO STORAGE
STORAGE TO PRELIMINARY FABRICATION
TO FIRST PRODUCTION DEPT.
TO TEMPORARY STORAGE
TO FIRST MACHINING OPERATION
TO SECOND MACHINE OR PROCESS OPERATION
TO THIRD MACHINE OR PROCESS OPERATION
TO PARTS INSPECTION DEPARTMENT
TO SUBASSEMBLY
TO SUBASSEMBLY INSPECTION
TO FINAL ASSEMBLY LINE
CONVEYED ALONG ASSEMBLY LINE
TO FINAL INSPECTION
TO PACKAGING DEPARTMENT
TO WAREHOUSE
TO SHIPPING PLATFORM

plant. A large part of the indirect labor [6] employed in manufacturing plants is engaged in the handling of materials (Fig. 10). For this reason, an analysis of materials-handling may reveal large opportunities for economy.

Types of Handling Devices. Equipment for the handling of materials may be classified as: (1) devices for lifting and lowering (vertical movement), (2) devices for transporting (horizontal movement), and (3) combination devices for vertical and horizontal movement. Figs. 10 and 11 illustrate application of a fork truck, a loaded pallet, a monorail, a roller conveyor, and a gravity chute.

Procedure for Establishing or Improving a Materials-Handling System. To establish or improve a materials-handling system industrial engineers conduct a survey involving five primary steps. They must:

(1) Define the goals to be achieved. The basic goals are, of course, *efficiency, adaptability,* and *economy,* but an identification of particular objectives directs the analysis toward specific savings and economies. These are:

(a) Elimination of handling wherever possible

(b) Reduction of travel distance in handling

(c) Increased speed of processing, uniform flow (elimination of bottlenecks), effective co-ordination of production operations, and rapid filling of orders

(d) Reduction of goods in process, faster turnover of working capital, and lower overhead cost per unit of output

(e) Minimum loss, wastage, and spoilage of materials during processing, handling, and storage

(2) Compile data on the scope of the handling problem and on the available handling devices. Relevant data are:

(a) Nature of the items to be moved or handled: bulk or unit, weight, size, care required in moving, type of containers necessary

(b) Quantity and rate of movement: the volume of materials to be moved or handled, the number of times movement will be required, and the duration (days, months, or years) the handling service will be needed

(c) Distances the materials are to be moved (indicated by flow lines on floor plan drawings)

---

[6] "Indirect labor" (e.g., repairmen and inspectors) is that which facilitates production but is not easily assignable as a cost to a given unit of the product; "direct labor" (e.g., machine operators) is that which works on the product and is readily allocable as a cost to a given item.

(d) Direction and variability of the travel (horizontal, vertical, or combination of the two) and of the available routes (floor, overhead, basement, outdoor)

(e) Limitations of the buildings: number of floors, ceiling heights, floor loads (i.e., carrying capacity), inclines of ramps, obstructions

(f) Available handling equipment—including that currently employed and that available but unused

(3) Analyze the handling problem on the basis of the principles and procedural approach outlined below which guide the survey toward the development of an efficient materials-handling system.

(a) The plant layout should be studied with the aid of the flow diagram and the flow process chart, and facilities should be arranged for the most economical materials-handling and production [7]

(b) Wherever practicable, operations should be eliminated or combined to reduce handling

(c) Machinery should be located and arranged for minimum handling and shortest travel distances between operations (See Figs. 30 and 31.)

(d) Definite routes of travel should be provided for the movement and processing of work. Such channelization of the flow of materials makes possible the installation of low-cost, fixed-position handling devices (e.g., roller conveyors, monorails, chutes)

(e) Delays, bottlenecks, and congestion should be eliminated

(f) Unit loads of materials and parts should be as large as practical

(g) The flow of materials, parts, and assemblies should be co-ordinated, and handling should be effectively integrated both interdepartmentally and between plants

(4) On the basis of the foregoing analysis select the handling methods and devices best suited to the operating needs and properly integrate these in the over-all plant handling and processing system.

(a) The most adaptable standard handling equipment and containers should be used where feasible, but special devices should be employed for unusual handling conditions

(b) When alternative handling devices are available, equipment should be chosen on the basis of suitability for long-run

[7] See Ch. 17 for a discussion of flow diagrams and process charts; also see Figs. 28 and 29.

needs, capacity, ease and reliability of operation, low purchase price, and economy in installation, operation, and maintenance

(c) Gravity methods (e.g., chutes) should be introduced wherever possible

(d) Handling should be mechanized whenever strenuous and costly manual handling or possible damage to materials may thereby be prevented

(e) Piling, loading, and unloading time should be reduced through mechanization

(f) Wherever practical, conveyors should be adapted or designed to hold the material during the work cycle, to pace the rate of production, to perform operations (such as conveyorized etching and dip painting), to temporarily store materials in process and conserve floor space (e.g., by overhead handling), and to inspect goods while in transit (the automatic checking of size and weight, for example)

(5) Appraise the proposed handling system by comparing its overall performance and cost (purchase price and installation and operating cost) with the performance and cost of any pre-existent system. Compute how long it will take for the new system to pay for itself from the savings it achieves.

Questions

1. (a) When can special-purpose machines be economically used in production? (b) What are the advantages and disadvantages in the use of such equipment?

2. When can general-purpose machinery be used to advantage?

3. Explain what is meant by "tooling up" and "retooling" and illustrate the classes of tools that may be involved.

4. Illustrate managerial policies that guide the selection and organization of equipment.

5. Explain how the expenditure of depreciation funds for the "replacement of old facilities" can keep an establishment technologically up-to-date without need for new (net) investment from retained profits or outside sources.

6. Explain why, during the establishment of a new plant, service equipment should be selected only after production machinery has been chosen.

7. What factors would you consider in appraising the relative performance of several competing makes of a given type of machine—e.g., a five-ton press or an automobile?

8. Explain and illustrate how product specification data (blueprints and bill of materials) and the projected volume of output determine the kind of

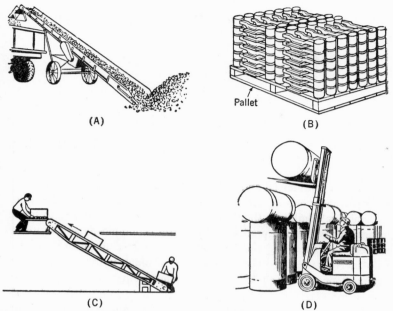

Fig. 11. (A) and (C) Belt conveyors. (B) A loaded pallet. (D) High stacking by a fork truck. ("B" and "D" courtesy Towmotor Corp.)

machinery needed and the extent to which mass-production methods are economically feasible.

9. Explain how you would achieve a "uniform flow of work" and "balanced capacity" in the selection of equipment.

10. Illustrate handling devices for horizontal movement, vertical movement, and combined horizontal and vertical movement.

11. What are the advantages and disadvantages of combining traffic management and management of materials handling in one department?

12. What data must be compiled before a plant materials-handling problem can be analyzed for the improvement or setting up of a handling system?

13. What are the successive steps for setting up or for improving a system for the handling of materials?

14. What are the steps for selecting specific handling methods and equipment?

12: Buildings, Lighting, and Air Conditioning

M odern commercial and industrial buildings are designed to fit the particular requirements of a business' operations and the layout of its facilities.[1] Buildings should be appropriately designed (1) to house business activities and production processes economically and to insure efficient operation and protection from weather damage or theft, (2) to conserve land area (when it is costly) through multistory and mezzanine floor space, (3) to support overhead equipment (e.g., bridge cranes, monorails, water tanks), (4) to separate internal departments and processes, thus shutting off heat and fumes, and (5) to provide for the most suitable installation of lighting, air-conditioning, and noise-control facilities.

SELECTION OF A BUILDING

The building should be selected or designed to offer maximum long-run operating advantages at minimum cost in land and improvements, construction, maintenance, and depreciation. Those selecting a building should not overlook its adaptability and resale value. Effective design of the building involves a consideration of the location and kind of site to be used and the type of layout plan developed for the establishment (see Ch. 17 for discussion). Layout objectives and the value of the land will largely determine whether a single- or multistory building should be used, the amount of floor space required, the necessary carrying capacity of the floor, ceiling heights, mezzanine requirements, size and location of elevators and stairways, and location of partitions,

---

[1] "Plant layout" is the arrangement and location of machinery, work centers, and service facilities and activities (shipping and receiving, storage, inspection, handling of materials) for the purpose of achieving efficiency in the manufacture of products or the supplying of consumer services.

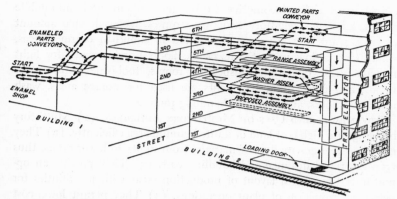

Fig. 12. Multistory buildings housing facilities for the manufacture of Universal electric ranges and washing machines. Conveyors travel at ceiling height. (Courtesy American Machinist, April, 1948)

doors, skylights, and windows. The design detail in the structural plans (width and shape of building, columns, necessary walls and exits), on the other hand, may make necessary some modifications in the layout.

Single- vs. Multistory Buildings. The requirements of the layout, value of land, and cost of construction generally determine whether a single- or multistory building is best suited for a given plant. Before a final selection is made, however, management must carefully weigh all the advantages of one kind of structure against those of the other.

ADVANTAGES AND USES OF SINGLE-STORY BUILDINGS. (1) Single-story buildings afford greater floor-bearing capacity. Adequate foundations can be provided for heavy equipment with comparative freedom from vibrations. (2) They make available more usable floor area because there are fewer columns and sidewalls, no elevators, and few stairways. (3) Because they are built with fewer obstructions, they also provide floor space that is more suitable to the requirements of an ideal layout and routing of work in process. (4) They are flexible enough to permit layout revisions and easy expansion of the existing building. (5) They generally can be erected faster, at lower cost per square foot of usable floor space, than multistory buildings. (6) They make available better natural ventilation and more daylight. (7) They facilitate effective supervision.

Single-story buildings are best for plants that use heavy equipment requiring firm foundations and that turn out heavy products; for example, steel mills, locomotive works, and aircraft and automobile plants. Since a single-story structure requires a considerable amount of land, plant sites are generally located in suburban or rural areas, where land is low in cost. Mezzanine floors provide space for light manufacturing operations, inspection rooms, tool-issue cribs, locker rooms, and offices; and basements are used for storage areas, wash rooms, corridors, and materials-handling routes.

ADVANTAGES AND USES OF MULTISTORY BUILDINGS. (1) Multistory buildings use high-cost land or limited ground area efficiently. (2) They make possible gravity flow of material from upper to lower floors, thus reducing travel distance and handling cost. (3) They provide an opportunity for vertical layout of production areas with possibilities for better co-ordination of plant operations. (4) They permit lower-cost air conditioning and heating because there is less roof area for escape of cold or heat. (5) Their upper floors are freer from dirt, odors, and noise.

Multistory buildings are generally advantageous for businesses located in areas of high land value (e.g., urban sites) and using comparatively lightweight material; for example, textile mills, food industries, and some chemical industries. They are especially beneficial for plants that can employ gravity flow for handling materials.

Shape of Building. The shape of the building (e.g., U, H, T, L, E, F, or solid block) should be selected to fit most appropriately the requirements of the layout plan, the plant site, and the needs for future expansion.

Type of Foundation. Solid foundations are essential to prevent settling, sagging, possible collapse, and costly repairs. The total weight of the plant and its distribution must be calculated before an adequate foundation can be designed. Bedrock, hardpan, or gravel generally provide satisfactory foundations. When such solid ground conditions are not present, piling (steel, concrete, or wooden posts driven into the earth) must be prepared to insure an adequate foundation for the structure.

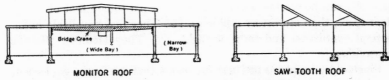

MONITOR ROOF   SAW-TOOTH ROOF

Fig. 13. Roof types. Note overhead bridge crane.

Type of Roof. A saw tooth, monitor, or flat roof may be used for a plant building (see Fig. 13). The windows and openings of the saw-tooth roof and the monitor roof provide for overhead natural lighting and inexpensive natural ventilation. The flat roof is structurally more appropriate to multistory buildings; artificial lighting and ventilation will be needed for all floors.

BUILDING CONSTRUCTION

Types of Construction. Reinforced concrete, steel-frame, and mill constructions are the three main types of structures. A building may be designed as a skeleton structure (rigid framework with "curtain" or "panel" walls) or as a bearing-wall structure (with the weight of building largely supported by walls).

REINFORCED CONCRETE. This type of building may be constructed from concrete poured at the site and reinforced by steel rods or it may be assembled from precast slabs. Such buildings, which are fireproof, can be rapidly erected (material being readily available from stock) with wide bays between columns. Maintenance cost is low and noise and vibrations are at a minimum, but the high cost of alteration and demolition are disadvantages to be considered.

STEEL-FRAME. Steel-frame buildings with masonry, wood, or sheet-steel sidewalls, roofs, and floors are comparatively free from vibrations and are relatively inexpensive to maintain or alter. City building laws, however, may raise construction costs by requiring cement encasement of the steel framework to forestall buckling and collapse of the structure in case of fire.

MILL. Mill construction dates back to the beginning of the New England textile industry. It consists of brick or masonry walls and massive timberwood columns, roofs, and floors. When sprinkler systems, encased stairways and elevator shafts, and various other fire-resistant features are provided, it is known as "slow-burning" construction.

First-, Second-, and Third-Class Structures. *First-class buildings* (constructed largely from noninflammable materials) include structures made of reinforced concrete and structures made of steel frames encased in concrete or masonry. *Second-class buildings* (partially inflammable) include both the slow-burning mill and the steel-frame structures when the walls and floors of the latter are made of inflammable materials. *Third-class buildings* are light-duty, one- or two-story frame structures made of wood or other inflammable materials. Although such buildings can be erected quickly at low cost, they are combustible and costly to maintain.

Standard Structures. The architects of firms selling structural steel have designed basic units of building construction consisting of standard ceiling heights, widths, units of length, floor loads, etc. Through combinations of these basic units, a wide variety of structures can be assembled to meet the individual needs of commercial establishments. Low cost and rapid erection are the prime advantages of standard buildings: little time is needed for design; materials of the required specifications are carried in stock; and experienced construction crews are generally available.

ACQUISITION OF A BUILDING

A number of considerations influence a firm's decision on whether to lease, purchase, or build a structure. Firms that are short of capital funds may be compelled to lease, particularly if their location is temporary. A firm may find it advantageous to lease a building on a time-staggered basis if its volume is subject to fluctuations—e.g., when there are strong seasonal fluctuations in sales or when goods are being produced for defense contracts which are expected to run out after a few years. A firm in light manufacturing requiring a general-purpose building may find an opportunity to purchase a suitable building at low cost or at a sacrifice price. A firm can sometimes secure from a construction company a long-term lease with a purchase option on a building specially erected to fit its needs.

LIGHTING

Poor lighting is both costly and wasteful. Good illumination means economical provision of the right amount and proper kind of light in the right place. An efficient lighting system in a plant or office reduces eye fatigue, helps prevent accidents, and improves morale; it decreases spoilage, raises the quality of workmanship, and increases production.

Features of Good Lighting. Effective lighting is gained by providing adequate intensity for the work and activities at hand and uniform diffusion free from marked shadows and glare.

PROPER INTENSITY. All operations and work areas in the room should be classified according to the number of foot-candles [2] necessary for

---

[2] Intensity of light is measured by a light meter in terms of "foot-candles," the amount of illumination produced on a given surface by a standard candle at a distance of one foot.

optimum lighting conditions. Progressively more light is needed for those operations that require greater discrimination of fine detail and a higher degree of accuracy.

PROPER DIFFUSION. Proper diffusion is an even spread of light over the working plane. It depends upon the distribution of light fixtures and upon the kinds of reflectors used.

Elimination of Abrupt Contrasts. If eyestrain caused by constant adjustment to varying intensities of light is to be avoided, all parts of the room must be illuminated. There should be no strong contrasts in the intensity between working areas and the remainder of the room.

Elimination of Glare. Direct glare and reflected glare can be eliminated by analyzing their sources and taking corrective action. Excessive concentration of light, which may cause discomfort and eye fatigue, is a result of too great intensity, poor location of light fixtures, and improper diffusion. Such glare can frequently be corrected by changing the position of the fixtures or of the reflecting objects, by diffusing the illumination at the light fixtures through the use of frosted globes, or by placing shades around the light sources.

Procedure for Achieving Good Lighting. (1) Design buildings for good daylight lighting; (2) select and arrange fixtures for an effective combination of artificial and daylight lighting; (3) paint the interior with the proper color combinations; and (4) provide for continual maintenance.

Daylight. When natural light is to be the principal means of illumination, the building should be designed for a uniform distribution of light, and the intensity should not fall below ten foot-candles. The window area should be equal to about 30 per cent of the floor area. With this ratio ten or more foot-candles will be transmitted into the interior of the building for a distance equal to twice the height of the windows. The use of glass blocks in the wall construction makes possible the scattering of light farther into the room. New types of glass keep interiors cooler by absorbing sun heat, eliminate the need for painting windows, and reduce glare. A saw-tooth or a monitor roof with skylights should be used to supplement window light. A saw-tooth roof facing north provides a uniform distribution of light for the center of the building. Although not so effective as the saw-tooth roof, the monitor roof also supplements the window light. Because seasons, weather, and time of day effect its intensity, natural light must be supplemented by artificial lighting.

Artificial Light. The factors to be considered in designing a system for artificial lighting are: (1) the required intensity and quality of illumination, (2) the arrangement and location of lighting equipment, and (3) the selection of the most suitable kinds of lighting equipment.

Lighting equipment may be located and arranged to provide general lighting, supplementary lighting, and local lighting. *General lighting* should supply the required minimum throughout the room or plant so that all parts of the floor area can be used for production. The light fixtures for general illumination should be placed at a uniform height and should be so spaced that adequate diffusion and intensity are attained. The kind and size of lamp used should determine the locations. *Supplementary lighting* is applied to those work areas that need greater illumination than that offered by general lighting, and should be properly located and directed with reference to the areas that need the extra illumination. *Local lighting* is used when a high intensity of light is required for detailed or fine work at a specific workplace—e.g., for sewing, precision machining, and close inspection. When local lighting is applied, an effort should be made to minimize abrupt contrasts with the remainder of the room in order to avoid eyestrain.

Reflectors producing direct and indirect lighting are generally suitable for industrial purposes; semi-indirect and indirect lighting are better for offices. Lamps with incandescent bulbs are widely used in industrial lighting. Special daylight bulbs, although they give less illumination, provide the right quality of light for purposes of color identification. In recent years the fluorescent lamp has been widely adopted in industry because it produces a high level of light at comparatively low temperatures. Fluorescent lights are available in many colors, and they can also approximate daylight.

Proper Painting. Gray or dull ceilings, walls, and equipment cause a marked decrease in intensity of light. With no additional investment in lighting, the repainting of plant and office interiors with a suitable combination of colors can increase the intensity of illumination, reduce glare, and improve vision with less eyestrain. Intensity can be increased by repainting in lighter colors, since these reflect rays whereas darker colors absorb them. Glare can be reduced by using a flat instead of a glossy paint finish. Vision can be improved by avoiding the monotonous effect of a uniformly colored surrounding area: "perceptive seeing" is enhanced by comfortable over-all color contrast. Walls, ceilings, and other surfaces that are continually in the line of vision can be made restful by means of weak colors of low chroma (e.g., vista green). Small equipment and tools may be painted in bright colors (e.g., corn yellow). Floors and bench tops should be painted in light colors to gain greater reflectivity. Workplaces should be painted in colors that produce a satisfactory color contrast of the machine parts against the material processed.

Good Maintenance. Once an efficient lighting system has been installed, it must be conscientiously maintained. Films of dust and dirt on windows and the absorption of light by dirty and dull surfaces can account for as much as a 50 per cent loss in interior light. Deterioration of bulbs and dirt on reflectors also reduce effective illumination. The continuation of good lighting demands regular maintenance schedules for washing windows, repainting walls, cleaning reflectors and lamps, and changing bulbs when their illumination output drops below standard.

AIR CONDITIONING

An air-conditioning system controls the circulation, temperature, and humidity of air and removes foreign substances in an enclosed area. To insure good atmospheric conditions inside the plant or office, it may be necessary to install a complete air-conditioning system for simultaneous circulating, heating or cooling, humidifying or dehumidifying, and cleaning of the air; on the other hand, it may be possible to obtain satisfactory results by using either natural or mechanical ventilation (fans and ducts for removing excess heat and fumes).

Objectives of Air Conditioning. Maintaining employee efficiency, safeguarding health, keeping production costs low, and protecting the product or equipment often depend upon adequate control over circulation, temperature, humidity, and purity of the air.

PROPER CIRCULATION OF AIR. Air movement is necessary, but excessive circulation or draft should be avoided.

CONTROL OF TEMPERATURE AND HUMIDITY. It is frequently necessary to control both the temperature and the humidity—the ratio of the moisture content of air to that which the air could contain at a given temperature. Air at 80° temperature and 20 per cent relative humidity is more comfortable than air at 80° temperature and 70 per cent relative humidity. Various humidifying and dehumidifying methods and devices are available.

CLEANING OF AIR AND REMOVAL OF DUST. When manufacturing processes and materials give off obnoxious or poisonous gases and harmful substances such as soot and bacteria, the contaminated air must be purified. It can be cleaned by such methods as mechanical filtration and washing (by being forced through a spray of water). Washing is also used to increase the humidity and lower the temperature. Dust-collecting systems are often necessary to maintain a clean plant and good working conditions for employees and to prevent excessive wear and abrasion of motor bearings and other moving parts. In woodworking, metal fabrication, and rubber plants, dust-collecting and blower systems are installed at various machine operations to collect and dispose of such elements as shavings, metal particles, dust, fumes, and lint.

PROTECTION OF MATERIALS DURING PROCESSING. Some manufacturing processes—e.g., those pertaining to textiles, tobacco, plastics, and precision instruments—require the control of atmospheric conditions to increase the workability and to maintain the quality of the product. If the humidity is too low in a textile mill, for example, the yarn becomes dry and breaks during weaving; on the other hand, if the humidity is too high, the working conditions are intolerable. Similarly, if the air is dry in a tobacco factory, leaves become too brittle for handling without breakage; but if the air is excessively humid, the leaves will become moldy and spoil.

Factors Influencing the Choice of an Air-Conditioning System. The objectives and benefits of an air-conditioning system should be carefully weighed against the cost of its installation and operation.

PURPOSES. As previously stated, an air-conditioning system may be designed and installed (1) to create favorable working conditions or protect employees from obnoxious or dangerous gases, foreign particles, the excessive heat and humidity, (2) to facilitate production processing and operation of machines, and (3) to protect materials and products. These purposes and, consequently, the need of air conditioning will be more important in some plants than in others.

CLIMATE. Climate and surroundings affect all places of business, but the need for air conditioning is generally the most pressing in hot, humid regions.

NATURE OF MATERIALS AND PROCESSES. Meeting the proper atmospheric requirements is more expensive when the materials or production processes give off large amounts of steam, dust, dangerous fumes, or noxious gases.

COMFORT OF WORKERS. When many workers are concentrated in one room, comfort standards are difficult to determine: individual preferences and group differences (arising from differing cultural and climatic backgrounds) must be considered. Workers engaged in manual operations prefer lower temperatures than sedentary workers. The outside temperature should also be taken into consideration: employees should not receive a physical shock when they enter or leave an air-conditioned building.

BUILDING AND AIR-CONDITIONING METHODS. Well-constructed and well-insulated buildings are less expensive to air condition than inferior ones since they hold heat longer and are easier to cool. When a central air-conditioning system is planned in advance, air ducts can be readily built into the columns and walls of the building. This eliminates the need for installing overhead ducts and equipment (which frequently obstruct lighting and overhead handling of materials). A central unit draws air into the conditioning apparatus, cleans, cools or heats, humidifies or dehumidifies, and then distributes it in the building by a system of ducts. On the other hand, when only one or a few rooms are to be cooled, the installation of self-contained cooling units at windows will suffice. Such units may cool the air by passing it over a cold surface chilled by ice or cold water or they may cool the air through mechanical refrigeration involving the use of a refrigerant.

NOISE CONTROL

Noise and vibration, as well as inadequate lighting and heat and poor ventilation, unnecessarily increase employee fatigue. Noise and vibration are best handled during the initial layout of the plant and design of the building. Impact equipment and excessively noisy operations should, when other considerations permit, be located where their effects will be minimized (perhaps in a specially designed structure) and properly screened off by sound-resistant walls. Machinery which causes strong vibrations should, whenever possible, be located on the ground floor and installed on proper foundations to absorb noise and counteract vibrations. Lighter equipment may be mounted on springs, cork pads, and other noise-dampening materials. Some mechanisms may be economically redesigned for elimination of noise and vibrations. Administrative, engineering, accounting, and other offices should be properly insulated by sound-resistant walls and ceilings.

Questions

1. What are the functions of buildings? What business operating needs should be provided for in the design of buildings?

2. Explain and illustrate how the location and site and the layout plan for the factory influence the type of building to be selected or designed.

3. Explain the factors that should be investigated to determine the suitability of a site for the erection of a large building.

4. Discuss the kinds of manufacturing for which single-story buildings are suitable and the kinds for which multistory buildings are suitable.

5. What are the relative advantages of a single-story and a multistory building for a medium-sized shoe manufacturing plant to be located in a suburban area?

6. Discuss the factors that should be investigated to determine the suitability of an existent building for purchase by a manufacturing firm.

7. Discuss the advantages of the "standard building" type of construction over an individually-designed type for a large firm engaged in light manufacturing.

8. What is meant by a "complete" air-conditioning system?

9. What are the various objectives of air-conditioning systems?

10. List the factors that should be appraised and provided for in the design and installation of air-conditioning systems.

11. Illustrate the ways noise may be minimized.

12. Illustrate how answering the following *procedural questionnaire* can lead to the establishment of an efficient lighting system.

(a) What are the benefits to be gained by a good lighting system?

(b) What are the features of good lighting?

(c) How should the building be designed for maximum daylight lighting?

(d) How can the required intensity and quality of light for various types of activities be determined?

(e) What are the considerations in locating and arranging "general," "supplementary," and "local" lighting?

(f) What are the ways that proper painting and maintenance enhance good lighting and "perceptive seeing"?

13: Power and Heat

I t is on the basis of economic appraisal and business judgment, rather than on strictly technical considerations, that management must choose how to provide for power and heat. Various chapters in this book show how such appraisals influence other decisions involving technical considerations—for example, those dealing with product engineering, plant machinery, and production planning.

POWER

Procedure for Selecting an Economical Power Supply. (1) Carefully determine the amount of power the firm will need to operate machinery; supply heat, steam, hot water, and compressed air; and provide light, ventilation, and air conditioning; then decide whether it will be cheaper to produce or purchase electricity. (2) If the firm is to produce all or part of its power, set up an efficient power plant and steam-boiler system. (3) Choose suitable power drives—methods of conveying power to plant equipment.

Decision Whether to Purchase or to Produce Power. Whether a firm should buy electric power from a utility company or should generate its own power is best determined by a comparative cost study. The prime factors affecting a firm's ability to produce power economically are (1) the amount and steadiness of its power consumption; (2) the amount of steam which it needs for manufacturing and heating purposes; and (3) the availability of waste materials that can be used as "free" fuel for power generation. Many firms find it advantageous to buy a part of their power and to generate the balance.

ADVANTAGES OF PURCHASING POWER. A firm finds it advantageous to buy electricity when it needs only small amounts of power, when its requirements fluctuate, when it uses no steam, or when it has an uncertain business future.[1]

[1] Central power stations attain efficiency and low cost because of their superlative equipment and large-scale operation and because they have the

ADVANTAGES OF PRODUCING POWER. A firm can economically produce its own electricity if it steadily requires large amounts of power,
needs steam in its operations, has wastes that can be used to generate
electricity, or can produce and sell surplus electricity.

ADVANTAGES OF COMBINING THE TWO METHODS. It is sometimes
desirable to purchase part of the power needs and to generate the balance in the firm's own plant. Although arbitrary rules are not applicable, since each power-supply problem is individual, the following
plans illustrate possible arrangements. (1) A fixed quantity may be purchased at a favorable rate for normal needs and additional power may
be generated by the company for peak requirements only. The company-owned power plant can also serve as a stand-by unit to satisfy minimum power needs in case of interruption of supply from the public
utility. (2) When exhaust steam is essential for processing purposes,
it may be desirable to generate a constant quantity of power for
normal needs and to buy additional energy for peak requirements.
(3) The need for exhaust steam for heating during winter months may
make it economical to operate a power plant with a boiler during part
of the year and to purchase electricity during the balance of the year.
(4) Joint ownership of a generating plant by two firms whose power
and steam needs complement one another may be an economical plan.

Installation of an Efficient Power Plant. Economy can be achieved
by accurately determining service needs, by properly calculating the
size of the power plant, by selecting the most suitable kind and design
of equipment, and by controlling operations and reducing wastes.

DETERMINATION OF SERVICE NEEDS. Management must carefully
calculate its needs in terms of kilowatt-hours of current, pounds of
steam and air pressure, and gallons of hot water. Peak requirements as
well as normal needs must be carefully determined, and provisions must
be made for heavy demands during seasonal upswings.

Alternating-current and direct-current needs must be determined.
Alternating current is commonly employed because of the ease and
economy of its distribution and because of the flexibility of voltage

---

advantage of top engineering specialists. Through the interconnection of power
lines among several power plants forming a "superpower system" or "grid,"
companies can effect economies (and a reliability of service) which enable
them to deliver current to customers' switchboards at low cost. The comparatively steady over-all demand of a large market permits a low overhead
charge per kilowatt-hour, and the grid system enables companies to operate
only the more modern and efficient of their plants during periods when the
power demand is low.

changes. A high voltage is generated at the power plant and distributed to the point of use, where it may be stepped down by transformers to a lower voltage. This practice reduces line losses and also reduces investment in cables. *Direct current* is necessary for equipment that operates at varying speeds (e.g., bridge cranes) or for processes that require extreme constancy of power (e.g., chemical processes).

SELECTION OF APPROPRIATE EQUIPMENT. The types of equipment commonly employed for power generation are (1) a boiler and a steam turbine or steam engine, (2) water turbines (in cases of hydroelectric plants), and (3) internal combustion engines using liquid or gas fuel. The selection of the most appropriate kind and design of equipment is best made after securing competent engineering counsel. Simple, inexpensive equipment is adequate for most firms. The capacity of the power plant should be sufficient to meet the company's particular requirements with some allowance for the needs of expansion when these can be reasonably anticipated. Since depreciation charges are a high cost factor in power generation, the initial investment should be kept as low as economically practicable.

REDUCTION OF OPERATING COSTS. Management should strive to attain not only low cost per kilowatt-hour but also low power-cost per unit of product turned out. High load factors, high power factors, efficient use of fuel, and elimination of wastes insure economical power.

Attainment of a High Load Factor. The "load factor" of a plant is the ratio of the average power to the peak power used during a given period. A plant requiring as its peak load one thousand kilowatts each day and an average load of five hundred kilowatts has a load factor of one-half.[2] A plant with a low load factor, generating its own power, must have sufficient power-generating capacity to meet its peak requirements: for such a plant, investment would be costly and depreciation charges per kilowatt-hour would be excessive.

Management should plan power use with a view to decreasing maximum demands. The load factor may be raised (i.e., peaks may be reduced and consumption made steadier) by using one motor to drive a group of machines wherever practical, by staggering the operation of equipment requiring high electrical loads, and by proper scheduling of production to avoid the simultaneous starting of heavy machinery.

Attainment of a High Power Factor. The "power factor" is the ratio

---

[2] One-half would be a relatively low load factor. As the factor approaches unity, economy improves.

of the real power (energy-producing current at machines) to apparent power (initial current generated and put into circuits). Because of induction (presence of idle power) in the line, the power factor is always less than one (unity). A low power factor requires a large investment in the power plant since big generators, lines, and transformers are necessary. When a firm's power factor drops below 85 per cent, it generally pays a higher rate per killowatt-hour than it would have to pay for current purchased from a utility company. A low power factor can be corrected by selecting motors of the proper size and by using synchronous motors and corrective devices whenever their installation is practical.

Economy in the Use of Fuel. A power plant may use one or more of the following fuels: bituminous or anthracite coal, oil, gasoline, natural or manufactured gas (e.g., coke-oven gas), or combustible wastes from manufacturing processes. It should regularly use whichever fuel is most economical, but should be set up for substituting a suitable alternative in case of scarcity or interruption in the supply. If coal is used, the most suitable grade should be purchased under standard specifications which designate the B.T.U. (British thermal unit [3]), ash, and moisture content. When suitable, mechanical stokers should be set up for boilers; and modern coal and ash handling equipment should be installed. Power-plant efficiency can be measured by calculating the ratio of pounds of coal burned to kilowatt-hours of energy produced.

Regulation of Operations and Elimination of Wastes. Power production and consumption can be controlled by setting up standards of efficiency to cover temperature and pressure and to cover consumption of electricity, steam, fuel, water, and air. Measuring instruments should be installed to record and chart operating conditions, point out situations requiring attention, and guide personnel in making adjustments and corrections to conform to established standards. In short, meters can serve as a check on the performance of men and equipment. Equipment failure or poor performance, leaky pipes and valves, inadequate insulation, soot-coated flues, and other inefficiencies and wastes can be reduced by comparing actual performance with accepted standards and taking corrective action where necessary.

Selection of a Power Drive. There are four basic types of drives (methods of conveying power to machines): single-motor drives, unit

---

[3] A "British thermal unit" is the quantity of heat that is required to raise the temperature of one pound of pure water one degree Fahrenheit.

(or individual-motor) drives, fractional drives, and group drives. There is also a combination of group and unit drives.

SINGLE-MOTOR DRIVE. In a single-motor drive system, all the machines in a shop are geared by overhead shafting and belting to one large motor.

Advantage. Low initial investment in equipment is possible: the motor can operate at its maximum load much of the time.

Disadvantages. (1) Efficient machinery layout is difficult. (2) Friction losses in power transmission are considerable. (3) Motor or shaft breakdowns disrupt shop operations as a whole. (4) Shafting fastened to ceiling interferes with plant lighting and overhead materials handling. Because of these disadvantages the single-motor drive is not used in most modern plants.

UNIT (OR INDIVIDUAL-MOTOR) DRIVE. Under the unit-drive system each machine is powered by an individual motor. This system is the one most widely used because for most plants its advantages outweigh its disadvantages.

Advantages. (1) Because of its flexibility the unit drive makes it possible to lay out and arrange machinery efficiently. Because of the absence of overhead transmission, it makes for good lighting, good ventilation, and minimum interference with overhead handling. (2) Each machine can be driven at the speed best suited to its needs. (3) Friction losses will be at a minimum, and a motor failure will disrupt the operation of only one machine. (4) It is economical for large machines that operate steadily at approximately full load. (5) It is suitable for mobile equipment that is shifted from workplace to workplace. (6) It is particularly economical for seasonal industries and job-lot production where some machines may be idle for many days.

Disadvantages. (1) The initial investment is high because each motor must be of sufficient size and capacity to take care of the maximum demands of the machine its drives. (2) Power use can be inefficient (low power factor) because of the low average load of many individual-motor drives. (3) Maintenance charges are higher than those of the group drive because the repair cost for small motors is relatively greater than for larger and more rugged motors.

FRACTIONAL DRIVE. To gain greater individualized powering and flexibility, modern equipment frequently employs fractional drives— two or more motors powering different parts of a machine. The fractional drive—a refined application of the unit drive principle—simplifies the design and construction of equipment and reduces wear on the machine. Moreover, it saves the workers' time and motions and frequently it results in better control over the whole machine. The disadvantages of this system are the same as those of the individual-motor drive.

GROUP DRIVE. One motor can be used to drive a number of similar or related machines. Such a "group drive" is adaptable to layouts where machines can be symmetrically grouped or where similar machines can be arranged in a line or "battery."

Advantages. (1) A few large low-speed motors are less expensive and more efficient than numerous small motors. They can reach a high load factor and a high power factor because the size of motor selected can be proportioned to the average load requirement of the machines. (2) They permit better layout of machinery than do single-motor drives. Additional flexibility is possible in that any section of the shop can be run independently of the rest of the shop. (3) They reduce the shaft and belt friction losses of single-motor drives. (4) They reduce maintenance costs because fewer breakdowns occur when large motors are used.

Disadvantages. (1) Power costs can be high when only a few machines in the group are operated at one time. (2) Power transmission losses may be high. (3) Ceiling transmission (shafting) may obstruct overhead handling. (Such obstruction may be minimized by placing transmission installations beneath the floor in tunnels or by suspending them from the ceiling of the floor below.)

COMBINATION OF GROUP DRIVE AND UNIT DRIVE. Both group and individual-motor drives can be advantageously employed in the average manufacturing plant. Some equipment lends itself favorably to group drive, whereas other machines can be more conveniently arranged for individual drive.

HEAT

Industrial plants use heat for many manufacturing processes as well as for maintenance of a comfortable working temperature. Hot-water, steam, or unit heaters, or any combination of these, can be used to regulate temperature. A heating-cost and heating-performance study should be made to determine which of the heating systems is best suited for a given plant.

Hot-Water Systems of Heating. Hot-water systems are more expensive to install than steam systems because they require larger radiators and more piping. Although heating a room with a hot-water system is initially slower than with steam, the amount of heat given off is more readily controllable, since one has only to vary the temperature of the feed water.

Steam Systems of Heating. It is sometimes practical to use exhaust steam from a power plant for both heating and processing purposes, but dual-purpose power and heating plants are not always advisable from the point of view of cost. A firm located in an industrial center may find it economical to purchase steam from a central station or from a manufacturing firm which produces a surplus of exhaust steam.

A low-pressure steam system heats radiators to higher temperatures and warms rooms faster than a hot-water system. For this reason, a steam system can utilize smaller radiators and pipelines, thus reducing initial investment. It can provide more nearly uniform heat in all radiators, and each unit is more readily adjustable.

Unit Systems of Heating. Individual heaters installed at strategic points on the floor, or suspended overhead, employ fans to discharge warm currents of air from units consisting of coils heated by steam, hot water, gas, or electricity. The temperature, direction, and velocity of air currents can be controlled. Unit heaters are adaptable to the needs of many situations since they are comparatively economical, flexible, variable in capacity, and easy to install.

Questions

1. What are the steps for acquiring economical power and heating?
2. Explain why it is generally more economical to buy than to produce power when the demand for electricity is small, when steam is not needed, when power consumption fluctuates appreciably, or when the long-run need is uncertain.
3. Explain why it is generally cheaper to produce power when large quantities of steam are needed, when consumption is large and steady, or when "waste" materials can economically be used for fuel.
4. When is it advantageous to adopt a combination plan for power supply?
5. Explain how the setting up of standards of performance and the use of measuring instruments aid in the provision and maintenance of efficient power production and consumption.
6. What are the advantages of the unit drive over the single-motor drive?
7. What are the advantages and disadvantages of unit heaters?

14: Maintenance of Plant and Facilities

As mechanization in industry and capital investment per worker have increased, the maintenance of equipment has become as important as the supervision of workers. Uninterrupted operation of integrated manufacturing processes is essential in keeping production costs at a minimum and in meeting delivery dates. When machinery is run-down and difficult to keep in adjustment, production and quality decline.

METHODS OF ACHIEVING CONTINUITY OF PRODUCTION

Management can adopt a number of policies to promote the continuity of production operations and to minimize the seriousness of equipment failures. In its program, it can give the maintenance department full responsibility for the prevention of breakdowns and for the making of emergency repairs.

Replacement of Equipment. The company program for the purchase of replacement equipment should be forward-looking in order to keep plant facilities new and technologically up-to-date and thus insure their reliability during operation.

Provision of Substitute Machinery and Routing of Work. "Stand-by" equipment should be available and alternative processing and routing of work should be prepared for key machines and operations whose breakdown would cause serious interruption.

Reserve Stocks for Manufacture. An inventory of fabricated parts and finished goods adequate to meet emergencies should be kept on hand. Then if key equipment fails or major machines must be shut down for repair, manufacturing can be continued and shipments to customers can be made for a time at least.

Plant Engineering for Preventive Maintenance. Machine breakdown can be reduced and continuity of production better assured through a policy of preventive maintenance than through a policy of allowing equipment to fall into disrepair until every repair is an emergency. Careful scheduling of periodic overhauls and renewals can minimize interruption of production; and systematic inspection of equipment can indicate probable failures that frequently may be prevented by prompt repairs. Moreover, the seriousness of breakdowns can be lessened if the firm employs a well-managed crew of high-caliber repair specialists and keeps on hand an ample supply of replacement parts and repaired subassemblies (motors, pumps, instruments) for all important machines.

ORGANIZATION AND DUTIES OF THE MAINTENANCE DEPARTMENT

The maintenance (or plant-engineering) department performs a service function: it is responsible for the upkeep of physical facilities. Setting up such a department calls first for determining its place in the organization and then for delegating duties to it.

Organization. The place of the department in the organization structure and its scope of activities vary with the type and size of the plant (see Fig. 14). The plant engineer, generally designated as the head of the department, may report to the plant superintendent, to the chief engineer, to the head of manufacturing, or directly to the works manager. In a medium-sized manufacturing plant the primary subdivisions of the maintenance function are the mechanical, electrical, building, and planning sections. Outside organizations may be employed to perform specialized work, such as installing heavy machinery and power equipment.

Duties. The maintenance department is expected to provide information about plant and facilities, to study equipment and undertake plant revision, to perform emergency repairs, to take care of preventive maintenance, and to provide routine upkeep of property and premises.

PROVISION OF INFORMATION ON PLANT AND EQUIPMENT. (1) The department compiles the data necessary for the effective study of equipment and for the maintenance or possible modification of the plant. The records kept include maps of the property; drawings of plant layout and buildings that show the location of equipment, operating activities, the piping systems, and the power-distribution system; and equipment information consisting of an inventory of plant machinery, blueprints and parts lists, instructions for installation and operation, and history of repair and inspection. (2) It supplies equipment information to the industrial engineers, process engineers, and accountants; and it also provides information to foremen and workers about the proper operation and care of equipment. (3) It secures co-operation among the production-planning section, foremen, and other groups for proper scheduling of maintenance work.

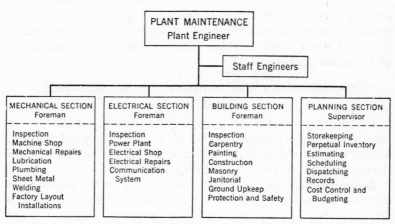

Fig. 14. Maintenance department of a medium-sized manufacturing firm.

EQUIPMENT ENGINEERING AND CONSTRUCTION. (1) The plant engineer participates with plant superintendents and with industrial and process engineers in equipment studies. On the basis of careful analysis, he makes recommendations to management for the replacement of equipment when machines are obsolete, when their repair costs become unduly high, and when new models of machinery show substantial savings in production.[1] (2) The department builds, improves, and installs equipment, undertakes construction projects, or arranges for the work of outside contractors if this is cheaper and more convenient.

EMERGENCY REPAIRS. The department gives top priority to emergency breakdowns in order to minimize interruption of the firm's cur-

---

[1] Management may choose to forego replacement of the given facilities if business is declining; if new or redesigned products are planned and new facilities are to be purchased for their output; or if expenditures can more profitably be made in some other phase of business such as sales promotion or industrial research or in modernization of plant in general.

rent operations. Repair specialists are expeditiously shifted from routine and less important work to emergency work.

PREVENTIVE MAINTENANCE. (1) The department makes periodic and expedient overhauls and renewals on the basis of equipment records and engineering judgment. The aims are to keep machinery in prime running order, to maintain continuity of production, and to stabilize employmei t of the maintenance force. (2) The department makes timely preventive repairs and adjustments to stave off serious machine failures which would disrupt production. It does such work following scheduled inspection of plant facilities to detect probable failure or needs for repair or replacement (machinery can be checked during routine lubrication). Its written inspection reports call for upkeep (frequently of a minor nature) which will forestall the need for more serious repairs.

MAINTENANCE OF BUILDINGS AND GROUNDS AND PLANT PROTECTION. (1) The department provides routine maintenance of property and premises through periodic painting; repair of walls, roofs, drainage system, roadways, and walks; cleaning of windows; removal of rubbish; and upkeep of buildings, grounds, and fences. (2) In addition, it frequently takes care of fire protection and policing and guarding the premises.

OPERATION OF THE MAINTENANCE DEPARTMENT

Procedure for Improving and Operating the Maintenance Department. (1) Analyze the physical facilities and select the maintenance specialists needed; (2) set up a budgetary system for the overall planning and control of maintenance; (3) establish a method for planning and scheduling maintenance work; and (4) develop a suitable method for compensating the maintenance force. (The survey for improving the maintenance department of any establishment—e.g., department store, hospital, or university—is the same as that for a manufacturing firm.)

Assignment of Maintenance Activities. A survey of plant and equipment can determine the kind and amount of maintenance work required—i.e., the kind and number of maintenance crafts and repair specialists needed (millwrights, electricians, welders) and the repair facilities required (tools, welding machines, lathes). For planning, maintenance work is grouped into these categories: (1) *routine work:* inspection, lubrication, upkeep of building and grounds, and protection; (2) *nonroutine work:* repairs arising from inspection reports, overhauls, and renewals; (3) *special work*: emergency breakdowns, installation of equipment, modification of plant facilities, construction.

DELEGATION OF RESPONSIBILITIES. All the aforementioned types of work should be clearly delegated to the respective repair specialists (see Fig. 14). There must be an orderly distribution of the maintenance force to meet the needs of all categories of work. Whenever possible, each man (or crew) should be assigned to a territory or a given class of equipment in order that he may become an expert. Overlapping and conflicting assignments should be avoided.

RESPONSIBILITY FOR SETTING UP RECORDS FOR CONTROL. The maintenance department should keep records showing the available men (man-days or man-hours) in the various maintenance crafts, the available repair facilities (e.g., tools, ladders), and the available replacement parts and materials needed for plant and equipment upkeep. In addition it should keep an account of the planned long-term maintenance work and special projects.

Budgetary Control of Maintenance. Management uses the budget for planning and controlling the total amount of maintenance work for a given future period.[2] The plant engineer usually draws up the budget, classifies the necessary work, and estimates the funds required to cover the cost of the various categories. Before giving approval, management collates his computation with past maintenance expenditures and with future production plans. The over-all activity as well as the specific work are controlled by means of periodic comparisons of actual expenditures with budgetary allocations—i.e., with planned expenditures. If maintenance costs exceed budgetary allocations, management can look for causes and take corrective action. For cost-accounting purposes, maintenance expenses are apportioned to the various departments using repair services.

To supplement budgetary control, management can regulate maintenance expenditure for specific purposes and jobs by establishing allowable limits. Supervisors may be permitted to authorize expenditures up to $50, plant superintendents and department heads may authorize amounts up to $500, and the works manager or the general manager may authorize higher expenditures.

Planning and Scheduling of Maintenance Work. The plant engineer prepares a yearly or semiannual plan for a well-balanced maintenance program which will reduce trouble during periods of peak production and will also stabilize the work of the maintenance force.

[2] See Ch. 26 for a discussion of budgeting.

MAINTENANCE WORK ORDER				
				Date _____
Order No.			Equipment	Location
Written by			Material (check one): ☐ Available ☐ Requisitioned ☐ None	
Approved by			Work to be Performed	
Date to be Started				
Date to be Completed				
Date Completed				
Account No.				
Cost:	Estimate	Actual		
Labor				
Materials				
Total:				(see other side)

Fig. 15. Maintenance work order or job ticket.

The program (or master schedule) outlines routine work, major over-hauls and renewals, and special projects (e.g., revision and rearrange-ment of facilities and installation of new equipment) since these can be planned in advance. The program also allocates man-hours for emergency work and for repairs arising from inspection reports. With careful planning, the plant engineer should be able to stabilize over-all maintenance work by dovetailing routine and long-term jobs with the demands of current emergency breakdowns and other repair needs. Authorization for all maintenance work is best made through repair orders or job tickets.

ORIGIN OF MAINTENANCE REPAIR ORDERS. Repair orders generally specify the work to be done, the dates of beginning and completion, and the account number (identifying the department or activity) to which the repair cost is to be charged (see Fig. 15). They are usually initiated by the plant engineer or maintenance foremen, but may originate from the written requests of production foremen and super-visors of other departments, as in the case of emergency repairs. Main-tenance work involving plant revisions may be initiated by management or the engineering departments.

SCHEDULING OF REPAIRS. The maintenance planning and dispatching office carries out the details of scheduling maintenance job orders. Emergency work gets first call. Overhauls, renewals, and special projects are scheduled for slack periods, when possible, and in such a manner as to minimize disruption of business operations. When emergency and nonroutine tasks increase beyond the anticipated amounts, men

119

are shifted from less urgent work to repair work that must be done so that plant and business operations can continue. Proper time allowance should be made for maintenance work so that an orderly assignment and disposition of the force can be attained.

The maintenance dispatcher [3] can plan and control current maintenance work by using a simple control board or a tickler file to classify job tickets as: (1) jobs to be done—i.e., the backlog of work; (2) jobs in process—i.e., the current work program showing the assignment and distribution of men according to the kind and location of jobs; and (3) completed jobs. Men completing repairs are given tickets for the next job as indicated by the control board. Before the dispatcher issues tickets for the next job, he makes sure that replacement parts and materials are on hand and that tools and repair equipment are readily available.

Compensation of Maintenance Force. Although maintenance men are generally paid on an hourly basis, it is desirable and practical to pay an incentive wage for specific tasks on the basis of work accomplished. This requires the setting up of time allowances [4] (standard tasks) for routine and general maintenance work. Infrequent and unusual maintenance jobs, however, obviously require compensation on the hourly basis.

ESTABLISHMENT OF TIME STANDARDS. Job-instruction sheets specifying a sequence of operations can be prepared for routine tasks (e.g., lubrication, painting, installation of rebuilt motors) and for nonroutine tasks (e.g., typical overhauls and renewals and installation of familiar machinery) much in the same manner as for factory production work. Then on the basis of job-instruction sheets and time study, time standards (allowances) as well as cost standards (for labor, material, and overhead) can be determined for each category of work. Time studies must consider the working conditions and the kind of repair equipment and methods employed. Time standards for emergency repair jobs can be estimated by an experienced maintenance foreman.

INCENTIVE-PAYMENT PLAN. [5] A common incentive plan for maintenance is that which pays a man or crew of men a guaranteed hourly wage rate plus a bonus computed as a percentage of time saved in the performance of a given job. Although incentive-payment plans require additional clerical work and place extra demands on foremen who de-

---

[3] See p. 217 for a discussion of the dispatcher's duties.
[4] See Ch. 16 for time-study procedure.
[5] The procedure for designing an incentive plan is discussed in Ch. 24.

termine standard tasks for nonrepetitive work and inspect completed work, they make for substantial savings. The use of standard tasks and incentive plans enables management, through performance reports, to compare the actual hours spent for maintenance work with the standard hours allowed for the work and thus to gauge the efficiency of its maintenance department.

Questions

1. Explain why successful maintenance of plant facilities is as vital today as successful supervision of factory labor.

2. What policies can management adopt to achieve continuity of production operations and to minimize the seriousness of machine failure?

3. List the major functions of the plant engineering department.

4. Distinguish between preventive and corrective maintenance.

5. How is preventive maintenance achieved?

6. What is the purpose of repair schedules and what factors should be considered in the preparation of overhaul schedules? Inspection schedules?

7. What are the procedural steps for improving and operating the maintenance department?

8. In what categories can maintenance work be classified?

9. How does management achieve over-all control of maintenance through the use of a budget, through the regulation of repair expenditures, and through the use of the task standards of incentive plans?

10. How do maintenance repair orders originate?

11. What is the procedure for scheduling current maintenance work?

15: Work Simplification: Process, Operation, and Motion Study

Although a business firm should be initially well organized and its production facilities, processes, and procedures efficiently set up, such a level of development is not immediately possible. Processing methods and procedures must be improved, whipped into shape, and followed up. The organization must be tightened to insure smooth functioning. In a going concern, moreover, new situations and problems arise that require managerial attention.

Management, in medium-sized and large firms, establishes an *industrial engineering* or *methods department*—a staff of management experts [1]—to solve problems and improve business operations (see Fig. 16).[2] Management, aided by the head of industrial engineering, reviews the scope of business operations and draws up a company-wide program for improvements to be made on a continuing basis. Depending on their magnitude and urgency, management determines the priority in which problems should be studied—e.g., it may give priority to modernization of plant, to improvement of production planning, and to improvement of efficiency through work simplification. When industrial engineers study a problem, they consult with and receive suggestions from the department heads and supervisors concerned. During their surveys, successful engineers gain acceptance of their suggested improvements from department heads, thus assuring ultimate adoption of their plans.

[1] These management experts are identified in some firms as "industrial engineers," in others as "method analysts" or "methods men."
[2] In a small firm improvements are made by the general manager and heads of departments, whenever they have the opportunity, without benefit of the expert knowledge of management or industrial engineers except on a consultive basis from outside firms (see discussion in Ch. 1).

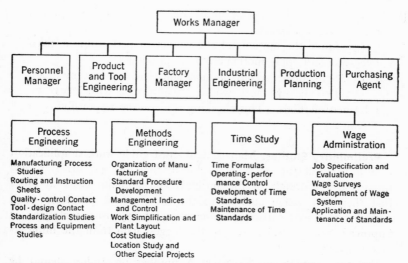

Fig. 16. Scope of studies undertaken by the industrial engineering department.

A work-simplification survey (i.e., process analysis, operation analysis, and motion study as presented in Fig. 17) achieves these *benefits:* (1) more effective processes and layout of plant facilities which increase production capacity at lower unit cost, attain greater standardization of operations, and maintain closer uniformity in the quality of products; (2) more effective production planning and managerial control; and (3) more accurate task standards which increase the effectiveness of the wage-incentive plan and result in higher labor productivity and higher earnings.

Procedure for a Work-Simplification Survey (Methods Analysis).[3] Observe the logical analytic procedure and survey techniques: first study the general and over-all aspects and then progressively move to the finer degrees of detailed analysis noted in A, B, and C in Fig. 17.

(1) Make preliminary studies to identify the goals so as to gear the improvement program to the needs of the firm; compile cost data to guide the analysis for maximum savings.

(2) Analyze the production process (or office procedure) in its entirety by means of the flow-process-chart device.

[3] Work simplification of one scope or another can be applied by anyone in the organization versed in the analytic approach (supervisors, assistants to department heads). Many firms train foremen to conduct work simplification.

(3) Analyze the operation of key and expensive machine stations and workplaces.

(4) Study the motions of the worker in performing a given operation and apply motion-economy principles.

(5) Standardize, record, and introduce the improved methods.

(6) Periodically check workers' compliance with newly established methods. (This checking is a routine responsibility of foremen.)

Preliminary Studies. Management must guide work simplification if it is to meet the needs of the firm; therefore executives review the scope and trends of the business and appraise costs in order that they may assign analysts to the most urgent problems (e.g., need for increased capacity, conservation of expensive materials, or improved quality) and thus reap the biggest gain from the improvement survey.

PRODUCT AND PLANT FACTORS. A number of studies should be conducted in order to clarify the objectives and properly direct the work-simplification program toward the needs of the business: (1) A product-simplification program should be undertaken to reduce fixed- and working-capital needs and to lower unit cost (see p. 82). (2) The plans (and the need) for redesigning existing models or introducing new models should be reviewed. Such product programs generally require a revision of the physical facilities of a plant. (3) Trends in sales should be reviewed to determine the need for increased capacity in some lines of ouput and the possible existence of idle capacity in other lines of output. (4) The desirability of greater adaptability in plant facilities should be considered. (5) The need for greater stabilization of production should be ascertained.

COST GUIDES TO ANALYSIS. Data indicating the relative magnitude of various cost factors are valuable in directing the analyst's time and effort to those aspects of production wherein substantial improvements and savings can be made. (1) The analysis should consider the proportions contributed by direct labor, materials, and overhead to the unit cost of the products. Industries with high labor costs pei unit of output (e.g., shoes and pottery) obviously afford good possibilities for the reduction of labor costs; whereas industries with high material costs per unit of output (e.g., pig iron and aluminum) offer good opportunity for the reduction of material costs. (2) Facilities and departments expensive to run should be singled out for improvement before

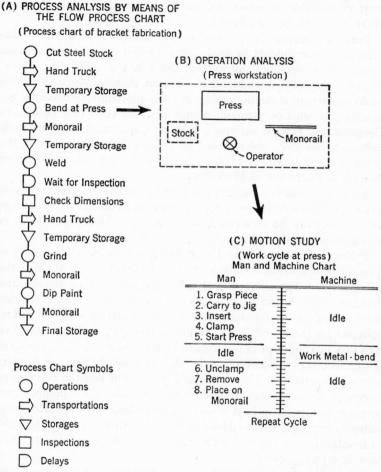

(A) PROCESS ANALYSIS BY MEANS OF
   THE FLOW PROCESS CHART
(Process chart of bracket fabrication)

- Cut Steel Stock
- Hand Truck
- Temporary Storage
- Bend at Press
- Monorail
- Temporary Storage
- Weld
- Wait for Inspection
- Check Dimensions
- Hand Truck
- Temporary Storage
- Grind
- Monorail
- Dip Paint
- Monorail
- Final Storage

Process Chart Symbols

- ◯ Operations
- ⇨ Transportations
- ▽ Storages
- □ Inspections
- D Delays

(B) OPERATION ANALYSIS
   (Press workstation)

Press
Stock
Monorail
Operator

(C) MOTION STUDY
   (Work cycle at press)
   Man and Machine Chart

Man	Machine
1. Grasp Piece 2. Carry to Jig 3. Insert 4. Clamp 5. Start Press	Idle
Idle	Work Metal · bend
6. Unclamp 7. Remove 8. Place on Monorail	Idle

Repeat Cycle

Fig. 17. The degrees and procedure of analysis in work simplification.
(A) *Process analysis* by means of a flow process chart. (B) *Operation analysis* of selected key machine stations or workplaces in the process.
(C)*Motion study* of the worker's movements at a selected operation.

less costly activities are analyzed. (3) Plant facilities turning out expensive products sold in large quantities should be surveyed before facilities putting out inexpensive products sold in small quantities. In single-product plants, more intensive analysis should be given to facilities that turn out expensive parts and subassemblies. (4) Comparative costs of available processes and machines should be studied before alternative methods are selected.

Process Analysis. A "process" may be defined as a method of creating a definite product or service; it is broken down into operations performed by machines and workers (see Fig. 17A). *The flow process chart* is a graphic tool used for the collection, classification, and analysis of an entire manufacturing process or office procedure (purchasing, accounting, production planning, recruiting). The chart may be used to designate the flow of materials, men, or paper work. The data are collected, classified, and recorded on process charts by following the progress of the activities and observing the actual steps (from beginning to end) in the process or procedure.

STUDY OF CURRENT PROCESS FOR IMPROVEMENT. The process or procedure is broken down and carefully analyzed to determine what steps or activities can be eliminated, rearranged, combined, simplified, or further subdivided to advantage.

PREPARATION OF A NEW FLOW PROCESS CHART. Thorough flow-process-chart analysis invariably results in improvements through the elimination or reduction of operations, delay, inspection, storage, and handling. The layout of plant facilities is improved—i.e., machines, work stations, inspection cribs, and storerooms may be relocated and regrouped for greater efficiency. Shipping, receiving, and storage activities may be combined in one area to better advantage. The amount of goods in process is generally reduced, and faster turnover and better control are attained. The more rapid production and the consequent increased output lower overhead charges per unit of the product, particularly in firms with high overhead costs. Moreover, with production capacity increased, the need for additional investment in plant facilities is forestalled. The improvements made in the process are recorded on a new flow process chart.

Operation Analysis. An "operation analysis" is a disciplined procedure that subjects a single machine or workplace tended by an operator or a crew to a thoroughly detailed improvement study.

SELECTION OF HIGH-COST WORK CENTERS. Operation analysis, a time-consuming survey, reaps substantial cost-reduction benefits when applied to high-cost work centers—those operations that are repetitive, relatively permanent, and involve high labor input.

PROCEDURE. Every aspect of the operation is questioned and examined for improvement and cost reduction. Bottlenecks are removed and better balance in production capacity is achieved. The analyst employs a systematic procedure, surveying each point in logical order as listed in the following *guide:*

(1) Question the purpose of the key operation. Is the operation necessary? Can it be eliminated in whole or in part, perhaps by a redesign of the component? Can it be better accomplished in some other way?

(2) Review all the operations performed on the component. Can any be combined, performed during the idle time of another operation, or advantageously subdivided into simple tasks?

(3) Review inspection requirements and quality standards. Can work on the given operation be speeded up and scrap reduced by liberalizing inspection standards or by redesigning the part without lowering the quality of the product or reducing the ease of assembly? Can sampling inspection replace costly 100-per-cent inspection? Can the measuring gauge be designed into the jig or fixture and inspection performed during the operation?

(4) Review the materials used. Can more suitable, cheaper, or more workable materials be used? Can a better size, form, or shape of materials be used to speed up the operation or reduce waste?

(5) Review the methods of handling materials. Could new or specially designed handling devices, special containers, or pre-positioning of materials be used to reduce handling and delay? Would rearrangement of the workplace and machine reduce handling?

(6) Investigate new machinery, auxiliary equipment, and tooling. Would a new and improved machine pay for itself in a few years from the savings obtained? Would investing in the modification and improvement of the machine or purchasing special attachments be advisable? Would more elaborate or automatic tooling prove profitable?

Motion Study. The motion study of a work cycle (i.e., the sequence of steps) should be undertaken only after the improvement based on operation analysis has been achieved. To undertake motion study in advance of operation analysis is illogical because operation analysis invariably alters the method of work (e.g., eliminates tasks or necessitates changes in tools, material, and design of parts) making the results of a previous motion study inapplicable.

Procedure for a Motion Study of an Operation. First, chart the current cycle of motions and then analyze and improve the cycle (i.e., prepare a new cycle) by applying motion-economy principles: (1) to develop a normal and maximum working area, (2) to use the fewest basic motions, (3) to eliminate delay, (4) to achieve rhythm and automaticity, (5) to improve the workplace, and (6) to better working conditions.

CHARTING OF CURRENT CYCLE OF MOTIONS. The sequence of motion elements in the cycle of work should be recorded on a *man-and-machine chart*, which shows the balance of working time and idle time for both man and machine (see Fig. 17C), or on an *operator right-and-left-hand chart*, which presents the motions of both hands while performing the cycle of work (as illustrated in Fig. 18).

IMPROVEMENT OF CYCLE. An improved cycle of work can be developed by careful analysis and the application of the *motion-economy principles* outlined below.

(1) Develop a normal and maximum working area. The work (materials, parts, tools, and controls) should be located close to and in front of the operator so that motions can be made with the least effort within a normal and maximum area (see Fig. 19).

(2) Use fewest basic motions. Develop a sequence of the simplest and fewest basic motions. Tools, work, levers, and other controls should be arranged and located to enable their manipulation with the easiest hand, arm, and body movements and with the greatest mechanical advantage. The Gilbreths classified bodily movements into seventeen basic elements called *therbligs* (search, find, select, grasp, position, etc.).[4] Motions from the simplest to the most complex are:

> Finger motions
> Finger and wrist motions
> Finger, wrist, and forearm motions
> Finger, wrist, forearm, and upper-arm motions
> Finger, wrist, forearm, upper-arm, and body motions.

(3) Eliminate delay. Pauses and delays should be eliminated or minimized, and barriers in the motion path should be removed. Hands should be relieved of work that can be performed by tools and jigs or by feet and other body members—e.g., foot-

---

[4] Frank B. Gilbreth and Lillian M. Gilbreth were the first to analyze comprehensively the nature of bodily movements and to develop the field of motion study.

OPERATOR CHART

Operation __riveting corners to crosspiece__   Date __Jan. 6, 19--__

Department __assembly__   Chart by __O. W.__

Operator __Walters__   Sheet no. __1 of 1__

__new__ Method

Left Hand			Right Hand
hand to rivet	①	①	hand to rivet
slide to depression	②	②	slide to depression
position rivet	③	③	position rivet
hand to crosspiece	④	④	hand to corner
pick up crosspiece	⑤	⑤	pick up corner
crosspiece to fixture	⑥	⑥	corner to fixture
position crosspiece	⑦	⑦	position corner
hand to corner	⑧	⑧	hand to hammer
pick up corner	⑨	⑨	pick up hammer
corner to fixture	⑩	⑩	hammer to rivet
position corner	⑪		
hold assembly	⑫	⑪	hammer rivet
		⑫	hammer to 2nd rivet
		⑬	hammer rivet
pick up assembly	⑬	⑭	hammer to side
assembly to shute	⑭	⑮	release hammer
release assembly	⑮		

repeat ‡ cycle

Symbols:

◯ = operation

◯ = transportation

Fig. 18. Operator right-and-left-hand chart.

Fig. 19. Maximum and normal working area. (Both figs. reprinted by permission from John A. Shubin and H. Madeheim, *Plant Layout*. Copyright, 1951, Prentice-Hall, Inc.)

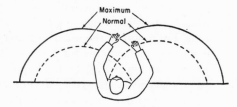

Maximum
Normal

pedals and controls activated by knees can free arm movements for other work. Additional work may be provided to use the time of unavoidable delay. With proper arrangement, an operator may be able to tend more than one machine.

(4) Achieve rhythm and automaticity. The workplace should be arranged to enable maximum natural rhythm and automaticity. Motions of arms should be in opposite directions over

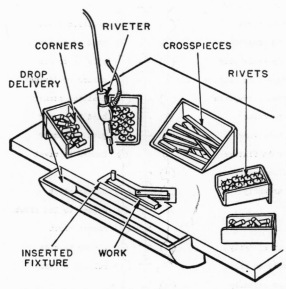

Fig. 20. Workplace layout developed from motion-economy principles presented in the improved right-and-left-hand chart, Fig. 18. Note the prepositioned, suspended riveter and the drop delivery arrangement for disposal of completed work.

symmetrical paths. Zig-zag movements and sharp changes in direction should be avoided. To achieve continuous, smooth, and balanced sequence of movements, both hands should, wherever possible, begin and complete their motions at the same time. For example, the use of jigs and fixtures for the holding of work frees and permits the use of both hands for manipulation of tools and materials or for the installation and assembly of parts. Balance is achieved by having each hand perform the same amount of work or number of movements.

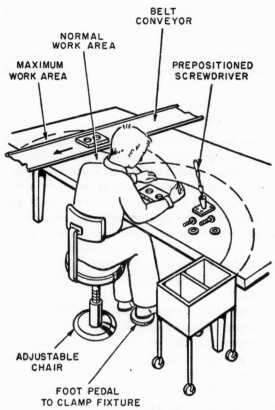

NORMAL
WORK AREA

BELT
CONVEYOR

MAXIMUM
WORK AREA

PREPOSITIONED
SCREWDRIVER

ADJUSTABLE
CHAIR

FOOT PEDAL
TO CLAMP FIXTURE

Fig. 21. A workplace layout developed from motion-economy principles. Note belt conveyor delivering work to next operator.

(5) Improve the workplace. The workplace should be arranged to conform to the principles of motion economy (as shown in Figs. 18, 20, and 21). Tools and materials should be located and arranged so as to permit the use of the best sequence of motion elements. Tools and supplies should be pre-positioned to facilitate grasp. Containers should be designed to facilitate the grasping of materials or their delivery by gravity-feed to the point of use. Finished pieces should be disposed of by "drop delivery" or by ejectors, not carried by hand to the tote box at the workplace. ("Drop delivery" is accomplished by releasing completed work into a chute located close to the point where

work is finished.) Completed work may be moved to a tote box automatically by means of a mechanical ejecting device or a blast of air.

(6) Improve working conditions. Additional efficiency may be achieved by furnishing the worker with an adjustable chair and by providing the workplace with the proper lighting, ventilation, and temperature. Harmful dust, noise, vibrations, and hazards should be eliminated.

Micromotion Study. Micromotion study is the subdivision of an operation into therbligs and their analysis for the improvement of the work cycle. Detailed bodily movements, especially rapid skilled motions, are recorded and time is measured by taking motion pictures at a constant speed with a microchronometer ("wink" clock) in the background. Because of the expense involved, micromotion study can be economically employed only when several highly skilled operators are performing identical tasks. Improvements made on one operation can then be applied to the several identical operations. Micromotion study can also be employed to train motion analysts and make them "motion-minded."

Methods-Time Measurement. In the methods-time measurement approach industrial engineers establish standard time allowances for various body movements that go into the performance of manual operations. They determine the most efficient motions required to perform a given operation. Then, on the basis of the predetermined time standards for the various movements, they compute the over-all time required for performing a given operation.

This approach can be used (1) for the initial establishment of efficient work methods, (2) for the improvement of existent methods, (3) for compilation of data for time study and for estimating of job costs, and (4) for the development of designs (of machines, tools, or products) that make possible the efficient operation or application by the user.

Questions

1. Why must management draw up and periodically review a company-wide improvement program, including a priority classification of specific projects?

2. What specific projects would ordinarily be included in the improvement program of a large manufacturing firm during a recession period? During a period of prosperity? During a wartime economy?

3. Why are diplomatic approach and tact as important qualifications for a successful industrial engineer as analytic ability?

4. Why, during their consultations with department heads and supervisors on improvement studies, must methods analysts endeavor to educate and "sell" sound principles and latest practices?

5. What are the benefits of a work-simplification survey?

6. What is the over-all analytic procedure for a work-simplification survey?

7. Illustrate the preliminary studies that aid in gearing a work-simplification program to the needs of the business.

8. (a) Distinguish between process analysis, operation analysis, and motion study. (b) Explain why a work-simplification survey must start from over-all (i.e., process) considerations and then progressively move to the detailed considerations.

9. Explain how flow process charts can aid in improvement of procedures for purchasing, production planning, or employee recruitment.

10. On what basis should work centers be selected for "operation analysis"?

11. (a) Outline the procedural approach for an "operation analysis." (b) Explain why the "purpose" of the operation should be questioned before its materials-handling aspects are reviewed and why the suitability of the material must be examined before improved tool design is sought.

12. What are the steps for the "motion study" of an operation?

13. Illustrate how work simplification increases output per man-hour with less employee effort (i.e., without "speed up") and fatigue.

14. What is meant by "use fewest basic motions" in the development of a work cycle?

15. How may the "hands be relieved of work"?

16. How can "rhythm and automaticity" be developed for the work cycle?

17. Illustrate how the workplace can be arranged to conform to the principles of motion economy.

18. Explain how flow-process-chart techniques and motion-economy principles have contributed to the design of efficient dental chairs and dentist's workplaces, modern soda fountains, and modern kitchens.

19. What improvements in working conditions reduce fatigue and raise morale and output?

20. When can micromotion study be economically applied?

21. Explain how improved flow process charts and carefully written up instruction cards assist the foreman in his periodic review of workers' compliance with newly established standard methods.

22. Distinguish between a product-simplification survey and a work-simplification survey.

16: Time Study

"Time study" is the analysis and determination of the time necessary to perform a given task. It calls for careful improvement and standardization of the operations to be timed and the application of a well-developed technique and procedure for stop-watch timing of the work. Time study replaces the less objective practice of using past performance, judgment, or trial runs as a method of establishing the time allowed for the performance of a task.

Management employs time study (1) to determine a standard time for the performance of an operation and use the data for establishing a fair incentive-wage plan [1] (workers accomplish more when they are given definite goals and are paid according to work produced); (2) to estimate the time and cost involved in new production orders; (3) to achieve a uniform flow of work ("balanced" machine capacity) in developing or improving the layout of a plant; and (4) to aid the analysis of work methods during a motion study of jobs.

PREPARATION FOR TIME STUDY

Well-designed incentive-wage plans based on accurate time standards appreciably raise employee earnings while substantially increasing the volume of output at lower costs per unit of product. Before long-run benefits can be expected from the use of time study for wage-incentive purposes, however, plant operations should be improved for efficient production; jobs should be standardized as much as is practicable; and workers and the labor union should be properly advised of the time-study program.

Improvement of Production. Operations must first be improved and standardized through a work-simplification program (see Ch. 15) if stable time allowances are to be established for tasks. Though operations can to some degree be improved during the timing of tasks (i.e.,

[1] Discussed in Ch. 24.

without benefit of a prior methods improvement program) and though an incentive-wage-payment plan can increase output, best results are not obtained through such a procedure. If task times are set before a work-simplification program is conducted, the times will soon become too liberal or "loose" because workers, motivated by higher bonus earnings, tend to improve their work methods (e.g., through better arrangement of the workplace and construction of special tools) and speed up the operation. Then, when management retimes worker-improved jobs in order to eliminate obsolete time allowances, employees will feel that this retiming, which they call "rate cutting," is unfair, and their morale will be impaired.

Proper Introduction of Time Study. When time study is not properly introduced to employees, workers become suspicious of its purpose and resist the program, and foremen have difficulty in carrying out their supervisory responsibilities. Therefore, the purpose of the time-study program (whether for incentive wages, production planning, or plant layout) should be explained to the employees and to the labor union in order to gain their confidence, to make them receptive, and to enlist their co-operation.[2] Time study should first be applied in that part of the plant where operations are well standardized and comparatively simple. Foremen should periodically observe the timing of jobs in order that they may become familiar with the technique and appreciate its value as a tool of production management.

Selection of Equipment and Method. The equipment consists of an observation sheet, a decimal stop watch, and a clip board to hold the sheet and watch during the timing of jobs (see Fig. 22). Two common types of watches are used—the "decimal minute," with a dial calibrated into 100 divisions each representing 0.01 minute, and the "decimal hour," with a dial calibrated into 100 divisions to represent 00.1 minute and/or 0.01 hour. The decimal watch is equipped with controls that enable the time-study observer[3] to start the hand, to stop it, or to set it back to a zero starting point. The control mechanism on the watch makes it possible to use the *snap-back method* of timing whereby each motion step in the sequence of an operation can be timed separately. When two watches are attached to the time-study clip board,

---

[2] In recent years, time study, when properly administered, has been accepted by many unions as a comparatively objective method of determining a "fair day's work." Union-management labor agreements frequently provide for the review of time studies by union representatives when workers question the accuracy of time allowances.

[3] Also called a "time-study analyst" or a "time-study engineer."

135

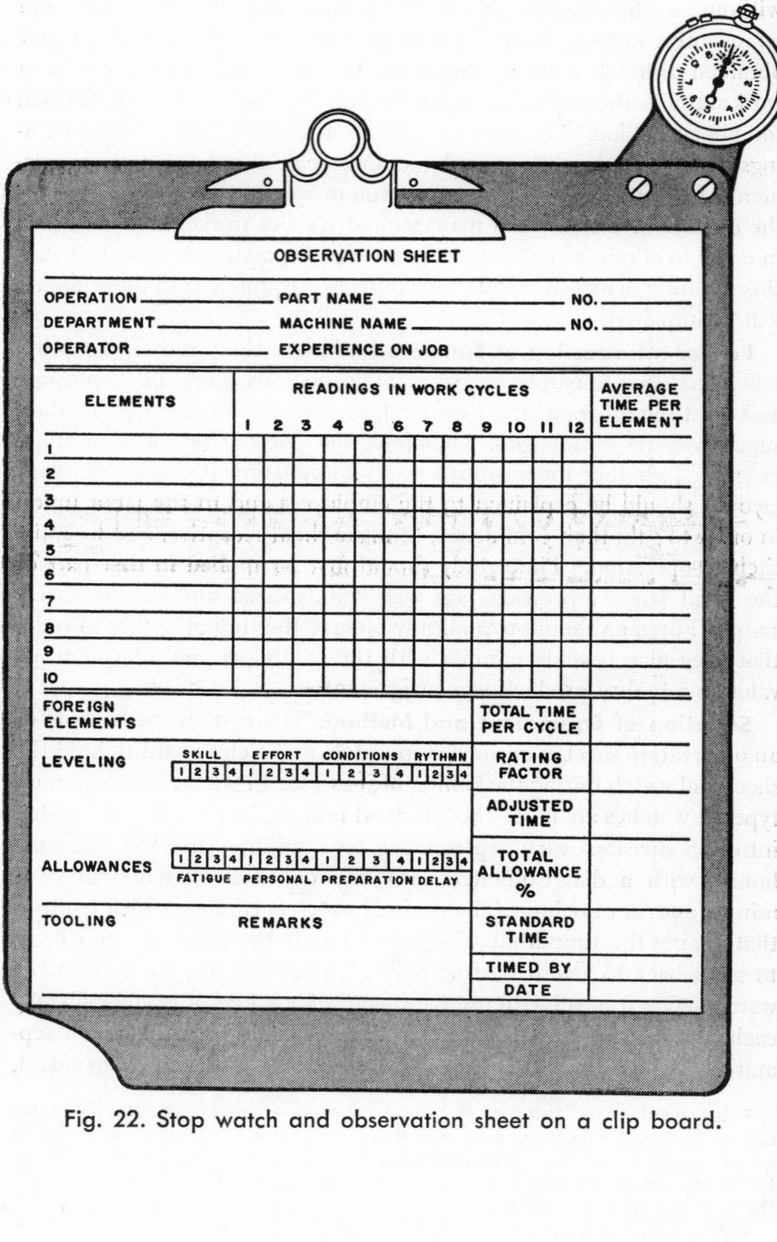

OBSERVATION SHEET

OPERATION _____ PART NAME _____ NO. _____
DEPARTMENT _____ MACHINE NAME _____ NO. _____
OPERATOR _____ EXPERIENCE ON JOB _____

ELEMENTS	READINGS IN WORK CYCLES												AVERAGE TIME PER ELEMENT
	1	2	3	4	5	6	7	8	9	10	11	12	
1													
2													
3													
4													
5													
6													
7													
8													
9													
10													

FOREIGN ELEMENTS — TOTAL TIME PER CYCLE

LEVELING — SKILL 1 2 3 4 — EFFORT 1 2 3 4 — CONDITIONS 1 2 3 4 — RYTHMN 1 2 3 4 — RATING FACTOR

ADJUSTED TIME

ALLOWANCES — 1 2 3 4 — 1 2 3 4 — 1 2 3 4 — 1 2 3 4 — FATIGUE PERSONAL PREPARATION DELAY — TOTAL ALLOWANCE %

TOOLING — REMARKS — STANDARD TIME

TIMED BY

DATE

Fig. 22. Stop watch and observation sheet on a clip board.

the second watch is used for *over-all timing* of the job with readings taken to cover all the steps of the operation. The over-all timing method can be used to check the accuracy of the snap-back method.

TIME–STUDY PRACTICE

Three types of time study are generally employed. The most common is *job time study*, which is applied to set an allowed time for each piece or unit of work turned out at a given standardized operation wherein the parts or material made are identical. *Operation time study* is applied to establish allowed times for an operation (e.g., welding or milling) wherein the materials or parts worked (welded or milled) vary in size and composition or alloy. *Production time study* is an all-day study of a given task for the purpose of acquiring detailed job information. Operation time study and production time study are, in general, supplementary to job time study.

Procedure for Making a Job Time Study. (1) Select the work and operator, (2) divide the job into steps (i.e., prepare a work cycle), (3) observe the job and clock and record the time, (4) analyze the job during time study, and (5) compute a standard time per piece or unit of work.

Selection of the Work and Operator. Time study is most easily conducted for routine jobs where appreciable labor costs are involved and, especially, where a number of workers are performing identical operations—e.g., assembling toasters, clocks, or instruments of given models, drilling standard parts, or sewing blouses of a given style. Not the highly skilled or the poor, but the better-than-average worker should be selected for time study. A better-than-average worker can be timed more easily than the average or poor worker because his motions are less hesitant and less erratic.

Division of the Operation into Steps. All information relevant to the study of a given job should be compiled in advance from the results of a work-simplification program and from job instruction sheets, quality specifications sheets, and blueprints. On the basis of these data and his personal observation, the time-study analyst subdivides the worker's operation into steps ("motion elements") in order that he may detect unnecessary motions and more easily identify hesitations and delays. If a group task (e.g., the erection of a large subassembly or the operation of a huge press) is being time studied, the observer subdivides the job into successive steps as performed by the crew of workers as a whole. The observer describes the work cycle (i.e., the

137

sequence of steps for the job) on an observation sheet. To avoid overlapping of steps, he establishes definite points ("break points") in the cycle to designate the end and the beginning of a step. Motion elements that are shorter than .02 of a minute are combined with other elements.

Observation, Clocking, and Recording the Time. The operator to be timed is notified in advance by his foreman. When timing the worker's task, the observer stands at that point near the job where he can get a clear view of the operation. If he uses the snap-back method of timing, he clocks and records on the observation sheet the exact time for each step in the sequence. If he employs the continuous-timing method, he records the cumulative times for each successive step. Then the exact time for each step is calculated by subtracting the reading for a given step from the reading for the following step.[4] The observer should clock a sufficient number of work cycles (e.g., nine) to get a representative sample. If the job is simple and of comparatively long duration (e.g., approximately 12 minutes per piece or work cycle) fewer cycles may be clocked. The average one-man task can be time studied in about 30 minutes.

Analysis During the Time Study. The time-study observer checks to insure that the machine is properly adjusted, that it is operating at the required speed, and that the work being turned out is of the required quality. This checking is particularly important for the more automatic types of machines. During the study the observer identifies machine-paced motion elements and worker-paced motion elements and he also notes the steps that are constant and those that are variable in time duration. After he has classified the steps of the work cycle, the observer can then easily note unnecessary motions, avoidable and unavoidable delays, and unusual conditions of work. He investigates the causes of delays and takes appropriate measures to eliminate those that are avoidable.[5]

[4] If the cumulative readings were 0.80 minute for the first step, 1.20 minutes for the second step, 1.70 minutes for the third step, and 2.15 minutes for the fourth step, the exact times for the second, third, and fourth steps would be 0.40, 0.50, and 0.45 of a minute respectively.

[5] A competent time-study observer (i.e., one who has had actual work experience in industry) secures an accurate time for jobs. The observer can not be easily fooled by a capricious worker since the observer can detect instances where a machine has been "adjusted" for slower speed, where the tool is unduly worn, where the worker takes unnecessary time to produce quality higher than that required, and where the worker adds extra movements and creates artificial delay. Moreover, to check the accuracy of the time set for a job, the

During the study the observer determines the *leveling factor*—that is, he evaluates and rates the better-than-average operator (as compared with the average) in respect to (1) the degree of skill possessed, (2) the effort expended, (3) the consistency of movements, and (4) the conditions of work. The observer uses the leveling factor (expressed as a percentage) to adjust the total time for the work cycle of the operator studied to that which will be expected of an average worker. Leveling is, in essence, a compensatory factor introduced to determine average performance. If the better-than-average worker studied is rated at 108 per cent, an average worker will require 8 per cent more time to perform the job. However, if a below-average worker has been studied and rated 90 per cent, an average worker will require 10 per cent less time to perform the job. The leveling factor is primarily a matter of judgment based upon the training and experience of the time-study observer.

Computation of a Standard Time. The observer records the data on a sheet and computes a standard time for the job in the manner outlined below.

USE OF REPRESENTATIVE READINGS. Readings (recorded times for steps) that are very high or very low should be eliminated as not representative of performance. Any time which varies more than 25 per cent from the average is usually stricken from the calculation.

CALCULATION OF THE TIME FOR THE WORK CYCLE. The acceptable times for each motion element are usually averaged arithmetically, though the median or the mode is sometimes a more suitable "average." [6] The total time for the work cycle is secured by adding the average time for all motion elements or steps.

ADJUSTMENT OF THE WORK-CYCLE TIME. The adjusted time is computed by applying the leveling factor to the total time for the work cycle. If the total time is 8.5 minutes per piece, a rating factor of 110 per cent will yield an adjusted base time of 9.35 minutes per piece.

ADDITION OF ALLOWANCES. Definite allowances should be itemized and added separately to the adjusted base time in order to establish the standard time (i.e., allowed time per piece turned out). (1) Fatigue allowance (generally 5 to 15 per cent) should be sufficient to

---

observer can (when duplicate operations exist) time study the identical task performed by another worker. The second worker cannot manipulate the job to extend the time in the same manner as the first worker.

[6] The "median" is the middle point or time in a series: half of the readings in the series are on one side of it, and half are on the other. The "mode" is the time, in the series of readings, which occurs most frequently.

enable the operator to perform the job from year to year without injury to health. (2) Personal time allowance (3 to 5 per cent) should be sufficient for the operator to meet his personal needs. (3) Preparation time (time needed for setting up the job and for inspection of first pieces) may be added as a percentage for each piece or as a separate time element when it precedes each operation. (4) Unavoidable-delay allowance (for example, gauging work, tool breakage, or machine adjustment) is generally determined by an all-day delay time study.

The foregoing "extra" time allowances establish a fair standard time—one that makes it possible for an average operator to produce the required quantity while working at a normal rate of speed and periodically taking his allowed rest periods.

Example of Job Time Study. Boring a hole of a given diameter in a given part can be used to illustrate the computation of a standard time. The operator goes through the following work cycle: (1) he picks up a part from a box near the machine and places it in a jig, (2) adjusts and clamps the part in the jig, (3) drills a 7/8" hole, and (4) removes the completed work and puts it away in a box for finished items. The circled readings below should be eliminated because they are too high or too low and are, therefore, not representative.

Motion elements	Readings (time in minutes) for each step in work cycle								Average time per element
	1st cycle	2nd cycle	3rd cycle	4th cycle	5th cycle	6th cycle	7th cycle	8th cycle	
Pick up; position	.26	.24	.26	(18)	.26	.26	(34)	.25	.25
Clamp in jig	.21	.20	.19	.17	.22	(28)	.21	.20	.20
Drill 7/8" hole	1.35	1.40	1.37	1.43	1.41	(1.69)	1.39	1.42	1.40
Put away	.30	(37)	.26	.29	.31	.29	(38)	.29	.28
					Total time (in minutes) per cycle				2.13

With a rating (leveling) factor of 110%, the adjusted time = 2.13 × 110 = 2.345

The allowances to be added are listed separately:

Fatigue	7%
Personal	3%
Preparation	5%
Unavoidable delay	5%
Total allowance	20% × 2.343 = .468 (additional time allowed).

Standard time per piece = 2.34 + .468 = 2.81 minutes (allowed time)

Operation Time Study. Operation time study is required when one machine performs work (e.g., drilling or milling) on a variety of materials and parts. Standard times are established for each of the various fundamental motion elements included in the operation on all of the types of materials worked; then the motion elements that make up the work cycle for the output of a specific part are compiled to determine the standard time per piece.

For example, the time required for a drilling operation depends on the thickness of the metal and the type of alloy. Therefore, time data must be compiled for fundamental motion elements on the basis of which time standards for turning out each type of drilling work can be computed. Time data for "constant" and "variable" motion elements which make up various work cycles are acquired through the timing of the drilling operation on a variety of materials. A *constant element* (e.g., "pick up stock and place on drill press table") remains fixed in time regardless of the material or quantity turned out. A *variable element* depends upon the material (e.g., the actual time for drilling a hole depends upon its diameter and the thickness and strength of the material).

The time data on variable elements are plotted graphically and smoothed into a standard curve showing the relation of time to diameter of holes, to thickness of material, to type of alloy, or to other variable. Once adequate basic data on fundamental motion elements have been compiled and presented in charts or formulas, the standard time for a specific job on a given material can be calculated by adding up the time of the motion elements required for the work cycle. In short, standard times can be computed "synthetically" in the office, thus obviating the need for taking time studies in the shop.

Production Time Study. Production time studies are all-day studies to uncover processing difficulties, delays and their causes, undesirable working conditions, and poor methods. These studies are conducted to determine necessary allowances for preparation of work, fatigue, and delay and to verify the accuracy of job time studies.

Maintenance of Standard Times. Standard times established through time study will not remain correct indefinitely. Changes in operations (due to redesign of parts, improved tooling, or changes in materials) should be reported to the time-study office so that jobs can be retimed, but the retiming of old jobs should be held to a minimum. The bases for retiming should be clearly defined by management and announced to the workers. In general it is good practice not to retime a job unless improvements in the operation are expected to produce more than a 5 per cent reduction in time.

16: Time Study

1. What are the purposes for which time study can be employed?

2. What preparations are necessary before time studies can successfully be carried out for wage-incentive purposes?

3. Explain how time study for wage-incentive purposes may best be introduced in a manufacturing firm.

4. What are the procedural steps for making a job time study?

5. What should the time-study man analyze and appraise during the actual stop-watch timing of a standardized job?

6. What is the meaning and purpose of "leveling"—that is, rating a worker during time study?

7. What are the steps for computing a standard time for a job?

8. What are some factors that would influence the percentage allowance for fatigue and unavoidable delay?

9. (a) When should jobs be retimed? (b) How can the retiming of jobs be systematically regulated for the mutual satisfaction of labor and management?

10. Distinguish between "job," "operation," and "production" time studies and explain how they are related.

17: Plant Layout

"**P**lant layout" is the arrangement and location of production machinery, work centers, and auxiliary facilities and activities (inspection, handling of material, storage, and shipping) for the purpose of achieving efficiency in manufacturing products or supplying consumer services. Its objective is to integrate machines, materials, and men for economical production. This function calls for careful analysis of the operational goals; of the process, facilities, and site to be used; and of the long-term plans for the growth of the firm. Moreover, plants must periodically be modified and improved to meet new production goals and to adopt technological developments.

FACTORS INFLUENCING PLANT LAYOUT

Company policies, location, types of processes, and types of machine groupings should be carefully studied before a plant layout is designed.

Managerial Policies. Policies that govern layout objectives are those stipulating the kinds and quality of products, the size of plant and the extent to which it is to be integrated, the amount and kind of plant flexibility desired, the plans for expansion (centralized or decentralized), the amount of inventory to be carried in stock, and the kind of employee facilities to be provided.

Location. Both the general location and the specific site will influence the kinds of processes that can be used and the patterns of layouts that can be developed. One region will have a combination of production factors differing from those in another region. (For example, a particular area may have numerous and diverse suppliers, whereas another may have few.) The size, shape, and topography of the site will affect the spotting of the building on the plot and the arrangement of the general layout for effective receiving and shipping (whether by truck or rail) and for the best flow of production in and out of the plant.

Manufacturing Processes. The manufacturing processes to be employed affect the type of plant layout that can be developed. The various types of processes are not mutually exclusive; two or more may be found in a single plant.

SYNTHETIC AND ANALYTIC PROCESSES. Processes may be classified as to whether they are synthetic, analytic, or a combination of the two. A *synthetic process* is one that combines several different ingredients (e.g., in the making of oleomargarine, medicine, or soap) or assembles numerous component parts (e.g., in the making of refrigerators or tractors) to manufacture a final product. An *analytic process* is one that starts with a basic raw material and breaks it down into various constituent products (e.g., in lumber milling or oil refining).

CONTINUOUS AND INTERMITTENT, REPETITIVE AND NONREPETITIVE PROCESSES. A *continuous process* is one characterized by an uninterrupted flow of operations from raw materials to the completion of the product through integrated facilities (or a series of integrated machines) in a distinct cycle, as found in printing, cement, and flour-milling plants. An *intermittent process* is one in which work is completed by stages—that is, it consists of a series of distinct work stations and operations functioning to turn out a product, as in automobile, television, and bicycle manufacturing.

Repetitive processes, usually found in the manufacture of standard products, are those in which operations are repeated in the same way. In the output of nonstandard products, such as job-order manufacture of special machines to the customer's specifications, the process is *nonrepetitive* since the same sequence of operations is not used for all manufacturing orders. See page 222 for "comparison chart" contrasting job-order and repetitive manufacture.

Arrangement of Equipment. There are three primary ways of grouping production machinery: product (or line) layout, process layout, and a combination of the two.

PRODUCT (OR LINE) LAYOUT. Under product grouping, all equipment and operations are arranged in a continuous line (though not necessarily a straight line) in the sequence required to manufacture the product (see Figs. 23 and 24). This arrangement is suitable for repetitive processes employed to manufacture a large volume of standard products.

The advantages of product layout are five. (1) Channelized flow of work permits low-cost mechanization of materials handling (e.g., monorails and chutes). (2) Semiskilled labor can be used to operate

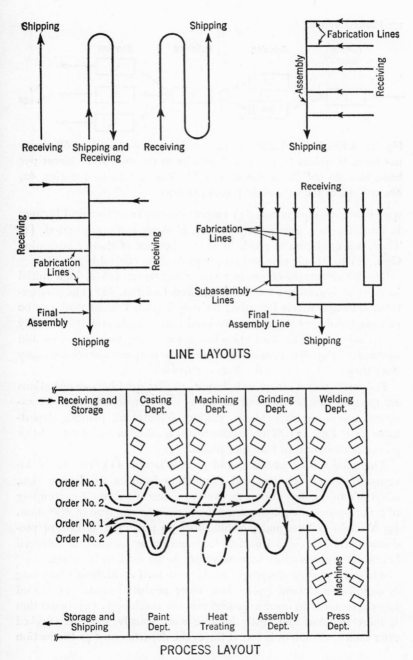

LINE LAYOUTS

PROCESS LAYOUT

Fig. 23. Types of layout arrangements that may be developed.

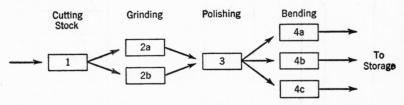

Fig. 24. A line layout balanced for a uniform flow of work at 60 pieces per hour. Machines Nos. 1 and 3 process at the rate of 60 pieces per hour; Nos. 2a and 2b, at the rate of 30 pieces per hour; and Nos. 4a, 4b, and 4c, at the rate of 20 pieces per hour.

special-purpose equipment. (3) Inspection may be economical because in an integrated line defective work is often easily segregated. (4) There is a minimum of goods in process because of shorter processing time. (5) Relatively easy and simple production control is possible.

The disadvantages of product layout are these: (1) A high initial investment is required for the specialized facilities. (2) The arrangement is comparatively inflexible, for only a given kind of work can be manufactured. (3) Aggregate overhead cost is high, and idle capacity is expensive. (4) The production line is vulnerable to interruption and shutdowns. (5) The demands on the supervisors are sometimes heavy since they are responsible for diverse activities.

PROCESS LAYOUT. In process layout, similar machines or operations are grouped functionally and set up as shops or departments—for example, machining department, welding department, painting department (see Fig. 23). This arrangement is suitable for nonrepetitive processes employed in job-order plants.

There are several advantages of process layout. (1) The initial investment is relatively low. (2) Production facilities are flexible (i.e., adaptable to the output of a variety of products) because the grouping of general-purpose equipment provides access to any type of operation. (3) Machine failures and job difficulties do not seriously disrupt production schedules. (4) Effective foremanship may readily be achieved because a supervisor can become expert in the work of his shop.

There are also disadvantages to this system. (1) Materials handling is more extensive and costly than under product layout. (2) Skilled labor is required to operate general-purpose machinery. (3) Inspection is more frequent and costly because work usually must be checked after each operation or before it leaves the department. (4) Production time is longer, requiring more goods in process. (5) Production control is complex and costly.

COMBINED ARRANGEMENT. Product layout and process layout can frequently be combined to good advantage. For example, a firm engaged in repetitive manufacture of standard products may group expensive machine units of a given kind for more intensive use, segregate shock and impact equipment for control of vibration, and segregate machinery requiring special service facilities (e.g., exhaust ducts or heavy-duty cranes). Such machine groupings may then be integrated with the over-all line arrangement in the plant. The firm may also use process arrangement for those fabrication stages that require flexibility— e.g., various types and sizes of grinders or welding units may be organized into groups since these facilities do work on a number of different parts of a standard product.

TOOLS AND TECHNIQUES FOR PLANT LAYOUT

Tools and techniques used for developing layouts include process charts and flow diagrams; machine-data cards; and templates, machine models, layout drawings, and plot plans.

Process Charts and Flow Diagrams. Charts and diagrams are used in work-simplification surveys for summarizing and analyzing production processes and procedures.

The *operation process chart* subdivides the process into its separate operations and inspections. (See Fig. 25.) It is generally used for the layout of a new plant. The *flow process chart* is a graphic summary of all the activities taking place on the production floor of an existing plant (from first operation to completion of product) (see Fig. 17).

The *flow diagram* is an aid to the visualization of the movement of material on a floor plan or layout drawing (see Figs. 23 and 30). A single line is drawn to scale on a layout drawing to represent the physical movement of material or a product through the entire plant.

Machine-Data Cards. The machine-data card carries an illustration of the equipment and the information necessary to lay it out (e.g., facts about output capacity; space, power, and foundation requirements; best-suited handling devices).

Techniques for Visualization. The layout can be represented by templates, models, and drawings.

TEMPLATES. The area taken up by a machine or other equipment is cut to scale from a sheet of heavy paper to form a template (see Fig.

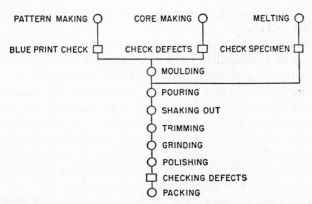

Fig. 25. An operation process chart for producing sand castings in a foundry. (Reprinted by permission from John A. Shubin and Huxley Madeheim, *Plant Layout*. Copyright, 1951, Prentice-Hall, Inc.)

26). Various layout schemes can be developed by locating and arranging templates on drawing paper.

Models of Equipment. Three-dimensional models of machinery, benches, handling devices, storage fixtures, and other equipment can be used for complex layouts when expensive installations are to be made. Scale models of layouts enable full visualization of plans and simplify the detection of weaknesses and the revision of plans.

Layout Drawings. Completed layouts are represented by drawings of the plant showing walls, columns, stairways, machines and other equipment, storage areas, aisle space, and office areas (see Fig. 27).

Plot Plans. A plot plan, either as a drawing or a model, shows the over-all arrangement of the site including buildings (see Fig. 27).

LAYOUT OF A NEW ESTABLISHMENT

A *sound layout achieves efficiency* in seven ways: (1) it uses labor and equipment effectively by reducing delays, bottlenecks, waste capacity, and operators' working time; (2) it obtains high output capacity from a given floor area through a wise arrangement of facilities and use of space; (3) it achieves low-cost materials handling by eliminating or reducing travel distance and by employing economical handling methods and devices; (4) it gets maximum production flexibility (including ease of future expansion) consistent with low-cost operations; (5) it makes easy production control possible; (6) it simplifies supervision; and (7) it attains "built-in" safety and desirable working conditions for employees.

Layout Procedure. (1) Acquire a statement of the objectives and compile process and equipment data; (2) develop an over-all plan for the general arrangement of the process, building, and site; (3) develop a template arrangement of production machinery; (4) arrange plant service departments to facilitate the production process; (5) prepare building specifications to fit the needs of the layout; and (6) prepare layout drawings, flow process charts, and flow diagrams, and make a test run when the facilities are installed.

This layout procedure can also be employed for laying out service establishments such as restaurants, automobile repair and service stations, department stores, railroad depots, hospitals, and university campuses.

Statement of Objectives and Compilation of Data. (1) Policy statements outlining layout goals with respect to capacity, production flexibility, and plans for future expansion must be obtained. (2) An operation process chart (or a number of such charts) must be developed for the machinery and processes selected to manufacture a standard product (or several products) in the required volume. For job-order production, a "generalized" operation process chart should be made for each category of representative work. A few such charts can summarize the sequence of operations required to produce a large percentage of job-order work. When necessary, "load" charts should be prepared to show the capacity demands on specific machines, operations, or departments.[1] (3) Machine-data cards and templates of selected equipment will be needed. As the layout is being developed, templates should also be provided for the additional equipment that will be selected—e.g., materials-handling devices and storage facilities. (Equipment selection, discussed on pages 87–89, is best made while the layout is being devised, because the proper sizes of machines for a uniform flow of work, the required capacity of cranes, the kind and length of roller conveyors and monorails, and the kind and amount of storage facilities needed can be accurately determined only as these are calculated from floor plan drawings and flow process charts.)

Development of an Over-All Plan. A general plan, including the flow of production and the arrangement of service activities, the best-suited type of building, and the arrangement of the plot plan, must be formulated. (1) First, a floor arrangement and flow plan must be made

[1] For a discussion of load charts, see pp. 213–214.

for production machinery and processes (see Fig. 23). Production machinery may be grouped according to product layout, process layout, or a combination of the two—depending upon the degree of standardization in manufacturing and upon which plan will best achieve management's objectives (e.g., decentralization of plant or rapid processing and the layout efficiencies enumerated on page 148). After a floor plan has been developed for production machines, service activities should be arranged to facilitate the manufacturing process. (2) Next, the kind of building that will be most economical to construct (e.g., steel frame or reinforced concrete), yet best suited to the needs of the layout and to the location (single-story or multistory), should be chosen. (See Ch. 12 for a discussion of the selection of an appropriate building.) (3) Finally, a tentative plot-plan arrangement suited to the plant layout, the building, and long-run utilization of the site should be prepared.

The most efficient over-all layout plan evolves only after experimentation with alternative arrangements: at least two plans should be drawn up and compared to determine which offers greater opportunities for achieving sound layout objectives in terms of economical processing and materials handling, production flexibility, provision for expansion, and minimum investment (see Fig. 23).

Template Arrangement of Machinery. Templates, representing machines and operations, should be located on the floor plan according to the sequence or groupings indicated on the operation process charts and in conformance to the over-all plan developed. There should be sufficient space around each machine to allow for the operation of the equipment, the movement of work, the convenience of the worker, the

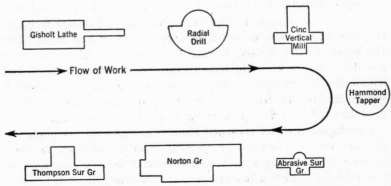

Fig. 26. A "U" layout arrangement of machine templates.

storage of goods in process, the installation of handling devices, and maintenance and repair needs. The output capacity of the successive machines or groups of machines in line layout must be comparatively equal (i.e., "balanced" machine capacity must be achieved) in order to assure an even flow of work and avoid bottlenecks and waste machine capacity. The best machine layout is obtained when a flow process chart is prepared in conjunction with the arrangement of the equipment.

Arrangement of Service Activities. Service and auxiliary activities should be located to facilitate the manufacturing process and aid production workers. (1) A materials-handling system can best be developed by observing the procedure discussed on pages 92–94. The amount of space to be provided for floor handling (including an area for aisles) should be determined by studying the size and movement of material being transported on roller and belt conveyors, hand trucks, and fork trucks. (2) Receiving and shipping areas should be combined wherever possible and should be located for economical movement of materials and finished goods to and from storerooms. (3) Inspection is generally most effective when a combination of the centralized (crib) and decentralized plans is used (see page 165 for discussion). Wherever practical, inspection stations and cribs should be integrated with the production line. (4) The maintenance shop should be located for an effective servicing of the entire production floor. Sufficient space should be provided around equipment to permit repair work; means of transport should be furnished for equipment that has to be moved to repair and overhaul areas. (5) The kind and quantity of utilities needed and the best manner of providing them can be determined by studying the process and equipment (see Ch. 12). The power plant, because of its comparative permanence, should be located where it will not obstruct future expansion of the plant. (6) Offices which do related work requiring frequent personal contact should be located adjacent to one another. Shop offices (such as those for production control, process engineering, inspection, and maintenance) should be near the plant floor. (7) Employee facilities (locker rooms, toilets, washrooms, first-aid clinics, cafeteria, and parking lots) should be adequate and appropriately located; and safe working conditions should be provided (for discussion, see end of Ch. 23).

Building Specifications. After the production process and service and auxiliary activities have been laid out, building requirements—total floor space, floor-load capacities, ceiling heights, mezzanines, location

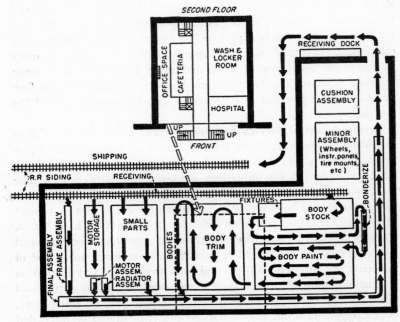

Fig. 27. The layout of the Lincoln-Mercury plant at Los Angeles. It was planned to attain a smooth flow through processing and assembly. (Courtesy *American Machinist*, April, 1948)

of partitions, size and location of doors and windows, elevator size and capacities, and ramps—can be specified. Columns, elevator landings, and stairways usually necessitate minor modifications of the layout.

Completed Layout: Drawings, Charts, and Test Run. The final results of the project will be represented by layout drawings, process charts, and diagrams. A detailed floor and plot plan, or layout model, must be prepared and its efficiency tested by means of a flow process chart and a flow diagram. The effectiveness of the layout of auxiliary departments and service activities should be similarly appraised. When the final plans are submitted to management, layout drawings should be supported by process charts and flow diagrams, as these make layout drawings easier to understand. After the building has been acquired and the equipment installed, test production runs should be made. The layout of plant and equipment can then be adjusted where required.

REVISION OF AN OBSOLESCENT LAYOUT

Poor layouts can result from inaccurate original planning, from use of an unsuitable site or building, from failure to make periodic work-simplification surveys, from rapid expansion without prior plans for it, or from piecemeal, makeshift plant changes necessitated by redesigned products or new models.

Procedure for Improving a Layout. (1) Carefully identify the goals to be accomplished and compile data; (2) conduct a work-simplification survey to eliminate flaws in the layout and to make revisions and provide for installation of new facilities (if required); and (3) develop an improved layout plan, flow diagram, and flow process chart.

Statement of Objectives and Compilation of Data. The objectives of the survey are outlined in managerial plans and policies concerning future expansion, location, quality standards, new products, and capital expenditure for new facilities. The purpose of the survey may be to enlarge plant capacity, to modify or convert facilities for the output of new models or products, or to improve an inefficient layout and adopt technologically up-to-date facilities.

Floor-plan and plot-plan drawings, together with the original building specifications, must be acquired and the drawings checked for accuracy. Templates should be made of machinery to be purchased and of equipment that may be rearranged during the survey.

Analysis by Means of a Work-Simplification Survey. A work-simplification survey for improvement of a layout involves the use of a checklist of typical weaknesses in conjunction with a flow diagram, a flow process chart, an operation analysis, an equipment replacement study, and a review of service activities and of floor-space utilization.

CHECKLIST OF TYPICAL WEAKNESSES. Nine types of weaknesses generally need to be guarded against: (1) inefficiency in the over-all process—for example, wasteful use of facilities, too much work in process, uneven flow or production (poor capacity balance), illogical sequence, and unnecessary operations; (2) poor combination of product layout and process layout; (3) uneconomical handling of materials—long hauls, congestion, backtracking, and lack of efficient methods and devices; (4) wasteful allocation of floor space—too much space for service activities (storage, shipping, receiving, offices) with accompanying congestion on the production floor—and unprofitable use of overhead space and outdoor areas; (5) inflexible facilities and inadequate provision for future expansion; (6) excessive production-cycle time

FLOW PROCESS CHART

IDENTIFICATION

SUBJECT CHARTED __fabrication of spare parts boxes__
DRAWING NO. __426 ass & 427 ass__ PART NO.s __model 26 &27__
POINT AT WHICH CHART BEGINS __receiving area__
_____ LOCATION __first floor__
POINT AT WHICH CHART ENDS __final storage__
_____ LOCATION __first floor__
QUANTITY INFORMATION
__continuous run__

CHART NO. __1__
TYPE OF CHART __process__
SHEET NO. __1__ OF __1__ SHEETS
CHARTED BY __W. Williams__
DATE __Jan. 9,'50__
APPROVED BY __G.B.S.__
DATE __Jan. 25,'50__
YEARLY PRODUCTION __280,000 appr__
COST UNIT __1.18__

PRESENT METHOD

QUANTITY UNIT CHARTED	SYMBOLS	DESCRIPTION OF EVENT	DIST. MOVED IN FEET	UNIT OPER. TIME IN min.	UNIT TRANSP. TIME IN min.	UNIT INSPECT. TIME IN min.	DELAY TIME IN min.	STORAGE TIME IN min.
skid		unload sheet steel at receiving area		4.81				
"		by hand truck to storage	197		5.10			
"		stock storage room						
lot		by hand truck to shear	7		1.15			
"		at shear						95
sheet		shear into four piece		2.47				
lot		by hand truck to press	52		2.03			
"		at press						115
"		raise to table	2	.36				
blank		press work		.66				
lot		by hand truck to brake	93		2.50			
"		at brake						120
"		raise to table	2	.36				
piece		brake work		1.11				
lot		by hand truck to spot weld	47		1.87			
"		wait for delivery of work					27	
"		at spot weld						124
unit		spot weld		2.82				
lot		by hand truck to finishing table	76		2.14			
unit		finish		1.15				
"		functional check				.48		
lot		by hand truck to degreaser	54		1.27			
"		at degreaser						121
unit		degrease		2.64				
"		by hand to priming tank	5		.22			
"		prime		.47				
"		by hand to oven	2		.21			
"		dry in primer oven	83	4.76				
lot		by hand truck to paint room	24		1.05			
unit		at paint room						120
"		spray paint		.56				
"		by hand to oven	4.5		.21			
"		dry in paint oven		5.16				
lot		by hand truck to final storage	67.5		1.98			
"		final storage						

Fig. 28. Flow process chart of the old method. (Reprinted by permission from John A. Shubin and Huxley Madeheim, *Plant Layout: Developing and Improving Manufacturing Plants.* Copyright, 1951, Prentice-Hall, Inc.)

SUMMARY .

<table>
<tr><td rowspan="2">TOTAL YEARLY SAVING—DIRECT LABOR

$42,500   ($28,400)</td><td rowspan="2"></td><td colspan="2">PRESENT METHOD</td><td colspan="2">PROPOSED METHOD</td><td colspan="2">DIFFERENCE</td></tr>
</table>

	PRESENT METHOD		PROPOSED METHOD		DIFFERENCE	
UNIT COST DIRECT LABOR & INSP.	.56		.44		.12	
DISTANCE TRAVELED IN FEET	716		271		445	
	NO.	TIME IN min	NO.	TIME IN min	NO.	TIME IN min
○ OPERATIONS	13	27.31	11	22.27	2	5.04
▢ TRANSPORTATIONS	12	19.74	12	22.52	0	2.78
▢ INSPECTIONS	1	.48	1	.22	0	.26
D DELAYS	1	27.00	0	.00	0	27.00
▽ STORAGES	4	695.00	4	36.00	4	659.00

Other summary items:
- INSTALLATION COST OF PROPOSED METHOD: $15,200
- ESTIMATED NET SAVING—FIRST YEAR: $27,300

PROPOSED METHOD

QUANTITY UNIT CHARTED	SYMBOLS	DESCRIPTION OF EVENT	DIST. MOVED IN FEET	UNIT OPER. TIME IN min	UNIT TRANSP. TIME IN min	UNIT INSPECT TIME IN min	DELAY TIME IN min	STORAGE TIME IN min
skid		unload sheet steel at receiving area		4.81				
"		by hand truck to storage	29		1.18			
"		at stock storage room						
sheet		conveyor to shear	5.5		2.21			
"		shear into four pieces		1.20				
blank		conveyor to press	6.5		2.19			
"		press blank		.32				
piece		conveyor to brake	7		2.67			
"		brake work		.31				
"		conveyor to spot weld.	5		2.25			
"		at spot weld						18
unit		spot weld		1.62				
"		conveyor to finishing	5		2.24			
"		finish		.62				
"		functional check				.22		
"		conveyor to degreasr	27		3.05			
"		at degreaser						18
"		degrease		2.64				
"		by hand to priming tank	5		.22			
"		prime		.47				
"		by hand to oven	2		.26			
"		dry in primer oven	83	4.76				
"		conveyor to spray paint	24		3.05			
"		spray paint		.36				
"		conveyor to paint oven	4.5		1.21			
"		dry in paint oven		5.16				
lot		by hand truck to final storage	57.5		1.98			
"		final storage						

Fig. 29. Flow process chart of the new method. (Reprinted by permission from John A. Shubin and Huxley Madeheim, *Plant Layout: Developing and Improving Manufacturing Plants.* Copyright, 1951, Prentice-Hall, Inc.)

because of delays, excessive temporary storages, and bottleneck machine operations; (7) service activities and auxiliary departments not located and arranged to aid the production process; (8) poor lighting, heating, and housekeeping facilities in the plant (e.g., lack of scrap and waste removal equipment, steam-cleaning equipment, and gravity drainage system); and (9) inadequate safety provision—e.g., unnecessary hazards at workplaces and at storage and handling places.

FLOW DIAGRAM. A diagram should be drawn to scale on the original floor plan to show the movement of work (see Fig. 30). A number of colored lines can represent the flow of several standard products in repetitive manufacture or the flow of typical work in job-order manufacture. The diagram is used to analyze the effectiveness of the over-all arrangement of plant activities, the location of specific machines, and the allocation of space. It will show how a more logical arrangement and economical flow of work can be devised through the elimination of long lines for handling, wasteful backtracking, crisscrossing, congestion, and confusion.

FLOW PROCESS CHART. The preparation and study of a flow process chart (see Figs. 28 and 29) will point to places where operations can be eliminated, rearranged, combined, simplified, or subdivided for greater economy. It will point out inflexible processes (i.e., those insufficiently adaptable to the output of redesigned models or related products) and indicate how more process-layout features can be introduced to good advantage. Some of the machines and operations may be segregated and profitably grouped, while other operations may be more efficiently reorganized into a line layout.

OPERATION ANALYSIS. An intensive study of machine operations (see pages 126–127) can increase plant capacity with a minimum of investment and can eliminate bottlenecks at specific operations through the introduction of better methods and the development of more effective workplace-layouts and work cycles. It is unwise to replace equipment before operation analysis has been conducted.

ANALYSIS FOR EQUIPMENT REPLACEMENT. Purchasing equipment for replacement purposes frequently calls for reorganization of other facilities—for a new machine unit generally has greater output capacity, turns out better work, is able to perform additional operations, and requires less labor; and it may have different floor-space requirements. The larger capacity and additional operations of the new unit must be integrated with the improved layout.

ANALYSIS OF SERVICE ACTIVITIES. A study of storage areas, inspection cribs, shipping and receiving zones, office space, and employee facilities frequently leads to their rearrangement for better servicing of the production floor or to make room for installation of additional equipment. The preparation of flow process charts of specific service activities (e.g., flow of office paper work, recruitment and induction of new workers, or routine overhaul of equipment) offers the best means for improving the layout of auxiliary departments.

ANALYSIS OF FLOOR SPACE. Greater "production density" and additional floor area can be acquired by eliminating waste space and unnecessary racks and benches, reducing goods in process, eliminating temporary storage areas, using "high-stacking" methods in storage, using overhead handling methods (e.g., monorails and bridge cranes), constructing mezzanine floors, and providing for joint use of space by two activities. The additional area acquired can be used for installation of new equipment or to relieve congested departments.

Development of an Improved Layout. As the survey proceeds, experiments with various layout plans are made by rearranging templates and reallocating space until an *improved* floor plan is developed. A new flow diagram and flow process chart are then made to check the elimination of layout weaknesses (enumerated on page 153) and the achievement of sound layout benefits (enumerated on page 148). The benefits gained by layout changes should be weighed against the cost of making the revision.

Illustration. The Coe Manufacturing Corporation originally was a strict job-lot firm engaged in the fabrication of diverse sheet-metal products. During the war years, the firm acquired a sizable backlog of orders for the fabrication of spare-parts boxes. Since it expected a large number of these orders to continue in peacetime, the company considered improving the layout and converting to a line-type arrangement. The over-all layout, however, would have to be adaptable to the output of the special orders that would continue.

THE ORIGINAL LAYOUT. The existent process layout did not permit line flow in the fabrication of spare-parts boxes. As a result output capacity was low and unit cost of production high. The inefficiency of the layout for the output of spare-parts boxes is indicated in Fig. 30. In the old layout, steel stock was delivered to the plant at the receiving area at (1) and from there moved to the storeroom at (2) by hand truck. The material was later drawn out of storage and moved by hand truck to the shear for the first operation at (3). The sheared blanks were stored temporarily in (3), then notched at (4). After the notching operation, the work was moved to the steel brake for temporary storage before the bending operation at (5). After it was bent, the work was moved by hand truck for temporary storage in the spot-welding section at (6). After joining, the boxes were finished and inspected at (7) and then moved by hand truck to the degreasing unit at (8) for cleaning preparatory to priming. Having gone through the priming tank at (9), the boxes were placed on the automatic conveyor, which moved the work in process through the primer-drying oven at (10). After drying,

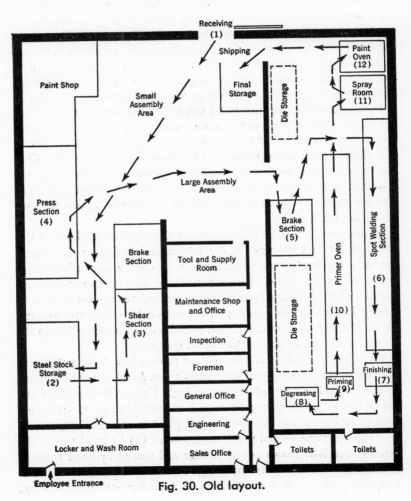

Fig. 30. Old layout.

the boxes were spray painted at (11) and put through the paint-drying oven at (12). Completed boxes were then moved to shipping area.

ANALYSIS AND IMPROVEMENT. The layout in the old arrangement was studied by means of the flow process chart (Fig. 28), and the survey resulted in the development at one end of the building of a line layout for the fabrication of spare-parts boxes. The over-all layout, however, still permitted output of many kinds of job-order work (Fig. 31).

The conversion to line layout required merely the relocation of

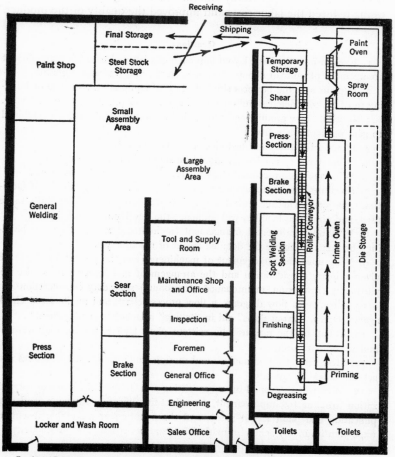

Fig. 31. Revised and improved layout.

storage areas and the rearrangement of certain equipment to conform to the sequence of operations indicated on the process chart. After detailed planning, the change was made in one week end at comparatively low cost. The improvements in the new layout, illustrated in Fig. 31, are summarized by comparing the new and old flow process charts in Figs. 28 and 29. The new layout arrangement, together with the installation of roller conveyors, made possible a substantial reduction in materials handling, in the amount of materials in process, and in temporary storage. Handling by the hand truck and lifting from floor to tables were practically eliminated. Tooling up for volume processing reduced the labor costs and improved the quality of the product.

Questions

1. Explain how the basic layout approach can be used to achieve an efficient arrangement of railroad depots, hospitals, stores, and recreation grounds.

2. Explain why the business site, selection of equipment, and type of building must be considered simultaneously in the development of a plant layout.

3. Illustrate how product and process layout arrangements may be combined to gain particular benefits.

4. Identify the tools and techniques of plant layout.

5. What types of efficiencies should be sought in plant layout?

6. What are the procedural steps for laying out a new establishment?

7. Illustrate how company policies covering degree of adaptability of facilities, expansion (whether centralized or decentralized), number of shifts to be used, and employee facilities will influence the development of a layout.

8. Why must an over-all arrangement (including selection of type of building) be prepared before the detailed layout of machinery is developed?

9. Why must the arrangement of machinery (i.e., the production floor) be given primary consideration and the arrangement and location of service departments (inspection, maintenance, storerooms) secondary consideration?

10. How can a flow diagram, a flow process chart, and an itemized check against typical "layout flaws" aid in "selling" a layout to management?

11. What are the reasons why existent plant layouts require improvement and periodic revision?

12. How can operation analysis and motion study eliminate bottlenecks and achieve balanced capacity?

13. Why will an over-all survey consisting of a study of the company organization structure for improvement, a product-simplification survey, a work-simplification and plant layout study, and the adoption of a suitable incentive-wage plan *invariably* achieve a marked increase in capacity and productivity?

18: Quality Control and
Inspection

Quality control and inspection are important technical and economic considerations in manufacturing. Though engineers and customers specify quality standards, it is the responsibility of the manufacturing division to produce work of satisfactory quality.

The *quality* of a product is defined by a set of specifications governing functional performance, composition, strength, shape, dimensions, workmanship, color, and finish. Quality is meaningful only in relation to the purpose and end use of the product. "Good quality" is attained when a product or a service fully satisfies the purpose for which it is designed.

Quality control means the recognition and removal of identifiable causes of defects and variations from the set standards. When a product is substandard, statistical techniques can be used for the systematic observation of quality and interpretation of variability; then corrective action can be undertaken. Proper standardization and effective control of materials, machines, and workmanship insure uniform quality in the product.

Inspection is the application of tests and measuring devices to compare products and performances with specified standards. Inspection determines whether a given item falls within specified limits of variability and, therefore, is acceptable or unacceptable (defective). Acceptance inspection (screening), per se, can not "inspect good quality into" the product; it merely identifies nonacceptable units after defects occur. By detecting substandard work during and after processing, however, inspectors help control quality by providing foremen and engineers with information useful in eliminating assignable causes of defective work.

Through quality control and inspection, management gains five *benefits:* (1) adequate maintenance of quality necessary to satisfy customers and to meet the competition of rival producers; (2) uniform quality of work necessary for the interchangeable-parts method of manufacture (parts must be fabricated within specified limits of variability in order that they may fit properly during assembly); (3) economical production achieved through the reduction of defective work and the consequent increase in utilization of facilities and labor; (4) prevention of waste of labor and machine time on work already known to be defective; and (5) the required checking of work necessary for piece-rate compensation (under incentive-payment plans, operators are paid only for work accepted by inspectors).

ESTABLISHMENT OF STANDARDS AND SPECIFICATIONS

A product must be appropriately designed for its intended purpose and for economical manufacture—i.e., definite quality attributes must be established in terms of standards and specifications.

Determination of Standards. Quality standards are determined by engineers in co-operation with sales, manufacturing, inspection, and purchasing departments. Standards defining the measurable characteristics of a product cover performance, composition, dimensions, weight, and finish. Since absolute uniformity is not economically attainable in production, standards take into account permissible variations from the ideal. Production men know that perfection is not merely impossible to attain but costly to approach. In establishing the permissible amount of variations (*tolerances*) from the ideal, the engineers weigh the higher cost of precision production against the advantages of better quality and superior performance of the product. In order to minimize reliance upon judgment and to avoid problems of interpretation during inspection, standards must, at the outset, be concisely presented in complete, accurate drawings and blueprints, specification sheets, formulas, or samples so that manufacturing and other departments will have no doubt as to what is required. Standards must, therefore, be reasonable, definite, understandable, and achievable.

Tolerances. Standards are expressed in terms of tolerances, or permissible variations from the basic criterion. The "zone of acceptability" is bounded by upper and lower limits. On a dimensional blueprint it consists of a specified size plus or minus an acceptable tolerance and is indicated in this fashion: $2.00 \pm .008$. The tolerance limits should be broad enough to include *chance* variations (those variables that are inherent in the production process). Deviations in quality resulting from assignable variables (those not inherent in the process) may be caused by improperly adjusted machines, worn tools, or careless workmanship. When product standards are scientifically established for the given process, variations (covered by the tolerances) in the product that go beyond the limits attributable to chance factors can be assumed to be due to assignable causes removable through proper shop practice.

When close precision fitting of given parts is necessary, high fabrication cost can be avoided through the use of broader tolerances and *selective assembly*. Under "selective assembly," companion parts of a product are gauged and sorted into classes according to size; the units of each class are fitted during assembly with mating parts of the corresponding class or size bracket.[1] By permitting the use of liberal tolerances, the selective-assembly method not only reduces the cost of fabrication but also makes for ease of inspection. The decision whether or not to employ selective assembly can be determined by balancing the savings gained in fabrication and assembly against the difficulty of replacing parts when the finished product comes up for repair.

DEVELOPMENT OR IMPROVEMENT OF AN INSPECTION SYSTEM

Procedure for Developing or Improving an Inspection System. (1) Determine the status of inspection in the company organization; (2) establish the points where checking of materials, parts, and product is needed in the process; (3) develop a floor layout for inspection activities; (4) select the methods to be used for checking; and (5) set up the department.

Status of Inspection in the Company Organization. The type of product and the importance of its quality and the size and divisional breakdown of the plant itself determine the status of inspection in the company organization.

FACTORS DEPENDING UPON PRECISION OF MANUFACTURE. In the output of precision products (aircraft, medical, and other scientific equipment) where rigorous exactness is obligatory, the inspection department should report to a high executive (works manager or general manager) whose authority will give sufficient weight to maintenance of specification standards. Though inspection may be established as a separate unit, it should be co-ordinated with the production-control,

---

[1] In the production of ball bearings, balls are sorted into groups according to size. This sorting facilitates the assembly of any bearing with balls of uniform size.

the manufacturing, and the engineering departments. With inspection set up as an independent function in the plant, quality will not be sacrificed to quantity under the spur of "rush" production orders. In cases where precision is less important, as in the manufacture of washing machines or vacuum cleaners, the chief inspector may report to the plant superintendent. When inexpensive products (hardware and low-grade china) are turned out in large volume, the inspection function may logically be placed under production foremen.

Factors Depending upon Size and Layout of Plant. In large plants inspection is commonly set up as a specialized function with a higher organizational status than the same function has in small plants. The divisional breakdown of a plant into shops or production departments also affects the organizational setup and status of inspection.

Determination of Points of Inspection. Where and when work is to be inspected can be determined by analyzing the various stages in the manufacture of the product. Low-priced products will require fewer points of inspection than high-priced items.

Inspection of Incoming Materials. Receiving inspection consists of checking raw materials, fabricated parts, and supply items before they are stored or used in manufacture. When material and parts are procured in large quantity and involve high transportation costs, inspection may be economically conducted at the vendor's plant.

Inspection of Work in Process. The amount of inspection required can be determined by studying the production process and by weighing the cost of carrying out inspection against the savings in the reduction of scrap. Defective items should be rejected at points which will lower the cost of production.

The points at which work-in-process inspection may be required are these: (1) before or after key operations where there is a high probability of defects—usually this means at each major machine; (2) before costly operations where checking the accuracy of the fabrication of parts will prevent trouble and delay in their assembly; (3) wherever succeeding operations would conceal defects; (4) at the last step of any series of operations that are logically grouped (this allows a convenient interval between inspections); (5) after each setup of a job on a machine (automatic machines generally require less frequent inspection than manually controlled equipment because they are less susceptible to variation, but first-piece inspection is always important); (6) anywhere along a single fabrication or assembly line ("floating" or "roaming" inspectors may sample the work; such sampling is inexpensive and it helps maintain the high level of workmanship required to turn out a desired quality); and (7) at the close of departmental responsibility.

FINAL INSPECTION. Finished goods generally require examination before storage or shipment. Inspection may range from a mere visual check of appearance to "functional inspection" involving a test of the product in a trial run or operation.

Layout of Inspection Activities. After inspection points have been selected, an effective inspection layout plan can be developed. The layout plan may call for either "floor" or "centralized" inspection, or, as it most often does, for a combination of the two.

FLOOR (OR "PATROLLING") INSPECTION. Under the floor-inspection system quality is checked at machines or at operations. This system achieves these advantages: (1) defects may be quickly discovered and corrected; (2) handling of materials may be reduced; and (3) line layout of machinery need not be disrupted.

The disadvantages of floor inspection include these: (1) the checking of quality may be hampered by vibrations, poor lighting, and possible "pressure" from workers for acceptance of work; and (2) costs may be high because of the need for skilled inspectors and many sets of gauging devices.

Floor inspection is suitable when heavy products are involved, when individual inspection stations can be effectively integrated with line layout of production, and when "roaming" inspectors can effectively check first pieces and periodic samples thereafter.

CENTRALIZED (OR "CRIB") INSPECTION. Under the centralized system quality is checked in cribs located at one or more places in the plant to which work to be inspected is moved.

This system has certain advantages: (1) a large quantity of work can be economically checked because the subdivision of inspection into simple tasks makes possible the employment of less skilled inspectors than would be required for floor inspection; (2) conditions are ideal: inspectors, free from the influence and interference of production operators, can check work impartially; (3) expensive and delicate instruments can receive proper care and can be used more accurately and intensively than would be the case under floor inspection; (4) the production floor can be kept orderly by the removal of completed material from machine areas.

The disadvantages of crib inspection include the following: (1) a large amount of spoiled work may accumulate at the crib before the defect is corrected at the machine and (2) the handling of materials and the total production processing time are increased.

Centralized inspection is suitable for receiving inspection and for final inspection, and for plants manufacturing relatively small and inexpensive parts; it is also suitable when the inspection point logically falls at the end of departmental responsibility—when the crib can be effectively integrated with line layout—and when the crib can be used for temporary storage as a station for materials control as well as for inspection.

In many manufacturing processes some work can be conveniently inspected at production machines while other items can best be checked at cribs. A combination of patrolling and crib inspection can, therefore, be used to good advantage by many plants.

Determination of Methods of Inspection. Inspection methods should be selected on the basis of the importance of maintaining quality at each selected point or stage of manufacture and their suitability for checking materials received, work in process, and finished goods.

INSPECTION OF EACH PIECE. Although costly, inspection of each piece is sometimes imperative when a particular detail or a high degree of accuracy is necessary. The need for and the cost of such 100-percent inspection can often be reduced through redesign of parts, application of statistical quality control, and the use of special inspection devices.

INSPECTION OF SAMPLES. Sampling inspection is often more practical and economical than 100-per-cent inspection. To be representative, samples must be taken at random from a batch of material or directly from current production. Although experience and judgment frequently form the basis for determining sample size (i.e., the number of pieces required to represent current output adequately), tables developed from mathematical formulas provide a more accurate basis.[2] Management must stipulate an "acceptable quality level"—i.e., an allowable percentage of defective pieces. When the percentage of defective pieces exceeds the acceptable quality level, the entire lot may be rejected and each piece may then be inspected for acceptance.

Sampling and 100-per-cent inspection can employ either "destructive" or "nondestructive" testing. *Destructive inspection* tests such fac-

[2] Tables developed in 1950 by the armed services of the United States are widely used in industry for various statistical purposes including that of determining sample size for a given quantity of product or material.

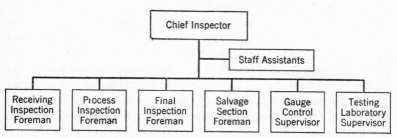

Fig. 32. Typical divisions of an inspection department.

tors as tensile strength, compressibility, and chemical composition to determine whether the material or product meets quality standards. *Nondestructive inspection* does not harm the product; it often involves only such tests as the checking of dimensions and the visual examination of color.

INSPECTION JOB METHODS. Inspection tasks should be studied and efficient procedures and workplace arrangements should be set up for checking quality. Reliance on individual judgment (which is often a matter of opinion) can be minimized by selecting or developing efficient inspection instruments or machines (automatic gauging devices, whenever economical). A procedure for the disposal of borderline cases (which generally require some type of review by the inspection supervisor) should be provided, especially where costly parts and operations are involved. Inspection *job instruction sheets* should be written up to specify the quality standards, gauging devices, and inspection methods. The output of inspectors can be increased by an incentive-wage plan, particularly when inspection has been made comparatively foolproof through the use of automatic gauging devices.

Organization of an Inspection Department. The inspection department (or section) should be set up to fit the status given to it in the company organization. Its internal structure will depend upon the amount of inspection that is necessary, the inspection methods to be employed, and the layout arrangement. Its particular activities should then be subdivided according to functions (see Fig. 32), specific duties should be assigned to the department, and personnel should be selected and trained.

DUTIES. The scope of inspection activities includes: (1) co-operation with engineering and other departments in product design, in the determination of quality standards, in the selection of production processes, and in statistical quality control; [3] (2) acceptance or rejection of purchased items (materials, parts, and supplies), work in process, and finished goods; (3) inspection of tools and purchased equipment; (4) selection, control, and maintenance of gauges, templates, instruments, and machines used for inspection and production purposes; (5) co-operation in, or complete supervision of, the salvaging of defective parts and materials; (6) jurisdiction over a testing laboratory set up for checking quality and for accepting materials; and (7) compilation and issuance of defective work and scrap reports to management.

PERSONNEL. The chief inspector should be an individual of executive ability who is familiar with the quality standards and production processes of the industry. He should be able to develop inspection methods and practices, to keep abreast of the latest inspection devices, and to uncover the causes for substandard work.

The number of inspectors required will be determined by the organizational setup, the inspection layout arrangement, the number of inspection points, and the inspection methods employed.[4]

The qualifications for inspectors vary, depending upon the nature of the work, from shop or technical experience to a college degree in engineering. In general, personnel selected for this work should be conscientious, should be exacting about details, and should have good eyesight and manual dexterity. Young women are suited for many inspection positions since they are adept at work requiring keen perception and nimble fingers. Since inspectors frequently stop operations when work is substandard, they must have the ability to "get along" with production workers. The training of inspectors should cover the techniques required (for example, use of instruments and reading of blueprints) and the purpose and importance of the quality specifications in the manufacture of the product.

[3] Statistical quality control is discussed later in the chapter.
[4] Firms generally requiring a high proportion of inspectors are those that manufacture precision products, those involved with frequent model and style changes, those engaged in job-order manufacture and employing general-purpose equipment, those expanding rapidly, and those with a rapid labor turnover. Firms generally requiring a small proportion of inspectors are those that manufacture low quality products, those that manufacture related standardized products, and those that employ special-purpose equipment or continuous-process type facilities.

STATISTICAL QUALITY CONTROL

Statistical quality control, which is based on the mathematical law of probability, indicates the limits beyond which variations in the quality of the product should not go without correction. The law of probability applies to the behavior of the chance variables in a standardized process. Variations in quality beyond the limits based on probability are attributed to factors which can be brought under control or eliminated.

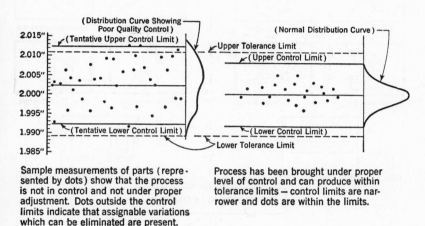

Sample measurements of parts (represented by dots) show that the process is not in control and not under proper adjustment. Dots outside the control limits indicate that assignable variations which can be eliminated are present.

Process has been brought under proper level of control and can produce within tolerance limits — control limits are narrower and dots are within the limits.

Fig. 33. Statistical quality control chart used to identify assignable causes of defective work that can be removed, thus bringing the process into control and reducing defective work.

Setting up statistical quality control requires the measurement of samples of the product for quality. By means of a simple statistical computation involving the use of tables, the measurements are plotted on a chart to show the range or control limits for the quality measurement of subsequent production. The control limits of the chart segregate the variations in the product that are due to random or chance causes (variables inherent in the process) from those variations that are due to assignable causes and can be removed. When points plotted from the measured samples of the work fall outside the control limits of the chart (see Fig. 33), the process is out of control and it is assumed that the variations are due to assignable causes that can be tracked down and eliminated by foremen and other plant technicians.

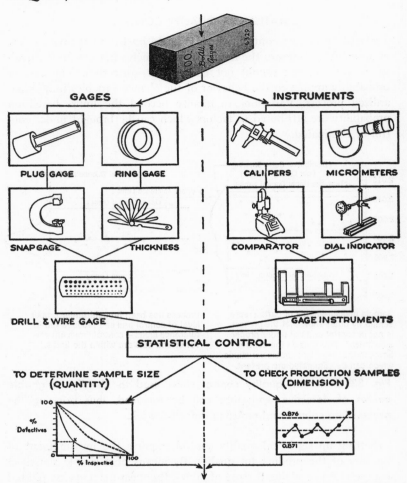

Fig. 34. Measuring instruments and gauges. Measuring instruments and gauges do not maintain their original accuracy, but are subject to wear, warpage, shrinkage, and damage in handling. Consequently, they must be calibrated with gauge blocks (such as that at the top of this illustration) at frequent intervals, and adjusted to gauge block standards. (Courtesy the DoAll Company, Des Plaines, Illinois; copyright, 1952)

The systematic removal of assignable causes (e.g., a machine or a fixture in disrepair, an inexperienced worker, or the use of the wrong material, tool, or sequence of operations) reduces defects and improves the quality of the product, brings the process into control, and narrows the control limits.

Statistical quality control secures several *benefits:* (1) it indicates whether the quality standards (tolerances) for a process are proper or should be changed, and also whether the production method should be replaced by a more suitable process; (2) it lowers the cost of inspection through the reduction of poor work, elimination of some inspection points, and substitution of sampling for 100-per-cent inspection; (3) it reduces needless confusion and interruption of production; and (4) it provides a record of the quality of work produced.

Fig. 35. Left: A bore gauge. Below: A thread gauge. (Courtesy the DoAll Company, Des Plaines, Illinois; copyright, 1952)

INSPECTION DEVICES

Accuracy of measurement, a prime factor in inspection, is attained by use of various types of measuring devices. There has been a gradual transition from manual to mechanical inspection. Mechanical inspection is economical when the volume of output is large, when manual gauging is tiresome, or when great accuracy must be attained. Mass-production types of inspection devices can generally be designed and constructed for any inspection activity where the volume of work justifies the cost. In fact, high output of precision products is made possible largely because of progress in the development and use of inspection machines.

Types of Inspection Devices. Inspection devices vary in type and complexity from the simple plug gauge to the elaborate mechanical and electronic machines.

Dimensional Gauges. Dimensional gauging instruments include such devices as micrometers; fixed-sized gauges; comparator-type gauges; air gauges; and gauge blocks.

AUTOMATIC TESTING EQUIPMENT. Electronic mechanisms are used to further automaticity in inspecting and sorting, in checking internal characteristics of products, in gauging thickness of liquids, and in measuring and recording temperatures and humidity.

LABORATORY TESTING EQUIPMENT. Laboratories generally contain machines and checking setups to perform a variety of inspection tasks ranging from tensile-strength tests and hardness tests to complex chemical analyses.

Control of Inspection Devices. A "gauge supervisor" is often charged with the responsibility of maintaining a systematic inventory of measuring instruments and periodically examining, repairing, and resetting all inspection devices, whether the equipment is used by production operators or inspectors.

Questions

1. Explain what is meant by "quality" of the product, by tolerances, by selective assembly, and by assignable variations.

2. What are the purposes and benefits of quality control and inspection?

3. What is the relationship between the quality of the product and the cost of the product?

4. Outline the procedural steps for developing or improving an inspection system for a given firm.

5. Enumerate the points at which inspection may be required during the processing and production of goods.

6. What are the relative advantages of floor (decentralized) inspection and centralized (crib) inspection?

7. (a) What are the manufacturing conditions to which floor inspection is best suited and the manufacturing conditions to which centralized inspection is best suited? (b) Can these layout arrangements be combined to advantage?

8. Distinguish between acceptance sampling and 100-per-cent inspection and indicate when each may be applied.

9. What factors should be taken into account in determining the place (status) of the inspection function in the company organization structure?

10. What manufacturing conditions tend to increase the amount of inspection needed—that is, the proportion of inspectors relative to production (direct) workers?

11. Explain the method of "statistical quality control" and list the benefits it obtains.

12. Under what manufacturing conditions can highly mechanized inspection devices be economically employed?

19: Purchasing

Acompany's procurement function becomes particularly important when its purchased items account for a high proportion of the unit cost of the product, when the prices fluctuate widely, when numerous diverse items are needed, and when the quality of the material appreciably influences the cost of manufacturing.

Efficient procurement is achieved by purchasing the required quantity and quality of raw materials, parts, supplies, tooling, and equipment at the right time and at the lowest prices. But buying at low prices is uneconomical if the required quantity of materials is not received when needed, if the quality does not measure up to specifications, or if the supplier fails to make satisfactory adjustments for his errors, as in delivery or price.

The "quantity," "quality," and "time" factors are defined for the purchasing department by engineering, manufacturing, and other departments that specify and request procurement. The "best price" and "vendor service" factors necessary to satisfy the requests for procurement are the responsibility of the purchasing department.

Procedure for Establishing or Improving the Purchasing Department. (1) Outline the scope and functions of the purchasing department. (2) Formulate purchasing policies to cover the quantity, price, and time of purchase; the selection of vendor; and the form of purchase. (3) Set up the purchasing department, determining the status of the department in the company organization, the degree of centralization, and the internal structure of the department. (4) Develop effective purchasing routine to cover specifications, purchase requisitions, the selection of vendors, the placing of orders, the method of follow-ups, and maintenance of records.

SCOPE AND FUNCTIONS OF THE DEPARTMENT

The purchasing agent and his staff (1) participate in the formulation of company procurement policies; (2) participate in seeking out new and improved materials which will reduce costs, improve products, or

173

serve as substitutes for scarce items; (3) study business and market conditions and analyze information on materials supply, price trends, and governmental controls; (4) co-operate with the engineering and other departments in carrying out simplification and standardization programs and in preparing rational specifications which will contribute to economical procurements; (5) maintain data on sources of supply, on prices, and on quantities available; (6) procure requested materials, equipment, and services at the best prices; and (7) attend to the details of purchasing: analyzing quotations, choosing suppliers, placing orders, following up, and maintaining records on purchases.

POLICIES OF THE DEPARTMENT

In formulating policy, the company takes into account such factors as quantities to be procured, capital and inventory carrying charges, the frequency and magnitude of price fluctuations, business trends, and scarcities caused by governmental regulation and defense production. In accordance with any or all of such factors, management should adopt specific policies for particular items or classes of items (raw materials, parts, supplies, tools, and equipment). With the participation of the purchasing agent, management should formulate policies to cover quantity, price, and time of purchase; selection of the supplier; and form of purchase.

Quantity, Price, and Time of Purchase. All items purchased should be classed on the basis of type, regularity of need, quantities required, and degree of price fluctuations. Policies that can be adopted to cover these considerations include "purchasing by requirement," "purchasing for a specific period," "market purchasing," "hand-to-mouth buying," "speculative purchasing," and "hedging."

PURCHASING BY REQUIREMENT. Items used infrequently or essential to emergency production needs are purchased by requirement. Accurate information on reliable and reputable sources must be on hand, since purchases cover only immediate requirements.

PURCHASING FOR A SPECIFIED PERIOD. Materials and supplies used regularly but not in large quantities are generally purchased for a specific period. Production schedules are usually the controlling factor in the determination of the period.

MARKET PURCHASING. Market purchasing endeavors to take advantage of price fluctuations while procuring sufficient materials to meet the needs of production schedules. The purchasing department, guided by a careful study of price trends, engages in *forward buying* (i.e., stocks up inventories in advance of future need) when prices are low and will rise, and thus simultaneously obtains large savings in purchase price and consolidates purchases in one transaction. High inventory carrying charges and deterioration should be constantly balanced against price advantages.

HAND-TO-MOUTH BUYING. Frequent purchases in small quantities are wise when prices are falling or unsteady or when a company's requirements are uncertain. Sometimes *averaging-down-on-the-market* can be advantageously practiced—that is, materials can be bought when the price drops sharply in the course of a general downward price change. Among the advantages of hand-to-mouth buying are limitation of losses from price declines, low carrying charges, decreased capital investment, and reduced deterioration of materials. Such advantages must be balanced against these disadvantages: possible losses occasioned by an upward jump in prices; a higher unit price because of loss of quantity discounts; possible interruption of production schedules because of errors in estimating inventory requirements, market shortages of materials, or delays in delivery; and higher clerical costs of frequent purchases and higher delivery and handling charges.

SPECULATIVE PURCHASING. Speculative purchasing is an attempt to gain considerable profits by buying an excess of materials at greater than normal risk when prices are considered to be at a low point. Unlike market puchasing, it makes price trends the primary factor in buying and gives less regard to the strict material requirements of the business. Since there is danger of large losses, speculative purchasing should be under the control of a major executive. Other disadvantages of speculative purchasing include the possibilities of obsolescence of material, interruption of production, large investments in inventory, and heavy carrying charges.

HEDGING. Hedging minimizes potential inventory losses arising from future price changes in raw-material commodities held and used by the firm. To hedge, the firm purchases for immediate delivery commodities to be used in production and at the same time sells a like amount of the material on the commodity exchange [1] for future delivery—i.e., it

---

[1] A "commodity exchange" is an organized open market (i.e., one maintained by a board of governors) for standard primary products for which there are many buyers and sellers wherein prices are determined by market supply and demand. Professional speculators, operating through such exchanges, endeavor to make a profit (but are prepared to take losses) on fluctuating prices by buying and selling *futures*—agreements to deliver at a given price at a future date.

sells "futures" contracts. Then, later, when the firm sells its finished goods, it fulfills its futures contract by covering—i.e., buying the commodity to make good the delivery.

What the firm loses (or gains) in finished goods sales, because of price changes, is offset by the gain (or loss) in its futures (or hedge) transaction. That is, if the finished-goods price drops because of a decline in the commodity price, the firm makes up this loss by the gain in its purchase of the commodity at the current low price to cover its "futures" sale which was made at a higher price. On the other hand, if the finished-goods price goes up because of a rise in the commodity price, the firm's extra gain in sales cancels its loss sustained in covering the futures contract. Thus the firm avoids the risk of price fluctuations, but makes its usual profit margin on the sales of its goods. The firm, however, can hedge only in the purchase of such items as cotton, copper, lead, rubber, coffee, and sugar for which there exist organized commodity exchanges.

Selection of Supplier. Although the supplier offering a given quantity and service at the lowest price is generally the vendor selected, purchasing policy may also call for "splitting orders," favoring local suppliers, giving special consideration to the reputation of a vendor, and practicing "reciprocity."

SPLITTING ORDERS. Buying from multiple sources tends to assure a reliable supply, especially if the vendors are limited in their capacity to provide important items.

FAVORING LOCAL SUPPLIERS. Local vendors may be favored when quick delivery is required or when the resulting good will is valuable to the firm.

CONSIDERING REPUTATION. The reputation of a vendor may be given prime importance, especially when quality and service are particularly valuable.

PRACTICING RECIPROCITY. Reciprocity is the practice of placing orders with suppliers who are customers. Such a policy may be acceptable if price, quality, and delivery tend to approximate competitive levels.

Forms of Purchase. Forms in which purchases are made include the following.

GROUP PURCHASING. Group purchasing is a sound policy for the procurement of goods bought in small quantities. Savings in clerical and delivery costs are made when one order is placed for a number of varied small items instead of an individual order for each type of item.

176

SCHEDULED PURCHASING. In scheduled purchasing, the supplier is given estimates of procurement needs covering a period of time; he can then effectively plan his production on a long-term basis. Both vendor and buyer enjoy the savings resulting from regularity of production and smaller inventories.

CONTRACT PURCHASING. A contract specifying periodic delivery can assure a continuous supply of goods and also obtain price advantages. Under contract purchasing both buyer and vendor avoid tying up funds in large inventories and are spared heavy inventory carrying charges. Lower prices are obtained through quantity discounts and greater bargaining.

ORGANIZATION OF THE DEPARTMENT

Setting up the purchasing office necessitates decisions as to the status of the department in the company organization, the degree of centralization desirable, and the most suitable internal structure.

Status in the Company Organization. The place of purchasing in the company organization depends upon the nature of the business. (1) If materials are to be resold after minor, inexpensive processing, purchasing may be placed under the sales department. (2) If procurement of materials is not complex and if prices are comparatively steady, purchasing may logically be a subdivision of the manufacturing department. If this situation prevails in the medium-sized firm, procurement and storeroom operation may be combined. (3) In larger firms, especially where materials account for a high proportion of the unit cost of the product, procurement should be set up as an independent department with the purchasing agent responsible to the president, general manager, vice-president, or treasurer—depending upon the magnitude and complexity of the purchasing function and the size and organizational features of the firm.

The Degree of Centralization. Procurement is inefficient if the purchasing function is scattered or "excessively decentralized"—that is, if each branch or department buys its own materials and equipment. High costs result from lack of buying skill, numerous purchases in small quantities, poor financial control, overstocking, and delay in deliveries.

Centralized purchasing performed by a special department under a competent purchasing agent achieves these advantages: (1) Procurement experts can consistently employ uniform policies and procedures and be held responsible for results. (2) They can eliminate needless variety in items purchased, thus reducing inventory investment; and by setting up rational specifications, they can widen sources and get better quality. (3) They can secure additional economies through the elimination of duplicate buying in small quantities, through central supervision over deliveries, and through such fiscal control of expenditures as central regulation of purchase requisitions, effective and prompt checking of invoices for cash discounts, and elimination of overpayments. (4) They can secure low prices and good vendor services, particularly on large orders providing for the aggregate needs of the company, through effective bargaining, use of vendor competition, and quantity discounts. (5) They can effectively regulate the time and quantity of purchases through advance information on the trend of company sales, on inventory stocks, and on material scarcities in the market, and through knowledge of governmental regulations.

The degree of centralization of purchasing should be greater if the products of a multiplant company are fairly uniform or are identical. Excessive centralization, however, should be guarded against. If the materials are highly diverse and if the company's plants are widely scattered, the attempt to carry out all purchasing from the home office may lead to difficulty in achieving proper control and vendor service. In such cases, the central purchasing office should control policies and undertake contract buying of important materials, while local purchasing agents (responsible to the manager of each branch) should place orders against the contracts and also buy miscellaneous items locally.

The Internal Structure. The quantity and variety of items purchased and the size of the company (including the number of its branches) largely determine the internal organization structure of the purchasing department. If purchases are large and varied, a greater degree of functionalized subdivision can profitably be employed; however, if purchases are small and not very complex, related activities (e.g., storeskeeping, receiving, or traffic) may be combined with purchasing. A representative purchasing department of a medium-sized firm is illustrated in Fig. 36.

THE PURCHASING AGENT. In addition to being in charge of the purchasing department, the purchasing agent has special duties requiring particular qualifications.

The purchasing agent has a major role in formulating and implementing departmental policies. He prepares a budget to show the total purchases necessary to meet production requirements. When approved by management, the budget establishes his purchasing authority and

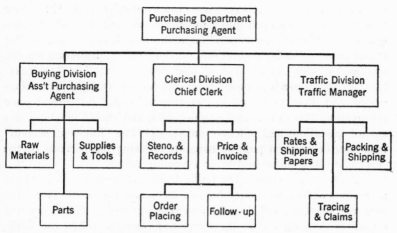

Fig. 36. A representative purchasing department (including the traffic division).

defines its financial limits. Within the general limits of the budget, the purchasing agent co-operates with other department heads in determining quantities of materials to be procured. He interviews important salesmen and personally negotiates the purchase of commodities involving large expenditures. In managing the functions of the purchasing department, he endeavors to secure advantageous prices, regular deliveries of goods meeting the required quality standards, and a maximum turnover of inventory (nonetheless keeping the inventories adjusted to business demands and seasonal fluctuations).

The purchasing agent has to have a good knowledge of the manufacturing processes of his firm and of the kinds of materials that are suitable. He has to have an understanding of economics in order to appraise market developments properly, to determine the effect of governmental regulations on supply, and to forecast price trends. He must also have a knowledge of commercial law governing purchasing and a knowledge of office procedure.

THE BUYING DIVISION. To the buying division is delegated the authority for selection of vendors, negotiation of purchase terms, and actual purchasing. A large firm requires a number of buyers, each a specialist in purchasing one type of commodity (e.g., raw materials, parts, supplies, or tools and equipment).

THE CLERICAL DIVISION. The clerical division provides office services to the buyers, and thus relieves them of much routine work. The service activities may be grouped into a number of sections. (1) The "stenographic and record-filing section" maintains records of past and present transactions—including requisitions, purchase orders, inspection reports, approved invoices, supply sources, and catalogs. (2) The "order section" writes up purchase orders from data on approved purchase requisitions. (3) The "price and invoice section" maintains current price information, checks bids against price data, and checks invoice prices against quotations and purchase orders. (4) The "follow-up section" facilitates delivery on promise dates by checking the progress of the vendor in filling orders and by investigating delays.

THE TRAFFIC DIVISION. The traffic division is charged with handling all matters dealing with outgoing and incoming shipments. This function may be placed either under purchasing or under sales, depending on which department has the larger traffic needs. When the traffic function assumes sizable proportions in large firms, it may be set up as an independent department.

To obtain economical and reliable shipping, the traffic division (1) selects the types of shipping service (railroad, express, steamship, motor, parcel post, or air) and the specific carriers on the basis of the lowest total charge, greatest dispatch, best care of goods, and "in transit" and other services; (2) prepares instructions for packaging and shipping to guarantee the lowest freight rate charges, protection of goods, and ease of handling; (3) prepares bills of lading (contracts between shipper and carriers); (4) traces overdue, and expedites urgently needed, shipments; (5) audits and approves freight bills for payment; (6) files and collects claims against carriers and insurance companies for loss, damage, delay, or overcharge; (7) investigates railroad-car delay (loading and unloading time) on company sidings to avoid demurrage charges—that is, carrier charges against the company for holding cars overtime; (8) prepares "rate charts" from carrier records to aid the purchasing department in calculating transportation costs and to aid salesmen in quoting shipping costs to customers; (9) supervises company-owned local motor-transport service and any required hauls to and from railroad depots; and (10) supervises receiving and shipping wherever such activities are under the traffic division.

PROCEDURES OF THE DEPARTMENT

Procurement procedures should be simple and definite, yet sufficiently flexible to handle varying volumes of purchases. An effective inventory-control system [2] must be set up and precise specifications of materials established before purchasing can be economical.

Specifications of Materials. Specifications concerning materials should be the result of a product-simplification and standardization program (see Chs. 10 and 18).

Good specifications are accurate, clear, and definite descriptions of materials with special reference to their properties, intended use, and permissible tolerances. They should stipulate quality standards that a buyer can easily check, and, whenever possible, the specifications should be capable of being met by several vendors.

Well drawn-up specifications secure the combination of properties desired in materials, gain uniformity of quality, avoid undue variety in items and thus reduce inventories, facilitate quotation comparisons, and promote efficient purchasing and rapid deliveries.

The responsibility for drawing up specifications falls on the engineers, particularly when close precision and questions of a technical nature are involved. Although the requirements of product design and manufacturing determine the properties and quality of materials needed, specifications should nonetheless correspond to trade terms and practices. The purchasing agent should, therefore, co-operate in the preparation of specifications, suggest modifications, or at least edit the final draft.

There are several *forms of specifications:* blueprints (usually employed for such items as parts and tools), brands or trade names (used when one or more brands have a reputation for superiority), physical properties and chemical formulas (used for many raw materials), method of manufacturing (when necessary for such items as special alloy steels), descriptions of use or purpose (employed for equipment and machinery), and samples (when other forms of specifications are not available).

Requisitions for Materials. Heads of departments, authorized supervisors, inventory-control clerks, and plant foremen originate purchase requisitions. Each requisition (a well-designed, serially numbered form) authorizes the purchase department to buy; specifies by name and description the item needed, the quantity, the time of delivery,

[2] For procedure see Ch. 20.

and the place to which it is to be delivered; and contains both the name and signature of the requester. It may also indicate the quantity on hand, why the item is needed, and the account number to be charged. Purchase requisitions are usually made out in multiple copies—one kept by the originator and at least two sent to the purchasing office.

Management can *control purchases* not only through the budget device but also by authorizing only certain individuals to make out or sign requisitions and by requiring the general manager, treasurer, or president to countersign requisitions exceeding a specified value or volume.

Quotations, Proposals, and Selection of Vendors. After receiving an authorized purchase requisition, the buyer reviews sources of supply and the quotations of various vendors. With a knowledge of current prices and discounts, he studies the market to determine the best time to buy. He checks the files and perhaps selects as many as four or five prospective vendors. He sends requests for quotations (specifying kind of material, quantity, delivery date, and other terms) to each of these and ordinarily selects the lowest bidder who meets the require-ments. Commodities purchased under contract or purchased repeatedly do not generally require requests for quotations.

Purchase Order. Since a purchase order is an agreement to buy, it must be carefully drawn up on a standard form. The purchase order stipulates kind of material (description and quality), quantity, delivery date, where to ship, order number, discount, billing instructions, and other terms. Copies of the purchase order go to the vendor, the re-ceiving department, the reference file, and the follow-up section. The placement of an order should not be considered complete until an acknowledgment of it is received from the vendor.

Follow-Up, Receiving, and Checking. The follow-up section makes sure that vendors deliver commodities on agreed dates. To facilitate follow-up, it keeps a tickler file of purchase orders arranged according to due dates. Through mail, telephone, telegram, or visits to the suppliers' plant, it expedites delivery of important purchases. When received materials have been checked for quantity and quality, the receiving clerk submits a "materials-received" report to the invoice clerk of the purchasing department. The invoice, having been already checked with the purchase order for price, computation of figures, and purchase terms, is then checked with the "materials-received" report for quantity and quality. Discrepancies are generally adjusted with the vendor before the invoice is approved for payment by the purchasing department.

Maintenance of Records. An effective purchasing routine requires the maintenance of up-to-date information on sources of supply, prices and quotations, purchase orders, and deliveries not yet received (follow-up file). A file of the *sources of supply* (classified as to commodity and as to manufacturers and dealers) is used for selecting a vendor since it includes information on the size of order that firms can fill, the time needed for receipt of shipment, shipping data, and freight rates. A *prices-and-quotations* file (consisting of all returned request-for-quotations forms, catalogs, price lists, and discount sheets) is used for appraising new quotations, negotiating prices, and reviewing discounts and other terms. A file of *purchase orders* is used for adjustments, rating of vendor performance, and study of price trends.

Questions

1. When is procurement particularly vital to a business, requiring a high-caliber purchasing agent and high organizational status in the company?

2. What are the procedural steps for establishing or improving the purchasing department?

3. (a) What aspects or phases of purchasing should be covered by procurement policies? (b) What factors should be taken into account in the formulation of such policies?

4. Under what external conditions would a firm practice "forward" buying and under what conditions would it practice "hand-to-mouth" buying?

5. What are the relative advantages and disadvantages of "hand-to-mouth" buying?

6. (a) Distinguish between "speculative" purchasing and "hedging." (b) When can a firm practice "hedging"?

7. Can "group" purchasing, "scheduled" purchasing, and "contract" purchasing be used simultaneously? Explain.

8. What are the advantages and disadvantages of centralized procurement by the home office?

9. (a) What are the principal duties of the traffic division? (b) What would ordinarily be the organizational status of the traffic function in a small firm?

10. (a) What are the various forms of specifications for items purchased? (b) Who should draw up or select the specifications? (c) What benefits do well-drawn-up specifications achieve?

11. What are the steps in the procurement cycle?

12. What are the various ways whereby management can achieve over-all control of its procurement function?

20: Inventory Control

When management neglects the control of inventories, its operations and costs invariably get out-of-hand. Shortages in inventories and tools, for example, interrupt production, making machines and men idle and causing sales loss. Unintentional excess buying and overstocking, on the other hand, result in unprofitable investment, high inventory-carrying charges (e.g., storage and deterioration expenses) and possible losses caused by price declines. Inadequate procedures result in misdirection of materials and a need for additional stock expediters.

Management gains over-all control of its inventories through (1) simplification and standardization of products, materials, and tools; (2) maintaining inventory records and furnishing data for accounting; (3) planning and determining total inventory requirements to meet the needs of production and sales; (4) procuring the required quality of items in the proper quantities and at the right time; (5) controlling the storage and issue of materials and tools and the flow of goods in process; and (6) conserving and substituting materials and supplies, particularly during periods of scarcity.

An effective inventory-control system secures numerous *benefits*. (1) It assures proper execution of policies covering procurement and use of materials and makes possible rapid shifts in business to meet changes in market conditions. (2) It obtains economies through a reduction in needless variety of items carried in stock. (3) It eliminates delays in production caused by nonavailability of required materials and tools. (4) It avoids overaccumulation of inventories and tools, and thereby maintains the minimum investment consistent with production needs and procurement policies. (5) It reduces inventory losses caused by inadequate inspection of incoming materials, damage, deterioration, obsolesence, waste, or theft. (6) It provides "balance-of-stores" records to serve as a reliable basis for effective production planning, economical procurement, cost accounting, and preparation of financial reports.

Procedures for Establishing an Efficient Inventory-Control System. (1) Determine the place of inventory control in the organization; (2) develop a method for classifying and identifying inventory; (3) set up and secure control through balance-of-stores records (perpetual inventory cards) for planning inventory needs and allocating materials, requisitioning purchases, taking physical inventory, and preparing financial statements; (4) establish the steps in the materials-control cycle for the regulation of the flow of items from requisitioning procurement to the completion of the product; (5) set up procedures for tool procurement and for its control; and (6) secure physical control of inventory through an effective system of keeping stores.

The major responsibility (and authority) for control of inventory should normally be placed in the manufacturing division under the chief of production planning and control. This means that all phases of the inventory-control cycle (requisitioning procurement, receiving, storage, allocation, processing, and replenishment) will have centralized direction—even though the execution of the cycle concerns the purchasing, engineering, inspection, and sales departments.

CONTROL OF MATERIALS

Classification and Identification of Inventory. In order to save time and simplify identification and allocation and control, the various types of inventory should be classified by means of symbols. Indeed, an identification system should be set up for all aspects of the business —departments and sections, machines, operations, positions, etc.

Types of Inventory. Inventory includes tools, standard supply items, raw materials, goods in process, and finished products. *Tools,* which will be discussed later in the chapter, include fixtures, dies, patterns, gauges, and "hand tools" used with machines and operations. *Supplies* are items (e.g., abrasives and lubricants) used to aid production but do not go into the product. *Raw materials* are commodities (steel, lumber, asbestos, fabric) and purchased parts (machined forgings and casting such as gears and pistons) that go into the final product. *Goods in process* are materials that have been partly fabricated but are not as yet completed. *Finished goods* are completed items ready for shipment.

Symbols for Identification. The numeric and mnemonic are common systems of symbolization for classifying and identifying inventories (including tools). The *numeric system* identifies and classifies items and subgroups by numbers and decimals. When the system is properly set up, the various digits and decimal positions have significance in designating models, location, sizes, or physical properties. The *mnemonic system* classifies and identifies items and subgroups by employing letters and numbers which assist the memory. The first letter may designate the general class, and successive letters the subclass (e.g., "Z" for model, "SA" for subassembly, and "P" for component part).[1] Stores may also be identified by use of tags, paint color, or distinctive markings.

Balance-of-Stores Record (Perpetual Inventory). The balance-of-stores record plays the central role in the inventory-control system, particularly in a job-order plant. In essence, it controls the movement of each item as it goes in and out of stock and shows the current balance on hand. Since the record is closely associated with production planning, it is generally best kept by a balance-of-stores clerk in the production-planning office.

PERPETUAL INVENTORY FORM. The stores record must be specially designed to serve the particular needs of the business (see Fig. 37). A loose-leaf ledger or card is kept for each item in terms of unit quantities (pounds, pieces, or gallons) and, usually, in terms of monetary value. The data frequently carried on the record include the name and identification of the item, location in storage, rate of consumption, ordering point, ordering quantity, and the following balance columns:

Ordered—quantity placed on order by a purchase requisition.

Received—quantity supplied to the storeroom.

Issued—quantity released to the plant in response to requisitions for materials.

Balance on hand—current quantity and value of stores.

Allocated or applied to orders—quantity apportioned to a production order but not as yet issued for use in the plant.

Available—quantity still available for allocation.

ORDERING POINT AND ORDERING QUANTITY. To prevent shortages and high costs due to under- or overbuying and to determine "when" and "how much" to order, a minimum quantity (ordering point) and a maximum quantity (ordering quantity) should be established for

[1] In a combined mnemonic-numeric system, for example, "Z2–SA08–P96" might identify a component part of a washing machine. "Z2" would mean the second model of the product; "SA08," the eighth subassembly of the model; and "P96," the ninety-sixth part of the subassembly.

PERPETUAL STOCK RECORD

Part _____ Location _____ Ordering point _____ Ordering quantity _____

RECEIVED				ISSUED					BALANCE	
DATE	PURCHASE ORDER NO.	QUANTITY	UNIT COST	DATE	REQ. NO.	DEPT. OR PROD. ORDER	QUANTITY	UNIT COST	QUANTITY	UNIT COST

Fig. 37. Balance-of-stores record (perpetual inventory).

each item and should be indicated in the stores record. The "ordering point," indicating the minimum quantity which must be kept in stock and thus the time at which the item must be reordered, is determined by the rate of use in production and the time necessary for purchasing or fabricating the item. The "ordering quantity" is determined by striking an economic balance among the following factors that influence procurement costs: (1) inventory-carrying charges (e.g., storage, insurance, and interest), (2) clerical costs of ordering for purchase or for fabrication in the plant, (3) transportation costs, and (4) quantity discounts on purchases. The increase in carrying charges accruing from larger ordering quantities must be balanced against the resulting savings in terms of clerical and transportation costs and quantity discounts. The ordering quantity should be periodically revised to meet the financial situation of the company and to meet seasonal fluctuations in production and market trends—rising or falling prices.

METHODS OF EVALUATING MATERIALS. In order to show a conservative figure on the balance sheet and to keep inventory value in proper relation to other current assets, controllers formerly often used "market or cost, whichever is lower" to evaluate inventory. However, inventory evaluation also affects operating profits, particularly during periods of price inflation or deflation. In selecting a method for evaluating materials, management should consider acceptability for tax purposes, pattern of price fluctuations, and suitability for the preparation of financial statements. The first-in-first-out and the last-in-first-out methods are most commonly employed for evaluating materials, but the standard cost, the cumulative average, and the normal stock methods are also used.

First-in-First-out (FIFO). The FIFO method takes the oldest material cost—that which was incurred when the materials were procured—for the computation of the unit cost of the product. During a period of rising prices, FIFO shows a higher profit figure; during a period of declining prices, a lower profit figure.

Last-in-First-out (LIFO). LIFO takes the current cost of material for the compilation of the unit cost of the product. Hence price fluctuations of materials recently procured are absorbed currently in the cost of operations. When prices are on the upswing, LIFO results in a reduced profit figure; and, conversely, during declining prices, it results in a higher profit figure.

USES OF THE PERPETUAL INVENTORY RECORD. The perpetual inventory serves these purposes. (1) It facilitates production planning since the stores record is a means for allocating material to production orders; and it enables the scheduling and release of orders with full assurance that materials will be available when required. (2) It enables timely procurements of purchases with accurate specifications as to "how much" and "when." (With accurate information on the rate of consumption and balance on hand, procurement can be planned to take advantage of price fluctuations.) (3) It facilitates allocation of material costs to manufacturing orders or to production departments using the items. (4) It makes it possible to prepare financial statements without taking physical inventory. (5) It establishes a basis for taking physical inventory and for controlling misallocation, waste, obsolescence, and theft of materials.

Physical Inventory. Since discrepancies between inventory records and quantities on hand can not be avoided, an actual count of all items on hand is periodically necessary for effective inventory control and is required for tax purposes. The method selected depends upon the size and diversity of stocks, the degree to which work in process is standardized, and the processing methods employed by a given plant. The following are among the common methods.

CONTINUOUS COUNT OF BALANCE ON HAND. Through an established routine, items approaching the ordering point are counted by a few specially trained men, including stock clerks when possible.

PERIODIC COUNT. All inventories, grouped by type and at various locations, are regularly checked by trained personnel at least once a year.

ANNUAL OR SEMIANNUAL TOTAL COUNT. All stocks are counted annually or semiannually at one time. The drawbacks of the total count method are the cost of the necessary shutdown of operations and the errors (e.g., duplications or omissions) that inevitably occur because of the speed of counting.

Control of the Cyclic Flow of Materials. An efficient system must be designed for the control of materials from the time of requisitioning of purchases to the storage of the finished product. A step-by-step standard routine must be developed, authority and responsibility for the execution of each step must be clearly delegated to specific individuals, appropriate forms must be drawn up to facilitate control of various activities.

The steps in the *materials-control cycle,* outlined in their usual procedural order, include these: (1) Stores-record clerks make out purchase requisitions for the procurement of needed materials, parts, supplies, and tools and transmit the forms to the purchasing office; and they file "requests for manufacture" with the planning office for those parts and tools to be fabricated in the plant to replenish stocks. (2) The purchasing office procures requisitioned items by placing orders with vendors and by following up deliveries. (3) The receiving department unloads incoming items and checks the materials against purchase orders for quantity and condition. The inspectors check the materials and parts for quality and forward "receiving and inspection" reports to the purchasing department. (4) The purchasing office audits invoices and (when necessary) takes up with vendors adjustments for discrepancies. (5) Handling men move materials received and parts fabricated to the storage areas. Clerks make appropriate entries on stores records, bin tags, or stores cards for items placed in the storeroom. (6) Stores-record clerks in the planning office make out materials requisitions, allocate materials for production orders, and make appropriate entries on perpetual inventory records. (7) Storeroom clerks issue materials and parts as specified on requisition forms received from the planning office. The clerks make entries on bin tags and send a record of materials issued to the accounting office for cost-accounting purposes. (8) Plant dispatchers control the flow of goods in process by means of route sheets (manufacturing orders) and "move orders" which direct the travel of work through the plant. Control boards in the planning office show the progress of work in the plant. (9) Dispatchers return unused materials and parts to the stock rooms. Clerks on the basis of "stores-return" slips make appropriate entries on bin tags, perpetual inventory records, and cost-accounting sheets. (10) Dispatchers direct the movement of finished goods to storerooms, and, on the basis of work-completed forms received from the plant, office clerks make appropriate entries on finished-stock records.

CONTROL OF TOOLS

There are four categories of tools, which may be either standard items or special devices designed for specific operations in the manufacture of a part or product. (1) *Holding tools* (jigs, fixtures, dogs) are work-holding and work-guiding devices used in conjunction with machine operations. (2) *Forming and cutting tools* (dies, drills, milling cutters) are used with machines to change the shape or form of materials. (3) *Measuring tools* (gauges, micrometers) are devices for checking the conformance of work to standards. (4) *Auxiliary tools* (screwdrivers, wrenches, pliers) are devices used for building up or tearing down products or machines.

Tooling and Retooling Procedure. "Tooling up"—the planning and acquisition of tools—is required when a new product is to be manufactured. "Retooling" is necessary when product-design changes are to be made or a new model is to be produced.

There are six steps in tooling: (1) Break down the product into its subassemblies and parts and analyze the bill of materials, drawings, and other specifications to ascertain the amount of tooling required. (2) Select and study the method of processing (machinery and sequence of operations) and, on the basis of the quantity to be produced, determine the type of tooling to be used for each operation in the fabrication of a part and in assembly. (The process engineering, the tool-design section, and the manufacturing department participate in this activity.) (3) Design the required special tools (jigs, fixtures, dies, templates, patterns, and gauges) for specific operations and select the standard tools needed in manufacturing. (4) Purchase or fabricate the tools according to their design drawings. (Standard tools are usually cheaper to buy, whereas special tools may be produced by the company toolroom or ordered from outside tool-and-die shops. The plan to be used generally depends upon the quantity of special tools required and the importance of prompt delivery. Many firms produce only part of their tools, but do all their tool-repair work.) (5) Inspect tools for conformance to specifications. When necessary, try out special tools on machines before releasing them for use in production. Properly indicate on route sheets and other instruction sheets the tools provided for each operation and, whenever necessary, include instructions for the use of tools. (6) Follow up the performance of tools in production and keep a record of tool costs, rate of output achieved by each tooling method, tool life, and causes of tool wear and damage. Use the information for improving the design of tools to be replaced and for the design of new tools needed in similar operations.

Control System. An effective tool-control system facilitates production planning by assuring the availability of proper tools when needed; and it attains economies by avoiding overaccumulation of tools, by securing proper maintenance and repair of tools, and by achieving efficient storeroom management.

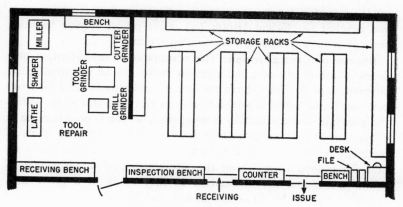

Fig. 38. Tool crib layout.

A tool-control system may be set up by this method. (1) Establish tool records (perpetual inventory with description, classification index, and quantity) to be maintained by the production-planning office. (A simpler, duplicate record should be kept in the tool crib.) (2) Select the location for tool cribs for the receipt, storage, repair, and issuance of standard and special tools (see Fig. 38). (3) Develop a system for the issuance of tools and for the return of tools not continuously used in production. (The production-planning office regulates the use of special tools through the release of tool requisitions, whereas plant operating departments regulate the use of auxiliary and other standard tools through the use of an appropriate method of "checking in and out.") (4) Establish a system for tool maintenance. After their use in production, tools should be adjusted, sharpened, and repaired before storage or reissue. (5) Establish a plan for tool replacement. Systematically replace worn and broken tools in order to assure constant readiness for production. Delegate the responsibility for restocking tools to the production-planning department or to the operating department. (6) Select the proper method for allocating tool cost either as an expense item or as a direct charge to specific orders. (7) Take a physical inventory to verify tool records, to avoid carrying tools in excess of needs, and to scrap obsolete tools.

STOREROOM MANAGEMENT

Procedure for Setting Up a Storeroom and Tool-Crib System. (1) Determine the proper degree of centralization and select appropriate locations for storage; (2) select an effective arrangement for stores and develop an efficient layout; (3) select proper storage facilities; and (4) achieve systematic storeroom operations.

Degree of Centralization. The advantages of centralization over decentralization of stores and tools are these: use of less total space; elimination of duplicate stores, equipment, and records; need for fewer personnel; and better supervision and control over inventory. When the principle of centralization is misapplied, service is poor because of congestion at the storeroom and delay resulting from long hauls of materials to the point of use. Storeroom and tool-crib locations are best determined by weighing the advantages and disadvantages of centralization and decentralization as they apply to a given case. Specific factors to be considered include the following.

PLACES OF RECEIPT AND OF USE. The incoming points for each type of inventory and the places where they will be used should be determined. When other factors permit, the storerooms should be easily accessible to those areas of the plant that have the greatest demand for materials.

SIZE OF PLANT AND NATURE OF PROCESS. The centralized storage plan is generally well suited to the small plant and to the single-story plant. The decentralized storage plan is generally more adaptable to multistory plants and to large plants with extensive floor areas wherein the points of material and tool use are scattered.

NATURE OF STORES. Heavy and bulky materials may be stored on the ground floor or outdoors. Inflammable materials frequently require isolated, fire-resistant storerooms. High-cost items should be stored with special consideration for their safety.

HANDLING METHODS. The availability of modern, economical handling methods (e.g., gravity chutes, monorails, fork trucks) make possible a considerable degree of centralization of storage, particularly in mass-production plants.

Layout of Storerooms. The development of a floor plan requires a comprehension of the benefits of good layout practice, compilation of data on materials, and the selection of appropriate equipment.

BENEFITS OF GOOD LAYOUT. A well-laid-out storeroom provides efficiently organized space; the flexibility required for accommodating changes in the amount of inventory carried; facilities for easy receipt, handling, storage, and issuance of materials; and an inexpensive means of controlling materials. It effects an appropriate classification and location for taking physical inventory, maintains turnover of inventory (first-in-first-out), and protects against misappropriation.

ANALYSIS OF STORES AND EQUIPMENT. The information that must be compiled before a storeroom can be logically arranged includes weight, size, and quantity (maximum and minimum) of materials to be carried; space, preparation, and protection required for the various materials; frequency and quantity of issuance of the various items; and available types of standard storage equipment.

POSSIBLE SYSTEMS OF ARRANGEMENT. The arrangement of inventory items in the stockroom may be based on the classification system, the index system, or a combination of the two. An analysis of the information compiled on materials will determine which system will provide the most efficient storeroom operation.

Under the *classification system* items are arranged and placed in the storeroom in an order corresponding to the numeric or to the mnemonic method of identification. Although this system generally makes items easy to locate, it has certain disadvantages: items frequently requisitioned may not be near the point of issue, extra space may be needed in a rack for expansion in stock volume, and bulky items can be located according to the classification only at extra cost. In general the classification system is more suitable for the arrangement of small supply items and auxiliary and cutting tools.

Under the *index system* items are arranged for ease of issue and convenience of storage, such factors as frequency of use, type, and size determining the placement. The drawback of the index system is the possible need for constant reference to an index of locations before a requisitioned item can be found.

Selection of Storage Facilities. Standard storage equipment (racks, bins, hoppers) should be selected whenever possible; all storage equipment should be suitable for the types of items carried and should provide the required capacity, flexibility, protection, durability, and safety. The storeroom should be functionally arranged with adequate aisle space, handling facilities, light, and ventilation. Sufficient room should be provided for receipt, inspection, and issuance of materials.

Systematic Operation of Storerooms. A well-organized stockroom makes possible, with a minimum of effort: (1) rapid receipt and placement of materials and tools in storage; (2) effective safekeeping, repair, and conservation (prevention of spoilage or deterioration) of stored items; (3) rapid preparation and issuance of stores and tools on authorized requisitions; (4) adequate maintenance of the required storeroom records: bin tags, stores cards, and tool index; and (5) effective supervision over the taking of physical inventory.

Access to the storeroom and tool crib should be allowed only to authorized personnel. If the stockroom is kept clean and in good order, the accumulation of "hidden" stock and obsolete tools is avoided, the oldest stock being used first. Whenever possible, storeroom clerks should be charged with the responsibility of taking physical inventory (preferably during time that would otherwise be idle).

Questions

1. What are the benefits of an effective inventory-control system?

2. What are the procedural steps for establishing or improving an inventory-control system?

3. Identify and illustrate five types of inventory.

4. What are the factors that must be taken into account in determining the "ordering quantity"?

5. Distinguish between the FIFO and LIFO methods of evaluating inventory.

6. What are the uses of perpetual inventory records?

7. What are the purposes and methods for taking physical inventory?

8. List the steps in the materials-control cycle in their usual order.

9. What are the steps in the provision and procurement of tools (jigs, dies, fixtures) for the manufacture of a new product?

10. (a) What are the procedural steps for establishing a storeroom and tool-crib system? (b) What are the benefits of a well-organized storeroom?

21: Production Planning and Control: Routing, Scheduling, and Dispatching

A firm plans on two levels: on the top-management level it formulates over-all plans that determine the line of products, facilities, plant size, and location (as in the business promotional survey discussed in Ch. 7); on the plant operational level it plans and controls production to meet sales requirements.

Company *over-all plans* must be adaptable: the enterprise must adjust its program to secular changes (long-run factors), such as basic shifts in consumer tastes and wants (which result in a demand for new products) or important technological developments and resource discoveries or depletions (which may make existing facilities and locations obsolete). The enterprise must also adjust its program to business cycle fluctuations—e.g., turns in business volume must be anticipated so that capacity can be appropriately expanded during the upswing of prosperity and so that undue idle plant capacity and excess inventories can be avoided during the downswing of recession.

Because of the organizational complexity of manufacturing and the time interval of production, management finds it necessary to plan current production programs systematically within the scope of company over-all planning noted above. Management sets up a *production-planning and control system* (identified in this book as the PPC) to integrate and co-ordinate the use of manpower, machines, and materials for efficient output of goods to meet its sales requirements. It organizes the PPC department to perform a planning function distinct and separate from the actual manufacturing function in order to relieve plant superintendents and foremen of such "nonoperating" responsibilities as inventory control, scheduling. and expediting. The PPC department, therefore, enables foremen to concentrate on production activities such as supervising the shop, getting work out, training operators, and maintaining efficient methods.

Production planning and control comprise a series of related activities, each predetermined and timed to co-ordinate manufacturing programs. The PPC department guides production by preparing and issuing manufacturing orders which direct the use of facilities and material and allocate labor to the output of the required quantity of products; in short, the department regulates and controls "how," "where," and "when" work is to be done.

To fulfill its function the department assumes these *PPC tasks:* (1) *inventory control*—regulating the quantities of stock and replenishing and issuing materials and tools; (2) *routing*—designating the processing methods and the operation sequence for the manufacture of each part, assembly, or product; (3) *scheduling*—establishing the rate of output and the beginning and ending dates of production; (4) *dispatching*—carrying out manufacturing orders through clerical control of work in the plant; and (5) *production control*—following up and checking to assure achievement of the planned output goals.

ESTABLISHMENT OF THE PPC SYSTEM

To establish or improve a PPC system, management (1) must know the benefits to be gained from a well-designed system; (2) must take into account and assess the peculiarities of the business (processes, products, organization, and policies) that will influence the design of the system; (3) must determine the proper degree of centralization of planning and control for the firm; and then (4) must observe the procedural steps outlined on page 200 for setting up the system to fit the needs of its business.

Benefits of Effective Production Planning and Control. A well-designed PPC system achieves five benefits: (1) it promotes sales through the maintenance of finished goods inventories adequate to meet the demand for its standard products and through accurate determination of delivery dates and costs of products (information which is necessary for the proper pricing of customers' orders); (2) it promotes steady production at high output levels by maintaining rapid processing, by minimizing the need for overtime and "rush" orders, and by reducing interruptions and idleness of men and machines caused by nonavailability of materials, parts, and tools; (3) it achieves low investment in inventory by keeping work in process at a minimum, by maintaining rapid stock turnover, and by avoiding over-accumulation of raw materials and finished goods; (4) it promotes efficient production by eliminating confusion in the plant and by relieving foremen of planning detail and "paper work"; and (5) it requires less planning effort (fewer man-hours) because it assigns the responsibility for operating the system to specialists.

An analyst can therefore identify a *poor PPC system* by noting such defects as these: sales losses caused by late deliveries or by an inadequate supply of finished goods; erratic production resulting from overtime work followed by, or intermingled with, machine idleness owing to material or tool shortages; the prevalence of an unnecessarily long production-cycle time; or the need for too many follow-up men and plant expediters.

Factors Influencing the Design of the Planning and Control System. A PPC system must be designed to suit (1) the type of processes utilized in the plant, (2) the type of work produced, and (3) the organization structure, size, and policies of the firm. These factors determine the complexity of the planning and control problem, the range and scope of activities to be included in the system, and the methods and techniques to be employed. Obviously, the greater the number of variables found in production, the more difficult the problem of subjecting them to routine and controlling them.

TYPES OF PROCESSES. Manufacturing processes may broadly be identified as continuous, assembly, or combination. A *continuous process* consists of an uninterrupted cycle of work, from raw materials to finished product, flowing through highly integrated facilities that are largely automatically controlled—e.g., oil refining. In *assembly process*, component parts are fabricated separately, usually by a series of machine operations, and brought together for the erection of finished products—e.g., automobiles. A *combination process* (widely prevalent in industry) is one that incorporates both continuous and assembly processes.

TYPES OF WORK PRODUCED. Plants utilize these processes to produce repetitive (standard), job-order, or semidiversified work.

Repetitive (Serialized) Manufacture. Repetitive manufacture is the production of one or more closely related standard items (a line of products) that generally go into storage from which sales shipments are made. Repetitive, continuous-process manufacture of a single standard product usually requires a relatively simple planning system.

Job-Order (Custom) Manufacture. Job-order manufacture is the production of goods to customers' specifications. (Typical job-order firms are equipment-manufacturing plants and tool-and-die shops.) Since each order is distinct and different, the work must be handled on an individual basis. Because it involves a large number of variable elements (separate blueprints, parts lists, and operations for each order), planning for job-order manufacturing is complex and requires an elaborate well-integrated system. Planning and control is most difficult when orders consist of a small number of units, each made up of many precision parts that must be fabricated and assembled in long, complicated processes. See page 222 for "comparison chart" contrasting job-order and repetitive manufacture.

Semidiversified Manufacture. Semidiversified manufacture is the production of custom and repetitive work on (generally) the same facilities. Though planning and control are ordinarily difficult, their complexity depends on the kind of products and quantities specified by customers' orders, the degree of similarity of work, and whether the process is predominantly of the continuous or the assembly type.

COMPANY ORGANIZATION AND POLICIES. The PPC system must be designed to fit the company organization and size of plant and it must be set up to implement managerial policies and practices dealing with production.

Division and Magnitude of Production. The sounder and more clear-cut the organization structure, the easier it is to design and operate a planning system with the assurance that delegated activities will be performed; and the greater the magnitude of production, the more elaborate the planning system must be.

The analyst must study the organization structure in order to assign planning activities properly (e.g., inventory control, order write-up, and dispatching) and in order to set up effective channels of communication. That is, he must take into account the particular breakdown of the manufacturing organization into shops or departments and the extent of centralization of control and supervision over production, storekeeping, inspection, and maintenance.

Policies Covering Production and Seasonal Variations. The planning system must be designed and operated in accordance with managerial policies and practices, which take into account such factors as whether a company budget is utilized, whether product simplification and standardization are emphasized, whether work simplification is stressed, whether an incentive-wage system is employed, and what method has been adopted to deal with seasonal variations affecting sales volume.

Management must determine the degree to which its sales and production fluctuate because of *seasonal variations* (those variations caused by climatic and institutional factors such as year-end holidays). If its seasonal variations are appreciable, management may adopt one or more of the following plans. (1) It may, to some extent, gear production to seasonal fluctuations by scheduling overtime work for the busy period and employees' vacations and long-term maintenance work for the slack period. This plan is feasible where investment in the plant is comparatively small and where the labor force consists largely of semiskilled and unskilled workers readily available on the market. (2) It may cut prices during the slow season and thus steady its volume of business. (3) It may stabilize business by producing complementary products (those that sell in the slack period and that can be put out on the same facilities) or by doing subcontract work for other firms. (4) It may stabilize business by producing at a uniform level the year round —building up inventory during the slack period and then drawing from the accumulated finished stock during periods of heavy sales. This policy, feasible when the investment in finished inventory is not high, when spoilage and style obsolescence are unlikely, and when storage costs are small, has certain advantages: it keeps investment in facilities low, assures a stable labor force and steady employment, and simplifies production planning.

Management must analyze the practicality, the cost, and the labor problem of each plan to determine which plan or combination of plans is the most economical and suitable for its firm. To the policy chosen, the planning department must conform.

Degree of Centralization of Planning and Control. The planning and control function is generally placed under the manufacturing division. Comprehensive (100-per-cent) control over all phases and elements of production may be uneconomical—excessive refinement of routing and highly detailed scheduling, dispatching, and recording of progress (involving much paper work) may prove too costly for the benefits derived. A PPC system should be only as precise and centralized as will be beneficial; systems may, therefore, range from the highly centralized to the widely decentralized. The degree of centralization depends upon the complexity of the planning and control problem.

THE CENTRALIZED PPC SYSTEM. A centralized system is generally suitable for small and medium-sized plants engaged in standard manufacture wherein a comparatively small number of variable elements and planning activities must be regulated. The engineering department in such cases can provide the planning department with complete information on routing, machine capacity, and production-cycle time, from which data the planning office can schedule exact production programs for all operations in the plant and maintain a close check over output and detailed control over materials and tools.

THE DECENTRALIZED PPC SYSTEM. Frequently the manufacturing activities and elements that must be predetermined and controlled are numerous and diverse. In such instances, a knowledge of production characteristics and of conditions necessary for the planning and regulation of these activities and elements is generally attainable only at the shop level and through close contact with plant operations. A greater degree of decentralization in the PPC system is, therefore, necessary where the enterprise is larger, work manufactured more diverse, and operating conditions less standard.

The PPC department should, in such cases, assume control over those phases of production and over those component parts and items whose regulation is vital to the effective fulfillment of the manufacturing program; and other departments and sections should assume control over regulatory activities that can not be adequately supervised by the planning office. The PPC department then regulates and co-ordinates only such major activities as routing and scheduling to shops and production departments as a whole. It thereby maintains control over the movement and co-ordination of work between departments, yet achieves the flexibility required for making adjustments to changing shop conditions.

Since only men in the plant have sufficient knowledge of, or familiarity with, equipment performances and capacities and the level of workmanship of various skilled operators, detailed routing and scheduling of work to machines are done in the shop. Every shop or department therefore performs its own planning and control in accordance with the general schedule or timetable laid down for the plant and reports on its progress to the planning office.

Procedure for Setting Up a PPC System. The development of a PPC system for practically all types of manufacture, or the survey of an existing system for improvement, calls for the following steps:

(1) Establish the following prerequisites (preparatory conditions) for PPC.

(a) Compile product specifications data on items to be manufactured.

(b) Set up an inventory record and control system.

    (c) Set up a tool record and control system.

    (d) Compile data on plant processes and machine output capacities.

    (e) Set up a sales-forecasting method to determine production requirements.

    (f) Decide which parts to make and which to buy.

(2) Design methods and procedures for planning and control.

    (a) Prepare route sheets (sequence of operations) for parts and products to be manufactured.

    (b) Set up a method for scheduling production.

    (c) Set up a procedure for preparing manufacturing orders for the authorization of production.

    (d) Set up a procedure for dispatching—putting production plans into action.

    (e) Set up a procedure for controlling output.

(3) Develop an organization structure for the PPC department.

    (a) Set up detailed routines necessary to operate the system.

    (b) Break down the PPC system (grouping related activities where desirable) into functionalized subdivisions and assign duties for the carrying out of activities.

Preparations. An effective PPC system is based on the thorough preparatory studies and preliminary procedures discussed in the following paragraphs.

PRODUCT SPECIFICATION DATA. Complete and accurate blueprints, drawings (Figs. 6 and 39), parts lists, chemical formulas, and bills of materials (Fig. 40) must be acquired. These data are used by the PPC department to specify to the plant exactly what is to be produced. If the firm manufactures its own standard products, the engineering department prepares the data; if the firm is engaged in job-order manufacturing, the customers usually provide the information.

INVENTORY RECORD AND CONTROL SYSTEM. A perpetual inventory record must be set up to show, for each item carried, such data as the balance on hand, amount allocated for production, and amount to procure. Product specifications data and sales requirements determine the kind and quantity of materials needed. An inventory-control procedure (cycle) must be established for effective issuance of materials, replenishment of stocks, etc. (See Ch. 20 for discussion.)

TOOL RECORD AND CONTROL SYSTEM. Process engineers, designers, or foremen specify the jigs, fixtures, dies, and other tools to be used in the manufacture of the products. A perpetual inventory record and

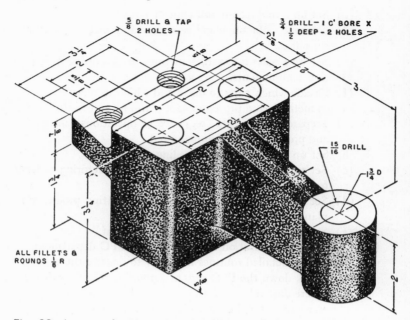

Fig. 39. A parts drawing of a clamp lever showing its dimensioning. (From Lombardo *et al., Engineering Drawing.* Copyright, 1953, Barnes & Noble, Inc.)

tool control procedure (cycle) must be set up to show the availability of the tools and to provide for their issue, replacement, and repair. (See Ch. 20 for discussion.)

MACHINE-CAPACITY DATA. Process engineers or foremen, on the basis of equipment analysis, compute the output capacities of machines in the processing of each part, type of material, or product. Capacity figures and machine-load records are used for routing and scheduling production. Over-all capacity figures determine whether the firm can fulfill the sales demand, whether there is need for overtime work, and whether additional equipment should be purchased and the plant expanded.

SALES-FORECASTING METHOD. Before production can be planned, sales must be forecast to determine "what," "how much," and "when" to manufacture. The longer the period for which sales can accurately be forecast, the easier it is to plan production and achieve a more uniform level of output. A suitable method must be selected to fore-

202

Pc. No.	Name	Quan.	Mat.	Size and Stock	Notes
1	Frame	1	C.I.		Casting purchased — surfaces to be finished and holes drilled
2	Base	1	C.I.		Casting purchased — surfaces to be finished and holes drilled
3	Plate	1	Hard rubber	4¾″ × 4¾″ × 5⁄16″	
4	Plate	1	Glass	4″ × 4″ × ¼″	
5	Conical ring	1	Hard rubber	¼″ thickness	See A.S.T.M. (American society for testing materials) specifications
6	Movable rod	1	Steel	½″ dia. × 12⅜″ length	See A.S.T.M. specs. for plunger end
7	Needle	1	Steel	Threads at each end ¼″ NF–28 × 7⁄16″	See A.S.T.M. specs. for needle
8	Graduated plate	1	Steel	1¾″ × 4½″ × 1⁄16″	See A.S.T.M. specs. for graduations
9	Indicator hex nut	1	Steel	⅝″ across flats	Holes drilled—stem-interference fit, plunger clearance fit
10	Indicator stem	1	Steel	3⁄16″ dia. × 7⁄16″ length tapped thru #4 NC–40	See above for fit
11	Indicator	1	Steel	⅝″ × 3⁄16″ × 1⁄32″	Solder to stem
12	Indicator set screw	1	Steel	#4 NC–40 × 9⁄16″ length	Knurled circular head — dia.
13	Rod set screw	1	Steel	#4 NC–32 × ¾″ length	Knurled circular head — dia.
14	Machine screw	2	Steel	#6 NC–32 × ¼″ round hd.	Fasten graduated plate to frame
15	Machine screw	7	Brass	#6 NC–32 × ⅜″ round hd.	Spaced to fasten frame and rubber plate to base

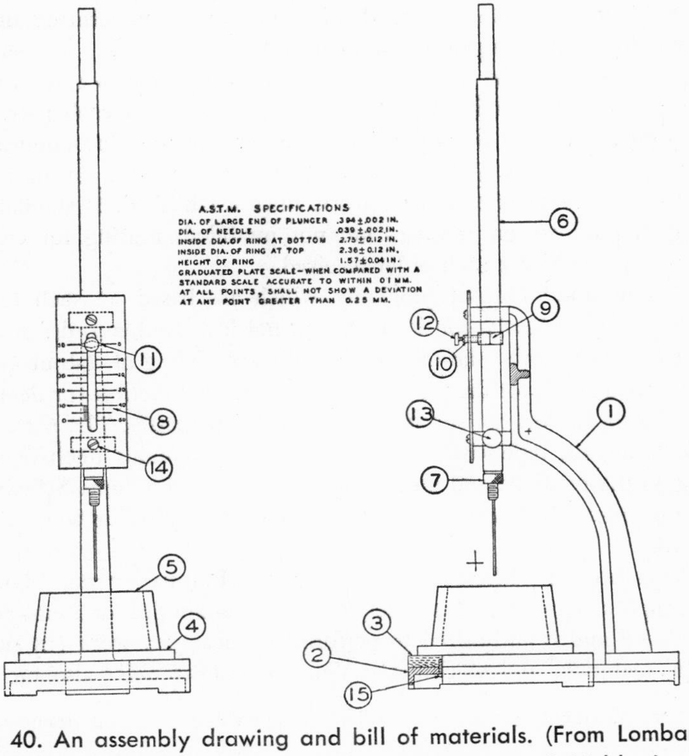
A.S.T.M. SPECIFICATIONS
DIA. OF LARGE END OF PLUNGER .394 ± .002 IN.
DIA. OF NEEDLE .039 ± .002 IN.
INSIDE DIA. OF RING AT BOTTOM 2.75 ± 0.12 IN.
INSIDE DIA. OF RING AT TOP 2.36 ± 0.12 IN.
HEIGHT OF RING 1.57 ± 0.04 IN.
GRADUATED PLATE SCALE—WHEN COMPARED WITH A STANDARD SCALE ACCURATE TO WITHIN 01 MM. AT ALL POINTS, SHALL NOT SHOW A DEVIATION AT ANY POINT GREATER THAN 0.25 MM.
1
2
3
4
5
6
7
8
9
10
11
12
13
14
15

Fig. 40. An assembly drawing and bill of materials. (From Lombardo et al., *Engineering Drawing*. Copyright, 1953, Barnes & Noble, Inc.)

cast sales (see page 246 for discussion) and to translate the data into a manufacturing program or production budget. In repetitive manufacture the sales department prepares an estimate (sales budget) showing the quantities that should be marketed in the next period—e.g., quarter or half year; in job-order manufacturing, it prepares a sales budget listing orders received (backlog) and expected orders (forecast) for various classes of work.

PARTS TO BUY AND PARTS TO MAKE. Production planners and process engineers, on the basis of comparative cost studies, reliability of quality and delivery, and backlog, determine which parts and subassemblies to buy and which to produce. In repetitive manufacture this decision is made when production is initially set up, but it is periodically reappraised. In job-lot manufacture, however, each customer's order must be analyzed individually.

Planning and Control Practice. Once these various preparations have been made, production programs can be planned and regulated through routing, scheduling, the issuance of manufacturing orders, dispatching, and the gauging and controlling of output.

ROUTING.[1] On the basis of their analysis of processes and capacity figures, engineers or foremen prepare route sheets for each part, subassembly, and final assembly. They specify the most economical sequence of operations (machines) for the output of work during manufacture. Routing for repetitive work, once established, is standard so long as products or processes are not modified; routing for custom work is prepared for each order received.

SCHEDULING.[1] Output programs, which are based on such factors as sales requirements, route sheet, and machine-load records, are prepared on two levels: *master (or over-all) scheduling* of output quotas of finished goods for the plant as a whole; and *production (or detailed) scheduling* of work for specific machines and processes. The pattern of scheduling for repetitive manufacture usually remains unchanged so long as the products and processing methods are the same. Scheduling for job-order manufacture must be done continually and in considerable detail.

AUTHORIZING MANUFACTURE: THE MANUFACTURING ORDER. Through a manufacturing order, the plant is notified of items to be produced and is authorized to perform the necessary work (by use of men, materials, and machines). A manufacturing order also provides

---

[1] A subsequent section of this chapter is devoted to a full discussion of this topic.

a starting point for control, states the rate of output or completion and delivery dates, and serves as a means for compiling and allocating costs.

In repetitive production, the manufacturing order originates in the master schedule and is drawn up and released to the various shops and departments as a production schedule which stipulates the rate of output of parts, assemblies, and products. Such data as blueprints, route sheets, and operation instructions (all of which technically are a part of the manufacturing order) are usually kept permanently in the plant by foremen and other personnel.

In job-order and, to some extent, in semidiversified production, the manufacturing order originates in a specific customer order. In this case, its preparation requires reference to information previously compiled (machine output rates, work in process, and work scheduled) and neccesitates the write-up of numerous forms such as job tickets, materials requisitions, and tool requisitions. A manufacturing order may give rise to supplementary orders such as a tool-making order or a casting order. Copies of manufacturing orders are distributed to shops and departments that will participate in the output of the specified products.

DISPATCHING.[2] The planning office releases manufacturing orders to dispatchers (planning clerks assigned to the various departments of the plant) who follow through on the orders and thus assist foremen in carrying out the planned production program according to schedule. Dispatchers issue job tickets, materials requisitions, tool requisitions, and other forms which authorize and direct the flow of work.

CONTROLLING PRODUCTION.[3] Planners control production by periodically checking "actual" output (quantities and completion dates) against "planned" output (production schedules) and, then, if work is behind or too far ahead of schedule, they take timely action to bring production back on schedule.

Organization of the PPC Department. Procedures must be devised to carry out interdepartmental planning activities and an organization structure must be designed for the PPC department.

PROCEDURES. Interdepartmental procedures must be set up for such routine planning activities as: (1) receipt of product specification data, including design changes, from the engineering department; (2) receipt of sales requirements from, and the forwarding of completion

[2] A subsequent section of this chapter is devoted to a full discussion of this topic.
[3] For detailed discussion see pp. 215–217.

dates to, the sales department; (3) the forwarding of purchase requisitions to, and the receipt of delivery promise dates from, the procurement department; (4) the issuance of manufacturing orders and schedules to, and the receipt of progress reports from, the plant; (5) receipt of information on machine availability (as affected by schedules of major repairs and plant modifications) from, and the forwarding of capacity requirements to, the plant engineering department, and (6) the forwarding of direct-labor and direct-material cost data to the accounting department.

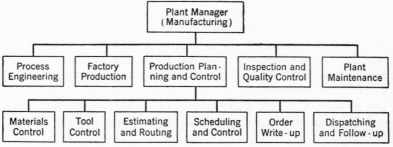

Fig. 41. A representative organization chart of a PPC department in a medium-sized firm.

Organization. The PPC department must be carefully organized to carry out the activities and procedures established in the planning system. Fig. 41 illustrates an organization structure for a medium-sized firm engaged in job-order or semidiversified manufacture.

Routing

Through *routing*, engineers or foremen determine, in advance of actual production, how work is to be processed and what machines are to be used; routing thus establishes the sequence of operations (see Fig. 43) and provides the basis for scheduling, writing up manufacturing orders, dispatching, and checking production progress. In repetitive manufacture, a "master" (relatively permanent) route sheet is developed when the plant facilities are initially laid out; in job-order manufacture, routing is developed for each new order (customer's sales order) received and is, therefore, generally used only for processing current work.

Routing Procedure. To develop routing, process engineers or planners (1) analyze the product, break it down into component parts and materials, and decide which items to buy and which to make; (2) determine the sequential order of completion of parts and subassemblies; (3) determine the operations and processing time required for each item, and the sequence in which operations will be performed; (4) determine the lot size for manufacturing orders; (5) determine the spoilage and stock allowance for each order; and (6) design a form and write up the route sheets.

ANALYSIS OF PRODUCT FOR MANUFACTURE AND PURCHASE OF PARTS. Product specifications data and the volume of goods to be produced should be analyzed to determine the kind and amount of parts and materials that are to be processed and to decide which parts and subassemblies should be purchased and which should be made.

ORDER OF COMPLETION OF PARTS AND SUBASSEMBLIES. The proper sequential order of fabrication and completion of the various parts should be determined so that the items may be available for assembly when needed—final assembly should not be held up for the lack of an item. An *assembly chart* may be prepared to show how the parts and subassemblies are synchronized and brought together in the manufacture of a product (see Fig. 42).

OPERATION SEQUENCE AND TIME. Plant equipment and machine capacity data should be analyzed to select the most economical operations (machines) for processing the work and studied to determine the best sequence in which the operations should be performed for the output of each part, subassembly, and final assembly. Where overloading of machines or failure of equipment seems likely to occur with some frequency, alternative machines or operations should be selected for processing the work. The material needed for the fabrication of each item should be carefully identified and the necessary jigs, dies, or other tools should be made or selected on the basis of the required volume of output. Route sheets should indicate the bringing together of two or more items at a given point in the process and they should also show when two or more parts take the same operation in processing so that these items may (whenever possible) be scheduled for processing together in order to save machine set-up time.

A *decentralized routing* arrangement, which is generally necessary when job-order manufacturing is complex, requires close familiarity with machines and operating conditions. In this case the planning office routes the work to the shops and departments and specifies the operations required, and foremen (because of their knowledge of the performance characteristics of equipment and the particular skills of their men) select the best machine and operator available for the work.

The *standard time* for each operation or process in the manufacture of a part or product should be computed and expressed in terms of minutes per piece or number of pieces per hour. The *total processing time* for a lot (a given quantity of work for an order) includes the

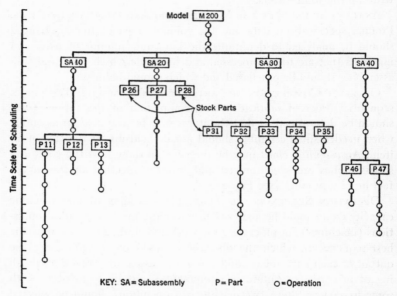

Fig. 42. Assembly chart (parts breakdown) and processing time for a lot. Together these establish the basis for determining the order of completion of items and scheduling within an order. Parts and subassemblies requiring more time for processing are started on an earlier date.

time required for the movement of material between work stations, the machine set-up time, and the machine operation time (i.e., the number of pieces in the lot multiplied by the standard time per piece). In repetitive manufacture the required processing time can be established by a time study. In job-order manufacturing, processing time can be computed "synthetically" [4] on the basis of the material and machine to be used, the operation method and tools to be employed, and the specified quality standards.

[4] For discussion see Ch. 16.

LOT SIZE FOR MANUFACTURING ORDERS. The proper lot size for a production order must be computed, particularly for repetitive multi-product manufacture and job-order manufacture involving large sales orders. Planners can compute an economical lot size (an optimum quantity to process at one time) by balancing the "preparation costs" of an order against its "carrying charges."

In repetitive multiproduct manufacture or in any manufacture where a number of different items are produced alternately on the same facilities (which require special setups for each order) appropriate lot sizes are best determined through cost analysis. Generally, the larger the lot size or quantity processed at one time, the lower the preparation costs (e.g., the clerical cost of preparing and issuing an order and the machine set-up cost) and the higher the carrying charges (e.g., interest on capital tied up in inventories, storage space, insurance, and deterioration). Hence, the optimum lot size for a manufacturing order is that quantity for which the sum of the preparation costs and the carrying charges are at a minimum.

In job-order production, large orders or groups of identical orders should whenever possible be combined and written up to formulate manufacturing orders which approximate the optimum lot size. When customers' orders differ in specifications and routing, the size of the order must of necessity be the lot size.

SPOILAGE AND STOCK ALLOWANCE. A spoilage allowance, determined on the basis of past performances, must be established for the anticipated normal scrap ("shrinkage" during processing) caused by substandard work and waste. Spoilage may be cumulative or it may occur largely at one point in the process. A *stock allowance* (required particularly for repetitive multiproduct manufacture) is an additional percentage (extra stock) for spares and repair parts or for an inventory reserve.

Planners can establish a *quantity factor* for both these allowances. This factor (e.g., 107 per cent) when multiplied by the number of units in a lot gives the quantity that should be scheduled for a specific order.

DESIGN OF ROUTE CARD AND WRITE UP OF SHEETS. The information included on the route sheet and the design of the route form (see Fig. 43) should suit the needs of the particular PPC system. It is sometimes necessary to provide a separate route sheet for each division of the plant.

Routing data carried on sheets made out for each part, subassembly, or final assembly generally include: (1) identification—the part number, blueprint number, order number, and materials specification; (2) lot size—the number of pieces in a lot and the number of divisions to a lot; (3) operations and machines—the department number, operations listed in sequence, machine names and numbers, tool number for each operation, and number of men per operation; (4) standard time—minutes per piece or pieces per hour, set-up time, and move

ROUTE SHEET

Model____ M 20 ____ Order No.__ 4-5252 __
Part Name__ Rocker Arm __ Material Chrome Nickel Steel
Part No.____ M 650 R ____ Size____ 2½" x 8" ____
Dwg. No.____ 64897-3 ____ Lot Size____ 1200 ____
Completion Date____ 6/30 ____ Spoilage Allowance____ 5% __

DEPT. NO.	OPER. NO.	OPERATION	MACHINE	TOOLS	NO. OF MEN	STD. TIME MIN./PC.	DUE DATES BEGIN	END
1	1	Cut stock	Power saw No.2	–	1	.50	6/1	6/2
2	2	Grind ends	Grinder No. 8	–	1	.70	6/2	6/4
8	3	Upset in press	Forge Press No.4	F 880	2	2.05	6/4	6/12
6	4	Trim	Press No. 16	P1205	1	.48	6/12	6/14
5	5	Grind	Grinder No. 10	–	1	.90	6/14	6/17
5	6	Heat treat	H.T. unit No.3	–	3	–	6/18	6/19
12	7	Straighten	Press No. 10	P1450	1	.57	6/22	6/23
5	8	Drill holes	Drill press No.2	0.1230	1	1.05	6/23	6/26
10	9	Mill slot	Mill No.3	L750	1	1.22	6/25	6/30

Fig. 43. A route sheet used as a production order. The schedule of due dates illustrates how operations may be dovetailed to reduce over-all processing time.

time; and (5) fill-in space—space for scheduling data, space for amount of defective work, and similar information. (The amount of such information carried on route sheets varies with processing needs.)

Data should be carefully typed on route sheets, and only authorized individuals should be allowed to make changes. When new route sheets are made up (e.g., because of production process changes), they should be carefully prepared, and obsolete sheets should be pulled out of circulation.

OTHER FORMS USED WITH ROUTE SHEETS. Depending upon the

needs of the PPC system, the "order write-up" section of the planning department may prepare: material requisitions, tool requisitions, job tickets, inspection tickets, or move orders. These papers are grouped with the respective route sheets and filed as a "manufacturing order" awaiting release to the plant in accordance with the schedule.

Master Route Sheets. Master route sheets (sometimes identified as "operation sheets") are prepared as a permanent record of the processing method for repetitive manufacture, and also for job-order manufacture when it consists of long production runs or repeat orders.

When only a few types of standard products are manufactured for stock, a master route sheet for each product is generally distributed to the various shops and departments and kept permanently in the plant for reference until superceded by new route sheets. Each manufacturing order released to the plant will then designate which master route sheet to use with the order.

For repetitive multiproduct manufacture, "job" route sheets are prepared for each manufacturing order from master route sheets kept in the planning office. (Or master sheets can be manifolded to serve as job route sheets.) Order number, scheduling information, and other data are added to the sheets before they are released to the plant.

Custom manufacture requires a job route sheet for each order received; master route sheets are prepared only for large volume orders and repeat orders. Job route sheets usually carry scheduling information: after consulting load charts and checking the processing time, planners inscribe on the route sheets the beginning and completion dates for each operation or for each phase of manufacture.

Scheduling and Control

Scheduling is the determination of when and at what rate products will be put out and the relative times at which specific activities shall occur in the manufacture of a given quantity of products. Scheduling aims to achieve the required rate of output with a minimum of delay and disruption in processing and to provide the quantities of goods necessary to maintain finished inventories at levels predetermined to meet delivery commitments.

Since sales forecasts and customers' orders provide the information for scheduling, close co-operation should exist between the planning department and the sales department. For example, the planning department should, when necessary, make special provisions to fill "rush" orders and thus aid in gaining new business; and the sales department should endeavor to forecast sales sufficiently far in advance to enable the PPC department to plan steady production, employment, and procurement.

Scheduling Procedure. Scheduling is usually carried out on two levels: master (or over-all) and production (or detailed).

MASTER SCHEDULING. In "master scheduling," total production requirements are balanced against available plant capacity so that manufacturing orders can meet sales needs. To carry out such over-all scheduling, planners combine figures from orders received with sales

MASTER SCHEDULE				
(Production Budget)				
First Quarter 19--				
PRODUCT MODEL	TOTAL QUANTITY	FACTORY COST	MONTHLY SCHEDULE	WEEKLY SCHEDULE
A-100	30,000	$ 60,000	10,000	2,308
J-200	12,000	120,000	4,000	924
N-300	24,000	48,000	6,000	1,846
W-400	9,000	27,000	3,000	692
COE-60	12,000	36,000	4,000	924
Job Orders				
No. 4292	1,300	32,000	425	100
No. 4293	650	22,500	213	50
No. 4294	3,000	63,500	1,000	231
Total		$409,000		

Fig. 44. Master schedule (also quarterly production budget) for a repetitive manufacturing firm which takes large volume job-order work.

estimate figures from forecasts, calculate the amounts of finished goods of each type that will be needed for the next (future) period, and balance this production demand against the manufacturing capacity available for the output of these products (see Figs. 44 and 46). Planners then set up production priority for the various items and the weekly or monthly output rates for each product. The primary aim in master scheduling is to meet sales requirements and delivery commitments and at the same time assure the operation of the plant at maximum effectiveness with production facilities working at high capacity as continuously as possible.

PRODUCTION SCHEDULING. "Production scheduling" involves setting the time of performance for the detailed operations of manufacture—

i.e., establishing the "order of work" at each machine or stage of process in the fabrication of parts and in the assembly of products. A careful distinction should be made between work (parts and sub-assemblies) which is to be purchased and work which is to be produced in the plant—it is often the latter which limits the possible output.

Objectives. Production schedules must be drawn up (1) to meet the output goals of the master schedule and to fulfill delivery promises; (2) to keep a constant supply of work ahead of each machine; and (3) to put out manufacturing orders in the shortest possible time consistent with economical operation. The schedules must, however, afford sufficient flexibility to accommodate the normal irregularities and interruptions that occur in manufacturing.

Data Necessary for Scheduling. If it is to achieve its objectives, a production schedule must be formulated on the basis of accurate information. Blueprints and bills of materials, master schedules, route sheets, inventory records, and machine-load records provide this basis. (1) Blueprints and bills of materials show the kind of items required and the detailed work to be put out. (2) Master schedules indicate the priority and the quantity of finished products to be completed within a given period and the amount of raw material required. (3) Route sheets stipulate the operations and machines to be scheduled and the processing times. (4) Inventory records show the availability of materials and tools and the time required for the procurement of items not carried. (5) Machine-load charts show the quantity of work already scheduled to various pieces of equipment and the amount of unallocated capacity available for use.

Preparation of Schedules. On the basis of available machine capacities, materials, and labor, planners convert data on the master schedule into calendar dates for the beginning and completion of work on various processes and operations. These dates (which are carried on production schedules) are then entered on route sheets and load charts to show machine allocation times. The planners, therefore, reduce the master schedule to detailed production schedules for the output of parts and subassemblies (Fig. 51).

Machine Loading. To aid in production scheduling as well as routing, planners prepare machine-load charts to show the amount of work (in terms of hours, days, or weeks) that has been assigned and scheduled to each machine, groups of identical machines, or shop departments (Fig. 45). They frequently employ the Gantt chart to indicate graphically the volume of work ahead of equipment and the amount of capacity still available for processing additional work.

Uses of Machine-Load Data. Machine-load charts are used for several purposes: (1) In master scheduling and in production scheduling (particularly in job-order and multiproduct manufacture) they are used in determining production rates and in fixing starting and ending dates for operating the specific machines listed on route sheets. (2) They are used to notify the sales department of the kind of plant capacity available (particularly in job-order manufacture) for new work (sales) which that department might negotiate. (3) They are

MACHINE LOADING

Machine __Radial drill No. 9__   Week Ending __June 5th__   Hrs. __40__

ORDER NO.	PART NO.	OPER. NO.	LOT SIZE	HOURS REQUIRED	BALANCE OF LOAD
6993	M410R	22	600	8	32
6994	M4507	34	600	12	20
7005*	T470	28	1200	26	—
*(6 hrs. carried to next week)					
				[for week ending-June 12th, Hrs.40]	
7005	T470	28	1200	6	32
7008	P847	16	600	10	22

Fig. 45. Machine loading form. Machine loading may also be shown on an appropriately designed Gantt chart.

used during plant layout and conversion (particularly in repetitive manufacture) for balancing capacity and achieving a uniform flow of work—i.e., for eliminating bottlenecks or excess capacity at specific machines and workplaces. (4) They show where and when machines are overloaded, or conversely, where the work load falls short of machine capacity.

Adjustments to Machine Overloading and Underloading. A machine is overloaded when the total amount of work assigned for a given period is more than the machine can put out with its current capacity. Depending on business conditions, overloading can be handled by rerouting work to machines that have unallocated capacity, by operating machines overtime, by subcontracting some work, or by purchasing additional equipment. Underloading can be handled by acquiring more sales orders, by scheduling work in anticipation of future sales, or, as a last resort, by selling the machines.

Production Control Procedure. In repetitive production the problem of control is largely one of maintaining the scheduled rate of output; in job-order production the problem is primarily one of meeting delivery dates on customers' orders. A PPC system regulates production on the basis of the following information: (1) production requirements—as shown by unfilled orders, sales estimate, and master schedule; (2) the amount of work scheduled to machines and the amount of unallocated capacity available for new work—as shown by machine-load charts; (3) status of current production with reference to the level of output and the meeting of delivery promise dates—as shown by schedule-control charts or control boards.

CONTROL OF PRODUCTION. "Production control" is achieved by comparing *actual* output with *planned* (scheduled) output and taking corrective action promptly to eliminate undue deviations before they become acute. Hence the progress of work must be periodically checked against the production schedule. Since a production schedule is not a rigid program but a working guide, minor divergences are to be expected. Schedules, therefore, provide for such contingencies as rush orders, minor design changes, and material shortages.

A control procedure must be set up to show production lags caused by serious machine failures, material and tool shortages, output of defective work, absenteeism, and the like. These delays or disruptions may be corrected through the use of standby equipment, temporary rerouting of orders, reassignment of operators, overtime work, hiring of additional workers, expediting procurement, or subcontracting work. When late delivery is unavoidable, customers should be notified promptly.

METHODS FOR SHOWING DEVIATIONS FROM SCHEDULES. An appropriate method must be selected to show deviations of actual from planned production and to provide a basis for analyzing the causes of delays and for taking remedial action. The methods employed range from the checking of plant performance against schedule sheets and route sheets to the use of control boards, also known as schedule-control charts.

Schedule Sheets and Route Sheets. For small plants and for plants whose production control is simple, schedule sheets can be drawn up to show the rates of output or the completion dates of orders for the various products. A supplementary control device is the filing of route

215

sheets according to the starting date of the first operation. The progress
of work can then be gauged by checking daily "completion of work"
reports from dispatchers or foremen against the schedule and route
sheets.

Control Boards (Progress Charts). For large plants and for plants
whose production control problem is complex, control boards (a form
of the Gantt chart) can be used to show work scheduled and to check

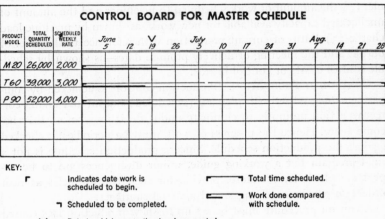

CONTROL BOARD FOR MASTER SCHEDULE

PRODUCT MODEL	TOTAL QUANTITY SCHEDULED	SCHEDULED WEEKLY RATE	June 5	12	∨ 19	26	July 3	10	17	24	31	Aug. 7	14	21	28
M 20	26,000	2,000													
T 60	39,000	3,000													
P 90	52,000	4,000													

KEY:

   ┌   Indicates date work is scheduled to begin.   ┌────┐ Total time scheduled.

   ┐   Scheduled to be completed.   ▭────┐ Work done compared with schedule.

   ∨   Date to which production has been posted.

Fig. 46. Control board (an application of the Gantt chart) and master
schedule for final assemblies of specified models of a repetitive manufacturing firm. On July 19 output of Model M20 is slightly ahead of
schedule. Model T60 is 1,000 units behind schedule—the inventory of
finished stock, however, is adequate to meet delivery schedules. P90 is
on schedule.

actual output against scheduled output. In such charts (see Fig. 46)
vertical columns represent an increment of output for a given interval.
The quantity figures (2,000, 3,000) opposite each product or part
indicate the planned output for a certain time period (e.g., a week).
The amount of work scheduled for the period is indicated by the
length of the thin line. Daily reports of the amount of work completed
are plotted by extending the thick line. The production status of a
particular product or part on the current date can then be readily
determined by comparing the actual cumulative output (thick line)
with the scheduled output for the given period (thin line). Such
charting establishes "control by exceptions," since poor accomplish-

ment relative to planned output of any item is easily noted and the need for investigation and corrective action is thus determined.

Advantages of Control Boards. Control boards (1) present an over-all picture of plant production and (2) provide a comprehensive and rapid means for plotting and showing production data in terms of (a) the detailed schedules in the manufacturing program and (b) plant performance in fulfilling the program.

Care must be taken in the installation and use of Gantt charts. Unless calculations and plottings are accurate, errors may be cumulative and difficult to detect. Gantt charts should not be used when information in tabular or other form would be more simple and just as effective.

PRODUCTION REPORT TO MANAGEMENT. Periodically, and when important operational shifts take place, planners submit to the general manager or to the works manager a production report which shows: (1) the size of the *production requirements* or backlog; (2) the *current rate of output,* expressed in terms of physical units (tons, barrels, meters) or as a percentage of "rated" plant capacity; [5] and (3) *capacity utilization*—(a) the amount of production lag and idle machine time, including causes of delays and action taken or recommended, (b) the percentage of the output rejected as substandard and the percentage scrapped, (c) the amount of overloading or overtime in various sections of the plant, and (d) the amount of unused or unallocated capacity (equipment).

Dispatching

Dispatchers put production programs into effect by releasing and guiding manufacturing orders in the sequence previously determined by route sheets and schedules. Though they are under the PPC department, dispatchers (also known as planning clerks) work out of "dispatch stations" in the plant. They assist foremen in carrying out production programs and report to the planning office on the progress of work. Planning clerks begin their dispatching function when the planning office transmits manufacturing orders (route sheets, materials and tools requisitions, etc.) to the plant.

To carry out the *dispatching routine,* planning clerks (particularly

[5] A firm can produce beyond "rated" capacity (e.g., at 106 per cent) if it postpones periodic overhaul of key equipment (e.g., blast furnaces and convertors) and "consumes" capital at a faster than usual rate, resorts to more overtime than ordinary, or turns out a smaller variety of products thereby reducing set-up time and achieving longer production runs.

in repetitive multiproduct and job-order manufacture) (1) assign work to machines and men, (2) release orders for the preparation and performance of work, (3) guide and control work in process, (4) record and report output performance, and (5) follow up and expedite production.

Assignment of Work. Dispatchers assign job tickets (work) to machines and operators according to the starting dates (order of work) specified on schedule or route sheets, and they maintain machine-load charts when these are economical to use. The clerks usually file the job tickets and related forms in dispatch racks or on bulletin boards that show the priority and load of work for each machine as (1) jobs

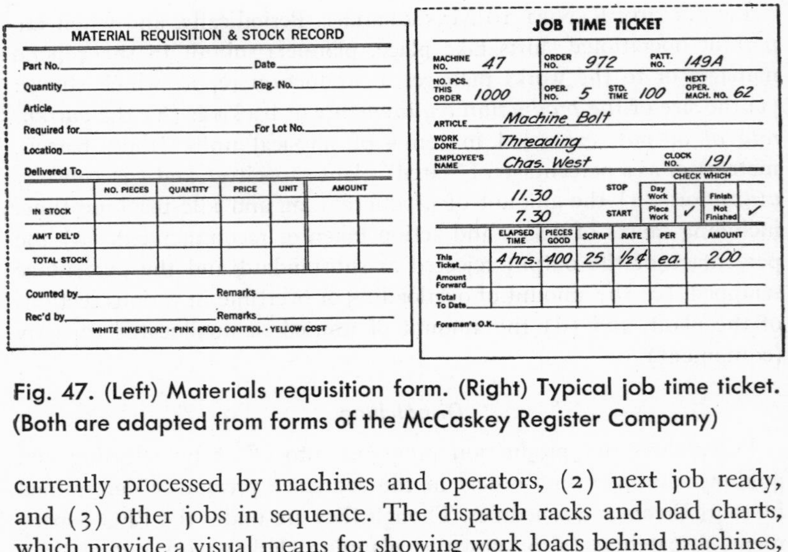

MATERIAL REQUISITION & STOCK RECORD

Part No. ______ Date ______
Quantity ______ Req. No. ______
Article ______
Required for ______ For Lot No. ______
Location ______
Delivered To ______

	NO. PIECES	QUANTITY	PRICE	UNIT	AMOUNT
IN STOCK					
AM'T DEL'D					
TOTAL STOCK					

Counted by ______ Remarks ______
Rec'd by ______ Remarks ______
WHITE INVENTORY - PINK PROD. CONTROL - YELLOW COST

JOB TIME TICKET

MACHINE NO. 47 | ORDER NO. 972 | PATT. NO. 149A
NO. PCS. THIS ORDER 1000 | OPER. NO. 5 | STD. TIME 100 | NEXT OPER. MACH. NO. 62
ARTICLE Machine Bolt
WORK DONE Threading
EMPLOYEE'S NAME Chas. West | CLOCK NO. 191

CHECK WHICH
11.30 STOP | Day Work | | Finish |
7.30 START | Piece Work ✓ | Not Finished ✓

	ELAPSED TIME	PIECES GOOD	SCRAP	RATE	PER	AMOUNT
This Ticket	4 hrs.	400	25	½¢	ea.	200
Amount Forward						
Total To Date						

Foreman's O.K. ______

Fig. 47. (Left) Materials requisition form. (Right) Typical job time ticket. (Both are adapted from forms of the McCaskey Register Company)

currently processed by machines and operators, (2) next job ready, and (3) other jobs in sequence. The dispatch racks and load charts, which provide a visual means for showing work loads behind machines, correspond to and duplicate the appropriate section of the control boards kept in the planning office.

Release of Orders for Preparation and Performance of Manufacture. Dispatchers start operations by issuing detailed orders which prepare for and direct production. (1) Material requisitions and identification tags are issued to storerooms (in advance of processing) to obtain raw stock, semifabricated materials, parts, or subassemblies needed for various jobs. (2) Tool orders (or requisitions) are issued to storerooms to obtain the required jigs, fixtures, dies, patterns, or gauges for various jobs. (Tool set-up orders may also be issued.) (3)

Time tickets (and blueprints when required) are issued to operators and inspectors. (4) Job tickets are issued to workers to authorize operations on the "next job" for which materials and tools are made ready. (Job tickets and time tickets can often be conveniently combined in one form; see Fig. 47.) (5) Inspection forms are issued to inspectors who will use them to report the amount of work accepted and the amount rejected. (6) Move orders are issued to transport materials and tools from storage areas to work stations and from machine to machine. (Move orders and identification tags can frequently be combined to advantage.)

Elaborate job tickets usually carry such data as order number, material specification, operation, machine number, quantity to produce, time allowed for operation, starting date, and blank space for recording the actual dates of the beginning and completion of work and the quantity of "good" and "bad" pieces produced.

Job tickets instruct workers as to the operations they are to perform, inform the planning office about the progress of jobs, and supply the accounting office with data for cost accumulation and payroll purposes.

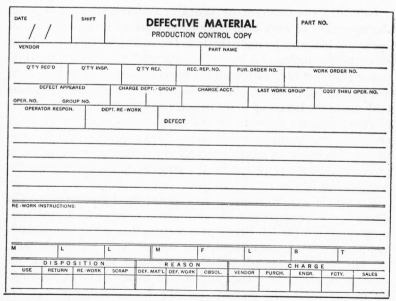

Fig. 48. Defective material slip. (Adapted from a form of the McCaskey Register Company)

IDLE MACHINE TIME REPORT

Dept. *Press*
Foreman *Williams*   Work Week *40 hrs.*   Week Ending *June 5th*

MACHINE NO.	HOURS IDLE	COST OF TIME (Burden)	REASONS
S20	3	1.35	Equipment break down
S70	1	.45	Wrong size stock delivered
S50	1	.45	No job ticket in rack
M10	4	2.80	Die broken; accident; no relief man available
M40	1	.70	Waiting for die change; crane overloaded
L20	2	3.00	Machine in poor adjustment; unable to hold work to
Totals	12	$8.75	tolerance

$$(Departmental\ time\ loss\ \frac{12\ hrs.\ loss}{600\ available\ hrs.} = 5\% - loss\ is\ normal)$$
Wms.

Fig. 49. Idle machine time report of a press department.

GUIDANCE AND CONTROL OF WORK IN PROCESS. Dispatchers direct the movement of work from machine to machine in the sequence of operations indicated by route sheets and according to schedules. When an operator completes his work, the dispatcher time-stamps the completed job ticket (i.e., he records the direct-labor working time of jobs) and issues a ticket for the next job. As work is processed, the planning clerk moves the tickets up in the dispatch rack according to the priority of orders, prepares the materials and tools for new work for machines, and issues the required detailed orders. He co-operates with the foreman to overcome or adjust the ordinary disruptions that occur in processing and keeps posted on the progress of work under his dispatching jurisdiction.

RECORDING AND REPORTING OF PRODUCTION PERFORMANCE. The dispatcher accumulates and forwards certain information to the planning office. (1) On job tickets he reports the beginning and completion times of work and makes special note of "late" and "rush" jobs. (2) On inspection or job tickets he transmits information on the quantity of acceptable pieces and spoiled pieces. (3) On "in slips" he reports completed products entering final storerooms. (4) On machine "downtime" sheets (Fig. 49) he reports idle machine time (giving reasons for delays).

Periodically the dispatcher "disposes" of completed jobs ("expended" orders) by collecting job tickets, timecards, blueprints, and other forms, which he sends to the planning office. He maintains contact with the planning office either by personal visits or through the use of telephones, messengers, pneumatic tubes, or teletypewriters.

FOLLOW-UP AND PREVENTION OF DELAYS. Dispatchers or specially assigned expediters assist in the prevention of delays in the maintenance of production schedules. They uncover and investigate such delays as late deliveries of purchased materials and tools, serious machine failures, errors in processing and inspection, and absenteeism. They make minor adjustments in schedules to overcome delays and recommend corrective measures and sometimes major adjustments to planning supervisors and to foremen responsible for the activities where serious delays occur.

PRODUCTION–PLANNING AND CONTROL SYSTEMS FOR VARIOUS TYPES OF MANUFACTURE

The designing of an effective PPC system for a given plant requires a clear comprehension of the nature of the manufacturing problem and an understanding of how the planning and manufacture of standard products differ from the planning and manufacture of custom products. The *comparison chart* on the following page contrasts job-order and repetitive manufacture.

Planning and Control System for Job-Order Manufacture. The survey for developing or improving a PPC system for custom manufacture necessitates the establishment of the required prerequisites and the setting up of procedure for estimating jobs, routing, scheduling, preparing manufacturing orders, dispatching, and production control.

PREREQUISITES. A materials-and-tool records and control system must be devised and machine-capacity data must be compiled before effective procedures can be designed.

ESTIMATING. In bidding for orders and in gaining new business it is essential to have an accurate estimate of cost (so that a *price* can be set) and of delivery dates. The customer usually provides the blueprints and other specifications that stipulate the kind and quantity of product to be manufactured. The engineering department sometimes redraws the specifications to provide blueprints of the required clarity for shop use or to supply the number of copies necessary for planning and manufacturing. Some job-order firms (e.g., machine manufacturers) design the product to suit the needs of the customer.

A Comparison Chart of Job-Order and Repetitive Manufacture

JOB-ORDER (CUSTOM) MANUFACTURE	REPETITIVE (STANDARD) MANUFACTURE
Planning is complex and costly because of the many variable elements that must be controlled.	Planning is comparatively simple and inexpensive because there are fewer variables to control.
Effective planning and control are vital to profitable operations and efficient use of labor and facilities.	Planning and control are important, but such programs as product simplification and work simplification offer more effective means for achieving efficient use of labor and facilities.
Estimating unit cost of the product and completion date are necessary and important.	Unit cost of the product is known and exact completion dates are usually less important since sales are made from stock.
Production aims to cover a backlog of customers' orders rather than to maintain finished inventories.	Production aims to replenish finished inventories and to cover sales estimate.
Inventories are generally highly varied and more difficult to control.	Inventories are generally less varied and more easily controlled.
Machine capacities are varied and usually must be estimated.	Machine capacities are less varied and are known in advance from past experience or time study.
Routing is done for each new order received.	Routing is done either when plant facilities are initially set up or when they are revised for a given product.
Scheduling is complex, usually requiring (a) the placing of an order in an appropriate priority category, (b) scheduling within-an-order, and (c) setting up the order of work for machines.	Scheduling is primarily concerned with establishing a rate of output sufficient to meet the sales requirement of the period.
Manufacturing is usually authorized through the release of a specific manufacturing order consisting of several forms.	Manufacturing is usually authorized through the release of schedules to various departments.
Dispatching is elaborate, requiring detailed regulation, and production control is primarily concerned with meeting delivery dates.	Dispatching is usually simple, and control is primarily concerned with maintaining the scheduled rate of output.

COST AND ESTIMATE SHEET

For	Address								Job No.	
Description									Date	
									Their No.	
Commenced	Finished				Quoted				Billed	

MATERIAL				LABOR					OVERHEAD		SUMMARY	
ITEMS	QNTY.	PER	AMOUNT	OPERATIONS	NO.	HRS.	RATE	AMOUNT	RATE	AMOUNT	DESCRIPTION	AMOUNT
											MATERIAL	
											LABOR	
											OVERHEAD	
											MATERIAL PROFIT	
											FACTORY COST	
											OFFICE BURDEN	
											NET INCOME	
											SELLING PRICE	

Fig. 50. Cost and estimate sheet.

The estimating procedure generally requires the participation of the engineering, the PPC, and the cost-accounting departments. *Job cost estimating* is basically the computation of material, direct-labor, and overhead costs for a particular order (see Fig. 50). In practice, however, it calls for an analysis of specifications, determination of parts to buy and parts to make, selection of materials and operations required, consideration of the quantity to be produced, forecasting of the cost (procurement price) of materials and labor, and consideration of the competitive situation and the need for repeat business. Estimating may also be based upon the cost of past orders (as in the case of repeat business), the cost of similar orders, or standard cost data (e.g., correlation between the weight of the product and its cost). *Delivery date estimating* is based on the scheduling procedure—job priority, processing time, load ahead of various machines (or departments), and time required for tooling up and procuring materials and parts.

ROUTING. Since it is a continuing activity, job-order routing is best prepared by competent personnel on the staff of either the engineering or the planning departments, following the standard procedure outlined earlier in this chapter. Routing is often complex and elaborate because general-purpose machinery is commonly used and facilities are arranged along the process-layout plan and also because machines are loaded to various degrees with diverse work. Owing to the fluctuating load on different machines, the most economical equipment and methods for processing work are not always available.

When routing requires special familiarity with machines and day-to-day shop operating conditions, it is best carried out on the decentralized basis whereby the planning office routing sheets specify the operations or process (sometimes only the department) and foremen specify the machine and worker best suited to turn out the work.

SCHEDULING. Because customers' orders differ as to specifications, quantity, routing, and processing time, scheduling for job-order manufacture is complex and necessitates much detail. Planners generally carry out scheduling in three steps: (1) they establish job priorities and completion dates of orders—i.e., they schedule an order in relation to other orders; (2) they schedule within-an-order; and (3) they establish the order of work for machine loading and for fixing the beginning and ending dates of operations on equipment. The first step involves master scheduling; the second and third steps involve production scheduling.

Master Scheduling. In master scheduling, planners balance the production requirements (based on customers' orders received and a forecast of new sales orders) against the available plant capacity and, as previously noted, establish approximate completion dates for customers' orders. Such over-all scheduling calls for the establishment of job priorities—e.g., the sequence in which new orders are to be put into manufacture is ordinarily determined on the basis of a classification of production into "rush," "regular," "repairs," or "stock" orders. The placing of an order in a given priority class establishes the relative importance of the order as compared to other orders received and, sometimes, as compared to work already scheduled but not yet in process.

Production Scheduling. Detailed production scheduling first requires scheduling within-an-order. The aim of scheduling within-an-order is to reduce the over-all processing time, to speed the turnover of work in process, and to minimize the storage and misplacement (loss) of completed parts by deferring their production until they are needed. Such scheduling involves fixing the relative times for beginning and ending the fabrication of parts and for processing the various subassemblies. The relative starting times for processing components is best determined by calculating processing time (as shown on route sheets) backward from the completion time of the final assembly (see Fig. 42). Scheduling within-an-order may include the setting of successive beginning times for engineering of products, tooling up, and procuring materials. Many of these activities could be dovetailed and scheduled to be carried on simultaneously.

The order is so scheduled that the various parts (both fabricated and purchased) will be completed and on hand for the beginning of the subassemblies, and the various subassemblies on hand for the beginning of final assembly. For example, if a considerable amount of time is required for processing a given batch of parts, that batch will be started in advance of a batch requiring less processing time. Total processing time may be reduced by overlapping or telescoping the processing of parts or assemblies—i.e., while one machine operation is turning out pieces (or batches of work), a second machine can begin processing the pieces (or batch) leaving the first machine. Such overlapping requires a "float" (a given minimum quantity of work between operations) and close co-ordination to avoid production interruptions.

Scheduling the "order of work" for machine-loading fixes calendar dates for the beginning and ending of operations on plant equipment. If only one manufacturing order were to be produced by the plant, the "ideal" relative time and over-all processing time determined by scheduling within-an-order would be converted into schedule dates for the order of work for machine-loading.[6] In a going concern, however, many diverse orders are in process and some machines are usually overloaded and others underloaded.

The determination of operation or process dates in order-of-work scheduling is based on: (1) the priority rating of the order and the approximate completion date determined by master scheduling, (2) the route sheets, (3) the relative times established by scheduling within-an-order, and (4) the load ahead of various machines. The dates established by the order of work are then entered on route sheets and the allocated machine times are entered or plotted on machine-load charts or schedule sheets. A comparatively accurate completion and delivery date for the order can thus be determined. The customer may be notified of the final completion date if it varies appreciably from the estimated delivery date initially given him.

---

[6] This would be the case if a job-order plant were awarded a defense contract that absorbed all of the output capacity for many months. Scheduling within-an-order would, then, be expanded into "scheduling a new project" to include the relative time required for process engineering, plant revision (conversion, where necessary), elaborate tooling up, and a test run (see Fig. 8).

PREPARING MANUFACTURING ORDERS. When two or more orders are identical or take identical routing, they should be combined, whenever scheduling permits, into a manufacturing order of the optimum lot size. After an order has been routed and scheduled, it is then written up as a manufacturing order well in advance of the scheduled dates for manufacture. Planners prepare manufacturing orders in this way: (1) After consulting the materials list and parts list, they allocate the required materials on the balance-of-stores records and they make out purchase requisitions for the procurement of items not carried in stock. (2) They check route sheets for tooling requirements and prepare tool fabrication orders or tool purchase requisitions. (3) In advance of the starting dates for the various activities, they write up the manufacturing order (which includes job tickets, route sheets, materials and tool requisitions) in the required number of copies and file these according to release dates for transmittal to planning clerks who will dispatch the order according to schedule.

DISPATCHING. Job-order dispatching is elaborate, usually requiring many forms for the control and use of machines, men, materials, tools, inspection activity, and handling equipment. Job tickets and other detailed orders are assigned and released to specific machines and individuals (storekeepers, movemen, set-up men, operators) to regulate their activity. A decentralized dispatching system is often more adaptable to job-order plants than a centralized system.

Whether centralized or decentralized, the dispatching procedures usually required are those outlined earlier in this chapter. Each department is held accountable for the completion of work as prescribed by the schedule. The dispatchers report to the planning office on performance and revise schedules when machine failures and other interruptions make revisions necessary.

CONTROLLING PRODUCTION. Control of job-order production is achieved by periodically checking and following up the progress of orders to assure that the work is being done on schedule. A column, "actual completion date," on route sheets or on schedule sheets may be used for this purpose. The dispatchers record the progress of work by observing the times and dates when work is completed and by making the appropriate notations on route sheets or schedule sheets. The planning office maintains a check on progress (employing charts whenever economical) by receiving daily reports (including "expended" order tickets) from dispatchers. The planning office keeps production on schedule through the initiation of corrective measures long before manufacturing orders can become critically late.

Planning and Control System for Repetitive Manufacture. The survey for establishing or improving a PPC system for standard manufacture calls for the development of routing and inventory control systems and the setting up of procedures for scheduling, authorization of manufacture, dispatching, and control.

PREREQUISITES. Management must analyze the product, develop routing, and set up inventory control systems concurrent with the establishment of plant facilities.

Product Specifications and Parts to Buy. After the product is designed and blueprints and bills-of-materials are available, a study must be conducted to determine which items to buy and which to make. From the study, items on the parts list can be designated as "purchased," "made," or "supply" items. The status of each item should be periodically reappraised since changes in the volume of output, in supply conditions, and in technology modify the relative advantages of purchasing or of fabricating a given part or assembly.

Routing. Routing is developed in conjunction with, and in conformance to, the layout of production facilities. The preparation of route sheets is comparatively simple since facilities in mass production plants are laid out in the operational sequence required to manufacture the standard products, and the capacities of machinery are balanced for a given volume of output.

The sequential flow of work in repetitive manufacture is, therefore, determined by the layout of production equipment and materials handling and other facilities, and remains unchanged so long as the products and facilities are not modified. Periodically, however, products are redesigned, or new models are added and old ones dropped; also, processes are modified or improved, and worn machines are replaced. These product and process changes should be regulated and planned in advance since they will call for new routing. The obsolete product specifications and route sheets should be systematically superseded by newly-developed ones in such a manner as to cause a minimum of confusion and disruption to planning and plant operations.

Where only a few standard products are manufactured, master route sheets are usually kept for reference by the various departments of the plant. Where many standard finished goods are put out in multi-product plants, master route sheets may be kept either by the shops or by the planning office. In the latter case the planning office prepares job route sheets from master route sheets for release with each manufacturing order or schedule issued to the plant.

Materials-Control and Tool-Control Systems. The materials-control system can be set up on the basis of the bills of materials and the projected volume of production; and the tool-control system can be set up on the basis of route sheets (since they specify the tools to be used) and the projected volume of production. The total quantity of the various kinds of materials, finished goods, and tools that will be kept in stock will be determined by sales and scheduling needs.

SCHEDULING. In repetitive manufacturing, scheduling determines the priority and rate of output of various standard products necessary to meet sales needs or to replenish finished stocks as they are depleted by shipments. Scheduling achieves economy in manufacture when it establishes a steady rate of output with a minimum of working capital—i.e., the shortest processing time, a rapid turnover of inventories, and minimum average inventories.

Scheduling is most simple for continuous process plants wherein a single nonassembly-type product passes through an integrated series of machines or processes. It becomes progressively more complex in repetitive multiproduct plants as a larger number of assembly-type products are alternately manufactured on the same facilities (Fig. 46).

Preparations for Scheduling. Before they can schedule repetitive manufacture, planners must (1) establish an effective sales forecasting method; (2) select a suitable scheduling period; and (3) ascertain the proper quantity of finished goods to be kept in inventory.

Effective sales forecasting as far into the future as possible is of prime importance in achieving efficient master scheduling and stabilized production. By interpreting business and market trends, top executives participate in the determination and approval of final production requirements (often adopting a formal production budget).

An appropriate scheduling period (annual, semiannual, quarter) can best be selected on the basis of such factors as the length of time required for the production cycle, seasonal fluctuations affecting manufacturing and procurement of raw materials, and the budgeting [7] period.

A quantity of completed goods must be maintained in finished stock to serve as a reserve or "buffer" from which sales are to be made; this stock is continually replenished by current production. If the finished

[7] See Ch. 26 for discussion.

inventory stocks are too large, unproductive working capital is tied up; if it is too small, some deliveries can not be made and sales will be lost. The "ideal" amount for finished stock is a quantity small enough to avoid needless use of working capital, but large enough to cover sales shipments and counterbalance the delays and interruptions that normally occur in the production of goods. The quantity of each product to be carried in inventory can often be determined on the basis of past experience.

Master Scheduling. For most repetitive manufacturing the master schedule is a comparatively simple form showing the quantities (or rate of output) of each type of product to be made in a given period. Output capacity and time required for the production cycle are known from past experience. If normal plant capacity is not sufficient to meet the estimated production demand, management must then decide whether to resort to overtime, employ an additional shift, purchase more parts from suppliers, or expand plant capacity.[8]

In multiplant firms the central planning office (located in the home office) frequently allocates the company's total production among the different branch plants. Finished stocks are generally reviewed each month and compared with the actual sales for the current month. Then, on the basis of forecasted sales for the next month, the schedule for each of the products is revised as necessary.

Production Scheduling. Planners break the master schedule down into component parts (items shown on the parts list) and plant departments and stipulate the rate of output (priority and starting date if necessary) for each part or item so that the assembly lines can be supplied with the components as needed (Fig. 51). They thus establish starting dates for each lot and weekly (or daily) output quotas for each item sufficient to meet the requirements shown on the master schedule. The completion date is automatically determined by the time required for the production cycle. Production scheduling for a going concern, therefore, is largely a matter of increasing or diminishing the rate of output of parts and assemblies to conform to the master schedule.

Where a single product is manufactured in a continuous process and where the same facilities are employed constantly in the output of a given item, production scheduling, as such, is not necessary since the master schedule designates the rate of output for all manufacturing

---

[8] Overtime and greater reliance on suppliers are short-run adjustments, whereas the multishift plan and plant expansion are long-run adjustments.

PRODUCTION (PARTS) SCHEDULE

Model __M 20__   Month __June__

Part No.	Per Assembly	Quantity Required on Dates Indicated							
		5	12	19	26				
M-410R	1	600	600	600	600				
M-420F	2	1200	1200	1200	1200				
M-430F	4	2400	2400	2400	2400				
M-440F	2								
M-450T	1								
M-460T	1								

Fig. 51. Production schedule for a repetitive manufacturing firm.

operations. Production scheduling is, however, necessary for multiproduct and single-product manufacture where machines are used alternately—i.e., when successive machine setups are made for the processing of various items.

Multiproduct firms require scheduling within-an-order to determine the best relative times for starting the fabrication of parts and the processing of subassemblies. Such scheduling aims to so synchronize the completion dates as to minimize processing time and maximize turnover and also to provide sufficient stock to avoid shortages of parts and delays in manufacture. The rate of output of parts must, therefore, be synchronized with the flow rates of subassemblies which, in turn, must be synchronized with the rate of output of final assemblies.

PREPARING THE MANUFACTURING ORDER. The manufacturing schedule, when approved by management, becomes the blanket manufacturing order that authorizes production for the next period. Copies of the manufacturing authorization are transmitted, in advance of the next period, to plant superintendents, foremen, inspection supervisors, purchasing agents, and plant engineers. The schedule, broken down by component parts and production departments, tells foremen the number of units they are required to put out in the next period. The schedules should be released sufficiently in advance of the future period to enable foremen to recruit needed labor and to prepare machines formerly idle and to enable the purchasing agent to procure needed supplies.

The schedule also can serve as the purchasing requisition for the required materials and parts to meet the stipulated rate of output (the

230

quantities required to cover the needs of the production period can be computed from the schedule). Purchase orders can then be placed for consecutive deliveries, timed to maintain the rate of output.

DISPATCHING. The specialized facilities, line layout, and channelized flow of work characteristic of mass-production plants usually make the dispatching of work between machine operations unnecessary. In highly repetitive manufacture, dispatching may consist merely of the release of the schedule to the various sections of the plant prior to the start of the manufacturing period. In multiproduct plants where facilities are alternately set up to process various kinds of work, dispatching is usually required for the beginning of the fabrication of a given part and the beginning of the processing of an assembly. Hence, dispatching is necessary only between process phases (series of machines). Some orders such as tool requisitions, material requisitions, scrap reports, and idle-machine-time reports are generally required. However, the amount of detailed dispatching and paper work needed is much less than that for job-order manufacture. Dispatchers and expediters must, nonetheless, uncover and rectify materials, parts, and tools shortages and other delays that make for interruptions and poor co-ordination in the flow of production.

CONTROLLING PRODUCTION. The control function becomes operative with the release of orders that set plans into motion. The plans establish flow rates for synchronized output of required parts for assembly.

Objective. The aim of control is to maintain the scheduled rate of output; that is, the rate of production must be sufficient to satisfy sales needs and also keep inventories of parts, raw materials, and finished goods at a practical minimum. The quantity selected for finished goods should serve as an adequate buffer to absorb the fluctuating demands of sales, while keeping the manufacturing output rate uniform. For example, finished stock must not be allowed to become exhausted because of a lag in production or excessive conservatism in sales forecasting; nor should finished stock be allowed to pile up because the output rate exceeds the planned rate or because sales estimates are over-optimistic.

Achievement. To achieve production control, planners compare "actual" with "planned" production and take prompt corrective action to rectify deviations (from schedules) that may become acute.

It is usually unnecessary to establish centralized control over the output of all items. Centralized control should be established primarily for over-all plant performance (output of finished goods); individual shop performance (output of key parts and subassemblies) is generally best observed and controlled on a decentralized basis.

Use of Control Charts. In assembly-type manufacture the control mechanism is usually best set up on two levels: first, for finished products and, second, for key parts and subassemblies.

The central (or finished goods) control chart is set up to compare actual output with planned output: weekly or daily reports on the amount of finished units produced are plotted against scheduled output. A control chart may also be set up to show how actual sales (orders received) compare with forecasted sales and thus to forewarn of changes in sales demand. A threatening depletion or the excessive accumulation of finished stock will be pointed up when the actual rate of output is compared with the actual rate of sales shipments.

Since the schedules for the output of parts are synchronized with the schedules for the output of assemblies, any serious lag in the production of a component part will disrupt the output of finished goods. It is not mandatory that daily (or weekly) rates of output of parts and assemblies correspond precisely with the planned rate, but it is necessary that the average daily (or weekly) rate of output closely correspond with planned rates. To take care of normal irregularities in output, reserve stocks of items are kept in intermediate stages of production and "banks" of parts and subassemblies are located at various points in the production line.

Control charts for key parts and subassemblies can show whether the rates of output for components and subassemblies are sufficiently synchronized and in balance; and a control chart for all items in production (finished products, parts, and subassemblies) can provide a comprehensive picture of plant output performance.

Planning and Control System for Semidiversified Manufacture. Semidiversified manufacture is exemplified by (1) plants that manufacture standard products for stock and also manufacture products to customers' specifications; (2) job-order plants where the customers' orders are repeated frequently or where customers' orders generally consist of a large volume of identical finished units; (3) job-order plants where many common parts and subassemblies are used in the manufacture and assembly of customers' orders, along with certain parts and subassemblies specially manufactured to customers' specifications. Common standard items are fabricated in advance of need and are drawn from stock for particular customers' orders.

Many of the features in the PPC systems outlined for custom and for repetitive manufacture can be combined in the development of procedures required for semidiversified manufacture. The following paragraphs illustrate the type of PPC procedures that may be employed in semidiversified manufacture.

ROUTING. For repetitive manufacturing (standard products), master route sheets should be prepared as outlined earlier in the chapter; for job-order manufacturing, procedures should be set up for job estimating and for routing customers' orders. When repeat orders are received, route sheets previously developed can be used again. Before reissue, however, they should be improved on the basis of the experience gained from past processing.

SCHEDULING. The scheduling procedure must be adaptable to the needs of mixed manufacture.

Master scheduling is formulated from sales forecasts as well as from customers' orders received. New work may be classified as "stock," "special," or "repair" orders. Special (customers') orders may be subordinated to stock orders, or vice-versa, depending upon the emphasis of the business. Both "priority" scheduling and scheduling within-an-order must be done.

Production scheduling determines the starting dates for the manufacture of stock items. The output rate for standard parts, subassemblies, and final assemblies is increased or diminished as stipulated by the master schedule. For the job-order phase of the business, production scheduling usually fixes the beginning and ending dates for each operation on the product. Such scheduling is done on the basis of the established priority of work, the delivery dates stipulated by the master schedule, and the machine-load charts. The repetitive phase and the job-order phase of production must be carefully co-ordinated, particularly when the same facilities are used for both types of output.

DISPATCHING. Manufacturing orders for stock as well as for custom items are transmitted to dispatchers in advance of the starting dates. Each type of order is made up of the required complement of forms—route sheets, materials issue, etc. After the preparatory dispatching work for stock orders, little intermediate dispatching is ordinarily required. Customers' manufacturing orders, however, generally demand detailed dispatching as previously discussed.

CONTROLLING PRODUCTION. Control of the repetitive phase of manufacturing is sometimes difficult because plant performance on job-order work can not be accurately predicted. For repetitive work, control boards may be set up to maintain a check on the rate of output. For job-order work, control requires periodic reports on each order at various stages of manufacture so as to assure meeting due dates.

1. Distinguish between over-all enterprise planning and production planning.

2. What factors would you check or investigate to determine whether a company PPC system is efficient?

3. Explain why the planning and control for a job-order manufacturing plant utilizing assembly-type processes is more difficult than the planning and control for a repetitive manufacturing plant using continuous-type processes.

4. (a) Discuss four methods of dealing with seasonal variations. (b) Explain how a firm's magnitude of overhead costs, inventory carrying charges, proportion of skilled labor in its working force, and need to provide steady employment would influence the selection of a plan to deal with seasonal variations.

5. (a) Differentiate between a centralized PPC system and a decentralized PPC system. (b) What factors determine the degree of centralization in a company PPC system?

6. Outline the over-all procedure for setting up a company PPC system.

7. (a) Explain the functions and purposes of a manufacturing order. (b) Enumerate the forms and type of data that would ordinarily make up a manufacturing order of a firm engaged in job-order production.

8. (a) Enumerate and briefly discuss the steps for developing routing. (b) Explain when master route sheets are used.

9. (a) Distinguish between master scheduling and production scheduling. (b) What are the objectives of production scheduling? (c) Enumerate the data that provide the basis for production scheduling.

10. (a) For what purpose can machine-load charts be used? (b) What four methods may be employed to deal with the overloading of specific machines?

11. What are the dispatching duties for job-order manufacture?

12. Contrast a PPC system for job-order manufacture with a PPC system for repetitive manufacture with respect to: estimating, computation of machine capacity, inventory control, routing, scheduling, make-up of the manufacturing order, and dispatching.

13. Distinguish between "priority" scheduling, scheduling "within-an-order," and "order-of-work" scheduling.

14. What factors would ordinarily be considered by a job-order firm in estimating the cost of a new order?

15. Illustrate three kinds of semidiversified manufacture.

16. How will a repetitive manufacturing plant differ from a strict job-order plant with respect to: layout of production machinery, handling facilities, inspection and quality control methods and devices, amount of skilled labor required, and ease of production planning and control?

22: Marketing: Pricing, Selling, and Advertising

A s increasing geographic and industrial specialization makes mar-kets [1] wider and more complex, business profits increasingly hinge on the existence of mass consumer demand and practical marketing (the process whereby goods and services flow from producers to ulti-mate consumers). To market commodities firms must select channels of distribution, price and promote products, sell (effect transfer of ownership), finance transactions, warehouse and ship goods, and serv-ice customers and products.

The high cost of marketing [2] as a proportion of total costs is due not only to increasing geographic specialization and rising expenditures for packaging, servicing, and advertising, but also to the fact that technological advances (e.g., mechanization and motion study) are more readily applicable to production than to marketing. Management can nonetheless improve the efficiency of selling through market re-search, product simplification, well-selected distribution methods, con-trol of expenses, and other means to be discussed.

Procedure for Developing or Improving Marketing and the Sales Department. This survey calls for the following procedural steps:

(1) Conduct continuous market research.

(2) Appraise and select channels of distribution.

(3) Set or adjust prices and discounts.

(4) Establish the organization structure for the department.

(5) Set up and control the selling activity.

(6) Advertise and promote the products.

[1] The *market* is best understood as the area wherein the forces of demand and supply for products and services operate in establishing prices and effecting exchange.

[2] For example, according to the Bureau of Agricultural Economics of the United States Department of Agriculture, the marketing function (including processing) takes approximately 61 cents of each dollar the consumer spends for food.

MARKET RESEARCH

Continuous market research must guide the development of the sales function. Market analysts appraise company products with reference to consumer needs and wants; and they study the market to identify and locate the likely buyers, to gauge the potential demand, to determine how and when to sell, and to forecast sales for the immediate sales period (forecasting is discussed later in this chapter). The large firm often sets up a separate merchandise office to co-ordinate the efforts of sales, engineering, and manufacturing departments with market research findings that deal with new products and simplification and redesign of existing products.

Product Research. The types of products desired by consumers can be determined and their effective planning can be facilitated by consumer surveys (opinion polls, panels, mail questionnaires), suggestions from the sales force and other employees, and the findings of industrial research and engineering. Proposed products and package designs may be tested for consumer acceptance through buyers' panels and trial sale in selected areas; and output cost may be checked through a manufacturing study.[3] Products may be redesigned to increase utility and to penetrate new markets. A study of "lost" sales may point to how a product, its packaging, or servicing may be improved. A product-simplification program can weed out slow sellers and needless variety.

Market Analysis. By analyzing the firm's products and appraising their marketability, analysts can ascertain their sales possibilities.

IDENTIFYING MARKETS. The nature of the goods to be sold identifies their markets. Consumers who buy given types of products can be identified (i.e., the market can be located) when the products are classified as to use (consumers' goods or producers' goods) and further subdivided as to price brackets and durability (high-priced durable goods or low-priced nondurable goods). The probable purchasing response may be determined by gauging the ease of sale at various prices and the variability of effective demand—inelastic [4] (for necessities) or elastic (for luxuries). Once the type of market and the likely consumers (housewives, farmers, chemical industries, government agencies) have been identified, the potential demand can be ascertained.

DETERMINING POTENTIAL DEMAND. The potential demand for proposed or new products or for currently produced items in a new mar-

[3] See p. 72 for discussion.
[4] See p. 240 for discussion.

ket area may be assessed through a compilation and analysis of such data as shipping rates and costs (to establish the geographic limits of the market), the number of consumers in the area, the share of national income going to consuming areas and to prospective buyers, purchasing habits of buyers (quantities bought, frequency, servicing, and terms of sale), and prices of substitute products. (For product and market analysis, also see Ch. 7.)

SELECTION OF CHANNELS OF DISTRIBUTION

In choosing a channel of distribution, management must consider the nature of the product (consumer or producer good, perishability, style, unit value, newness), the nature of the market (scope of distribution, size of average sale, the anticipated sales volume, consumers' buying habits), the availability and attitude of middlemen, and the effectiveness and cost of various outlets.

The firm must select the most profitable channel or combination of channels. Sales may be made (1) directly to ultimate consumers; (2) to middlemen who take title to goods—jobbers, wholesalers, retailers, industrial distributors; or (3) to middlemen who take a commission—brokers, dealers, manufacturers' agents. Management must periodically reappraise its channels of distribution and adjust the outlets to suit changes in business and economic conditions.

PRICE DETERMINATION

Because selling prices directly affect a firm's volume of business and profits, price policy is a prime concern of management. Though price behavior in the economy is interdependent and complex, management can make sound price decisions by analyzing the firm's particular pricing situation and then employing a systematic procedure for setting or adjusting prices.

A firm's pricing problem therefore is influenced by such factors as the degree of competition in the industry; types of products handled—i.e., consumers' or producers' goods, standard or custom-made products; [5] whether the firm is a producer or distributor; and whether its prices are subject to regulation by law.

Inasmuch as there are "going" prices for products and services currently sold, the primary managerial problem is one of anticipating market price fluctuations or of adjusting the firm's prices as much as

[5] See p. 223 for procedure for cost estimating and pricing of customers' orders in job-lot manufacture.

necessary to meet competition. Management adjusts its prices to market and business conditions and strives, at least for the long run, to maximize profits.

The Effect of Competition on Pricing. Markets may range from the highly competitive to the monopoly type. Imperfect competition (that which is intermediate between the two extremes and is identified as "monopolistic competition" and "oligopoly"), however, is the most typical in the economy, particularly in the manufacturing industry. The extent of competition in an industry affects a firm's power to fix the prices of its products.

COMPETITIVE MARKETS. A firm has progressively less freedom in setting its prices (and the industry is more competitive) if the products offered for sale by the various producers are more or less identical, if the number of sellers and buyers is comparatively large (numerous offers and bids narrow the price range of merchandise), and if the market is closely informed on prices, supply, and demand. When these conditions obtain to a high degree and competition is keen, the demand for the products of a specific firm is extremely elastic—that is, the firm can sell its products only at or near the market price.[6] Hence, if a firm which produces popular-priced garments for sale to stores, for instance, raises its prices above those prevailing on the market, it will lose sales since buyers can purchase from other firms at market prices. The firm can operate profitably only by reducing costs through efficiency and producing and selling (at or near market price) that quantity which will bring the largest surplus of sales receipts over total costs.

MONOPOLY AND IMPERFECT COMPETITION. A firm has greater latitude in setting its prices (and the industry is more monopolistic) when the products are not identical but are instead more differentiated (distinctive), when there are fewer rival firms, and when there is a larger number of buyers.

Although absolute monopoly—the exercise of complete control by a single organization over the supply of goods—is rare, a firm may gain considerable control over the market for certain products and achieve price-fixing power (even though it may not fully exercise such power) through control over the sources of scarce materials, ownership of patents, secret processes, or achievement of immense size which makes

---

[6] "Market price" is the actual day-to-day price on a given market which is established by supply and demand. The market price varies directly with demand and inversely with supply.

possible the economies of large-scale operations and thus discourages new producers from entering the field.

Under imperfect competition several firms (or a single firm), through substantial control over the supply of a given type of goods, may more or less regulate and stabilize prices. They gain such price-fixing power partly because new producers can not easily enter the industry owing to the heavy investment needed for plant and the high overhead and distribution costs which result when firms operate at low capacity, as they usually do in the initial years of business. Firms under imperfect competition also attain control over markets and gain price-fixing power by differentiating their products through trade-marks, stylizing, distinctive design, particularized service, advertising and promotional campaigns, and exclusive distribution methods. Although such firms may refuse to compete on the basis of price, they often do compete on the basis of quality, service, and terms of sale.

In the pricing of machinery and other capital goods, as contrasted with consumer goods, product differentiation is less important since sales are more contingent upon cost-reduction savings which accrue from the purchase of equipment for replacement purposes and upon business plans for expansion or retrenchment, which depend upon the phase of the business cycle and profit prospects.

Small manufacturers tend to follow the price leadership of the big firms in the industry. A small firm may set its prices at a level which will give it a competitive advantage over, or at least competitive equality with, the leading producers. Price-fixing power does not guarantee profits, since monopolistic as well as competitive industries sustain losses from declining markets during recessions and depressions.

Procedure for Price Setting by the Firm. When management, especially a manufacturer of consumer goods, revises its current prices or quotes a price for a new product, it must (1) consider the influence of price changes on sales volume or the quantities the market will take at various prices (i.e., elasticity of demand as shown by the buyers' response in the amounts purchased at each price level); (2) consider the influence of various volumes of output on unit costs and then set prices at levels which will yield the largest differential between total sales receipts and total costs; (3) decide whether the costs of servicing and shipping are to be included in the price or figured as separate charges; (4) set up the necessary discount allowances; (5) consider suggesting resale prices for retailers or other distributors; and (6) consider legal requirements, if any, dealing with prices.

Influence of Price on Sales Volume. A firm in a monopolistic position of one degree or another does not arbitrarily set its prices at the
highest possible levels. To do so might result in too large a loss in sales
volume. Hence, the firm must consider the *elasticity of market demand*
for its products and must appraise the influence of price changes on
sales volume. For example, a 10-per-cent increase (or decrease) in price
may give rise to a more (or less) than proportionate decrease (or
increase) in sales volume.[7] Sometimes a firm can satisfactorily test
buyers' response to price changes, thereby gauging elasticity, by quoting
different prices in selected areas.

To assess the possible sales volume at given prices, a firm must also
consider market changes in the *level of demand* for its products. The
firm can estimate its sales volume for the immediate marketing period
through a comprehensive forecasting method (see p. 246).

When the forecast indicates an increase in the level of market demand, a firm currently producing at peak capacity may increase profits
by raising its prices if the demand for its goods is comparatively inelastic. On the other hand, a firm producing at, say, 60-per-cent
capacity may improve its profit position by lowering its prices provided
the demand for its goods is relatively elastic.

Influence of Volume on Costs and Revenue. A firm can realize its
best income by regulating its volume of output, thereby adjusting its
unit cost to selling price (or its total costs to sales income). The firm
thus maximizes profits (or minimizes losses if purchasing power and
market demand are low) by producing and selling a quantity large
enough to spread its overhead costs over a large number of units,
thereby attaining low unit costs—so long as the addition to total cost
for producing the last lot is at or slightly below the addition to total
revenue (sales receipts) gained from marketing the lot. Obviously it
would be less profitable for a firm to push its output to the point
where the additional cost of producing more units is higher [8] than the
additional revenue gained—i.e., the point where marginal cost is higher
than marginal revenue.

---

[7] An "elastic demand" is one in which variations in price are accompanied
by comparatively great variations in the quantities that buyers will take; an
"inelastic demand" is one in which variations in price are accompanied by
comparatively small variations in the quantities that buyers will take.

[8] Costs may be higher because the employment of more workers as helpers
to machine operators will not yield the same addition to output as when
operators are initially assigned to unmanned machines.

Thus a firm should set its prices high enough to be profitable, yet low enough so that sales will be sufficiently large to make unit cost low, buyers will not shift to rival products, and potential competitors will not be encouraged to enter the industry.

Since most firms are confronted with a multiproduct pricing problem, they must consider the cost differentials of their products as well as the elasticity of demand for each item before they can establish the proper relationship among the prices of the group and maximize long-run profits for the entire line of products. The initial price of a new product can be set at a high level to tap the "luxury" market or at a low level to expand sales and lower output costs. The choice often rests on the degree of monopolistic control and the elasticity of demand for the item.

When firms consistently employ the *cost-plus pricing practice* [9] (always adding the same markup), they ignore elasticity of demand and the influence of volume on unit costs. Firms that use the *flexible markup practice* (i.e., regularly alter the original margin that they add to cost in the light of general business conditions) take into account elasticity of demand, changes in the level of market demand, and the influence of volume on unit cost.

In determining its "best" prices for profitable levels of output for the long run, therefore, a firm must consider not only the elasticity of demand and unit cost at various volumes of output, but also price trends of substitute products, the possible reaction (retaliation) of rival firms, possible wage demands, and, in the case of monopolies, possible government intervention.

Allocation of Customer Service Costs. A firm's price structure is affected by the manner in which it deals with guarantees, returns, and credit and collections; by practice regarding the absorption of shipping costs; and by the point where net price is quoted—f.o.b. factory, destination, or warehouse. A firm may service its products (e.g., install them, repair them, train operators in the use of them) to insure proper performance, to provide convenience to buyers, or to promote sales. Depending upon the purpose and expense involved, the cost of servicing may be included in the price, billed separately, or offered free of charge (and be absorbed as a promotion expense).

---

[9] Under cost-plus pricing a firm compiles unit costs of labor and material and computes the overhead expense at some arbitrary percentage of capacity. To this cost figure it adds its margin to arrive at the price.

The Discount Structure. The sales receipts and net profits of producers and wholesalers depend upon the quantities sold at various "real" (after discount) prices—not upon the published price lists. A firm should carefully design its discount structure (1) to fit the peculiarities of the selected market and distribution channels and the conditions surrounding sales to each class of buyers; (2) to serve as a means of adjusting prices to market changes and the competitive environment; and (3) to co-ordinate price quotations with promotional campaigns to increase sales or penetrate new markets.

By means of the discounts which it grants, a firm applies price differentials (quotes different prices) to suit particular selling situations. A *trade discount* offered to purchasers, for example, is a compensation for the performance of marketing functions. A *quantity discount* (made possible by the savings which accrue from bulk sales) is a concession to buyers of large quantities and is also used as a device to discourage small-order sales. A *cash discount* is an inducement to customers to pay promptly and a means of expediting collections. *Promotional, seasonal,* and *trade-in allowances* illustrate pricing practices adaptable to particular situations.

Retail Pricing Methods. Depending upon their preferences or the practice in their field of business, retailers may set prices (1) by observing suggestions of manufacturers and conforming to legal requirements dealing with prices; (2) by putting a flat markup on all items or a markup on individual goods in line with competition in the area; (3) by roughly estimating what the market will stand; or (4) by conforming to price levels set by leading firms in the area.

Government Regulations Affecting Price. A firm's prices may be regulated by laws. Resale price-maintenance laws (e.g., the Miller-Tydings Act and similar laws in forty-five states) allow producers to fix wholesale and retail prices below which distributors are not allowed to sell. Unfair trade-practice acts passed by twenty-two states prohibit a resale price below that of the middleman's own standard markup. Public utility commissions regulate railroad shipping, power, telephone, and other rates. Federal and state antitrust laws guard against price-fixing when it is monopolistic ("in restraint of trade").

ORGANIZATION OF THE SALES DEPARTMENT

A firm's size, the kinds of products sold, the type and size of the market, and the channels of distribution influence the organization structure of its sales department. The sales department of a manufacturing firm selling consumer goods nationally may have such divisions as market research, sales, customer service, and advertising directed by a manager whose personal duties require particular qualifications.

Duties of the General Sales Manager. As the executive accountable for effective marketing of products, the sales manager assumes the following direct responsibilities: (1) He plays an important role in the formulation of marketing policies covering lines of products (additions and revisions), the scope of marketing activities and territories, channels of distribution, pricing (preparation of price lists), and credit terms. (2) He formulates sales plans and promotional programs on the basis of company sales trends, price trends of similar and allied products, the trend of the company's selling costs, and the competitive standing of the firm, as determined by market research. (3) He prepares the sales budget through which he co-ordinates the marketing function with the activities of manufacturing, engineering, finance, and other departments so as to stabilize production, promote new or improved products, or revise credit terms, etc. (4) He assumes general direction over, and co-ordinates the activities of, the departmental divisions discussed below.

The Market Research Division. Set up to guide policy formulation and the marketing function, the market research division conducts studies in product analysis; in market analysis including distribution problems, pricing, advertising, and sales promotion; in sales performance; and in sales forecasting.

The Sales Division. Depending upon the size of the firm's market, the channels of distribution, the diversity of products, and the classes of buyers, the sales force may be subdivided along one of four lines. (1) A *territorial* subdivision (which ordinarily necessitates setting up branch offices responsible to local district managers) enables better control over outlets, permits closer supervision of the sales force, and facilitates contact with customers. (2) Subdivision according to *type of product* secures specialization in selling and is advantageous particularly for firms marketing diverse lines of technical products. A separate product sales manager may supervise the sales force for each line of goods. (3) A breakdown according to *class or type of customer* (e.g., commercial, industrial, institutional, governmental, and foreign) is effective when particular or unique conditions of sale exist for each class of buyer and when the products are not too technical. Each salesman thus becomes versed in a specialized outlet for a given type of customer. (4) A well-devised *combination* of the foregoing types of subdivisions is often suitable for firms selling diverse products nationally.

The Service Division. The successful sale of, and the expansion of the market for, some types of products necessitate setting up a customer servicing division under the sales or engineering departments. The scope of servicing varies, but it may include installation of products, instruction in the use and care of products, provision for repair and replacements, and the handling of consumers' complaints.

DEVELOPMENT AND CONTROL OF SELLING

When the over-all plan for marketing has been established, the stage is set for detailed planning and control of selling activities.

Procedure for Setting Up and Directing Selling Activities. (1) Develop an effective sales force; (2) co-ordinate activities of sales and other departments; (3) promote and advertise the products; (4) forecast sales; (5) plan and control the selling effort; and (6) analyze sales costs and appraise performance.

Development of a Sales Force. The sales manager can effectively direct and control the selling effort in the field only if he develops an efficient sales force through proper selection, training, and compensation of salesmen.

SELECTION OF SALESMEN. Since the qualifications for a salesman depend upon the type of product to be sold, the peculiarities of the geographic area and market, and the particular sales task to be done, a detailed job specification [10] must be prepared prior to recruiting personnel. A job specification, for example, may stipulate the technical qualifications and the commercial background necessary for selling machinery, steel, or chemicals to industrial purchasing agents; or, it may specify a familiarity with household needs and decorating trends and an ability to "comprehend" women. In short, the salesmanship needed to market the product determines the personal traits and qualifications required. The sales manager selects men not only for their selling ability but also for their aptitude for creating a favorable long-term relationship with customers. He can frequently find suitable recruits in the group currently employed by the company and from those who have selling experience in related fields and industries.

TRAINING. All personnel recruited require some instruction. The training program should cover company background, product use and

[10] See Ch. 23 for discussion.

performance, sales policies and procedures, terms of payment, customer service, and sales presentation. Sales managers often adopt a combination of *training methods* which may include company classes or lectures, assignment to various jobs in the plant and office (designed to school trainees in products, materials, and processes), enrollment in college courses, and understudy (apprenticeship) with experienced salesmen in the field. After the initial training period, instruction continues through informal sales conferences and sales letters which take up the problem of co-ordinating sales promotion and sales activities, new markets, product models, and selling methods.

COMPENSATION. The sales manager should design a compensation plan that attains maximum sales volume; advances the promotion program by emphasizing sale of profitable products, introduction of new products, and cultivation of new customers and markets; and keeps selling expenses low. Of the methods available, the *straight salary* plan does not offer the proper incentive and the *straight commission* plan does not provide stable enough earnings for salesmen. *Salary plus commission* (or bonus) and the usual traveling expenses provide stability of earnings and give the salesman an incentive to achieve sales quotas and other objectives. Commissions and bonuses, instead of being based on dollar volume of sales, should be differential payments based on the kind of sales work done: types of products sold (e.g., new products, profitable items), acquisition of new customers, or performance of services to customers.

Co-ordination between Sales and Other Departments. The sales manager must stress co-operation and exchange of information. He and the credit manager, for example, should co-operate in formulating or modifying the terms of sale in order to facilitate sales as well as minimize bad debts. The sales force can be helpful in supplying information to the credit manager for evaluating the credit worthiness of customers.

HOW THE SALES DEPARTMENT AIDS MANUFACTURING. By emphasizing accurate forecasting as far into the future as possible, the sales department assists the manufacturing department in its effort to minimize seasonal fluctuations and stabilize production. It carefully watches shifts in demand for various products so that slow-moving items will not be overstocked and poor-selling items may be dropped at the appropriate time. It seeks out new products that will minimize seasonal slacks and take up unused plant capacity. When the demand for particular products seems on the upswing, the sales manager gives timely notice to the plant manager so that he may have ample opportunity effectively to revise the layout, expand capacity, and lower unit cost through work-simplification surveys.

How the Manufacturing Division Aids Sales. The head of manufacturing should keep the sales manager posted on the contribution to earnings of each product sold so that he may promote the sale of those items with high profit margins. Information on the kinds and amounts of idle plant capacity will direct salesmen to seek the type of orders and business that will put idle machines to work. When the plant meets early-delivery promise dates, company good will is enhanced and the sales department can more readily obtain repeat orders.

Promotion and Advertising. Market studies and a careful analysis of the flow of company products through their channels of distribution should guide the preparation of sales promotion programs. Promotion through periodic and strategic introduction of new models, special pricing such as use of a "price" leader (a product sold at a loss) and extra trade-in and seasonal discounts, displays and demonstrations, and the various forms of advertising [11] should be co-ordinated with the efforts of personal salesmanship to stimulate a desire for purchase by customers.

Forecasting. An effective system should be developed to estimate sales for the immediate marketing period. A *combination of the following methods* should be employed to compile data which make up the sales forecast. (1) Salesmen, on the basis of their contacts and knowledge of customers' needs, can estimate the sales in their respective territories. (2) The research division can analyze past sales volume and arrive at a seasonally adjusted forecast figure which should be useful if market conditions are somewhat the same as in the past. Whenever possible, research should forecast sales figures through a statistical correlation showing the causal relationship between the firm's sales volume and some controlling factors which have predictive value and are more readily measurable (e.g., the sale of household furnishings and building supplies may be forecast on the basis of the number of building permits issued for dwellings in a given period). (3) The results obtained through salesmen's estimates and through statistical forecasting methods are appraised and revised (if necessary) by top executives on the basis of management's survey of general business trends as indicated by a regional breakdown of national income and employment figures, by turns in the business cycle, by shifts in the

[11] See p. 249 for procedure.

general price level and interest rates, by government economic and fiscal (taxes, borrowings, and expenditures) programs, and by consumer credit controls (see sales estimate or budget, Fig. 63).

Methods of Planning and Controlling the Selling Effort. By drawing upon the results of market research and forecasting, the sales manager, with the assistance of supervisors, develops programs and directs the selling effort. He aids salesmen through office services, encourages "selective" selling, plans sales routes, sets sales quotas, and appraises sales performance.

SUPPORTING SALES EFFORT. As previously noted, best vending results are obtained through careful selection of salesmen, continuous training, a well-designed incentive compensation plan, and the building of morale. In addition, the office staff should aid salesmen by providing them with records of customers' past purchases and with information on promotion plans and new product offerings, on the practices of competitors, and on market trends. Sales correspondents (special personnel in the sales office) assist by receiving customers' inquiries, by handling mail and telephone orders, by setting delivery dates, and by directing salesmen to prospective purchasers.

PROMOTING SELECTIVE SELLING. In order to maximize high-profit sales, the sales force should employ a selective selling approach. A study of territories and past sales to customers can point to where the potential demand for, and prospective sales of, profitable items are the greatest. The field force should cultivate sales to potential big buyers by carefully assessing their needs, by improving and expediting deliveries to such customers, by extending extra service to create good will, and by applying intensive personal sales effort. Proportionately less selling effort may be devoted to territories and customers with smaller potential demand; and inexpensive channels of distribution may be developed for the less profitable segments of the market.

PLANNING SALES ROUTES. To save time and effort the salesmen, aided by the office staff, should plan an economical route for thorough coverage of the market. The office can prepare a list of important calls and schedule these in co-ordination with the mailing of promotional literature to customers.

SETTING SALES QUOTAS FOR CONTROL. Managers should set up *sales quotas* to serve as an incentive, a measure of performance, and a basis for bonuses or commissions. "Sales quotas" are, in essence, a breakdown of the sales estimates by territories. To be equitable and readily attainable, sales quotas should be established for clearly defined territories and with consideration of the peculiarities of each territory—the number of outlets, past sales, the extent of competition, and promotional effort expended in the area.

ANALYZING SALES PERFORMANCE. The planning and control of sales effort must be based on records and reports compiled by salesmen or prepared by the sales office. Salesmen should be required to make daily and/or weekly performance (or summary) reports on total sales, number of calls, orders sold and orders lost, expenses, and market information. In order to uncover errors in forecasting and to evaluate the effectiveness of promotional campaigns and sales effort, the sales office should prepare reports comparing actual sales with sales estimates. It should also compare actual sales with sales quotas to evaluate the performance of salesmen and to arrive at a basis for "guiding" individual salesmen. Records on customers and prospective buyers should be kept to show volume, kind and time of purchase, discounts granted, and credit terms. A study of sales trends by products, areas, and classes of buyers may suggest modification of products, territories, outlets, price and discount structure, or customer service; improved selling methods may be introduced for more intensive selling and for opening up new fields.

Sales Cost Analysis. Distribution cost analysis as well as market research must be employed to develop and direct sales programs.

SALES EXPENSES. The cost of distribution includes such items as sales promotion and advertising, sales office overhead, compensation and expense accounts of the sales staff, shipping, and installation.

ALLOCATION OF SALES EXPENSES. The foregoing expenses do not serve as effective guides when they are lumped in a total. For cost analysis, sales expenses must be allocated to territories, products, and sales functions—e.g., costs of shipping to various areas, promoting various items, and handling sales orders. The degree of segregation of costs depends upon the analytic usefulness of the breakdown.

BENEFITS. Expense data provide a basis for comparing costs for each branch office, territory, product, or function. Such important questions as the contribution of each territory and of each product to profits can thus be answered and decisions made as to which territories to exploit more intensively, and which to reassign or drop. The sale of profitable products may then be pushed; "minimum" order quantities can be set on the basis of costs; the principle of selective selling can be more effectively applied; a useful sales departmental (expense) budget can be drawn up; and a logical basis for reducing distribution costs can be developed in terms of simplifying packaging, catalogs, record keeping, and clerical activities.

ADVERTISING AND PROMOTION

Advertising and promotion, as integral parts of the marketing effort, strive to realize the goals laid out by sales policy and programs. Advertising and publicity support the field sales effort by enhancing market acceptability of a firm's products and services. *Advertising* is the art of disseminating marketing information through various media of communication (such as newspapers, magazines, and radio) at the expense of the company for the purpose of increasing (or maintaining) effective demand and facilitating the sale of specific goods and services. It may be employed to promote the marketing of a product or it may be employed to promote an idea. *Publicity* is information concerning a firm and its product made available to the public by various media of communication without charge to the firm, because of its newsworthiness or other value to the disseminator. A firm's publicity office endeavors to promote favorable and suppress unfavorable news items.

Procedure for Establishing the Advertising Function. (1) Formulate advertising policy; (2) organize the function as an independent department or as a subdivision under the sales department; (3) delegate duties to the advertising office; and (4) develop methods for planning and conducting advertising.

Formulation of Advertising Policy. The sales manager and the advertising manager formulate advertising policy subject to the approval of the president or general manager. The policies stipulate the purpose and scope of advertising, the method of providing for advertising, and the amount of money to be spent for advertising.

PURPOSES OF ADVERTISING. Depending on its marketing objectives, management outlines one or more of the following as the goals of advertising: (1) to introduce a new product, model, or service to the market; (2) to facilitate or increase the sale of present products by constantly keeping the commodity before the market, thereby maintaining consumer awareness, offsetting the advertisements of competing firms,[12] and reducing the amount of personal sales effort re-

[12] When advertising is excessive or aims primarily to meet or offset competitors' promotional activities, it is considered by many economists to be a socially wasteful practice which raises the cost of commodities to consumers with no added benefits. However, since the expense of advertising is an allowable cost for tax purposes and because advertising is a widespread commercial practice, many firms spend large funds for essentially "defensive" advertising.

quired to secure an order; (3) to enlighten the public as to the features and uses of the products and overcome tradition or prejudices that may retard consumption; (4) to create or enhance company good will and thereby maintain or increase present and future market receptiveness to the firm's products or services.

The sales manager should periodically reappraise the advertising goals and co-ordinate them with the current promotional program and the shifts in the market.

SCOPE. Advertising may be done nationally or regionally. Its scope may be strictly confined to advertising or it may be enlarged to include such matters as public relations and participation in bettering employee morale.

USE OF THE ADVERTISING AGENCY. The company may conduct its own advertising or hire the services of an advertising agency. The growing popularity of the agency plan is due to the expert services offered by the agency at a low cost as compared with the cost to the company of handling its own advertising. The advertising agency can economically employ specialists for research, preparation of copy, and selection of media because of its volume of business and the substantial discounts (usually 15 per cent) which it generally obtains from the media that it selects. Such discounts are usually not available to individual company advertisers. Though a firm buys specialized services from an agency, it must nevertheless establish an advertising office for co-ordination, control, and liaison with the agency.

Manufacturers producing comparatively uniform products frequently find it advantageous to undertake co-operative promotion and advertising through their trade associations.

BUDGETARY APPROPRIATIONS. Although the amount to be expended is largely determined by the purposes of advertising, the sales promotion programs, the media selected, and the magnitude of corporate income taxes, management nonetheless places limits on expenditures. The advertising manager and the sales manager, with the participation of other interested executives, prepare the advertising budget. Appropriations to the various products may be distributed equally, on the basis of profits contributed by each item, or on the basis of the promotional plan for each line of products. Excessive advertising of a given item may be as wasteful as inadequate advertising.

Organization of the Advertising Department. Although the status of advertising in the organization varies, the advertising manager is generally placed under the sales manager. When a wide scope of activities is delegated to advertising and when the company is a multi-plant and/or multiproduct firm, advertising may be placed directly under the general manager or the president.

Duties of the Advertising Department. The advertising manager participates with the sales manager and other departments in developing sales promotion campaigns. Working generally through a carefully selected agency, he plans and develops the advertising phase of promotions and directs the activities discussed hereunder.

SUPERVISING ADVERTISING THROUGH BUDGETARY CONTROL. Appropriations, when broken down for each campaign and further subdivided by areas and products, aid in achieving the goals outlined. One or more members of the staff should assume responsibility for evaluating the effectiveness of advertising and for conducting research to develop ways and means of increasing the amount of actual advertising derived from expenditures. The company should make certain that the "appeal" of advertisements is tested before large sums of money are expended.

MAINTAINING LIAISON WITH THE AGENCY AND CONTACT WITH MEDIA. The advertising manager assumes the primary responsibility for clarifying company advertising policy and plans to the agency. When the products are varied and of a technical nature, he will maintain close co-operation with the agency, providing information on the technical aspects of the product (obtained from the engineering and research departments), on geographical coverage, on volume of business, and on promotional plans. When goods are nontechnical, he may largely delegate to the agency responsibility for the preparation of copy and the selection of the media.

The advertising department should nonetheless maintain direct contact with the media in order to further good relations and keep abreast of trends and developments in the field.

CO-ORDINATING ADVERTISING WITH SALES. Teamwork in executing sales policy and developing sales promotion and advertising plans is of paramount importance. Ineffective co-ordination leads to frustration and waste of funds. The sales force can aid the advertising office by providing helpful information for planning campaigns and by following up and reporting on the effectiveness of advertising. Advertising, when effective, can be of great value to the sales force in reducing the effort required to secure orders and in increasing sales.

Methods of Planning and Conducting Advertising. Advertising involves (1) locating the potential demand and the class of buyers to which advertisements are to be directed,[13] (2) ascertaining the buying motives, (3) selecting the most effective and economical media, (4) preparing advertisements, and (5) appraising the marketing effectiveness of advertising.

ASCERTAINING BUYING MOTIVES AND ADVERTISING APPEAL. After the market and class of buyers have been identified, the consumers' buying motives must be determined in order that an effective advertising appeal can be formulated and appropriate media selected. Typical buying motives (which vary with the nature of the product and the class of buyers) include economy, efficiency, quality and desirability, reliability, ease of operation, reputation, and quick delivery.

SELECTING THE MEDIA. The media selected should reach the largest number of prospective buyers and exert the greatest market influence at the lowest cost. For manufacturers of industrial goods such direct media as letters and catalogs and such indirect media as trade and technical journals are most effective. For general consumer goods the appeal is best made through appropriate mass media such as newspapers, popular journals, radio, and outdoor ads.

PREPARING ADVERTISEMENTS. Copywriters and layout and other artists collaborate to prepare advertisements. Ads may be of one color and contain copy only or they may feature color, illustrations, and slogans. Copy must always be carefully written and designed to appeal to the prospective customer.

APPRAISING RESULTS. The effectiveness and cost of various media per unit of sales or customer may to some extent be determined by keeping constant as many of the marketing factors as possible and then trying various media. Advertising effectiveness may also be tested by selecting two similar cities; running an advertising campaign in one, using the other for control; and then measuring the results by comparing sales in the two cities. A method of "keying" is also sometimes used to gauge the effectiveness of a medium or the pulling power of a given advertisement. For example, a newspaper or a radio ad may request a response (mailing of a clipping, presentation of a coupon, a telephone call) to a free offer. The effects of such advertising, however, are often cumulative and delayed.

---

[13] This study is usually undertaken by the market research office, as described earlier in this chapter.

Questions

1. What are the causes of the high cost of marketing as a proportion of the total costs of producing and distributing products?

2. What sources does "product research" investigate to determine the products consumers desire?

3. What are the primary considerations in selecting channels of distribution?

4. How may the potential demand for a new product be determined?

5. How do firms under imperfect competition gain some market control in the sale of a given type of product and thus acquire a degree of price-fixing power?

6. Outline the procedural steps for setting or adjusting prices in a manufacturing firm turning out consumer products.

7. (a) In setting its prices, why must a firm in a monopolistic position appraise the influence of price changes on sales volume—i.e., elasticity of demand? (b) Why must the firm also consider the effect of volume (rate) of output on unit costs before it sets its prices?

8. How may a firm's policies covering shipping and customer servicing affect its prices?

9. What are the purposes and uses of a manufacturer's price discounts?

10. What are the factors that influence the organization structure of the sales department?

11. What are four ways in which a field sales division may be broken down?

12. What duties are generally assumed by the sales manager?

13. Outline the procedural steps for setting up and directing sales activities.

14. What kinds of training methods may be adopted to develop personnel recruited for the position of field salesmen?

15. What factors should be considered in developing a compensation plan for salesmen?

16. Illustrate how the sales department can aid manufacturing and how the manufacturing division can aid the sales department.

17. What combination of methods may be employed to forecast sales?

18. How does "selective selling" reduce selling expense and how is such selling achieved?

19. How can sales performance be measured?

20. Why do many firms hire the services of advertising agencies?

21. What is the procedure for establishing a company advertising function and what are the steps in planning and conducting advertising?

22. Evaluate the following statement: "Countries of low income per capita (e.g., India) can raise their standards of living by large-scale nation-wide advertising which creates market demand and permits adoption of mass-production methods that lower costs and selling prices."

23: Industrial Relations: Public Relations, Labor Relations, and Personnel Management

Management directs its industrial relations through three closely allied programs. Through *public relations* it controls and improves company contacts with the public, professional groups, government agencies, and the business community; through *labor (or joint) relations*, it deals with the problems of union representation, collective bargaining, labor contract negotiation and enforcement, and grievance procedures; through *personnel management* it aims at increasing labor efficiency by studying and regulating such problems as recruitment, training, safety and health, job evaluation, and wage administration. When these three activities are properly integrated and co-ordinated, industrial relations are at their most effective level.

PUBLIC RELATIONS

Management has come to realize, particularly in the past few decades, that friendly relations with the general public and public understanding and appreciation of the objectives and aims of business are of prime importance to the welfare of its enterprise. Many firms now utilize a public-relations office to control external contacts in order to reduce misunderstanding, favorably influence public opinion, and create good will; this, in turn, brings about better stockholder, customer, and creditor relationships; lessens industrial disputes; and leads to more favorable governmental consideration.

Public relations is the art of communicating ideas and facts to promote better understanding. In the large firm, public-relations officers, accountable directly to top management, are educational and research specialists who are aided by a staff well grounded in journalism, press relations, social psychology, economics, and business practices. They study the firm's policies and trend of development, with special reference to public needs and attitudes, in an attempt to harmonize the two; they regulate contacts between the company and the public, serving as interpreters and disseminators of information for both. They advise top management in the formulation of company policies that will be accepted by the general public; and they "sell" company policies to the public by various means of communication, such as newspapers, radio, speeches, bulletins, and exhibits. They conduct a continual educational program from the public viewpoint to acquaint employees, stockholders, customers, creditors, educators, and the general community with the soundness of company practices and policies.

A company *public-relations program* is a plan for gaining acceptance of the firm's objectives and practices. Employees can be reached through the company magazine and the public address system, and their opinions about the company can be ascertained from attitude surveys. Stockholders' interest can be heightened through attractive, simplified annual statements. Open-house days will familiarize the public with the company and foster community interest. Special plant tours gain the sympathy of professional groups. News releases and radio and television programs help hold public interest.

LABOR RELATIONS

Labor relations involves joint participation of employers and employees in determining policy concerned with compensation, hours, and working conditions. There are three major areas of contact between management and labor: union organization activities, collective bargaining, and employee grievance procedure.

Union Organization. Unions acquire members by conducting organizational campaigns and by offering workers the prospect of obtaining these advantages: increased income; shorter working hours; paid vacations and holidays; improved working conditions; greater economic and job security through seniority, insurance, and pension plans; and higher status and prestige through participation in joint relations. Unions strive to gain these objectives by organizing workers into bargaining units; by increasing membership for greater bargaining power; by skillful collective bargaining; by applying economic pressure through strike threats, work stoppages, picket lines, and boycotts; by seeking favorable public opinion; and by promoting favorable government legislation dealing with labor relations. Unions endeavor to incorporate their demands in written agreements with management.

POSITION OF MANAGEMENT. Higher wages and rising indirect costs incident to welfare plans and to other labor benefits may place unionized companies at an economic disadvantage relative to nonunionized firms: excessive union demands may weaken the ability of management to fulfill its responsibility to pay dividends to stockholders. Management, therefore, strives to attach greater responsibility to unions for the well-being of the business, holding that both labor and management have a common interest in maintaining a healthy enterprise. Many employers view joint relations as a realistic means of communicating and dealing with workers; through such relations, an employer can ascertain the employees' attitudes toward the company and can take actions that will contribute to improving morale and long-run relationships.

PUBLIC POLICY DEALING WITH JOINT RELATIONS. The Supreme Court decision upholding the National Labor Relations Act in 1937 legally guaranteed collective bargaining to the vast majority of employees in interstate commerce.[1] Business groups are generally reconciled to the view that employees have the right to negotiate wages, hours, and working conditions through legal collective bargaining. Since the middle thirties, unions have expanded largely because of the Wagner Act and the competition for members between the CIO and AFL; by 1954 some 15 million employees belonged to organized labor. The vast majority of them were in transportation, construction, mining, and the mass-production industries—steel, automobile, electrical, rubber, meat-packing, glass, and clothing.

Collective Bargaining. "Collective bargaining" is the process of negotiating terms of employment and other conditions of work between the representatives of management and organized labor. When it is free of intimidation and coercion and is conducted in good faith,

---

1 Congress in the National Labor Relations (Wagner) Act of 1935 "legalized" union organizations and the right of unions to bargain collectively with management. It set up the N.L.R. Board to administer the act, certify bargaining units, and receive complaints of certain stipulated employer unfair practices. The Labor Management Relations (Taft-Hartley) Act of 1947 amended the N.L.R. Act; among other things it increased union responsibility, placed restraints on unions, provided protection for employer and employees against unfair union practices, and permitted government injunctions in industrial disputes affecting national health and welfare.

collective bargaining culminates in a workable contract.[2] The contract usually calls for joint enforcement and administration of the agreement. Responsible labor leaders and employers are increasingly settling their differences around the conference table rather than through industrial warfare. The process of bargaining and the settlement of disputes are often facilitated through outside assistance in the form of conciliation, mediation, or arbitration.[3]

REQUIREMENTS FOR SUCCESSFUL NEGOTIATION. The representatives or spokesmen of management and labor must have sufficient authority to bind each side in the negotiation. The representatives must have a thorough knowledge of the company wage scale and the wage scales of the industry and of the area. They should be versed in all points at issue and know past court decisions relating to similar cases. They should study all the proposed clauses to the contract and arrive at tentative agreements. The negotiators sign an agreement only after all outstanding issues are settled. *Contract provisions* in labor agreements generally stipulate details concerning union membership; the duration of agreement; the procedure for termination or amendment; wages and hours; overtime; shift differentials; insurance and other benefits; seniority; grievance procedure; and conditions for hire, promotion, or dismissal.

ROLE OF THE PERSONNEL DIRECTOR. Collective bargaining, a top management function, is generally the responsibility of operating executives, with the personnel director participating in a merely advisory capacity. When the personnel director takes an active role in negotiations, he should be given the title of vice-president. After a labor contract has been signed, the personnel director plays an active role in implementing the agreement, usually interpreting the contract provisions to foremen and supervisors, handling or participating in the grievance procedure, reviewing discharge and transfer cases, and activating various labor-management committees.

---

[2] A "labor contract" is a collective agreement between the representatives of labor and management for the sale of labor services at designated wage rates, hours of work, and other terms of employment and conditions of work for a stated period of time.

[3] Although conciliation and mediation are often used synonymously, in the strict sense *conciliation* is merely the bringing together by a third party of the two parties in dispute, whereas *mediation* involves the active participation of the third party in working out a compromise or a formula of settlement acceptable to both sides. *Arbitration*, on the other hand, is a semijudicial process wherein an impartial third party hears or receives evidence and then hands down a decision which, by advance agreement of the disputants, is binding upon both parties.

Grievance Procedure. The cumulative effect of employee griev-ances, minor irritations, and dissatisfactions disrupts business opera-tions unless a carefully worked out procedure is set up (regardless of whether or not a firm is unionized) to resolve dissatisfaction sys-tematically in such a manner as to eliminate the causes promptly and to relieve employee feelings of discontent or injustice. In unionized companies employees ordinarily present their grievances to their shop steward, who in turn takes up the unsettled matter with the super-visor. When grievances are not settled at the lower managerial level, they are dealt with at a higher level according to the procedure outlined in the labor agreement. Frequently the business agent or another union officer takes up the unsettled issues with a major company executive or the president. If no settlement is made at this juncture, arbitration or further collective bargaining is often necessary to effect a solution.

Employee Representation Plans. Management is generally more effective when employees enjoy a measure of participation in the affairs of the enterprise, particularly with regard to matters affecting employee welfare and conditions of work. In addition to the participation afforded by responsible unionism, *consultative management* may be extended in a variety of forms in both unionized and nonunionized companies. Labor-management committees, for instance, have been established in such areas as safety, shop rules, suggestion systems, waste reduction, job evaluation, credit unions, and recreation. Moreover, *multiple-management* plans have been established with varying degrees of suc-cess. This form of consultative management involves the setting up of a junior board of directors that studies operations and makes recom-mendations to the senior board. In general, these various forms of par-ticipation heighten morale and interest employees in their jobs.

PERSONNEL MANAGEMENT

When management has the unrealistic, narrow outlook that labor is primarily an adjunct to the machine and is to be purchased in the cheapest market, its organization will be ineffective—human resources will be wasted and workers will consider the company undesirable to work for. Not only will the organization be fraught with irritations and frustrations resulting in inefficiency; it will not be successful in recruit-ing the caliber of personnel necessary for profitable operation.

Personnel relations are effective when management realizes that employees are human beings with a number of motivating drives, who differ in emotional make-up, ability, and levels of aspiration. Progressive management, recognizing that employees respect leadership and executive ability, develops the talents and skills of employees and supervisors and creates a harmonious relationship within the organization. In this way, employees partially fulfill their drives and needs in the organization and thus not only experience a larger human reward but also make a more sizable contribution to company goals. Enlightened management, aware that specialists are required to deal with the technical aspects of the business (product, process and equipment, finance, and commercial law), also knows that experts should deal with the human aspect of production—one which is complex, dynamic, and volatile, particularly in the larger organization. With this knowledge management carefully selects for its personnel staff experts who have a mature understanding of, and sympathy for, people and who are versed in the findings of industrial psychology and other social sciences and in modern methods and techniques of *personnel administration*.

"Personnel administration," therefore, is the systematic recruitment of a competent working force whose human resources are effectively used through the control of the occupational environment in a manner that develops employees' potentials and enables them to contribute valuable services to the organization of which they are an integral part.

Prerequisites for Successful Personnel Administration. If personnel administration is to be successful, management must give it sincere support. Management tangibly expresses such interest by its willingness to hire a high-caliber staff of personnel experts; by adopting sound policies, programs, and procedures; and by training foremen in good personnel methods and seeing that the methods are put into practice.

Both management and labor are inseparable participants in the enterprise. Each has definite needs and obligations which require consideration and fulfillment. The employer wants efficient methods of production, high labor productivity, quality workmanship, co-operative labor, good morale, and industrial peace. The employee wants job and economic security, fair wages for work done, desirable working conditions, opportunity for advancement, self-expression through participation, and a sense of dignity stemming from his productive role in society.

Procedure for Setting Up the Personnel Department. (1) Outline the goals and objectives of the personnel program; (2) formulate sound personnel policies; (3) determine the status of personnel administration in the organization structure; (4) delegate duties to the personnel department; and (5) develop systems for recruiting and maintaining a working force, for training employees, for providing employee services, for keeping records and conducting research, and for maintaining health and safety.

Objectives of Personnel Administration. The goals of personnel administration are to increase the efficiency of the labor force, raise morale, and improve working relationships in the enterprise.

LABOR EFFICIENCY. A full-fledged personnel program justifies its existence by improving the effectiveness of employees and lowering labor costs in various ways. For example, the personnel department, as a central agency for recruitment, employee services, and records saves time for foremen and enables them to concentrate more effectively on the problems of production. Through a hiring program (e.g., labor budgeting) it avoids labor shortages and secures a high-caliber working force. By properly selecting and placing individuals in jobs suited to their talents, it eliminates misfits. Through training and the provision of a healthy working environment, it secures a high level of workmanship. By devising an effective wage system (including incentive payment where applicable) it increases labor output. Through an employee suggestion-box plan it improves production methods and secures worker interest and participation. By eliminating hazards and establishing a company medical service, it reduces accidents and injuries, absenteeism, and lost working time. Through exit interviews and attitude surveys, it reduces costly labor turnover. Through an effective grievance procedure and strict adherence to the labor contract, it reduces labor strife.

MORALE. "Morale," the intangible factor contributing to favorable working relations, is the attitude or frame of mind that grows out of an over-all occupational environment in which individuals integrate their personal desires in varying degrees with the ultimate goals of the organization and thereby experience personal satisfaction through identification with the organization. Such a working relationship— obtained by enlightened leadership and sound personnel policies and practices—raises labor productivity through increased employee co-operation and participation and continued industrial peace.

Formulation of Personnel Policies. Well-conceived company policies formulated by top management with the participation of the personnel director must guide the personnel program. Policies should be harmoniously integrated with the business goals of the enterprise and should avoid opportunism and paternalism. Sound policies recognize individual differences in interests, capacities, and desire for security as well as the tendency for employees to seek a voice in the phase of management in which they are vitally interested. Through collective bargaining and labor-management committees, employees participate in the determination of policies about which they are concerned.

Policies find their origin both in managerial acceptance of principles of personnel administration and in key managerial decisions relating to various phases of labor relations. Policies based on principles of personnel administration are exemplified by those (1) to provide safe working conditions and reasonable working hours; (2) to place workers in positions for which they are best suited; (3) to provide opportunity for advancement and to aid employee growth through effective training programs and promotion from within the organization; and (4) to encourage free communication of employees with executives concerning their interests or the company welfare.

Policies based on managerial decisions dealing with labor relations are exemplified by those (1) to compensate employees at the wage level prevailing in the area and industry; (2) to adopt individual and group incentive-payment plans; (3) to further economic security through the stabilization of production and employment, a guaranteed annual wage, union-management sponsored unemployment insurance, medical insurance, and pensions; (4) to encourage employee participation through the suggestion-box plan and joint committees.

To guard against ill-conceived actions at lower levels of supervision, which might distort or negate managerial decisions, policies must be implemented through an adequately staffed personnel department, through a well-devised system of procedures and practices, and through the education of supervisors to carry them out.

Status of Personnel Administration in the Organization. Set up as a staff department, the personnel office performs its duties as a service to the entire organization. Operating executives, foremen, and supervisors require the expert assistance and advice of the personnel office in dealing with the human relations aspect of business operations. Many personnel activities (recruiting, testing, counseling, and other services) are best provided through a central agency since they can not effectively be performed by line officers and supervisors in the course of their work. The personnel specialists generally work through department heads and supervisors, for they try not to weaken the authority of line men or to disturb the close relationship between line men and their subordinates.

The segregation of personnel administration from operating activities is almost universal in large firms. In most cases the personnel director, particularly if he performs a great variety of functions, is directly responsible to the chief executive of the company. A personnel director whose function is mainly that of dealing with the factory labor force may be responsible to the manufacturing executive. In a small firm, the personnel function may be assigned to the plant superintendent or to an officer with special aptitude for personnel administration.

Delegation of Duties to the Personnel Department. The types of activities that may be directed by the personnel officer, who develops and co-ordinates personnel policies and programs, are as follows (each of these is usually set up as a subdivision of his department): (1) *employment and maintenance of the working force*—development of labor sources, interviewing, testing, selection, placement, follow-up, transfer and promotion, and control of absenteeism and turnover; (2) *training*—instruction of new employees, apprentices, foremen, and minor executives; (3) *services*—provision or arrangement for cafeterias, rest rooms, counseling, group insurance, recreation, and an employee magazine; (4) *records and research*—maintenance of employee records, statistics, rules, and other data and surveys covering labor laws, labor audit, occupational trends, and employee attitudes; (5) *health and safety*—provision of health and medical services, a safety program, and good working conditions; (6) *wage and salary administration*—participation in job analysis, specification, and evaluation; employee merit rating; wage administration; and wage surveys (discussed in Ch. 24); (7) *joint (labor-management) relations*—collective bargaining, operation of labor contract, grievance procedure, labor-management committees, and group programs (discussed previously in this chapter); and (8) *public relations*—arrangements for, and control of, contacts with community and professional groups, business organizations, employees, government agencies, and publicity and communication media.

The collective bargaining phase of labor relations is ordinarily handled by the top (or other major) operating executive. The personnel director, however, serves as an advisor and aids in the implementation of the labor agreement. The public relations function in the large firm is often set up as a separate activity under top management.

Employment Practice: Recruitment and Maintenance of Force. To secure an effective labor force, the personnel department must (1) develop adequate sources of labor supply; (2) prepare and use job specifications; (3) appraise the results of application blanks and interviews; (4) conduct employee tests where necessary; (5) select candidates from screened applicants; (6) induct and follow up the placement of new employees; (7) make transfers and promotions for adjustment and maintenance of force; (8) control absenteeism and tardiness; and (9) control labor turnover.

Sources of Labor. The labor market should be carefully studied to select the best sources of labor supply for the firm.

Labor from Within the Company. It is ordinarily a sound policy "to hire from within." To fill a job opening through promotion or transfer, whenever possible, contributes to good morale since it indicates that employees have a future and can advance in the company. Former employees with a good service record can also be notified of a vacancy. (This practice reduces the cost of hiring and training and furthers good will.) And responsible present employees can be encouraged to recommend friends and acquaintances.

Unsolicited Applicants. Many firms can satisfactorily fill vacancies from individuals who apply in person or by mail. Files of these unsolicited applicants should be kept up to date.

Employment Agencies. The cost of recruitment can be reduced through utilization of carefully selected, reputable agencies that specialize in various classes of labor. Private, public, union, and fraternal employment agencies are available in large towns.

Schools. Scouting and selection of personnel from technical schools and universities have been found satisfactory by many firms.

Advertising. Newspapers, trade journals, and the radio are good recruitment media, particularly for skilled and professional labor.

Preparation of Job Specification. Job specifications developed through job analysis are an important aid in selecting the right man for the job, particularly in the large firm. The specification is a formal statement outlining the important characteristics of the job and employee qualifications. It generally includes the job title and number, equipment, tools and material used, a description of work to be done, working conditions, compensation, training required, the opportunity for advancement, and the qualifications for a satisfactory worker. Job specifications are also useful for transfer and promotion of employees, in training programs, in wage negotiations, for job evaluation, and for improving the organization structure.

Employment Application and Interview. Application blanks should be simple and clear, requesting all information necessary for evaluating the applicant. The applicant's suitability for a position can further be determined through a properly conducted interview. The interviewer should familiarize himself with the applicant's qualifications. In order more effectively to screen applicants he consults past records, test results, physical examination reports, and other objective data when these are available. The interviewer prepares a list of questions covering all aspects of the job as summarized in the specification. He conducts his interviews privately and is frank, yet tactful, courteous, and friendly. The interviewer puts the applicant at ease and ascertains the interviewee's qualifications in order to appraise his suitability for a position as objectively as possible.

TESTS. Many large firms use employment tests, in conjunction with application forms and interviews, for selecting, placing, and training personnel. When properly used, tests reduce guesswork; but they are of more value in identifying potential misfits and failures than in selecting probable successes. Moreover, unless tests are specially designed by industrial psychologists for a particular job, they are often of little value; and the high cost of preparing tests for many jobs makes them of but limited value for the small and medium-sized firms. The personnel director should decide which of the following kinds of tests are of sufficient practical value to be adopted by the firm.

Physical Examinations. Medical checkups are given by many firms since they aid in determining the applicant's physical fitness for a particular job. Physically handicapped persons, when they are properly placed and trained at suitable occupations, are not handicapped with respect to productivity on the job.

Intelligence Tests. IQ tests can help reduce misfits by identifying applicants who fall below minimum standards and those who have considerably more mental ability than is required for the job.

Trade Tests. Tests designed to measure proficiency in a given craft or trade are practical when they can be economically administered, as they can, for example, when they consist primarily of questions and pictures for identification and explanation, or when they involve a demonstration of work.

Aptitude Tests. Aptitude tests are used to determine whether an individual has certain minimum natural abilities or talents that can be developed through training. For example, they can measure finger dexterity, motor co-ordination, color blindness, and hearing acuity. Mechanical aptitude tests are those most commonly used.

Psychological Tests. Examinations designed to measure emotional stability, introversion-extroversion, interests, etc., are generally expensive to design and administer for specific jobs. When successfully applied, however, they aid in placing individuals in supervisory, sales, receptionist, or other positions for which they are fitted by reason of temperament and personality traits. They are also of value in employee counseling and vocational guidance.

FINAL APPROVAL FOR HIRE. After applicants have been screened through the evaluation of application blanks and the appraisal of interviews and test results, the best candidates for the job are hired. The employment office usually takes care of hiring for unskilled jobs. For skilled and semiskilled jobs the foreman or supervisor who originally placed the labor requisition generally has the right to select men from the applicants screened by the employment office. Applicants not selected are tactfully notified that the position has been filled.

INDUCTION AND FOLLOW-UP. A *planned induction* properly welcomes a new employee, creates a good attitude, and reduces labor turnover. It should include a friendly introduction to fellow workers, a tour to familiarize the new man with the plant and its employee service facilities, and a presentation of an employee manual giving a bird's-eye view of the company, its products, policies, rules, and privileges. It is the foreman's responsibility to help orient the worker, making him feel at home and a part of the working team. A periodic follow-up visit by the original interviewer to the employee on his job checks the success of the placement, furthers morale, and helps the employee to adjust.

TRANSFERS AND PROMOTION. Personnel placement is not fixed or static. Through periodic follow-ups, the personnel department will discover some errors in placement which should, whenever possible, be rectified through transfer. Good employees whose job interests have changed or who have become dissatisfied should be transferred. Business fluctuations and organizational, technological, or other changes frequently make it necessary to lay off men in one department and take on more workers in another department. Planned transfers in such cases contribute to job security and also reduce labor turnover.

When openings occur on higher job levels, qualified employees should be given an opportunity to better themselves through promotion; obviously, though, if properly qualified company personnel are not available, men should be hired from outside sources. Through an analysis of job specifications of all positions, the personnel department can work out a promotion scheme showing *lines of progression* from job to job. Such a policy will contribute to morale building and avoid the waste of employee talents and ability. Supervisors should send to the personnel department recommendations for promotions, but promotions should be made by the department on the basis of its personnel records and subject to the approval of the employee's immediate superior. Promotions should be made when employees at lower job levels are overqualified or have qualified themselves for a higher position through growth and experience, through a company training program, or through outside education. Merit rating [4] plans which periodically gauge employee progress are useful additions to a promotion scheme.

CONTROL OF ABSENTEEISM AND TARDINESS. A study of the causes of absenteeism and tardiness can reduce production interruptions. When the data are broken down by departments, occupations, sex, and frequency, analysis will point to corrective measures—shift changes, changes in bus schedules for commuting, elimination of job misfits, health promotion, or improvement of supervisory relations and morale in general. Tardiness can also be reduced by discontinuing privileges.

CONTROL OF LABOR TURNOVER. High labor turnover (replacements in the labor force) increases costs because it creates a greater need for recruitment and training and because it results in lower labor efficiency, increased spoilage, and poor use of machinery. High labor turnover may reflect a fluctuating demand for workers because of the seasonality of the business, or it may be the result of labor discontent and poor personnel administration practices. On the other hand, a very low labor turnover is not necessarily desirable since it may reflect stagnation in the working force.

The reduction of high labor turnover must start with statistical analysis. The number of "exits" or replacements in a given period per 100 employees should be classified as to layoffs, discharges, and quits and should be broken down by departments. Turnover figures are more useful when expressed in terms of "avoidable separations" divided by the "average labor force." Excessive turnover, determined by comparing actual replacements against reasonable turnover limits, may be reduced (1) by using the exit interview to uncover causes, (2) by controlling discharges, and (3) by stabilizing production and sharing work.

Exit interviews of employees who have quit may uncover some of the underlying causes for withdrawals. The causes may be external, such as poor means of commuting, inadequate housing, higher wages offered by other employers; or, they may be internal: for example, bad working conditions, poor foremanship, inequitable pay, lack of a future. The findings of exit interviews serve as a basis for corrective action.

Labor turnover can be reduced through the control of discharges. Under this policy a foreman has the right to discharge employees from

[4] See Ch. 24 for discussion.

his department but not from the company. An employee so dismissed would be interviewed by a member of the personnel department, who would also review the foreman's reasons for dismissal, before final action was taken. Competent employees would, whenever possible, be transferred instead of discharged.

Layoffs may be minimized by stabilizing production (see pages 198–199) and by working overtime during rush seasons and sharing work (using a shorter work week or workday) during slow periods.

Training. Building an efficient labor force requires not only proper selection but also effective training of employees. Employee talents are not fully productive without training. The need for a systematic training program has been increased by rapid technological changes which create new jobs and eliminate old ones and by the growing importance of semiskilled labor relative to unskilled—the plant labor force must absorb new techniques as they develop. Industry is frequently compelled, particularly during periods of business expansion, to hire unskilled labor and to train the new workers for specific operations or tasks. Many jobs in business consist of tasks which are unique and peculiar to the company. A *systematic training program* improves the quality and quantity of work, safeguards machinery, reduces costs, raises employee earnings and morale, and provides an effective means for imparting company policies and regulations.

ORGANIZATION OF THE TRAINING PROGRAM. The training program is generally placed under the personnel director who consults with a training committee of operating executives. When a large training program is organized, the personnel officer should appoint a director to carry out its activities and to work with a training staff in developing courses and methods of teaching. Such programs may be subdivided into (1) training for specific jobs and (2) general education—lectures and the development of plant library facilities.[5] The program must be designed to fit the needs of the company; its scope will depend upon the size of the firm, the nature of its operations, its expansion program and recruitment needs, and whether its establishments are centrally or decentrally located.

Kinds of Training. Based upon a survey of the company's immediate and long-run needs for qualified personnel, programs may be inaugu-

---

[5] Outside general education for an employee's personal needs should obviously be encouraged by the company. In some instances firms financially aid certain types of education—e.g., accounting, business management, statistics, economics.

rated for job training, trade training, supervisory and executive training, and general industrial training. Job training which involves teaching particular tasks is usually the type most in demand. Trade training, the mastery of the fundamentals of a complete trade (machinist, toolmaker, electrician) is, except for apprenticeship, less common.

Teaching Techniques. The instructional methods and techniques, whether demonstration, recitation, lecture, conference, or a combination, depend upon the material to be presented and the number of people to be taught. Effective teaching, nonetheless, emphasizes "learning by doing." The instructor must have not only a mastery of his subject, but also the ability and personality to impart his knowledge to others. The conference method, generally best suited for supervisory and executive training, encourages participation and the exchange of ideas, but conferences must be well planned and properly led. The effectiveness of any training program can be appraised by noting any improvements in workmanship, by analyzing reports or administering examinations, and by making an attitude survey.

METHODS AND PURPOSES OF TRAINING LABOR. Training, particularly "task" instruction, includes the teaching of inexperienced or new workers, retraining of workers who are to be transferred to another job, versatility or multiskill training to achieve flexibility in the labor force, and remedial instruction of old employees to improve their workmanship. In addition, promising individuals may be groomed for higher positions. The training methods discussed in the paragraphs below are among those that the personnel director should evaluate for suitability and economy before developing a company training program.

On-the-Job Training. On-the-job training—instruction given by the foreman, his assistant, or an experienced worker while the trainee works at a specific job in the plant or office—is widely employed because of its economy and convenience: no special training facilities and instructional staff are required. It is particularly suitable when the number of trainees is small; when the training period is short because of the simplicity of the job; or, conversely, when the variety of duties, the complexity of the work process, and the need for special equipment make other forms of instruction less suitable. With on-the-job training, a new worker is stimulated by the actual production situation and his suitability for the job can readily be ascertained by a competent instructor. The foreman, who is ultimately responsible for the workmanship of his men, should follow up the progress of the new employee to assure that the training is effective.

Vestibule School Training. Vestibule school training provides instruction in a special shop ("classroom") setup that is independent of the production floor. This method disrupts production less and causes less work spoilage than on-the-job training. Moreover, full-time instructors are able to apply good teaching techniques under controlled conditions and can increase the trainee's confidence. The vestibule method is desirable when the demand for training is large and when on-the-job training is not practical. Its major limitation is the expense both of providing costly equipment, which is sometimes needed for this purpose, and of maintaining a teaching staff when the demand for training fluctuates. Moreover, since actual shop conditions can not be reproduced under the vestibule method, the completion of training often finds the trainee still in need of adjustment to plant conditions.

Apprentice Training. Apprentice training is used to develop all-round skilled craftsmen (machinists, toolmakers, millwrights). It is generally best suited to the large firm with a steady demand for skilled labor and able to afford the expense of such a program. Candidates should be chosen for their perseverance, intelligence, and mechanical aptitudes and on the basis of their employee background, school records, references, and foremen's recommendations. The trainee devotes three or four years to mastering a trade while receiving a nominal though increasing wage. The training course usually consists of a predetermined schedule of factory work assignments (which generally contribute to production) and some related classroom instruction in the underlying principles of the trade. An *apprenticeship agreement*, drawn up between the firm and the trainee, stipulates the training period, wage rate, bonus, and other conditions.[6]

SUPERVISORY AND EXECUTIVE TRAINING. Upon department heads, superintendents, and, particularly, the foremen, falls the task of directing the great mass of industrial workers. The training of middle and lower management is therefore of paramount importance and should be a continual process, especially in expanding industry.

Foremanship Training. Foremen are best trained through planned

[6] A permanent federal committee on apprentice training was established in 1936 under the auspices of the Department of Labor. The committee in co-operation with state and local committees has established standards covering occupations which are apprenticeable, a minimum starting age (sixteen), work processes to be learned in the plant, number of hours to be devoted to related classroom instruction, wage scales, graduation date, and other apprenticeship standards. Labor contracts, particularly of craft unions, occasionally control apprenticeship in the industry.

conferences (or discussions) which may be supplemented by lectures and carefully selected textbooks. A homogeneous group of twelve to fifteen men from one plant constitutes an ideal conference group. Supervisors from small firms may enroll in general supervisory training courses offered by universities (usually in evening sessions) or by several companies jointly.[7] Foremanship courses should first deal with the immediate problems of supervision and then cover such topics as the techniques and responsibilities of shop management, company policies, production planning, methods of training workmen, terms of the union contract, job evaluation, merit rating, safety, and motion and time study and other methods of cost reduction.

Executive Training. Candidates for middle-management positions (such as plant superintendent, chief inspector, production planner, and district sales manager) ordinarily require intensive training as well as general business background. Off-campus courses covering business management, labor relations, and corporation finance are offered by universities in the larger cities. In addition "home study" can draw on trade and technical journals and other selected literature. Candidates for administrative positions may be assigned to various departments, placed on policy-making bodies, put in staff positions, or rotated from assistantship to assistantship. Such training should emphasize policy interpretation, the gaining of organizational perspective, and "consultative supervision," which requires that all levels of management consult with subordinates affected by policies and directives.

Policy of Training College Men. An important means for creating a backlog of talent to fill lower- and middle-management positions is to train young college men. Company representatives interview seniors or recent graduates and select high-caliber applicants for training to fill positions in general administration, controllership, industrial engineering, production management, product engineering, and industrial research. Trainees are often assigned to a succession of jobs in various departments so that they may learn various phases of business operation from first-hand experience. The program may include class sessions and study assignments. During the training period management can evaluate the various trainees' capacities for growth.

Employee Services. Service activities sponsored by personnel departments are designed to provide an occupational environment which

---

[7] Standard supervisory training courses may be purchased from industrial education organizations. Unless specially prepared to meet the needs of the firm, however, such courses are of limited value.

will advance the physical, mental, and emotional fitness of employees as well as afford a special incentive for better work. The activities may be grouped into (1) direct services such as cafeterias and lunch stands, rest rooms, counseling, co-operative purchasing, and parking space; (2) health and benefit programs such as medical attention on the premises, hospitalization, group insurance, and pension plans; (3) recreation, such as sports, dances, and hobby clubs; and (4) media of employee communication such as the public address systems, employee magazines, company letters, and posters.

Practical business motives should guide the provision of employee services just as they guide other personnel activities. Management must guard against paternalism, else the service programs will boomerang. Workers are sometimes suspicious of company motives and react negatively to welfare programs. For example, when expensive recreational programs (e.g., club houses, elaborate outings) are offered, workers cognizant of the cost to the employer may demand that the money be added to their pay, particularly if they feel that their wages are substandard. Employee service activities become an effective nonfinancial incentive to workers when they grow out of the occupational and community environment and when employees or the union actively participate in their joint inauguration and operation. Many of the services can be managed by the employees themselves with excellent results.

Personnel Records and Research. A central personnel-records file should be maintained to provide a running account of employment history and should include for each employee the application form, interview result, examination and test results, training received, merit rating (progress) scores, wage advances, transfers and promotions, accidents and sick leaves, disciplinary notations, termination notices, and result of exit interview. In addition, the personnel staff should conduct research. Periodic audits and surveys of employee attitudes should be made to appraise the performance effectiveness of personnel administration systems and activities. Labor information should be compiled and studied for wage and cost-of-living trends, labor legislation, union policies, labor supply, future manpower needs of the firm, accident trends, and developments in the safety movement.

Health and Safety. A well-organized health and medical program contributes to an efficient labor force by reducing absenteeism and labor turnover. Such a program includes pre-employment physical examinations repeated periodically thereafter, medical treatment and first aid, sanitary working conditions, and health education. Occupational diseases vary for each industry and area. The engineering and operating departments and the medical service must co-operate closely to ascertain the kinds and incidence of occupational disease in a given establishment and to lessen their effects. The health and medical service in the large firm is ordinarily directed by a full-time doctor assisted by a staff of full-time nurses. Medium-sized firms often find it necessary to maintain a part-time doctor or a full-time nurse.

Prompted by humane considerations and/or by workmen's compensation laws, employers have adopted safety programs for the prevention of accidents and occupational disease as a primary responsibility of management.[8] Management realizes that reduction of accidents lowers their high direct and indirect accident costs (insurance charges to cover employee compensation, damage to facilities, reduced productivity because of interference with output schedules, time loss of injured worker, and lowered morale) to more than pay for the expense of a continuing safety program. However, only when management sincerely supports the safety program with sufficient time and interest, adequate appropriations of funds, and qualified personnel, will foremen and employees fully co-operate in accident prevention.

Procedure for Establishing a Safety Program. (1) Set up an organization for accident prevention; (2) survey hazards and carry out safety engineering; (3) compile and analyze accident records; and (4) eliminate hazards through revisions of facilities, safety education, and enforcement of safety rules and practices.

ORGANIZATION FOR SAFETY. The size of the firm and the magnitude of hazards determine the type of organization needed. In the large firm a safety director or engineer, ordinarily reporting to the head of the personnel department, is charged with the responsibility for safety work and serves as motivator of safety and as advisor to operating executives. The safety director secures the co-ordinated participation of various departments and uses committees for inspection, accident investigation, and safety education. For the small firm a safety committee headed by the works manager or other executive is usually

[8] *Workmen's compensation laws* enacted by all states set forth the liability of employers for industrial accidents or disease resulting directly from certain conditions of employment. Since he is in a position to create and enforce safe conditions, the employer is required by law to assume direct financial responsibility for workers' loss of earning capacity resulting from injuries on the job. The cost of accidents is considered part of the expense of producing the commodity. Since insurance premiums are in general based upon the accident rate in the business, it is expected that employers will strive to reduce the severity and frequency rate of accidents and thereby lower costs.

sufficient. The committee should be made up of members from various departments and levels in the organization so that it may effectively direct the attention of the entire organization to accident prevention. Safety, in the final analysis, is a line responsibility of supervisors and foremen with safety engineers and committees acting primarily as motivators and co-ordinators.

SAFETY SURVEY AND ENGINEERING. Accident prevention should begin on the drawing boards: thus a firm may secure "built-in" safety in the plant structure, in the layout of facilities and flow of work, in accident-proofing and guarding of machines, and in proper handling and storing of materials. To eliminate hazards at the outset, the safety engineer reviews structural drawings, floor plans, and equipment drawings. He inculcates safety-mindedness in those who select equipment, develop processes, and design tools. The safety engineer and committee men periodically inspect operations and facilities to check compliance with rules and practices, and they call attention to and remove hazards.

ACCIDENT INVESTIGATION AND ANALYSIS OF RECORDS. The safety engineer (or safety committee) compiles accident reports which include such information as persons injured, time and place of the accident, nature and severity of the injuries, equipment involved, nature of the work, and causes as noted by witnesses, foremen, and persons injured. He personally investigates serious accidents and analyzes the reports and statistics as a guide to prevention since the information reveals points of danger and suggests remedial measures. Accidents may be caused by unsafe conditions (i.e., the environmental cause) such as inadequate machine guards, improper construction or designs, hazardous processes, poor illumination, and unsafe apparel. More often the cause will be recklessness or violation of rules (i.e., the human cause)—for example, improper use of equipment, overloading of machines, failure to use protective devices, or horseplay.

ELIMINATION OF HAZARDS. Accidents from identifiable causes may be prevented by instruction of employees and by engineering revision (for example, removal or reduction of the hazard or protection against it). Reducing accidents after the physical cause is ascertained demands continuous safety engineering; i.e., redesign of equipment and tools, improvement of workplaces, guarding at point of operation, development of safer handling and storage practices, better lighting and ventilation, specification of safety apparel and devices, and technical advice on protection from chemicals and on fire prevention.

Organizing a safe physical plant is of little avail if employees are

273

Fig. 52. Typical safety posters issued by the National Safety Council and reprinted here by permission of the Council.

improperly trained in safety, disobey rules, are negligent, take chances, show poor judgment, or play pranks. The removal of the human causes of accidents, therefore, requires application of industrial psychology and continual education of employees and supervisors. Safe work habits, for instance, should be ingrained in employees during their initial training period. Every employee should be made to familiarize himself with the safety handbook. Periodic meetings of supervisors should be held for safety lectures and films. Workers should be rotated on departmental safety committees. A competitive spirit on accident prevention should be aroused between departments. The plant magazine should print safety instructions and publicize safety. There must be a never-ending series of porters, exhibits, and other appeals. Workers must be shocked, shamed, and educated into safety-mindedness.

Questions

1. What is the content of a typical public relations program?
2. (a) What objectives do unions seek in collective bargaining? (b) What are the provisions of typical labor contracts?
3. What methods do unions employ to gain their objectives?
4. Distinguish among conciliation, mediation, and compulsory arbitration.
5. What role does the personnel director ordinarily play in negotiation of agreements and in implementation of labor contracts?
6. (a) What are the benefits of an effective grievance procedure? (b) What are the usual procedural steps in a grievance procedure?
7. What are the ways in which employees may participate in management?
8. Why are experts in the human relations aspects of production and business as vital to successful management as experts in technical aspects?
9. What are the steps for setting up the personnel function?
10. How does effective personnel administration achieve labor efficiency?
11. Illustrate some policies that guide the personnel program.
12. What are the duties of the personnel department?
13. How would the system for recruiting and maintaining a labor force in a large firm differ from that in a small firm?
14. How are labor requisitions, job specifications, application blanks, interviews, and tests used in screening and selecting men?
15. Explain how proper induction and follow-up aid placement of men.
16. How can transfers and promotions improve employee performance?
17. How can absenteeism and labor turnover be reduced and controlled?
18. How do the purposes and kinds of training in large mass-production firms differ from those in large job-order firms?
19. Compare and contrast foremanship training and the training of college men for key job..
20. Enumerate typical employee service activities and explain why labor should help to initiate and participate in such activities.
21. What types of labor research surveys may prove beneficial to firms?
22. What are the steps for establishing and operating a safety program?

24: Wage and Salary Administration:
Job Evaluation, Merit Rating,
and Incentive Plans

Both employees and management are keenly interested in the design and operation of the company wage system: it affects the level of workers' earnings, the ease of recruiting and maintaining an effective labor force, morale and efficiency, and the firm's costs and competitive standing in the industry. Though the problem is many-sided, management can nonetheless design a workable compensation system on the basis of careful analysis and systematic procedure.

Wages are the total earnings for the performance of services in a given period of time (a day or week); they are equal to the product of an hourly rate ($1.20 per hour) times the number of hours worked, or to the product of a piece rate (.12 per piece) times the number of pieces, plus any bonuses or premiums that may be earned. Thus the rate of pay may be based on time, output, or a combination of the two —e.g., a guaranteed hourly rate plus a bonus ordinarily based on the amount of "extra" work put out (or time saved) beyond a standard requirement. *Salary* refers to compensation on a weekly, monthly, or annual basis.

The worker's money wages must be distinguished from his real wages. His *money wage* is the actual number of monetary units (i.e., dollars, francs, pesos) he receives. His *real wage*, which is affected by changes in the general price level, is the amount of goods and services that he can buy with his money wage; a worker's real wage, then, determines his income and standard of living. Workers ordinarily regard "take-home pay," which is influenced by such factors as overtime, bonuses, and withholding tax, as more significant than their hourly or piece rate.

The factor of prime significance to the employer is the unit labor cost—the amount of direct and indirect labor cost required to turn out one unit of product. This depends not only upon the hourly or piece rate payments, but also upon supplementary wage payments such as shift differentials, paid vacations and holidays, sick leave privileges, and insurance premiums. Though an employer pays high direct and indirect wages, his labor costs per unit of product may be low because of the high output per man-hour accruing from efficient operations.

DEVELOPMENT AND ADMINISTRATION OF THE WAGE SYSTEM

In order to develop a sound wage and salary system, management must (1) clarify the objectives—i.e., what the wage plan should achieve; (2) formulate effective wage and salary policies to fit the firm's operating conditions; (3) delegate the responsibility for wage administration; and (4) apply the systematic procedure outlined on page 279 for the design and administration of the compensation plan; this procedure involves such measures as job evaluation, wage surveys, employee merit rating and the provision of financial incentives.

Objectives. The goals of an effective compensation plan are multiple. (1) The plan should be stable yet sufficiently flexible to permit adjustment to changing conditions. (2) It should emphasize low labor costs and increased production and a compensation level sufficiently high to enable recruitment and maintenance of suitable personnel. (3) It should pay fair and adequate wage and salary differentials that compensate for skill, training, experience, and other requirements of each job. (4) It should pay employees on the basis of merit and output or accomplishment (i.e., apply incentive payment wherever practical): hence management must (a) set accurate task standards so that a proper incentive will stimulate the workers to optimum performance without injury to health and (b) guarantee minimum earnings to protect incentive workers against delays in production over which they have no control (e.g., machine failures and material shortages). (5) The plan should establish a reasonable shift and work week and stipulate regular hours with minimum disruption to normal living. (6) It should be simple to administer—payment complaints should be easy to investigate and adjust, labor budgeting and cost control should be easy to carry out, and employees should be able to understand the plan.

Compensation Policy. Before it can formulate its policies and design a wage plan. management must analyze both the internal and external factors that influence the firm's labor costs, its demand for workers, the labor supply, and wage levels.

FACTORS INFLUENCING POLICY. Key *internal factors* are the proportion of labor cost to the total cost of production; the types of skills required and the extent to which reliance must be put on individual productivity for output; the suitability of the production process to incentive wage-payment methods; and the rapidity of changes in plant processes and technology that modify job content and the composition of the company working force.

External factors that management must appraise in formulating policy are the firm's competitive standing and the amount of monopoly control it has; its earning capacity and financial position; the stability of its volume of business and employment of labor; and its business prospects. Management, too, must consider the extent of unionization in the firm and industry; the size of the labor market from which it recruits workers; the level of wages prevailing in the area and industry; the trend in the cost of living; and government wage and hour laws.

POLICY COVERAGE. On the basis of the analysis of its particular internal and external situation, management should formulate policies to cover such matters as: the emphasis to be placed on recruiting the required caliber of personnel through high wages and salaries; the extent to which incentive payment plans should be adopted; the emphasis to be placed on supplementary wage payments; the extent to which nonfinancial incentives [1] should be adopted; how the firm's scale of wages should be related to, or set with reference to (i.e., placed above or below), the general level of wages prevailing in the area and industry; the extent to which union representatives will participate in the development of the wage plan; and how wage and salary administration is to be organizationally handled. These policy matters are discussed in the following pages under various topics.

Delegation and Organization of Wage Administration. An interdepartmental committee of high-ranking executives, under the chairmanship of the chief executive or personnel director, should be responsible for the over-all development of the wage system. If not chairman of the committee, the personnel director should at least participate in an advisory capacity; he should not, however, assume the responsibility for setting wages and changing rates.

---

[1] *Nonfinancial incentives* include records of achievement and employee recognition, opportunity for advanced training, opportunity for promotion, and other similar influences which stimulate performance.

The industrial engineering department (with the co-operation of the personnel and other departments) is generally best equipped to conduct specific studies for the wage system—job evaluation, wage surveys, design of incentive wage plans, and establishment of task standards. The fixing of wage rates and the adjustment of individual job rates should be approved by line executives who take final responsibility. The wage administration office, generally placed under the personnel director, should implement the day-to-day procedures covering wage problems.

In unionized firms, collective bargaining agreements obviously influence the alignment of job rates, supplementary payments, and periodic adjustment of the wage scale.

Procedure for Designing and Administering a Wage System. The survey for setting up a wage system calls for the following procedural steps.

(1) Conduct a job evaluation study (i.e., rate all jobs) to establish differentials that reflect the relative worth and mutual alignment of company positions—the occupational hierarchy.

(2) Establish a wage rate and a salary schedule (a base compensation rate for each job) by conducting a wage survey in the area and setting the company wage schedule at, or adjusting it to, the general wage level prevailing in the market.

(3) Establish the required supplementary compensation—overtime rates and shift differentials, paid vacations and holidays, sick leaves, severance pay, insurance and pension benefits.

(4) Adopt incentive (or premium) payment plans, whenever suitable to the work, on the basis of carefully established task standards.

(5) Maintain and administer the wage and salary system: rate new jobs, make transfers and promotions, and merit rate employees and adjust wages within the compensation range.

(6) Periodically review and, when necessary, adjust the company wage level to changes in the firm's business conditions and profit situation, to changes in the market wage level, and to collective bargaining and labor contract provisions.

Job Evaluation—Occupation Differentials and Alignment. Though it is obviously impossible to measure the relative value of company jobs with exact precision, it is possible to rate jobs [2] in an

---

[2] Job rating should not be confused with merit rating. Employee *merit rating* is used to reward individuals with a wage or salary increase within a predetermined wage-rate range for performing a given job with better than the average effort, skill, and conscientiousness required by the position.

objective, consistent manner on the basis of explicit criteria. *Job evaluation* (*or job rating*) is a systematic procedure for measuring the relative value and importance of occupations on the basis of their common factors (skill, training, effort) for the purpose of determining wage and salary differentials. Job evaluation deals with the occupation and not with the employee holding the position.

The establishment of proper wage differentials for company jobs is necessary to bring forth the required caliber of labor and to encourage men to train for skilled jobs. Moreover, ratings (occupation differentials expressed as labor grades or numerical point values) are necessary for the establishment of logical and practical company wage rate and salary schedules. In firms where such logical wage and salary differentials have not been established, compensation patterns are often irregular and chaotic since they will have evolved from traditional attitudes, arbitrary decisions, expediency, and favoritism. In such cases jobs that call for greater effort, skill, and responsibility may pay less than jobs requiring fewer of these attributes; and individuals in the same or similar occupations may receive widely varying compensation. Morale is consequently low and performance poor since employees keenly feel these inequities, and management can not explain the inconsistencies on a logical basis.

BENEFITS OF JOB EVALUATION. In addition to its role in wage setting and surveys, a job evaluation program (including job specification) clarifies the organizational lines of authority and responsibility; provides a basis for hiring, transferring, and establishing lines of job progression and channels of promotion; and serves as a basis for developing a training program.

JOB ANALYSIS,[3] A PRELIMINARY STUDY. *Job analysis* is the methodical compilation and study of work data in order to define and characterize each occupation in such a manner as to distinguish it from all others. In this procedure the job analyst (or a supervisor properly instructed in the technique) (1) collects information, (2) prepares job descriptions, and (3) works up job specifications.

The analyst compiles pertinent occupation data by observing the performance of jobs, by conversing with employees, and by interview-

[3] Job analysis should not be confused with methods analysis, operation analysis, and motion study. These studies improve and standardize operations, thus clarifying and fixing the skill, working conditions, and performance content of jobs; they are obviously a prerequisite to effective job evaluation since best results in job rating can be attained only after operations and processes have been improved and standardized.

ing foremen. He may gather his information, particularly for salaried and supervisory jobs, by circulating questionnaires and then investigating to check the accuracy of the data.

The analyst prepares *job descriptions* by condensing the data to represent an accurate and complete picture of the distinguishing features of each job in terms of task content and occupation requirements (see Fig. 54).

From the occupation data (and generally on the basis of group judgment subject to executive review), the analyst then draws up on a standard form *job specifications* which concisely stipulate the skills, operation routines, responsibilities, types of efforts, working conditions, and other requirements of a job and which serve as source data for job rating. The analyst reviews position and occupation titles and standardizes job names in order to facilitate the cross comparison of jobs.

PREPARATION FOR JOB EVALUATION. Though the analyst alone may rate jobs, ratings are more accurate when conducted by a committee since the pooled judgment of competent individuals is generally superior to that of one person. Foremen and other supervisors should participate in rating jobs in their departments; and it is sometimes necessary to have union participation in the study. The benefits of job evaluation should be explained to employees to secure their confidence.

In their procedure, job analysts (1) select factors common to all jobs, (2) define the factors, and (3) employ one or more of the available rating methods.

In order to measure one job in terms of, or with reference to, other jobs, it is necessary to select factors or features fundamentally prevalent in all occupations. Even though occupations vary in duties, operation routine, equipment, and material, the basic nature of all wage (production) jobs, for example, can be expressed and compared in terms of such attributes as "skill," "effort," "responsibility," and "working conditions." Thus the analysts can measure the relative degrees of skill, effort, and other factors contained in different jobs—e.g., the amount of skill and training required in an electrician's trade as compared to that required in an acetylene-torch-welder's trade. By breaking down and carefully studying key company jobs [4] as outlined in job specification

---

[4] "Key jobs" are labor grades which are comparatively stable in duties and content, are occupations in which a considerable number of workers are generally employed, are scattered throughout the ladder of labor classification, are familiar to many people in the industry, and are common to many firms. Owing to the aforementioned features, key jobs are important in job evaluation studies and wage surveys.

POINTS ASSIGNED TO FACTORS AND KEY TO GRADES

FACTORS	1st Degree	2nd Degree	3rd Degree	4th Degree	5th Degree
SKILL					
1. Education	14	28	42	56	70
2. Experience	22	44	66	88	110
3. Initiative and Ingenuity	14	28	42	56	70
EFFORT					
4. Physical Demand	10	20	30	40	50
5. Mental or Visual Demand	5	10	15	20	25
RESPONSIBILITY					
6. Equipment or Process	5	10	15	20	25
7. Material or Product	5	10	15	20	25
8. Safety of Others	5	10	15	20	25
9. Work of Others	5	10	15	20	25
JOB CONDITIONS					
10. Working Conditions	10	20	30	40	50
11. Unavoidable Hazards	5	10	15	20	25

Score Range	Grades
— 139	12
140—161	11
162—183	10
184—205	9
206—227	8
228—249	7
250—271	6
272—293	5
294—315	4
316—337	3
338—359	2
360—381	1

2. EXPERIENCE

Experience appraises the length of time usually or typically required by an individual, with the specified education or trade knowledge, to learn to perform the work satisfactorily from the standpoint of quality and quantity under normal supervision. Do not include apprenticeship or trades training, which has been rated under Education. Include under Experience only the time required to attain production standards.

1st Degree
Up to three months.

2nd Degree
Over three months up to one year.

3rd Degree
Over one year up to three years.

4th Degree
Over three years up to five years.

5th Degree
Over five years.

Fig. 53. An illustrative breakdown of factors into subfactors and degrees; distribution of points; designation of job grades; and the definition of the subfactor "experience." (Courtesy National Metal Trades Association)

forms, analysts select the required number of attributes—first major and then minor factors. They keep factors to a minimum, yet sufficient to cover the contents of jobs. Analysts must work up definitions for factors to stipulate the limits of each, to avoid overlapping, and to assure common understanding and proper evaluation of job content. Since factors ordinarily are not of equal importance, analysts assign relative weights to each.

Many firms find it necessary to conduct two job evaluation studies— one for production jobs and one for clerical and salaried jobs. The evaluation approach for each class of occupations varies in regard to the manner of compiling job descriptions, the factors selected, and the relative weights assigned to factors. For example, while physical effort and working conditions are important in rating production jobs, they are usually of little importance in rating clerical and salaried jobs. Moreover, since salaried positions are ordinarily not well standardized in job content, they are often difficult to evaluate.

JOB EVALUATION METHODS. Jobs may be rated by using one of three general methods: (1) ranking or grading, (2) factor comparison, and (3) point system. Job evaluation programs may, however, combine two or more methods for purposes of counterchecking and balance.

The Ranking or Grading Method. A committee, on the basis of its composite judgment, compares each job in its entirety with all other company occupations, arranging the jobs in order of importance from lowest to highest. Then the committee places each job, in accordance with its ranking, in one of ten or more categories or grades which indicate relative worth. Wage rates can then be assigned for each job on the basis of the findings of the wage survey whereby the company scale of wages for key jobs is set in relation to that prevailing in the market. The ranking method provides no record of the factors considered or of the basis for ratings, and, therefore, is not useful in explaining to employees or union representatives why one job is rated higher than another. While the ranking method has its limitations, it does provide an over-all review of jobs at one time and serves as a point of departure for job rating in a more systematic manner.

The Factor Comparison Method. Analysts select specific occupation factors to which they usually give equal point values. In the rating process, they compare each job with others (one factor at a time) and assign factor point values to each occupation. Analysts compute job ratings (i.e., differentials) by totaling the points received by each job. After minor adjustments are made to arrive at uniform wage-scale

```
┌─────────────────────────────────────────────────────────────────────────┐
│                                                  CODE NO   T 09           │
│                 JOB RATING SPECIFICATIONS                                 │
│                                                  DEPT   Tool Room         │
│                                                                           │
│                                                  GRADE        3           │
│                                                                           │
│   JOB NAME    TOOL MAKER                          CLASS  B                │
│                                                                           │
│   JOB DESCRIPTION:                                                        │
│                                                                           │
│        Lay out, construct, alter and repair a variety of tools; ordinary com- │
│     bination, blanking, piercing, drawing, bending, and forming dies; box │
│     and stand type drill jigs; milling and other fixtures for general type │
│     of machining operations and location and profile gauges where design  │
│     is available but involving ordinary development work as to mechanisms  │
│     and details.  Visualize finished job, make necessary mathematical     │
│     calculations and select allowances for spring, shrinkage, lapping,    │
│     grinding, scraping, fitting and finishing.  Recognize and report for  │
│     correction blueprint errors such as improper angles, radii, materials, │
│     etc., which would prevent economical production.  Perform difficult   │
│     and exacting machine operations requiring a wide variety of set-ups and │
│     methods to maintain close tolerances; skilled bench work involving    │
│     filing, scraping, grinding, lapping, fitting, assembling and adjusting │
│     to insure satisfactory performance.  Make tool try-outs, detect faulty │
│     operation or defective material and correct trouble.                  │
│                                                                           │
│   TYPICAL PARTS:                                                          │
│                                                                           │
│                                                                           │
│                                                   ┌──────────────────────┐│
│                                                   │       REVISED        ││
│                                                   ├───────────┬──────────┤│
│                                                   │    BY     │   DATE   ││
│   DATE                                            │           │          ││
└─────────────────────────────────────────────────────────────────────────┘
```

steps, the ratings are converted into a money scale which is set with reference to the prevailing wage level as explained on page 289. Since the factor comparison method usually gives equal weight to all factors, it tends to undervalue jobs that are high in the "skill" factor and to overvalue jobs that receive many points for the "working conditions" factor. Moreover, the process is laborious since it requires that a single factor for one job be compared to the same factor in a large number of different jobs.

The Point System. The point system, a widely used method, is based on a job evaluation manual. Separate manuals have been prepared for a number of industries. To design a rating manual for the factory labor of a firm, analysts ordinarily select the factors of skill, effort, responsibility, and job conditions and assign weights to each. In industries where workmanship and skill or mental application are important in contributing to productivity, analysts give proportionately more weight to skill and effort than to working conditions. After assign-

						CODE NO. **T 09**		

JOB RATING SPECIFICATIONS

DEPT. **Tool Room**

GRADE **3**

JOB NAME **TOOL MAKER**   CLASS **B**   TOTAL POINTS **325**

FACTORS	SUBSTANTIATING DATA	DEG.	PTS.
EDUCATION	Use shop mathematics, hand book formulas and trigonometry. Work from complicated drawings or sketches. Use all types of precision measuring instruments. Thorough knowledge of machine shop practice, principles of mechanics and machine tool operations, working qualities of materials. Equivalent to formal apprenticeship training.	4	56
EXPERIENCE	Over 3 and up to 4 years in the construction, alteration or repair of tools, dies and gauges.	4	88
INITIATIVE AND INGENUITY	Lay out, construct, alter and repair a variety of tools, dies, jigs, fixtures and gauges. Considerable judgment to select allowances, work out mechanism details, perform ordinary development work, fit and assemble mechanisms and parts to close tolerances.	4	56
PHYSICAL DEMAND	Light physical effort performing bench work or machine operations. Occasionally handle heavy tools or machine attachments.	2	20
MENTAL OR VISUAL DEMAND	Concentrate mental and visual attention closely, studying drawings, planning and laying out work, performing wide variety of operations requiring close attention and high degree of skill and accuracy.	4	20
RESPONSIBILITY FOR EQUIPMENT OR PROCESS	Use variety of machine tools such as engine lathes, jig borers, universal milling machines and grinders, etc. Improper set-up or operation may cause damage; seldom over $250	3	15
RESPONSIBILITY FOR MATERIAL OR PRODUCT	Improper construction, alteration or repair of tools, dies, jigs, fixtures or gauges may cause losses seldom over $200	3	15
RESPONSIBILITY FOR SAFETY OF OTHERS	Numerous and varied temporary machine set-ups, e.g., work mounted on face plate of lathes, grinders, etc. Improperly fastened work may fly out or tool try-outs may cause lost time accidents to others.	3	15
RESPONSIBILITY FOR WORK OF OTHERS	None.	1	15
WORKING CONDITIONS	Good working conditions. Use of machine involves some oil, dirt, chips, etc.	2	20
HAZARDS	Exposed to loss of fingers, hand or eye injury through operation of large variety of machines including making tool try-outs.	3	15
REMARKS			

9

Fig. 54. (On page opposite) A sample job description, a preliminary step to job rating on the basis of a job specification. (Above) The rating of a tool-maker's job (point system) on the basis of pertinent job specification data. (Courtesy National Metal Trades Association)

ing the proper weight to each factor, analysts break the factors down into subfactors and scale each subfactor into degrees of point value (Fig. 53). They then define subfactors and degrees in order to aid judgment and enable more consistent appraisal of job worth.

After the point system has been set up and the manual prepared, analysts use the scale of degrees for subfactors (the standard yardstick) to rate each occupation individually on the basis of its job specification data (Fig. 54). The total number of points they allocate to all factors of a given occupation determines its rating. Then, corresponding to points received, analysts place jobs into brackets (job grades designating differentials) for which wage rates are set with reference to the prevailing wage level as explained on page 289. The company can justify the rating of a job on the basis of the distribution of scored points on the rating sheet.

Setting the Company Wage Level. After job differentials have been determined, management can translate the resulting labor grades [5] (derived from point value brackets) into a final company wage rate (or salary) schedule through these steps: (1) by conducting a wage survey to determine the prevailing (market) wage-rate level for key jobs, (2) by comparing the company level of evaluated job grades with the prevailing level and establishing a new company wage-rate (or salary) schedule, and (3) by converting the old company wage-rate level to the newly designed schedule of compensation.

WAGE SURVEY. The prevailing rates of pay in the community can be determined by a careful wage survey conducted either by the trade association or (a more costly method) by the company. Analysts first select the key jobs or occupations to be covered and delineate the market area. Adequately prepared specifications must be available for key jobs; and if the survey is to be sound, rates must be uniformly compiled for essentially the same grades of labor. Wage data may be secured by mail or, preferably, by visits to firms in the area. The data for the prevailing wage should be acquired on a uniform basis, generally as straight hourly rates or total earnings in a 40-hour week (including average wages for incentive or piece-rate workers but excluding supplementary pay—overtime and shift differentials, paid vacations and holidays—data for which may be compiled for comparative study and collective bargaining purposes). The prevailing level of payment is the

[5] The number of labor grades and compensation levels selected should be based on the degree of simplicity desired in the wage structure and the need for adequate promotional gradation.

median or mode of the actual hourly rates paid on straight time by the various firms in the area. The prevailing level for the various grades of labor (occupations) can be shown as a *wage line* in a chart (see Fig. 55, line PL), the slope of the line indicating the steepness of the progression of rates from the lowest to the highest job grade. This market level of wages for key jobs is used to set the company wage scale. (Fig. 56 shows the prevailing occupational wage differentials for key jobs in the machinery industries in 1946. Though it realistically presents market wage differentials, it is too inclusive for practical use for a given industry in a given area. Fig. 57 shows the average 1950 hourly and weekly earnings of production workers in selected industries.)

Since salaried employees are recruited from a market different from that of hourly-paid employees, an independent scale of pay for salaried

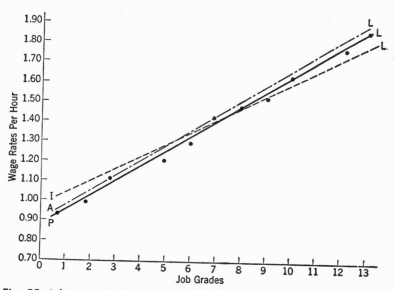

Fig. 55. Adjusting the firm's level of wages to the prevailing level. Line "PL" illustrates the prevailing (market) wage level based on median wage rates (represented by dots) for key jobs in the area. Line "IL" illustrates a firm's initial wage level; its slope does not correspond in steepness to the prevailing level. Line "AL" illustrates the firm's level after it has been adjusted by management to correspond in steepness with the prevailing level; note that it has been set slightly above the market level.

Fig. 56. Wage rates of male workers in key occupations in machinery industries as percentage of wages of janitors and hand truckers, January, 1946. The wage rates are expressed as a percentage of the wage for janitors and hand truckers which are set at 100 and designated as the unskilled wage rate. The horizontal bars represent the range of the middle half of such percentages recorded for occupations. The vertical lines through the bars mark the ratio of the median wage in the occupations to the average wage for janitors and hand truckers. Note that the median wage for production machinists was 58 per cent above the average for janitors and that of millwrights, 43 per cent above. (Based upon Bureau of Labor Statistics data; reprinted by permission from W. S. Woytinsky and Associates, *Employment and Wages in the United States.* Copyright, 1953, The Twentieth Century Fund)

Average Hourly and Weekly Earnings of Production Workers
in Selected Industries, Annual Average, 1950

Industry *	Hourly Earnings	Weekly Earnings
Tobacco manufactures	$1.08	$41.08
Retail trade	1.18	47.63
Leather manufactures	1.19	44.56
Apparel manufactures	1.20	43.68
Textile mill products	1.24	48.95
Furniture manufactures	1.28	53.67
Lumber basic products	1.35	55.31
Food and kindred products	1.35	56.07
Telephone	1.40	54.38
Paper and allied products	1.41	61.14
Stone, clay, and glass	1.44	59.20
Wholesale trade	1.48	60.36
Electrical machinery	1.48	60.83
Local railways and bus lines	1.49	66.96
Chemicals	1.51	62.67
Rubber manufactures	1.58	64.42
Machinery, except electrical	1.61	67.21
Iron and steel †	1.65	67.24
Automobiles and equipment	1.78	73.25
Products of petroleum and coal	1.83	75.01
Anthracite mining	1.97	63.24
Bituminous coal mining	2.01	70.35

* Industries arrayed by ascending order of hourly earnings.
† In 1950, primary metal industries.

Fig. 57. Average hourly and weekly earnings of production workers in selected industries, annual average, 1950. (Based upon Bureau of Labor Statistics data; reprinted by permission from W. S. Woytinsky and Associates. *Employment and Wages in the United States.* Copyright, 1953, The Twentieth Century Fund)

jobs should be constructed by means of a special wage survey. Surveys for occupations are difficult to conduct because of differences in company organization structures and the comparative lack of standardization in salary jobs. Moreover, salary payments tend to be influenced by such factors as individual talents (even though not required by the job), years of service, ownership interest in the firm (including nepotism), and company precedent.

RELATING AND ADJUSTING OF COMPANY WAGES TO PREVAILING WAGES. Management can establish a satisfactory scale of wage differentials at a level best suited to its purposes by relating its scale of job differentials (schedule of job grades) to the slope and level of wages prevailing on the market. To accomplish this, management first sets the steepness of the firm's slope of job grades so that it compares favorably with that of the market; and management then decides whether its wage level should be centered upon, above, or below the wage level (line) prevailing in the market.

If the company wage level is centered upon the prevailing level, the wage rates for both the lowest-rated and the highest-rated company job grades will be established at the going market rates for the same occupations. The wage rates for the intermediate occupation grades can then be set according to the differentials established by the job evaluation study.[6]

When management enjoys a secure competitive position in the industry, it may adopt a policy of centering its wage-rate level upon the prevailing level and thereby maintain a satisfactory labor force and good morale.

Sometimes management adopts a *high-wage policy* (i.e., sets the company wage level above the prevailing scale). It can do so without endangering its earning capacity (1) when its labor costs make up a small proportion of the unit cost of the product; (2) when its unusual plant and managerial efficiency attains low labor costs per unit of output; (3) when it has sufficient monopolistic control to pass higher labor costs on to consumers in the form of higher prices; or (4) when it desires to maintain top hiring specifications, ease of recruitment (important to expanding business), high morale, and above-average labor performance by its employees.

Management may, on the other hand, succeed in placing its wage-rate level *below the market level* without adversely affecting its ability to recruit and hold a satisfactory labor force (1) when it offers the advantages of steady earnings and job security through stabilized employment; (2) when it offers liberal supplementary wage payments; (3) when it happily enjoys the reputation of "being a good place to work" (perhaps because of enlightened personnel practices); or (4) when it is in a position consistently to offer longer hours and overtime and thus provide higher "take home pay."

After the company wage-rate level has been established, wages for the various labor grades may be paid as "flat rates" or as "rate ranges." If the production process and wage jobs are highly standardized and precisely defined, management ordinarily selects a *flat wage rate,* which is a fixed sum for each job. In other cases, management selects

---

[6] The wage rates of upper and lower anchor jobs are sometimes set by collective bargaining.

wage-rate ranges which establish steps for periodic pay increases to represent progress through the range. For salaried jobs, management usually selects the rate range method because of differences in the abilities of salaried personnel and the comparative lack of occupational standardization. To control favoritism and arbitrary wage advances, pay increases within the range should be based on periodic merit rating of employee performance.

CONVERSION TO THE NEW WAGE SCHEDULE. A comparison of the existing company rates with the new wage-rate schedule will show which jobs are underpaid and which are overpaid. Underpaid positions should be raised to the new rates as soon as is practicable. Though the rates for overpaid positions can not expediently be reduced, the new rates for these jobs should be applied to newly hired or transferred employees. Wage rates as a whole can gradually be converted into the new schedule and brought into proper alignment by arresting or reducing wage increases for overpaid positions when a cost-of-living or other general wage increase is granted.

Supplementary Compensation. Management should formulate a definite policy and practice concerning supplementary payments which in some cases may make up an appreciable portion of the total wage cost.[7] Among the well-established wage supplements are overtime pay, vacation pay, and shift differentials (i.e., premium pay for working undesirable hours; e.g., a bonus of 6 per cent per hour for the second shift and 12 per cent for the third shift). Largely under the pressure of union demands, supplementary compensation has been expanding in such forms as paid holidays, paid lunch periods, paid wash-up periods, sick leave, severance pay, group insurance, hospital benefits, and attendance, year-end, and other bonuses.

Incentive-Wage Payment. When production is comparatively standardized and output is measurable in definite units, management can use the incentive-wage payment method to the benefit of both employees and the company. Management should decide the extent to which incentives shall be applied; and then it must select or design the most appropriate incentive plan on the basis of a careful analysis of its production conditions. For satisfactory operation, the plan must be suitable to the work and simple to compute and administer; it must offer an adequate financial incentive and provide a guaranteed base

[7] Supplementary compensation in American industry probably averages not much more than 10 per cent of total employee earnings, though estimates for some firms run 25 per cent or more.

wage rate and protection against rate cutting. The incentive-wage payment scale for various occupations must be set up to contain job differentials and supplementary payments comparable to those of straight hourly paid jobs. The procedure for developing an incentive plan is discussed in the last section of this chapter.

Maintenance and Administration of the Wage System. Once the wage system has been designed and established, it must be maintained by the wage administration office. Though the wage structure may be modified and adjusted to meet new conditions, the system itself must be kept intact. This requires consistent administration and adjustment: first, in applying the wage schedule to existing jobs and, second, in keeping the wage structure up-to-date to meet job changes.

APPLICATION OF THE WAGE SCHEDULE. The wage scale is applied when employees are hired; when they are transferred from one job or department to another or from one shift to another; when wage-rate advances (those within the job rate range) are to be granted in accordance with employee merit rating results or on the basis of automatic progression; and when individuals are upgraded along the channels established by the promotional chart.[8] So that proper interdepartmental alignment in the wage structure may be maintained, an advisory committee on wages should be set up to receive and review wage complaints of employees. Unless the matter falls under a labor contract grievance procedure, the final decision on wage matters, dealing with specific jobs should be left to the executive concerned.

METHOD OF KEEPING THE WAGE STRUCTURE UP-TO-DATE. Organizational changes and revision, expansion, and modernization of plant facilities invariably modify or eliminate jobs and create new ones. Specifications should be prepared for all new or changed jobs, and these occupations should be rated on the same basis that jobs were initially evaluated. On occasion the company may require a particular grade of skilled labor which is in limited supply on the market; workers in that field are then able to demand higher wages than their rating warrants. In such a case management should put the job into an irregular classification for the duration of the shortage and pay the employees the wage rate necessary to recruit and hold them.

These various adjustments in the wage structure should not be confused with the general, periodic wage adjustments necessary to meet the external changes discussed below.

---

[8] The merit-rating procedure is discussed in the next section of this chapter.

Periodic Adjustment of the Wage Level. Even though adequate job differentials have been established, the size of the supplementary payment determined, and the level of wages set relative to the prevailing level, the resulting company wage structure can not remain static for an extended period of time and be effective. It will require adjustment to business and economic fluctuations and trends, particularly when such changes are strong and abrupt.

Compensation adjustment may take one or more of the following *forms:* an increase or decrease of wage rates by a definite percentage or sum, a change in supplementary payments, a change in the length of the workweek (affecting "take-home pay" only), or a gradual "loosening up" or "tightening up" of time standards which affect the ease of earning bonuses in incentive payment plans.

The immediate factors that generally call for adjustment in the firm's level of compensation are (1) changes in the prevailing wage level, (2) changes in the cost of living, and (3) changes in the company's ability to pay as reflected by its profits. These *short-run factors* are not in themselves the fundamental causal factors. They are merely the overt manifestations of more basic business and economic forces, such as rising productivity,[9] major shifts in consumer tastes, cyclical fluctuations (prosperity or recession), and rearmament and war booms and their associated dislocations (e.g., labor shortages and inflation). These forces affect the demand for, and the supply of, labor and thus influence the market level of wages. Labor markets, however, do not respond instantaneously and do not operate smoothly since they are influenced by such factors as union control of labor supply, worker ignorance of market wage levels, and varying degrees of labor immobility. Among the *long-run factors* underlying supply and demand for labor are the size and the growth of the labor force (population) relative to the abundance of natural resources and capital accumulation, the rate of fundamental technological advance, and the general economic organizational framework. Obviously the short- and long-run factors dovetail and are interrelated and any attempt to abstract a single factor for the purposes of a "wage theory" would be out of context and therefore unrealistic.

[9] The factor of increasing productivity in terms of output per man-hour has been used to justify a wage increase. Labor agreements in the automobile and other industries include an "annual improvement factor" clause which provides for a yearly upward adjustment in wage rates (e.g., 7 cents). This provision tends to reduce the amount of year-to-year bargaining over wages and to make possible the adoption of longer-term contracts.

Collective bargaining influences and modifies the impact of labor shortages and price level and profit changes on the unionized segments of the economy.[10] Thus organized labor, particularly during periods of a high level of business, seems to promote faster and more uniform adjustments in the wage levels in unionized industry than might otherwise be the case.

ADJUSTMENT TO CURRENTLY PREVAILING WAGE LEVEL. Prevailing wage rates are commonly supposed, particularly by employees, to reflect the actual market value of labor services in a given occupation; and these rates, therefore, are held to be reasonable and proper.[11] Management may, for a number of reasons, adhere to the policy of maintaining its wage level at a given position relative to the prevailing levels. Failure to pay comparable wages (keep up with the area) may increase the difficulty of recruiting a satisfactory labor force and maintaining labor efficiency and morale. Moreover, unions will apply pressure to induce the company to keep up with increases in the area and industry.

ADJUSTMENT TO THE COST OF LIVING. Pronounced inflation and deflation disrupt a firm's level of compensation and distort wage patterns in industry. In order to maintain the level of employees' income, management in general accepts the principle of adjusting wage rates to the rising cost of living as necessary for the upkeep of morale and efficiency. Upward or downward wage adjustments, however, tend to lag behind changes in the general price level, so that profit margins generally

[10] For a discussion of such criteria as "comparable wage rates," "productivity," "cost of living," "ability to pay," and "purchasing power" used in wage negotiations, see Bowman and Bach, *Economic Analysis and Public Policy*, Prentice Hall, 1949, pp. 681–686. The criterion used by labor in wage bargaining depends upon the phase of the business cycle, economic circumstances surrounding the industry, and company and union strategy. For example, management may hold that an excessively high wage level increases unemployment since it reduces profit margins and the level of business volume—labor "prices itself out of the market" relative to its productive contribution. Labor may hold that higher wage levels are required to maintain the level of purchasing power necessary for the mass consumption of the voluminous output of mass-production industry.

[11] This point of view is reflected in state and federal *prevailing wage laws* which require that employees working on construction financed by public funds be compensated at rates equal to the prevailing scales in the areas in which the work is done. Also, the Walsh-Healy Act of 1936 stipulates that firms supplying the federal government with commodities on contracts exceeding $10,000 must pay employees engaged in the output of these goods at prevailing wage rates and must maintain standard working conditions, such as the 40-hour week, a premium rate for overtime, and a policy of employing no male workers under sixteen years of age or females under eighteen.

294

widen during the earlier periods of inflation [12] and narrow during deflation. In nonunionized firms management ordinarily makes the upward adjustment in the form of a "cost-of-living" bonus. The provisional nature of this wage "increase" assures a measure of flexibility in that it can more easily be discontinued during periods of declining prices. Collective bargaining agreements have come to include a cost-of-living adjustment or "escalator" clause, whereby wage levels rise automatically as the cost of living increases. During periods of deflation, unions typically strive to eliminate such clauses in labor agreements and resist wage cuts.

ADJUSTMENTS TO ABILITY TO PAY. In the long run the upper limit in a firm's wage level is determined by its "ability to pay," that is, its net income above what it considers a normal profit margin. The application of this criterion for short-term wage adjustment, particularly during periods of fluctuating business, might make for disruptive fluctuations in wage schedules and wide discrepancies between firms in the area and in the industry. The lower limit in a firm's wage level is determined by the minimum rate required to recruit and maintain a satisfactory labor force.

Since the wage-paying capacity of many firms rises and falls more or less uniformly, the wage levels of companies frequently move in the same direction. Business establishments are often stimulated by, and respond to, the same market and economic forces: one firm adjusts its wages upward when other enterprises are also raising their pay levels. Moreover, the "key bargains" in labor-management agreements establish wage patterns in leading industries which contribute to uniformity in the wage levels of allied industries. Wage settlements in a given area are influenced by awards gained in other areas, particularly when they are in the same industry.

A firm with sufficient earning capacity may maintain a high-wage policy for a number of reasons: it may want to keep up its morale and labor performance; its labor cost may be a small percentage of the unit cost of the product; it may be sheltered from competition; or, it may anticipate a high level of business owing to a strong demand for its products. Marginal firms are frequently squeezed between their low wage-paying capacity and the minimum wage level necessary to hire

[12] There is a close interaction between wage increases and price increases during strong inflationary periods such as generally occur during and after wars. Rising prices, which decrease real wages, prompt demands for wage increases; and wage increases, since they raise costs, in turn lead to higher prices.

satisfactory workers and maintain an adequate labor force. Management can sometimes maintain a satisfactory "level of wages" by increasing the employees' take-home pay through an increase in the workweek.

EMPLOYEE MERIT RATING

Since company wage and salary systems generally provide for compensation within a range of pay for each position, it is important to determine the basis on which wage and salary increases within the limits of pay for each position should be made and the basis on which men should be selected for advanced training, promotion, layoff, etc. These decisions should not be left to the arbitrary judgment of supervisors, but should be made on the basis of explicit criteria consistently applied to measure employee performance of his work—i.e., on the basis of *merit rating*,[13] which is a systematic appraisal of the employee's personality traits and performance on the job and is designed to determine his contribution and relative worth to the firm. In deciding upon pay increases and promotions, therefore, management can not ignore such important employee performance factors as "quality of work," "capacity to learn," "co-operation," and "initiative." Moreover, enlightened management recognizes that employee merit rating brings positive advantages—it stimulates performance, makes possible a better understanding of employees, and uncovers special abilities of value.

Since merit rating often requires subjective judgments concerning such qualities as the employee's interest in his job, desire to learn, or reliability, it is subject to serious errors which can impair morale. A merit rating system must, therefore, be carefully designed, raters must be thoroughly trained, and employee performance scores carefully interpreted and followed up with constructive measures. An ill-devised or poorly administered plan defeats its purpose by permitting inconsistency, arbitrariness, or bias to creep into the rating of employees; results can be no better than the judgment or honesty of the appraisers. Partially because of experience with poorly devised or administered rating systems and partially on "principle," unions generally oppose employee rating as a "fancy scheme" for favoritism; they prefer flat wage rates or an "automatic progression" plan for wage increases within the pay limits; and they favor seniority as a basis for decisions regarding promotion and layoff.

[13] It must be noted that whereas "job evaluation" *rates the occupation* or position to determine job differentials, "merit rating" *gauges employee performance* to determine the employee's relative contribution "on the job."

Procedure for Designing and Administering a Merit Rating System. (1) Determine employee groups to be covered and the purposes of performance rating; (2) set up a rating method by selecting and defining performance traits to be appraised and preparing a rating scale; (3) select and train raters; and (4) check and interpret performance scores and use the information for granting individual wage advances, employee counseling, and training and the like.

Coverage and Purposes of Merit Rating. Management may apply performance rating to manual employees only; or it may extend the coverage (particularly after it proves successful with hourly-paid workers) to include clerical and office employees and supervisors.

A number of *benefits* accrue from merit rating: (1) merit rating provides a sound basis for pay increases within wage-rate and salary ranges; (2) it provides a basis for promotions, selection for higher training, transfer, or layoffs; (3) it checks the effectiveness of recruiting, training, and placement of employees and provides a basis for better job reassignment when employees have been improperly placed; (4) it promotes a desire for improvement and heightens morale by showing that management appraises and rewards individual performance and growth; and (5) it guides and aids employees in their self-improvement and makes possible a close follow-up on their progress.

Considerations in Setting Up a Rating Method. Employee performance factors must be carefully selected, defined, subdivided into degrees, and weighted; the data must be incorporated into a *rating scale* (i.e., scoring form); and instructions must be drawn up for its proper use.

SELECTION OF FACTORS AND PREPARATION OF SCALE. Merit rating requires the careful selection of traits or qualities to be considered in measuring the relative performance and worth of employees. Traits should be relevant to, and appear in varying degrees in, the classes of employees to be rated. The quality factors in the rating scale for supervisors will, therefore, differ to some extent from those in the rating scale for manual workers or office employees. The factors frequently used are (1) quantity and quality of work turned out; (2) dependability and attitudes as reflected, for example, in attendance and safety records and ability to co-operate; and (3) the employee's potential abilities as reflected by such traits as desire and capacity to learn, versatility, initiative, and leadership. Each factor should be precisely defined to secure a common understanding of qualities and a consistent standard of appraisal among raters and from one scoring period to

EMPLOYEE MERIT RATING				
NAME		DATE OF REVIEW		
POSITION		LOCATION		
DEPARTMENT	SUPERVISOR	DATE EMPLOYED		

FACTORS CONSIDERED	RATING AND COMMENTS				
1. QUALITY OF WORK ACCURACY, THOROUGHNESS; NEATNESS; CARE OF EQUIPMENT AND MATERIALS	☐ EXCEPTIONAL	☐ ABOVE AVERAGE	☐ AVERAGE	☐ BELOW AVERAGE	☐ POOR
	COMMENT:				
2. QUANTITY OF WORK AMOUNT OF ACCEPTABLE WORK ACCOMPLISHED; PROMPTNESS IN COMPLETING ASSIGNMENTS	☐ EXCEPTIONAL	☐ ABOVE AVERAGE	☐ AVERAGE	☐ BELOW AVERAGE	☐ POOR
	COMMENT:				
3. DEPENDABILITY ATTENDANCE; PUNCTUALITY; AMOUNT OF SUPERVISION REQUIRED	☐ EXCEPTIONAL	☐ ABOVE AVERAGE	☐ AVERAGE	☐ BELOW AVERAGE	☐ POOR
	COMMENT:				
4. ATTITUDE TOWARD COMPANY POLICIES; TOWARD FELLOW EMPLOYEES; TOWARD THE JOB; INITIATIVE	☐ EXCEPTIONAL	☐ ABOVE AVERAGE	☐ AVERAGE	☐ BELOW AVERAGE	☐ POOR
	COMMENT:				
5. ADAPTABILITY ABILITY TO DO OTHER TYPES OF WORK; TO ADJUST QUICKLY TO JOB CHANGES	☐ EXCEPTIONAL	☐ ABOVE AVERAGE	☐ AVERAGE	☐ BELOW AVERAGE	☐ POOR
	COMMENT:				
5. ADDITIONAL INFORMATION NOTEWORTHY DATA NOT COVERED ABOVE	COMMENT:				

Use Reverse Side for Additional Observations.

Fig. 58. A simple merit rating form.

another. To measure the relative influence of a particular trait upon the employee's performance and worth, each factor should be subdivided into appropriate *degrees* (usually five) and described in carefully stated phrases. The factors should then be weighted according to their relative importance and in terms of the purpose of rating. Because of the need to justify ratings to employees, the "objective qualities" (e.g., quantity and quality of output) since they are more easily

measured are sometimes given more weight than the "subjective qualities" (e.g., initiative and desire to learn) which, though significant,
are appraised mainly on the basis of personal judgment.

A variety of rating scales are used in industry (see Fig. 58). To
test its comparative validity or usefulness, the prepared or selected
scale should be tried out on a sample group of employees before it is
adopted.

FREQUENCY OF RATING. The frequency of rating is largely determined by its purposes—that is, how often decisions must be made for
merit pay increases, promotion, and layoff and how much stimulation
and counseling are required for employee improvement. Employees are
ordinarily rated semiannually (though sometimes annually or quarterly)
and all personnel are rated at the same time in a given department or
plant. The time intervals between ratings must not be too short; else
ratings will suffer from hasty appraisal owing to the annoyance and
irksomeness of the task.

Selection and Training of Raters. Raters should be carefully selected and properly instructed. Supervisors and foremen are usually
assigned as raters since they are on the supervisory level closest to
employees. Two or more raters should be used whenever possible.
Raters must know the work and performance of employees in order
to appraise and rate personnel accurately. Faulty appraisals are worse
than none at all. Foremen's superiors should check ratings for thoroughness.

The purposes, scale, techniques, and procedure for rating should be
thoroughly covered in training conferences. Practice ratings should be
made during the conferences. To assure maximum accuracy, rating
difficulties and weaknesses should be noted, and raters should be
guided in how to circumvent them. A number of *common deficiencies*
in ratings can be identified and guarded against. Poor judgment and
bias may result from racial and religious prejudice. There may be no
uniform standard for or definition of quality factors. There may be a
"central tendency" (insufficient spread) in ratings with the result that
too many employees are rated as "average." Some employees may be
rated exceptionally high on all traits simply because they are ex-
ceptional in one trait the appraisal of which overshadows and influences other traits (halo effect).

Interpretation and Application. By reviewing present and past
ratings the personnel department can check for obvious discrepancies
and unusual shifts in ratings. These may be reviewed with the rater

for possible inconsistency in the use of rating standards and other deficiences discussed above.

Employees should be notified of the performance factors by which they are rated so that they will know the basis for promotions and wage increases and how to improve their performance. Employee progress can be measured by comparing recent rating scores with earlier ratings. Completed ratings should be discussed with employees so they may be informed of their strong points, told of their weaknesses, and given constructive suggestions for improvement and self-development.

DEVELOPMENT OF A WAGE–INCENTIVE PLAN

Management can develop a sound wage-incentive plan through an understanding of the relative merits of timework payment and incentive payment, familiarity with the various "standard" incentive plans, and application of the procedure (presented on pp. 308–313) for designing an incentive plan to fit company needs and operating conditions.

Timework (Day-Rate) Payment vs. Incentive Payment. The simplest and most common method of compensation is timework, whereby employees are paid a definite wage rate per hour or day, or a salary per week or month. Although the time method of payment is widely applied, there are many conditions under which a properly designed incentive wage plan can be used to the advantage of workers and the company.

APPLICATION OF TIME PAYMENT. The time basis of payment is used in approximately three-fourths of the manufacturing industry. It is necessary when work is unmeasured or not readily measurable, as in the case of much office, professional, supervisory, and factory indirect work. Time payment can be satisfactory where close and intimate supervision is practical, as in small shops or small firms.

Time payment is satisfactory for production work (i.e., direct labor jobs) (1) when the speed of work is mechanically paced by the process or by the materials-handling equipment (as is increasingly common with the widening application of mass-production techniques); (2) when quality and precision are important and may be sacrificed under the stimulus of incentive payment; (3) when production is highly diversified (as in custom manufacture of small orders or in cases where operations are of a temporary nature); and (4) when production interruptions and delays are sufficiently extensive to make incentive payment less practical.

BENEFITS AND LIMITATIONS OF TIME PAYMENT. Time payment is easy to compute and assures employees of definite earnings for time put in. Time as a basis of payment merely measures employee presence on the job, not the effort expended or results produced. Except in cases where production is mechanically paced, the amount of work performed or services rendered largely depends upon employee willingness and the effectiveness of supervision. An inefficient or lazy worker is paid at the same rate as an efficient worker. The efficient employee tends to hold down or peg his output to that of his fellow workers since additional effort is often not immediately reflected in his pay check. Unless there is a prospect for a pay increase or promotion (as would generally be the case under employee merit rating), employees doing routine work sometimes stabilize their output or performance at a level sufficient to hold their jobs. To get work out, therefore, requires persistent supervision; and when output varies from worker to worker, accurate unit labor costs are sometimes difficult to compute.

APPLICATION OF INCENTIVE PAYMENT. Incentive payment can be successfully applied to work which is readily measurable—that is, whereever standard tasks can be established and the work inspected and counted; it can not be satisfactorily applied where standard tasks or levels of performance can not be established. Incentive payment can be used for various purposes: to compensate manual or clerical employees on the basis of measured output; to compensate salesmen on the basis of sales volume; or to reward foremen on the basis of labor and material savings.[14] Incentive systems are more frequently applied to direct labor than to indirect labor since the flow of work is steadier and more easily measured. Industries in which measurable direct-labor jobs are common and which use incentives on a wide scale include coal mining and those engaged in the output of apparel, hosiery, rubber, shoes, and cigars.

BENEFITS AND LIMITATIONS OF INCENTIVE PAYMENT. Maximum employee efficiency is achieved when men are assigned a definite task for a given time and are stimulated financially by compensation according to their performance. Both the employee and the employer gain their primary objectives under a well-designed and properly administered incentive system. By increasing his output, the employee increases his earnings, while the employer receives a higher output of

[14] Incentive payment may also be applied to activities which are supplementary to production—e.g., maintenance of quality standards, accident prevention, attendance record.

standard quality work at lower labor cost per unit and lower overhead charges per unit. Though work simplification, which is necessary before jobs can be accurately timed for incentive payment, initially achieves output efficiency, it is the financial incentive which releases human energy and makes for additional long-run gains.

Incentives, as has been previously indicated, are limited to work and performance that can be measured as standard tasks; they are often handicapped by employee and union attitudes; and, unless well designed and properly administered they may boomerang and impair morale.

UNION ATTITUDE TOWARD INCENTIVES. Labor groups frequently identify incentives as "speed up." This view is, in part, a carry-over from the earlier experience with incentive systems when tasks were not accurately measured and rate cutting was not uncommon. Unions generally favor the day-rate over individual incentive payment because it makes for greater labor unity and places the primary responsibility for increased earnings upon collective bargaining rather than upon the individual effort of workers. During World War II when the wage stabilization program was in force, however, unions supported group incentive compensation as a potential means of increasing earnings. In many cases, as temporary measures, plant-wide incentive plans have been set up on the basis of over-all output in relation to man-hour expenditure.

Types of Incentive Plans. All incentive plans offer extra compensation for output in excess of ordinary levels. All except the straight piece-rate plan compensate on the basis of time (i.e., guarantee wage rates) as well as output (provide bonus earnings). The plans differ, however, with respect to the basis or methods for determining and calculating bonus and premium compensation for extra performance. Though they have been designed to fit particular production conditions, many of the incentive plans have some identical features and can be applied to indirect [15] as well as direct labor.

The most suitable "standard" plan may be selected and (where necessary) modified, or a special plan may be designed to fit given production conditions by considering and arranging the *component elements* which generally make up a plan: (1) the task level (performance standard), (2) the level (amount) of the guaranteed base wage rate, (3) the point at which extra compensation (bonus or

[15] Incentive plans have been successfully applied to indirect jobs such as maintenance work, stores-keeping, materials handling, and inspection.

premium rate) is to start, (4) the percentage of the extra output (or time saved) above the standard task to be credited to the worker, and (5) the amount or size of incentive reward or bonus. (The representative plans presented in the following paragraphs illustrate the foregoing features, familiarity with which will aid in applying the procedure for designing a company incentive plan as discussed at the end of this chapter.)

THE PIECE-RATE. The straight piecework plan compensates on the basis of the number of units of work produced for the day multiplied by a fixed rate per piece (e.g., 6¢ per piece × 200 units produced = $12 earnings). Except for the minimum wage required by law, the employee makes his gains or losses in direct proportion to his performance—hence the incentive impetus is very strong.

Piece rates, in earlier practice, were set arbitrarily—usually derived by dividing the previously existing day wage by the average number of units that were produced and then selecting a piece rate somewhat less than this amount. Rates for new jobs were estimated. These inaccurate methods of rate setting frequently resulted in their being either too high or too low. High rates were identified as "speed up" and the raising of rates was dubbed "rate cutting." [16] The piece-rate plan is an effective, stable incentive only when rates are accurately established by time study (after jobs have been improved and standardized) and are guaranteed against revision or "rate cutting" so long as jobs remain substantially unchanged; and when there are comparatively few production interruptions.

THE 100-PER-CENT PREMIUM PLAN. Under the 100-per-cent premium plan, task standards are set by time studies, and rates are expressed in time rather than money (e.g., 0.10 hour per piece). A definite hourly rate is paid for each task-hour of work performed. The plan is identical with the straight piece-rate plan except for its higher guaranteed hourly rate and the use of task time as a unit of payment instead of a "price" per piece. The worker is paid *full value for time saved*. For example, if the standard task-hour is set at 10 units output and the worker completes the task in 40 minutes, he receives the full hourly wage. In essence, the plan provides a straight piece rate for all production above the standard task. Its introduction is made easier by

[16] Even when rates were more accurately set, efficient workers by improving their methods and workplace arrangement could increase their output and earnings until the employer identified the rate as "too low." In order not to "kill the job" workers would "hide" their improvements and protect "loose" jobs by pegging their output at what they considered to be a reasonable level.

the hourly rate and the premium piece-rate features. Its advantage over the straight piece-rate plan is the ease of raising or lowering the hourly rate—hourly rates can be adjusted while the time standards for output remain the same. Changes of rates under the straight piece-rate plan are cumbersome, and downward adjustments are invariably interpreted as "rate cutting."

THE STANDARD-HOUR PLAN. The standard task, ordinarily set by time study, is measured in man-hours representing 100-per-cent efficiency, or the standard hour. The plan, guaranteeing the hourly wage, is flexible in that the level selected for payment at full hourly wage rates (i.e., bonus earnings) is at a point less than 100-per-cent efficiency (e.g., at 80 per cent or 90 per cent of the standard task). When the worker's output rate reaches the designated level, he receives his hourly rate for all work put out at that rate. For example, if the task time is 0.20 hours per unit (or 5 units per hour) and the point for full hourly payment is set at 80 per cent of the standard hour, the worker will receive one hour's wage for every 4 units produced. Under the 100-per-cent premium plan, however, bonus payments start at standard task—i.e., 100-per-cent efficiency. In this case the worker receives the full hourly rate for every 5 units produced.

THE HALSEY PREMIUM (GAIN-SHARING) PLAN. The Halsey plan sets performance standards on the basis of previous average production, guarantees a daily wage, and rewards the worker for *time saved at a definite percentage* of the hourly wage rate (usually 30 to 50 per cent).[17] Since the worker shares the gains with the company, his earnings per piece progressively decrease as his output exceeds the standard; whereas in the piece-rate and the 100-per-cent premium plans he takes the entire savings or gains above standard. Though the Halsey plan sets a comparatively liberal task level, inaccuracies in time standards are not too serious since the bonus is modest. Because the company shares in the savings and thus reduces labor costs, it is less tempted to cut rates. In order to stimulate over-all performance, some Halsey-type plans give a portion of the company's share of the time

---

[17] For example, in a 50–50 gain-sharing plan with a guaranteed wage of $1.00 per hour and a standard task of 1 unit per hour or 8 units in an 8-hour day, a superior worker producing 11 units for the day (saving 3 hours) receives $8.00 as guaranteed wages and, in addition, a premium of $1.50 which is 50 per cent of the time saved multiplied by the hourly wage rate. Workers producing at or below the standard task (8 units a day) receive only the guaranteed wage ($8.00).

saved to foremen and a portion to indirect workers supporting production.

The Halsey plan is easy to introduce since the standard is based on past performance and no preliminary methods improvements and time studies need be conducted. Thus it is readily applicable to the less standardized production processes and to maintenance work, materials handling, and other indirect labor where the work can be estimated or roughly timed. With a guaranteed wage securing the base earnings for the worker, the plan uses the bonus feature to "coax" employees to produce more than past performance.

The weakness of the plan is the unevenness of task standards—some job performance standards are "easy," others, "hard." This weakness can be overcome by, first, improving and standardizing production methods and, then, setting task standards through time studies. Then, to generate sufficient incentive, a larger premium allowance (a greater percentage of the time saved) should be offered since accurate setting of tasks will tend to reduce the amount of time formerly saved on loosely set jobs and on jobs made loose by workers' own improvement of inefficient operations.

THE GANTT TASK-AND-BONUS PLAN. In the Gantt plan, after production methods have been improved and standardized, performance standards are set by time studies at high task levels (which require consistent application of effort and workmanship to attain) and workers are guaranteed a comparatively high hourly wage rate. Workers completing the task in the standard time or less are paid the hourly rate for the *allowed time plus a bonus* which is a fixed percentage (20 to 50 per cent) of the wage for the allowed time. For performance *above task*, however, the worker receives the *full labor savings*, which makes the plan at this point equivalent to a high piece rate.[18] Because of its strong incentive and wage security, the plan is suitable to production involving high overhead charges and susceptible to unavoidable delays. The plan uses the selective principle by rewarding superior workers with a sharp jump in earnings, while substandard and average

---

[18] For example, with a day rate of $1.00 per hour, a standard task of 40 units in an 8-hour day (0.20 hours per piece), and a bonus of 25 per cent of the wage for the allowed time, a worker producing 40 units will receive $10.00. A worker producing 39 units will receive only $8.00, the guaranteed day rate. A worker producing 45 units will receive the day rate ($9.00) for the allowed time (9 hours) plus 25 per cent of the allowed time ($2.25), resulting in earnings of $11.25.

workers, being discouraged, leave the job (or are transferred) and are systematically replaced by men who can earn the high task and bonus. The bonus percentage selected depends upon the nature of the work and the amount of incentive necessary to achieve the required response. The strong incentive is designed to secure uniformly high performance by superior workers, thus facilitating production planning and reducing over-all costs, particularly on machines with high burden rates. The system, as advocated by Gantt, offered foremen a bonus based on the number of the workmen attaining the task level, a feature which would encourage foremen to improve the performance of substandard workers and achieve more intensive use of facilities.

EMERSON EFFICIENCY-BONUS PLAN. In the Emerson plan, task standards are set by studies after production methods have been improved. With the day rate guaranteed, a *graduated bonus* starts at 67 per cent of efficiency, paying 10 per cent of the day rate at 90-per-cent efficiency, and 20 per cent at 100-per-cent efficiency. For output above the standard task the worker is *credited with all the time saved plus* 20 per cent *of the actual time worked.* The worker's efficiency and bonus are calculated over a pay period (usually a week) and not for a given job or a single day, thus giving the worker an opportunity to make up for work in which he fell behind. The plan offers a moderate incentive and provides a gradual pull for performance, rather than, as the Gantt task-and-bonus plan, strong incentive with a sharp jump in earnings.

THE BEDAUX POINT SYSTEM. In the Bedaux plan, operation methods and working conditions are first improved and standardized, and then, with the day rate guaranteed, time study is used to set allowed times for all work in terms of standard minutes, "Bs" or "points," the common denominator to which all tasks are reduced. If a particular work task is rated at 60 Bs (or one B-hour), the worker is allowed one hour for its completion and receives a *bonus for the number of Bs,* i.e., time, *saved.* A "B," therefore, represents the amount of work an average man performs in a minute while working at a normal rate of speed and effort; it consists of a fraction of a minute of effort plus a fraction of a minute allowance for fatigue (rest) and personal needs. The size of the fatigue allowance depends upon the physical demands of the work and hence varies from job to job.[19] Thus, the plan establishes comparable standards for all work throughout the plant.

A worker's accomplishment is measured by the number of B units

[19] A difficult task may be given $\frac{1}{3}$ of a minute for rest, while a less strenuous task may receive $\frac{1}{6}$ of a minute for rest.

produced in an hour, with 60 Bs as a standard hour's work and 480 Bs as a standard (8-hour) day's work. If a workman produces less than 60 Bs per hour, he receives a guaranteed hourly rate. For accomplishment in excess of 60 Bs per hour, the workman receives a bonus equal to the time saved [20] or, in some cases, 75 per cent of the time saved with the remainder divided between foremen and indirect workers.

The plan is particularly suitable for plants in which operators are assigned diverse work or are shifted from one job or department to another; and it is also useful for production control purposes. Since departmental output (including machine output) is reducible to a total number of Bs per day, the planning office can accurately load departments and machines, set exact completion dates, and measure accomplishment.

THE GROUP INCENTIVE PLAN. The group incentive plan, which compensates a number of workers for their combined output, widens the application of the incentive method of payment. Its suitability to given work must be be based on the analysis of the selected production and the appraisal of the benefits to be derived.

Applications. A group incentive may be applied when a measurable group task occurs as a logical divisional unit in fabrication, assembly, or indirect work in which operations are closely integrated and are at close proximity and employees are keenly aware of their interests as a group. In such cases individual incentives are not practical either because individual jobs are not readily measurable or a given worker's speed is limited by the output rate of preceding operators. The group task, controlled by a working group leader, is usually effective for incentive payment when it is limited in membership—e.g., a crew operating a large piece of equipment, up to 20 men fabricating given parts or products, or up to 100 men assembling an item. The character of the work and the size of the groups should be such that workers can be mutually helpful and able to see the results of their individual efforts (and thereby be effectively stimulated).

Bonus Payments. Many of the plans already discussed are suitable for group incentive purposes. For example, in the Gantt-type of plan, with day rates guaranteed and a standard group task set, the group bonus

[20] For example, if a workman with a day rate of $1.20 per hour accumulates 600 Bs on various jobs during an 8-hour day, he receives $9.60 for the hourly rate plus $2.40 bonus. The 120 premium points (600 Bs — 480 Bs = 120 Bs) or two B-hours saved by the worker are multiplied by the hourly rate. The workman keeps account of his current bonus earnings by checking a daily posting sheet which shows the individual's previous day's bonus earnings.

307

percentage is applied to each man's base wage rate.[21] The foreman and supporting indirect workers may be included in the bonus.

Benefits. Under the spur of incentive, production is greater and the workers' earnings larger than would be the case under the day rate. Little additional clerical work is required. Discipline and responsibility for accomplishment are assumed by all, and constant interest in achieving the group objective maintains high morale. Each worker's attentiveness is increased, and the slow worker strives to attain the performance expected of him. Stimulated by a common financial incentive, the members co-operate and work as an efficient team; they share the fine points of the trade, jointly improve methods, eliminate bottlenecks, and keep the operations in balance. New workers are quickly trained by the group. Less supervisory effort is required of the foreman since the working group leader assumes much of the direction and control over the details of the group task.

Limitations. When personal difficulties arise among the members, the group effort may be disrupted. If the group is comparatively large, a member may "lie down" unless group pressure is sufficient to keep him on the job. A highly experienced group is sometimes too impatient with a new worker, considering him "slow in learning."

Procedure for Developing a Company Incentive Plan. (1) Select and improve production processes and activities that are suitable for incentive payment; (2) identify (for inclusion in the plan) the features essential to the satisfactory functioning of incentive payment; (3) study the firm's particular operating conditions including the manner in which work is assigned and effort applied: (4) select and adopt a suitable "standard" plan, or design a special incentive plan to fit the firm's needs and operating conditions.

The design of the plan must take into account the company's experience with incentives and the employees' and unions' attitude toward incentives.[22] Plans should first be introduced in those departments where operations can easily be improved and standardized and time standards for workers' tasks readily determined. With the experience gained and employee confidence and acceptance secured,

[21] If the group achieves a 20-per-cent bonus, for instance, a worker with a base rate of $1.00 per hour will receive $8.00 on his day rate plus $1.60 bonus (.20 × $8.00), a worker with a base rate of $1.20 per hour will receive $9.60 on his day rate plus $1.92 bonus (.20 × $9.60), etc.

[22] Despite prevailing union opposition on the basis of principle, local unions in some industries co-operate in the operation of incentive plans. Some companies cover the basic principles of the incentive plan in collective bargaining and include the details in the contract.

management can then extend incentive payment to cover other production departments and, later, to the operations of indirect workers.

Selection and Improvement of Work (Prerequisites). Incentive wage payment plans can not function successfully unless processes, operations, and the quality requirements of production are suitable for incentive payment; processing methods are standardized; and individual or group output tasks (performance standards) carefully established.

SUITABILITY OF WORK. Incentives can be applied to work or activity where a sufficiently direct relationship exists between employee efforts and output results and where individual tasks or group tasks are measurable in terms of definite units of output, e.g., a given quantity of pieces, pounds, or gallons per hour.

SUITABILITY OF QUALITY REQUIREMENTS. The quality of work must not decline because of incentive payment. When quality is relatively unimportant or its effect on quality is negligible, wage incentives can obviously be applied with no need for additional inspection. However, if work can not be easily or inexpensively inspected, management must weigh the additional cost for quality control against the saving to be gained from incentive payment.

IMPROVEMENT AND STANDARDIZATION OF PRODUCTION. For best incentive results production methods and processes must, first, be improved through a work-simplification study, and operation sequence, equipment, material, and working conditions must be standardized and reasonably controlled. Delays and interruptions in the flow of work should be eliminated or, at least, held to a minimum. Workers' output and performance should not be hampered or held down by irregular or retarded output from preceding operations.

ESTABLISHMENT OF TASK STANDARDS. Output standards (time allowed for workers' tasks) should be set by time studies so that employee effort may be accurately measured and rewarded.

Essentials of a Satisfactory Plan. The plan must offer an adequate financial reward, be simple and acceptable to employees, provide a guaranteed base pay, provide protection against rate cutting, and be easy to administer.

ADEQUATE INCENTIVE. The amount of financial incentive offered should be sufficient to stimulate effort and essentially reward the worker for quantity and quality of work turned out. To maintain an effective inducement, incentive earnings should be computed frequently (bonus slips issued daily or weekly) and promptly paid (or credited) at the end of the period in which they were earned.

SIMPLICITY AND ACCEPTANCE. The plan must be sufficiently simple for the worker to understand the basis for compensation and reward and to compute his bonus earnings. Excessively complicated plans as well as indefinite task standards do not create the required inducement or incentive "pull" and, in fact, often breed suspicion and mistrust. In order to secure confidence and acceptance, the plan should be carefully explained to employees and union representatives.

GUARANTEED BASE PAY. The plan should provide adequate guaranteed base compensation or hourly wage rates as security against delays over which the worker has no control. Straight piece-rate plans when applied to the proper kind of work essentially "guarantee" the going base pay since production delays are sufficiently infrequent for the worker to "make his rate."

PROTECTION AGAINST RATE CUTTING. The plan must protect the worker against rate cutting or "tightening" of task standards. The rate, time allowance, or standard task should not be revised unless a substantial change has been made in production methods—e.g., machine or tool improvement, material change, or product design change. In general, alterations which change output in excess of 5 per cent from that of the previous standard should justify a retiming of the job.

EASE OF ADMINISTRATION. The plan should be comparatively inexpensive to operate and easy to administer—i.e., it should be simple to check, count, and record output of acceptable quality; to compute earnings and bonuses; to notify employees of results; and to adjust errors in bonus computations. Whenever possible, the plan should be integrated with production-control and cost-accounting procedures.

Analysis of Operating Conditions and Use of Labor. A suitable incentive plan must be selected and adapted or specially designed to suit the operating conditions and the manner in which labor effort is applied.

OPERATING CONDITIONS. In designing an incentive plan the analyst should take into account and appraise (1) the magnitude of the firm's overhead charges, (2) the degree to which operating conditions have been standardized, (3) the extent of time loss owing to interruptions and delays, and (4) the suitability of the work for individual or group tasks and incentives. High overhead charges and comparatively standardized conditions, for instance, tend to favor a plan which emphasizes the selection of superior workers and the attainment of low costs primarily through intensive use of, or high output from, the expensive facilities. These objectives may be attained by using a moderate guaranteed base wage rate, a high task level, and a strong incentive (large bonus) paid at task level with all time saved above task accruing to the worker. Low overhead charges and less standardized conditions, on the other hand, tend to favor a plan which stimulates workers at all levels of output and stresses low labor costs through the use of an intermediate task level (or a graduated bonus starting below 100-per-cent efficiency of a high task), sharing of time saved above task, and a comparatively high guaranteed base rate.

Assignment and Application of Labor. The conditions involved in assigning work and applying effort that must be considered include (1) the amount of diversity in work assignments and the extent to which workers are shifted to various jobs, (2) the extent to which foremen and indirect workers directly aid in furthering the output of incentive workers, (3) the extent to which new workers are hired or the manpower force expanded, and (4) the extent to which employees are trained before assignment to regular work. If assignments are comparatively diverse and conditions are standardized, a "point" incentive system with a guarantee against delays (Bedaux-type plan) is suitable. When foremen and supporting indirect workers materially facilitate and improve output, their inclusion in bonus earnings may be recommended. If the firm is constantly expanding, or if labor turnover is comparatively high, a temporary day-rate basis of payment will be necessary until new men are ready (fully trained) for inclusion in the incentive system.

Selection or Design of the Incentive Plan. After work suitable for incentives has been selected and prepared, features essential to successful incentives identified, and operating conditions and application of labor analyzed for incentive purposes, a plan may be selected (and, when necessary, adapted) to fit the needs of the firm. Or a plan may be specially designed by arranging or determining the task level, the level of the guaranteed base wage rate, the point at which the bonus starts, the percentage of the time saved (or extra output) going to the worker, the amount (size) of incentive bonus offered, and the level of total earnings. Since these factors are mutually influential, all must be analyzed and arranged to fit the operating conditions of the firm.

Task Level. A comparatively high task level should be set when conditions are standardized, accurate time studies can be made, overhead charges are high, a high guaranteed base rate is used, and the attraction and retention of superior workers are desired. The task level should be lower when conditions are less standardized, when accurate time studies are difficult to make, and when a gain-sharing feature is to be employed.

THE LEVEL OF THE GUARANTEED BASE WAGE RATE. The level of the guaranteed wage must meet the requirements of minimum-wage laws, and it must be set with reference to the problem of recruiting labor. In general, the level should be higher when delays are extensive or when a high task level is used with bonus starting at task.

THE POINT AT WHICH THE BONUS STARTS. The point at which bonus payment starts should be lower when the guaranteed base wage rate is low, and higher (e.g., at task level) when the base wage rate is high, when production delays are less prominent, or when the selective principle is to be applied.

THE PERCENTAGE OF TIME SAVED GOING TO THE WORKER. The percentage of time saved going to the worker should be greater (usually 100 per cent) when conditions are standardized, task levels high, and overhead charges large. The gain-sharing feature should be adopted when opposite conditions prevail.

THE AMOUNT OF INCENTIVE BONUS OFFERED. The size of the bonus provided, whether at or below the task, and its effectiveness as a stimulus can be determined on the basis of the level (or difficulty) of the task and the level of the guaranteed wage rate.[23] The "pull" of the bonus ("extra earnings" above guaranteed wage) tends to be greater when it makes up a larger portion of the total earnings that can be made. The stimulus of the bonus will, obviously, vary from worker to worker.

LEVEL OF TOTAL EARNINGS. Earnings of workers under incentive wage systems should be, and customarily are, higher than those of day-rate workers on equivalent jobs since the output of the former is greater. But the problems to be solved are how much higher the earnings should be and how large an incentive should be necessary for adequate inducement. In principle, incentive wage rates and earnings for various job grades should be derived from the wage rates established by job evaluation and wage surveys for the same or equivalent jobs. Incentive wages should be at least high enough for the average incentive worker to be able to attain earnings slightly above (ordinarily 10 to 15 per cent) the upper limit of the pay range established for an equivalent

---

[23] For example, if the guaranteed base rate is set at a moderate level and the level of the task is high, the bonus (to be paid at task level) should be large enough to induce the worker to achieve the task. On the other hand, if an intermediate task level is set, a smaller bonus may be sufficient to induce the worker to achieve the task. The incentive pull of the bonus is obviously influenced by the level of the guaranteed base rate.

day-rated job. However, the level of earnings as well as the bonus should be higher when the task level and overhead charges are high. When the financial stimulus is effective, earnings of most workers will substantially exceed the upper level of the wage range of the timework wage, but the amounts will vary because of individual differences in response to the incentive pull, in ability, and in experience. Actual incentive earnings are sometimes lower than they should be (even though the incentive plan is well designed and time standards properly established) because workers hold down their output as a result of the "lump-of-labor" attitude—i.e., the notion that there is only so much work (e.g., sales orders) available and that if the point of exhaustion is approached some workers will be laid off. Thus employees sometimes hold down production because they "don't want to work themselves out of a job." This attitude partly stems from experience with technological, seasonal, and cyclical types of unemployment.

Questions

1. What aspects or phases of company operations may be favorably or adversely affected by the design and administration of their wage systems?

2. Identify and distinguish among real wages, supplementary pay, take-home pay, wage rates, and labor cost per unit of output.

3. What internal and external factors should management take into account and appraise in formulating its wage policies?

4. State four wage policies and show how internal and external factors influence the formulation of these policies.

5. Outline the over-all procedural steps for designing and administering a company wage system.

6. What personnel and compensation problems develop when company wage and salary differentials are not established on a rational, consistent basis such as obtainable through job evaluation?

7. Distinguish among operation analysis, job analysis, job rating, and merit rating.

8. What are the advantages of the point system of job evaluation over the ranking method?

9. What factors are commonly used to evaluate manual jobs?

10. Since job evaluation seeks to determine wage differentials for occupations, what is left for collective bargaining on wages?

11. Explain how a wage survey is conducted.

12. What is meant by "key jobs," "labor grades," and the "wage line"?

13. Distinguish between occupation differentials and geographic differentials.

14. Under what conditions may management adopt a high-wage policy (i.e., set wages above prevailing levels) without endangering its earning capacity?

15. When may management succeed in paying a wage below the prevailing level without seriously affecting its ability to recruit a satisfactory labor force?

16. When should a "flat wage rate" be adopted and when should a "wage rate range" be adopted?

17. Identify and distinguish among automatic progression, escalator clause, and the annual improvement factor.

18. How does "keeping the wage structure up-to-date" differ from "periodic adjustment of the wage level"?

19. How may changes in the prevailing level of wages, cost of living, and ability to pay affect a firm's wage level?

20. Outline the procedural steps for designing a merit rating system.

21. How would you determine what employee traits or qualities to rate?

22. Under what conditions is time payment a satisfactory basis of compensation for production workers?

23. What are the benefits and limitations of incentive payment?

24. Why do unions favor day-rate payment over individual incentives?

25. What are the common elements making up incentive-wage plans?

26. What is the essential difference between the "piece-rate" plan and the "100-per-cent premium" plan?

27. Describe the Halsey premium (gain-sharing) plan and explain why it is easy to introduce.

28. Describe the Bedaux point system and explain the operating conditions to which it is particularly suited.

29. Explain the "selective," "time-saving," and "gain-sharing" features of wage-incentive plans.

30. Distinguish between individual and group incentive-wage plans.

31. How may indirect workers be included in such plans?

32. (a) Under what conditions may the group incentive plan be successfully used? (b) What are the particular benefits of the group incentive plan?

33. Outline the steps for developing a company incentive-wage plan.

34. What prerequisites must exist or be established before incentive-wage plans can function satisfactorily?

35. What features are essential to a satisfactory incentive plan?

36. What production conditions must be taken into account and appraised before a wage-incentive plan can be selected or designed?

37. What factors in work assignment and application of labor must be appraised before a wage-incentive plan can be selected or designed?

38. What are the component elements of incentive-wage plans that must be analyzed and arranged in designing a plan to fit the particular operating conditions of a plant?

39. What are the causes of the "lump of labor" attitude among workers?

40. Evaluate "profit sharing" against the criteria of a sound incentive-wage plan and explain why it is comparatively ineffective in inducing workers to increase efficiency on a day-to-day basis.

25: Controllorship and Cost-
Accounting Control

In a going concern, management controls business operations, studies trends, and formulates plans on the basis of comprehensive reports prepared from financial, cost accounting, and operational records. It establishes a controller's department to compile and summarize records and prepare reports so that its business activities and developments can be duly brought to the attention of executives and supervisors. Managerial reliance on comprehensive factual information becomes progressively more important as its organization increases in size and complexity and when business is uncertain and economic change rapid.

THE CONTROLLER'S DEPARTMENT

Procedure for Setting Up the Controller's Department. (1) Determine the place of controllership in the company organization structure; (2) determine the type of information and reports to be included in the centralized records-keeping system—i.e., outline the scope of the controller's department; and (3) break down the department into functionalized divisions and delegate duties to each.

Place of the Controller in the Organization. The position of the · controller in the organization structure varies, depending upon the needs of the business, the caliber of the person holding the position, the specific functions assigned to the office, and the size of the firm. In the large firm, he ordinarily heads up a separate department directly under top management—the president, general manager, or board of directors. In the small firm, the controller's functions may be combined with those of the treasurer.

The Controller's Functions. The controller is in charge of the department responsible for company-wide records and reports—accounting, tax liabilities, auditing, budgeting, credit and collections, and statistics. With the co-operation of associate executives he organizes, determines standards for, and controls and co-ordinates the interdepartmental records system from which he provides timely reports to management. Though departmental records are not within his jurisdiction, the controller nonetheless assists company executives in developing records systems for their offices—e.g., for engineering and production planning.

DETERMINATION OF TYPES OF REPORTS. Periodically or for a special purpose, the controller prepares *analytic reports,* which evaluate, interpret, or propose recommendations for action, and *informational reports,* which merely summarize data without recommendations. His *periodic reports,* which are carefully selected for their usefulness to management, include financial statements (balance sheet, profit and loss and manufacturing statements), annual reports to stockholders, tax returns, budgetary statements, and production summaries. His *special reports,* often initiated by executives, are usually the results of investigation and analysis of problems dealing with particular phases of business operation—e.g., cost studies of engineering projects and governmental tax, credit, and other regulations. The controller may also directly participate, or advise executives and staff men, in the preparation of their special reports—e.g., proposals for new products, marketing outlets, plant revisions, or equipment replacement.

The controller sees that effective techniques and proper form in report preparation and writing are observed. He sets report-writing standards, taking into consideration the purpose of the report, the scope of the presentation, and the knowledge, interest, and comprehension of the reader; he may require that the content and organization of reports consist of a summary, text material, conclusions, and recommendations.

CONTROL THROUGH REPORTS AND STANDARDS. To increase the value of periodic reports for purposes of analysis and administration, the controller establishes or participates in setting up realistic standards of performance for every important phase of the business. His current records and reports, prepared with reference to and in comparison with the selected standards, provide a basis of regulation and control through the "principle of exceptions." Hence, when company activities and developments deviate from established standards, the records-and-reports system promptly reveals the abnormality. For example, *operating standards* establish control limits for inventory turnover, scrap percentage, absenteeism, ratio of distribution expense to sales for each area and salesmen, etc. *Procedural standards*, set up for departmental and interdepartmental routine activities (e.g., procurement and materials control), implement policies, attain co-ordination and control, and reduce errors. *Financial standards*, expressed in terms of ratios, show changes in the relationships among the various parts of the financial structure—e.g., ratio of current assets to current liabilities.

Departmental Breakdown and Control. In a representative firm the controller breaks down his functions into the following specialized divisions, which he administers: (1) the *general office*, which develops and co-ordinates office procedures and provides company-wide clerical services; (2) the *general accounting division*, which sets up and operates the company accounting system and prepares financial statements and reports; (3) the *cost-accounting division*, which compiles production and distribution costs, computes the value of inventories, and conducts special cost studies; (4) the *tax division*, which prepares and files company tax returns and advises management on tax matters; (5) the *auditing division*, which examines and verifies the accounting books, transactions, and financial statements; (6) the *budgeting division*, which assists in the preparation of budgets, carries out the procedure, and works up departmental performance reports; (7) the *credit and collection division*, which approves customer applications for credit and collects bills; and (8) the *statistical division* which compiles and analyzes internal data (e.g., output, quality, and accident figures) and external data (e.g., population trends, income distribution and price trends necessary for managerial planning and control).

The General Office Division. As the company specialist, the general office manager prepares, co-ordinates, and issues standard procedures and systems for the office work of the firm. To relieve the various departments of clerical burdens, he provides such *routine office services* as switchboard operation, messenger delivery, mailing and telegraph, duplicating, stenography, typing, and filing.

The general office manager achieves efficiency by establishing the proper degree of centralization of company office work, by designing effective record-and-report systems, by developing economical office practices through work simplification, and by effectively planning and scheduling office work.

CENTRALIZATION OF OFFICE WORK. The extent to which common clerical work should be concentrated in the general office depends upon the practicability of separating routine office work from the various departments, the amount of clerical skill required, and the economies to be obtained.

Effective concentration relieves executives of part or all of their responsibility for office supervision through the employment of an expert (the office manager) in office work; permits greater specialization in office tasks and thereby lowers labor costs; and affords an opportunity for installation of efficient procedures and elaborate office machines that save many man-hours of clerical work.

DESIGNING OF AN EFFECTIVE RECORDS SYSTEM. In designing efficient systems for records and reports, the general office manager employs the following criteria.

(1) *Useful Purpose.* Reports should be made and records kept only when the information is important. To be useful for managerial control and to serve as a basis for action, they must also be timely, and the recording procedures should automatically single out "exceptions" requiring attention.

(2) *Logical Presentation of Data.* Essential information should be presented simply yet completely and accurately. Important data should "stand out" so that they can be easily identified.

(3) *Appropriate Forms.* In order that the data may be logically arranged for easy interpretation and compilation into reports, forms should be designed (standard forms should be purchased when suitable) to fit the special needs of the company.

(4) *Effectiveness and Economy in Use.* Record systems should be designed for multiplicity of use, maximum correlation with other information, and minimum duplication of clerical work.

(5) *Convenience and Accessibility.* Filing methods should be developed for speed and accessibility. Files should be centrally located and controlled by responsible personnel.

WORK SIMPLIFICATION. The general office manager with the assistance of the industrial engineer applies the principles of work simplification and motion economy, particularly to the routine work that absorbs many man-hours. As he develops efficient standard clerical procedures, he purchases special office equipment suitable for the routine, thus attaining "mass-production" economies. Since his office work is

Financial Statements

specialized, he can recruit and easily train comparatively inexperienced personnel for the various simplified tasks.

The manager develops an efficient office layout by applying the principles and techniques (flow process charts, diagrams, templates, floor plans) outlined in Ch. 17.

The Accounting Division. The chief accountant assumes responsibility for designing an accounting system, keeping accounts, and preparing and interpreting financial statements through which management measures the results of past operations and plans and controls the conduct of the business. In the large firm the chief accountant subdivides his function into general accounting, cost accounting, tax accounting, and auditing.

THE COMPANY ACCOUNTING SYSTEM. The chief accountant sets up a classification of accounts,[1] breaking down assets, liabilities, costs, and income to reflect the firm's particular business operations. On the basis of this classification he can make up financial statements in the form most useful for managerial purposes. He specifies the procedure for recording all transactions that add to or subtract from the capital assets of the firm and those that add to or subtract from the income of the business. He then organizes his system into functionalized sections—e.g., the general ledger, accounts receivable, accounts payable, payroll, etc. Because assignments are specialized, bookkeepers responsible for each section become proficient in their work.

FINANCIAL STATEMENTS. Accountants prepare three primary statements—the balance sheet, the profit and loss statement, and the manufacturing cost statement showing financial position and operating results (i.e., net worth and profit or loss). The *balance sheet* (Fig. 59), prepared from the classification of accounts, is a statement of assets, liabilities, and net worth (or owner's equity, the difference between the assets and liabilities) arranged to show the financial condition of the firm on a given date. The *profit and loss statement* (Fig. 60) reports income from operations and the expense involved in producing and distributing goods and services; it indicates the financial progress or regress during a given period. The *manufacturing cost statement* (Fig. 61) summarizes production costs for a given period and supports and supplements the profit and loss statement.

[1] The items listed on the balance sheet, on the statement of cost of goods manufactured, and on the profit and loss statement illustrated in Figs. 59, 60, and 61 show a representative classification of accounts for a medium-sized manufacturing firm.

BALANCE SHEET
December 31, 1953

ASSETS			
Current Assets:			
Cash..............................		$30,000	
Accounts Receivable............	$35,000		
Less Reserve for Bad Debts..	1,000	34,000	
Inventories:			
Finished Goods..................	$17,000		
Goods in Process...............	11,000		
Raw Materials..................	9,000	37,000	
Total Current Assets........			$101,000
Fixed Assets:			
Land..............................		$13,000	
Factory Buildings...............	$70,000		
Less Reserve for Depreciation	15,500	54,500	
Machinery and Equipment...	$60,000		
Less Reserve for Depreciation	21,000	39,000	
Furniture and Fixtures........	$ 5,000		
Less Reserve for Depreciation	2,200	2,800	
Total Fixed Assets—Depreciated Value......		109,300	
Deferred Charges:			
Unexpired Insurance............		300	
			$210,600

LIABILITIES AND NET WORTH			
Current Liabilities:			
Accounts Payable................		$ 22,800	
Accrued Salaries and Wages......		4,325	
Total Current Liabilities......			$ 27,125
Net Worth:			
Capital Stock....................		$100,000	
Surplus..........................		83,475	
Total Net Worth.............			183,475
			$210,600

Fig. 59. A balance sheet.

COMPARATIVE STATEMENT OF PROFIT AND LOSS FOR THE THREE
MONTHS ENDED DEC. 31, 1953, AND DEC. 31, 1952

		1953		*1952*
Sales		$152,879.67		$147,389.30
Less: Return Sales	$ 1,719.50		$ 1,480.50	
Discount on Sales	2,654.54	4,374.04	2,374.80	3,855.30
New Sales		$148,505.63		$143,534.00
Cost of Goods Sold (per Statement 1) *		101,200.00		97,914.72
Gross Profit on Sales		$ 47,305.63		$ 45,619.28
Expenses:				
General Expenses (per Statement 2) †	$20,767.60		$18,592.60	
Selling Expenses	6,470.38		7,482.50	
Total Expenses		27,237.98		26,075.10
Income from Operations		$ 20,067.65		$ 19,544.18
Other Income				
Scrap (sale)	$ 690.00		$ 830.20	
Dividend on Whiting Co. stock	115.00		—	
Interest Earned	—		47.50	
Total Other Income		805.00		877.70
		$ 20,872.65		$ 20,421.88
Deductions from Income:				
Interest Expense	$ 396.25			
Loss on Sale of Drill	125.00			
Total Deductions from Income		521.95		
NET PROFIT		$ 20,350.70		$ 20,421.88

OPERATING RESULTS SHOWN BY FINANCIAL RATIOS

	1953	*1952*
Sales, net of returns	$148,513.76	$143,534.00
Gross Profits	47,305.63	45,619.28
% to Sales	31.9%	31.8%
Selling Expenses	6,470.38	7,482.50
% to Sales	4.4%	5.2%
General Expenses	20,767.60	18,592.60
% to Sales	13.8%	13.0%
Total Selling and General Expenses	27,237.98	26,075.10
% to Sales	18.3%	18.2%
Income from Operations	20,067.65	19,544.18
% to Sales	13.5%	13.6%

Though sales for the period in 1953 were higher than in 1952, selling expenses were lower.

* For Statement 1, see Fig. 67.
† General Expense Statement includes such costs as social security, income taxes, insurance, and salaries.

Fig. 60. Comparative statement of profit and loss.

CONTROL THROUGH FINANCIAL REPORTS. Financial reports and the classification of accounts aid management in directing current operations and making decisions, and they facilitate the analysis of, and place responsibility for, failure or success in performance.

STATEMENT OF COST OF GOODS MANUFACTURED FOR THREE
MONTHS ENDED DECEMBER 31, 1953

Materials:

Inventory, September 30, 1953...............		$12,000	
Purchases.........................	$44,000		
Less Returned Purchases and Allowances...........................	1,500		
Net Purchases.....................	$42,500		
Freight In........................	800		
Total.................................		$43,300	
Total Inventory and Purchases...........		$65,300	
Less Inventory, December 31, 1953...........		9,000	
Remainder—Cost of Materials Used...............			$ 46,300
Direct Labor...			44,100
Manufacturing Expenses:			
Indirect Labor.............................		$ 4,100	
Heat, Light, and Power.....................		3,500	
Building and Machinery Repairs.............		300	
Depreciation:			
Buildings.............................		3,500	
Machinery and Equipment..............		6,000	
Insurance.................................		1,000	
Taxes.....................................		1,400	
Factory Supplies...........................		3,500	
Miscellaneous Factory Expense..............		2,500	
Total Manufacturing Expenses....................			25,800
Total Materials, Labor, and Manufacturing Expenses.....			$116,200
Add Goods in Process Inventory, September 30, 1953......			5,000
Total...			$121,200
Deduct Goods in Process Inventory, December 31, 1953...			10,000
Cost of Goods Manufactured...........................			$111,200

Fig. 61. Statement of cost of goods manufactured.

Through *financial ratios* that compare one aspect of the business (as reflected in financial statements) with another against a selected standard, management observes trends, gauges performance, and controls activities. It selects the activities that should be controlled and employs such ratios as ratio of expense to sales; percentage of gross profit on sales or percentage of net profit on sales; working capital turnover (obtained by dividing sales by the difference between current assets and current liabilities); and turnover of finished inventory (obtained by dividing the cost of goods sold by the average finished inventory).

Management also analyzes trends through *comparative financial statements*—a compilation of a series of profit and loss statements or balance sheets of past operating periods (see Fig. 59). By comparing figures and ratios of one period with the corresponding figures of past periods, executives gauge trends in the various phases of the business— e.g., the trends of accounts receivable, bad debts, accounts payable, working capital, or size of inventory.

The Cost-Accounting Division. Although cost accounting is generally placed under the controller, in many cases it can logically be placed under the chief industrial engineer, production manager, or some other executive connected with manufacturing operations who is versed in cost accounting. Cost accountants compile all the elements (direct labor, direct material, and overhead) that make up the unit cost of the product; and, upon request, they undertake special cost studies (as explained later in this chapter).

The Tax Division. Tax accountants compute the tax liabilities (e.g., levies on profits, property, payroll, and sales) and make out federal, state, and municipal returns. They keep abreast of the latest tax regulations, practices, and pending revenue legislation in order that they may properly advise management on measures to reduce tax liability (often in anticipation of new levies). For example, they recommend reassessment of property value; location (or relocation) of sales offices, warehouses, or other company establishments in low-tax areas; and proper cost computation, such as valuation of inventories and allowable expense limits for advertising and promotion (particularly under excess profits tax laws).

The Auditing Division. A full-time specialist is generally employed to conduct an *internal audit*—i.e., periodically to verify records, statements, and reports through a systematic checking and examining of journal ledgers, books, and such accounts as cash, securities, inventories, and receivables. The auditor submits the results to management in a formal report.

PURPOSES OF INTERNAL AUDITING. Management audits accounting books to achieve discipline and a high accounting standard. Auditing (1) insures the observance of company policies and procedures; (2) guarantees compliance with the company's standard accounting practices and principles; (3) reduces errors and promotes accuracy in financial records, and (4) guards against misappropriation of funds, materials, and supplies.

PURPOSES OF EXTERNAL AUDITING. In the interests of the stockholders management generally employs a public accounting firm to conduct an annual audit of financial records and statements; and it often finds external auditing necessary when it plans to sell securities or apply for a bank loan.

The Budget Division. The controller often serves as budget officer. He sets up the budgeting system,[2] and his staff provides executives with financial and other data necessary for drawing up their departmental budgets. When the company budget has been adopted, the staff makes progress reports (i.e., it measures actual departmental performance against budget estimates) and if certain departments exceed their budgetary limits, they try to find out why.

The Credit and Collections Division. The credit manager formulates policies and procedures (with the approval of the controller and the treasurer) which will facilitate and expand sales and yet avoid losses from bad accounts—i.e., keep bad debts within reasonable limits. He consults with the sales manager on credit standards, co-ordinates his credit policies with sales campaigns, and periodically adjusts credit policies to fit changing business and selling conditions, such as seasonal changes in sales volume and recession or recovery turns in the economy.

The sales manager gets credit information on his customers from his salesmen (a profit and loss statement, a balance sheet, or a questionnaire); in addition, he may find it necessary to secure financial ratings from the credit bureau of the trade association or from such organizations as Dun and Bradstreet. His staff watches the current credit standing of customers, passes upon their credit ratings, and secures payment of bills through an adaptable collection procedure which includes an effective follow-up routine for collection of overdue accounts. The credit division works in close harmony with the *cashier* who receives, deposits, and disburses cash and keeps necessary records.

COST CONTROL

Cost accounting accumulates and studies all expenses (actual or estimated) chargeable to a given unit (e.g., an engineering project, a product, or a process) for purposes of measurement and control, analysis, or planning of business operations. Since cost-accounting problems are generally common to the member firms in a given industry, trade associations have developed, through research and experience, uniform cost-accounting principles and methods for their industry. By adopting these principles and methods, a firm may improve its price practices and

[2] See the next chapter for a discussion of budgeting.

keep itself better informed on competitive developments in the industry. The Chamber of Commerce of the United States defines *uniform cost accounting as* ". . . . a set of principles, and in some cases, accounting methods which when incorporated in the accounting systems of the individual members in an industry will result in the obtaining of cost figures by the individual members of the industry which will be on a comparable basis. Uniform cost accounting does not mean the preparation of average or standard cost figures for the industry, nor the inclusion in costs of predetermined or fixed elements of cost."

Procedure for Setting Up a Cost-Accounting Program. (1) Clarify the purposes for which cost studies are to be conducted, (2) make sure that the correct cost classifications (concepts) are used for each study, and (3) see that sound methods and procedures are observed when computing actual costs of production or applying standard (i.e., carefully estimated) costs in the computations.

Purposes of Cost Studies. Management uses cost computations (1) to gauge efficiency and control operations, (2) to appraise improvement programs, and (3) to assist in formulating price, wage, and other policies and in making administrative decisions.

MEASUREMENT AND CONTROL OF OPERATIONS. On the basis of organized cost data management can gauge the results of operations. It can tell where and when poor performance occurs and what corrective measures need be taken. If unit cost of production is rising, for example, detailed cost information may indicate that it is due to poor production planning or to excessive waste of material or machine time.

APPRAISAL OF IMPROVEMENT PROGRAMS. If they are to make substantial improvements, executives and industrial engineers must single out expensive operations and activities for analysis on the basis of cost data; and they must select proposed methods which will yield the biggest cost-reduction savings. Through this cost-and-savings approach engineers can recommend plans for modernization (e.g., purchase of facilities for the replacement of old units or revision of floor layout) that show the highest return for the capital expenditure.

GUIDE TO POLICIES AND DECISIONS. Through cost computations management can more accurately decide when changes in prices and wages should be made, when inventory stocks should be increased, when new products or new orders can advantageously be added or old products dropped, when the plant can be economically expanded, which production lines or branch establishments should be shut down, or which locations for new establishments should be selected.

Classification of Costs. Depending on the purpose of the computation, costs may be classified as material, labor, or overhead elements; as to the degree to which costs vary with changes in the rate of output; or as past costs or future costs.

MATERIAL. Material used in business may be direct or indirect. *Direct materials* are items which go into, and are easily traceable (chargeable) to, the product. *Indirect materials* are items (e.g., lubricating oil and abrasives) that either do not go into the product or are not easily traceable (chargeable) to specific products.

LABOR. Workers employed in the enterprise are either direct labor or indirect labor. *Direct labor* is that which is applied to the output of goods and can easily be charged to specific products. *Indirect labor* (e.g., maintenance and storeroom services) is that which can not easily be charged to specific products.

OVERHEAD (EXPENSE). A firm's overhead consists of factory expense, administrative expense, and selling expense. Management selects an appropriate method of distribution to apportion these expenses to the cost of the product.

Factory Overhead. The factory overhead consists of cost items that can not be directly charged to the product—i.e., indirect labor (salaries of factory clerks and supervisors), indirect materials, power, factory insurance, depreciation.[3]

Administrative (or General) Overhead. Administrative expense consists of the "front office" executive costs such as public relations, salaries to officers, research men, and secretarial staff.

Sales Overhead. Selling expense consists of the cost of marketing— for example, advertising and promotion, salaries, transportation, storage.

FIXED, VARIABLE, AND SEMIFIXED COSTS. The classification of costs as to the degree to which they vary in total with changes in the rate of output is useful for budgeting, for estimating costs of new orders and quoting prices, and for break-even analysis. *Fixed costs*, such as executive salaries, depreciation, fire insurance, and property taxes, remain constant regardless of the rate of output. *Variable costs*, such as direct material and direct labor, vary in total amount directly with changes

[3] *Depreciation* is an allowance for the decrease in the economic usefulness or value of a product (e.g., machinery) owing to exhaustion, wear and tear in business use, passage of time, action of elements, and obsolescence or inadequacy. Various plans (e.g., straight-line, machine-hour) are used to apportion the cost of the physical asset to current production. Such plans gradually convert the cost of the physical asset into current expense (included in overhead) by a suitable method of apportionment.

in the rate of output. *Semifixed costs,* such as power and maintenance, vary in total amount but not directly with the rate of output.

Computation of Actual Cost. Accountants segregate and compile actual costs by component parts or products, by departments, by major divisions of the enterprise (manufacturing, administration, and distribution), or in other ways depending upon the purpose to be served.

PRODUCTION COSTS. Figs. 10 and 62 show the costs that go into operating the enterprise.

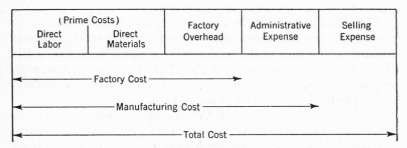

Fig. 62. Cost breakdown.

To compute the cost of producing a commodity, accountants compile (1) the cost of direct material used as shown by material requisition slips, (2) the cost of direct labor used as shown by time tickets, and (3) the portion of factory overhead allocable to each item as determined by a suitable method of distributing expenses.

METHODS OF DISTRIBUTING FACTORY OVERHEAD. The chief accountant (with the approval of management) selects the most accurate practical method for applying factory expense to the product so that each unit will bear its proportionate share of the overhead burden.[4] He does this by selecting a factor which is common to all products and which varies in direct proportion to the amount of the burden that should be charged to the products—e.g., cost of direct labor, direct labor hours, cost of direct material, and the cost of machine hours. Overhead is obviously more difficult to apply when diverse products are put out or

---

[4] Since the total expense to be distributed in a given future period is necessarily estimated and depends upon the anticipated volume of production and cost changes, the factory burden may be underestimated or overestimated. The resulting plus or minus balance in the manufacturing accounts is usually applied to the surplus account at the end of the period. This practice of "correcting for" or absorbing the actual factory overhead makes it possible to maintain a steady apportionment of burden to output from period to period without disturbance from temporary fluctuations in expense accounts.

when joint products or by-products are manufactured. The accountant may achieve accuracy by applying a special distribution method for each product or for each department.

The Direct-Labor-Cost Method. Where product, equipment, and wages are comparatively uniform, the factory overhead can be accurately charged to the product on the basis of direct-labor costs. For example, if $100,000 is the estimated factory burden and the direct-labor cost is $50,000, a burden rate of $2.00 would be applied to each $1.00 of direct labor charged to the product.

The Direct-Labor-Hours Method. Where the type of work and the pay rates are comparatively stable, the burden can be satisfactorily distributed on the basis of the total number of hours worked on a job. For example, if 300 man-hours of direct labor were expended on a job or product at a burden rate of $.50 per man-hour, the overhead charged to the job or product would be $150.

The Direct-Material Method. Where continuous-process manufacture is used or where the processing methods and materials are common to all products turned out, the burden rate may be satisfactorily based on the cost or amount of direct material used in the product.

The Machine-Hour Cost Method. Though the machine-hour rate method involves detailed computations, it is a comparatively accurate means of allocating burden and is important in plants where investment in equipment is heavy and machine operating costs are high. To compute the machine-hour rate (cost), the total estimated expense involved in operating a specific machine for a given normal output (depreciation, average maintenance, and the prorated cost of power, heat, floor space) is divided by the estimated number of hours the machine will be used. For example, if the total monthly overhead for a machine is $1,000 and the machine is to be operated 500 hours during the period, the hourly burden rate would be $2.00.

Control Through Standard Costs. When actual (i.e., past or historical) costs are compiled, the cost of the product can not be determined until the item is finished. Past costs, moreover, do not provide an effective basis for measuring the efficiency or controlling the use of labor and materials.

By analyzing past cost behavior, however, it is possible to predetermine what cost ought to be (i.e., standard costs) for materials, labor, and overhead. Since they represent the proper costs of conducting business, these costs serve as a basis for gauging efficiency and attaining control of operations. Though they are most readily applicable to manufacturing (particularly standardized repetitive production), standard costs can also be effectively applied to the administrative and sales phases of the business.

PROCEDURE FOR DETERMINING COST STANDARDS. The standard is selected on the basis of the lowest attainable cost for materials, labor, and overhead under normal operating conditions. *Standard materials costs* (computed at anticipated prices) can be determined by an analysis of the quantity required for the manufacture of the product, including an allowance for scrap. *Standard labor costs* can be determined from the established wage rates and the standard times set for work by time studies. *Standard overhead costs* can be derived from the selected method of apportioning the estimated expense for a given normal volume of output.

Special accounts must be set up to record the *variances*—i.e., amount over or under standard costs. These accounts are eventually cleared (incorporated) into the profit and loss statement. When variances are persistent, the particular process or item should be analyzed to determine the cause. If the variance is due to inefficiency, the poor performance should be remedied. If it is due to a change in wage rates or in prices of items purchased, or if it is due to an improper initial computation, new cost standards should be established.

BENEFITS. Standard costs offer these advantages. (1) They simplify and reduce the amount of detailed work required for cost accounting (cost analysis and estimates can be quickly made); and they serve as an effective guide for pricing since they reflect the predetermined cost which management expects to attain. (2) They provide a means for gauging and controlling the efficiency of operations *during* manufacturing. When actual costs deviate from standard costs, the causes for such discrepancies can be analyzed and eliminated. Since only variations from the standard costs need be analyzed, the application of the "principle of exceptions" makes for easy managerial control.

Use of Decision-Making Costs. Many business decisions are made on the basis of cost concepts that differ from accounting (i.e., historical) costs. For example, in deciding whether to shut down a branch or cut back production, management computes the "escapable" cost as compared with the "unavoidable" cost to arrive at the actual "savings" gained by the contraction. In measuring the performance or efficiency of an operating executive, management will separate "noncontrollable" from "controllable" costs (costs that are susceptible to economy and can be regulated by the executive). To compute the outlay required for expanding the plant or for adding a new service, management uses "incremental" costs—the added estimated (future) cost of the new project. In choosing a venture among alternatives (expanding capacity, modernizing the plant, or setting up company-owned sales outlets), management considers "opportunity" cost—i.e., the profits foregone by using funds for a particular venture instead of for other ventures.

Questions

1. (a) What factor should be considered in determining the degree of centralization of office work? (b) What economies may be achieved by such centralization?

2. Explain how a work-simplification program can increase the efficiency of office work.

3. What are the criteria for designing an effective system for records and reports?

4. How do reports prepared with reference to carefully selected standards provide a basis for control through the "principle of exceptions"?

5. How does the chief accountant set up the company accounting system?

6. Define three financial statements and explain their uses.

7. Enumerate four financial ratios and illustrate their uses.

8. What are the purposes of internal auditing and external auditing?

9. What are the meaning and purpose of "uniform cost accounting" developed by trade associations?

10. What are the purposes for which cost studies be made?

11. Break down "total cost of operations" into its major components.

12. Enumerate four types of cost classifications (i.e., cost concepts) and illustrate when and how they may be used.

13. Distinguish among factory overhead, administrative overhead, and sales overhead.

14. (a) Distinguish among the "direct-labor cost," "direct-material cost," and "machine-hour cost" methods of distributing machine burden. (b) To what plant operating conditions is each method best suited?

15. How do variations in capacity utilization affect the distribution of overhead expense?

16. What are three methods of apportioning depreciation charges?

17. What are the advantages of using standard costs instead of actual (historical) costs?

18. How may standard costs be determined for materials and labor?

19. What are typical items (accounts) that make up the "cost of goods sold" in a representative manufacturing firm?

20. What factors should be considered in establishing or adjusting company credit policies?

26: Over-All Planning: Budgetary Control and Break-Even Analysis

The president or chief executive of any organization who personally attempts to investigate or review all business matters and pass decisions on them and who delegates only nominal or minor authority to his officers and department heads invariably becomes the primary bottleneck and obstacle of the firm. Such "concentration of authority," particularly in the larger firm, usually means that there is no effective leadership, planning, or control, that the enterprise is adrift, and that executive talent is wasted and morale impaired. How, then, can effective over-all planning and control of the enterprise be achieved? A number of methods and time-saving devices have been discussed in earlier chapters. To recapitulate the most significant of these will focus attention on this over-riding managerial function and responsibility.

Top management effectively *achieves over-all planning and control* of the business when it (1) formulates and periodically reviews policies covering all major phases and aspects of the business; (2) maintains a sound, up-to-date organization structure with a system of procedures that assures the execution of policies and programs; (3) fills all key positions with, and delegates full authority to, the caliber of men who can dynamically administer departmental functions; (4) regularly analyzes its financial statements and ratios and reviews the primary operational reports; (5) initiates comprehensive research and forecasts market demand, business conditions, and economic trends that affect the firm; (6) formulates long-term, company-wide programs (e.g., those dealing with product coverage, facilities, distribution channels, and plant relocation) that effectively direct and promote the enterprise; and (7) employs "master budgeting" and "break-even analysis" to plan and guide the business toward profitable goals. Budgeting and break-even charts, the primary profit-making tools that have not been previously discussed, are the subject of this chapter.

BUDGETARY CONTROL

A *budget* is a comprehensive, over-all plan in which management, on the basis of estimated sales volume and receipts, establishes cost and expense allowances for future operations, in this way effectively integrating and directing activities toward carefully determined goals. Through *budgetary control* (periodic comparison of actual performance as reflected in current costs with planned performance expressed as established expense allowances) management co-ordinates and guides executive activities and, when necessary, takes corrective action to keep operations running along predetermined lines.

Procedure for Setting Up a Budget System. (1) Gauge the benefits and the limitations of budgeting as they apply to the firm's type of business; (2) establish the prerequisites for budgeting; (3) select the type of budget best suited to the business (fixed, variable, or a combination); (4) determine the length of the budget period; (5) draw up a classification of departmental budgets to cover all important phases of the business; and (6) outline the steps for preparing and administering the company (master) budget.

Benefits and Limitations of Budgeting. The preparation and the administration (i.e., application) of a well-designed company budget achieves these beneficial results: (1) it necessitates systematic analysis of all the factors affecting the business so that the required policies can be formulated (or revised) before the actual budgeting is begun; (2) it translates policies and decisions into co-ordinated programs of operation; (3) it carefully outlines departmental goals which provide executives with a guide to performance and serve as an incentive; (4) it unifies in one comprehensive plan (the master budget) all departmental programs and thereby assures executive co-operation and integrated performance; (5) it is a device for securing centralized control: by comparing current performance with planned performance, management can take appropriate corrective action when actual performance deviates from the budgetary plans; and (6) it improves morale by clarifying departmental tasks, by using fair standards to measure performance, and by promoting stable employment through the co-ordination of production rates with sales estimates.

Though the budget is a primary managerial tool for business planning and control, it can not function automatically or take the place of executive review of primary functions. Moreover, budgeting is difficult to apply when the firm puts out products characterized by rapid style changes or does special-order work and when the enterprise is subject to uncertain market conditions and strong shifts in the economy. The budget is, in addition, limited by management's ability to forecast the market, prices, and costs; to interpret valid data; and to maintain effectiveness in its over-all administration.

Prerequisites for Budgeting. Before it can hope to budget successfully, management must establish (or review for their effectiveness): (1) a sound organization structure with clearly defined lines of authority and responsibility; (2) policies which clearly outline departmental and business aims and serve as a basis for preparing budgets; (3) a system for adequate forecasting of sales, prices, costs, and other trends which provide the information necessary for preparing budgets; and (5) cost records (broken down according to areas of executive responsibility) suitable for estimating departmental expense, checking with past periods, and comparing current performance with budgeted levels.

Types of Budgets. Depending upon the peculiarities and needs of its business, management may adopt (with the advice of the budget officer) a fixed budget, a variable budget, or one combining features of the two.

THE FIXED (STATIC) BUDGET. When sales (production requirements) and income can be predicted with a reasonable degree of accuracy, management adopts the fixed-type budget. In such cases, on the basis of past or standard cost, it computes the cost of direct material and direct labor and the overhead expense to operate departments for a "known" volume of business.

THE VARIABLE (FLEXIBLE) BUDGET. When the market for its goods is uncertain or when, for any reason, its production volume will vary during the budget period, management adopts the flexible-type budget. Because of its automatic adjustment to changes in production volume, the variable budget is, for many enterprises, a more effective control device than the fixed budget, which would require a revision for each change in the volume of business during the budget period. Management, however, can utilize special fixed budgets for definite programs— e.g., engineering projects, promotion and advertising, plant modernization or expansion.

Through the flexible budget, management anticipates and systematically provides for changes in business volume by computing the cost of operations for various volumes on the basis of standard costs. Direct material and direct-labor costs can easily be calculated since, within limits of plant capacity, they vary as a total directly with changes in the volume of output. Management classifies overhead items as fixed or semifixed expenses and computes semifixed expense from data derived from studies of the impact of various rates of production on each overhead item.

Management can achieve budget flexibility by using either a "step budget" or a formula for overhead expense. In the *step-budget method* it sets up budgets for various volumes of output—e.g., a budget for each 10-per-cent change in the volume of output or for each level of output where abrupt changes occur in the cost of operations because of overtime work, an additional work shift, or other cause. In the *formula method* it computes budgets for any volume of output by adding to fixed cost the total variable cost for the units produced. For example (to use a simplified illustration), if the fixed cost per month were $100,000 and the total variable cost (direct material, direct labor, and semifixed overhead expense) were $10 per unit of output, the budget would allow $200,000 for 10,000 units of output and $220,000 for 12,000 units of output.

The Length of the Budget Period. To determine the time duration for its budget, management considers the periodicity of its business activities and the frequency with which important decisions must be made and then selects a period (say, four months) that best fits the conditions. In this study it considers such factors as the time period over which forecasts of sales and business trends can effectively be made, the duration of the production cycle, the time required for financing sales and purchases, and the interval selected for accounting and financial statements.

Many firms budget a year in advance and then, if necessary, adjust the budget to the new conditions that have developed in the immediate period (e.g., four months). Through progressive forecasting (i.e., adding a future month and making the required adjustments) they constantly project and maintain a budget for a year in advance. They use the long-term budget to co-ordinate long-range plans (those dealing with finance, research, plant expansion) and they use the short-term (four-month) budget to deal with immediate conditions and thus gain flexibility.

Classification of Budgets. Management selects separate but related departmental and special budgets which are suitable for the size of the firm and its organization structure, its type of business operations, and the various phases of the business that it desires to control. Its master budget is the consolidation (summary) of the separate budgets.

Management introduces the budget system gradually; and as executives and supervisors become educated to the budget program, management refines and extends the budget system to cover all aspects of the enterprise. It usually starts with the sales budget. When this is working satisfactorily, it introduces the manufacturing budget, then the budgets of service departments.

THE SALES BUDGET. The sales budget (Fig. 63) consists largely of the sales estimate, which is generally based on past sales, salesmen's estimates, and a forecast of the market and business conditions. In preparing the budget the sales manager balances sales estimates against the existing or anticipated production capacity of the firm, and the results, when approved by management, make up the budget. The

SALES BUDGET										19___
									Third Quarter	

PRODUCT MODEL	PAST QUARTER		QUARTERLY ESTIMATE		MONTHLY ESTIMATES					
					June		*July*		*Aug.*	
	VOLUME	VALUE	VOLUME	VALUE	VOLUME	VALUE	VOLUME	VALUE	VOLUME	VALUE

Fig. 63. Sales budget form.

sales budget foretells sales receipts and, when total costs are computed from other budgets, it is a basis for estimating the firm's earnings. A breakdown of the sales budget into quotas by districts and salesmen and a comparison of actual sales with quotas provide a means for controlling sales performance. In addition a *sales expense budget*, prepared from accounting records, controls selling costs through the comparison of actual costs with the expense allowances for advertising, warehousing, salesmen's salaries, offices, and other activities of the department.

THE MANUFACTURING BUDGET. The general manager with the assistance of the production manager prepares the manufacturing budget, which comprises a number of special budgets. He takes the sales budget as the output goal and from this he prepares the production budget and then the materials, purchase, labor, and manufacturing expense budgets, and, in part, the plant-and-equipment budgets.

PRODUCTION BUDGET							19___	
							_____ Quarter	
PRODUCT MODEL	FINISHED STOCK BEGINNING OF PERIOD		PRODUCTION		SHIPMENTS		FINISHED STOCK AT END OF PERIOD	
	ESTIMATE	ACTUAL	ESTIMATE	ACTUAL	ESTIMATE	ACTUAL	ESTIMATE	ACTUAL

Fig. 64. Production budget form.

The *production budget* stipulates the monthly or weekly rates of output—i.e., the quantities of the various products to be manufactured in order to meet production goals (see Figs. 44 and 64). Serving as the firm's over-all output schedule,[1] it aims to stabilize production,[2] use plant capacity and labor efficiently, and at the same time meet the requirements of the sales budget.

The *materials budget* specifies the kinds and quantity of raw materials, parts, and supplies and the time that they will be needed to meet the requirements of the production budget.

The *purchase budget* establishes the financial allowances for procurement. It is computed from the materials budget and lists of other needs (tools, fixtures) and is influenced by price trends of the various items and the financial position of the company. A well-designed purchase budget assures a timely placement of purchase orders, procurement of inventories at low costs, and the maintenance of adequate stocks to meet production needs.

The *labor budget* specifies the amount of direct labor required to maintain the over-all production schedule. When properly broken down by job classifications, this manpower forecast enables the personnel department systematically to recruit, train, transfer, or lay off personnel. The treasurer uses the labor budget, plus wage and overtime rates, to estimate the payroll funds necessary to meet the wage bill.

The *manufacturing expense budget*, prepared from an analysis of the forecasted volume of business and past costs or standard costs, establishes expense (overhead) allowances for each production depart-

---

[1] For discussion see p. 212.
[2] For discussion see p. 199.

ment (foundry, machining, assembly). Then, for control purposes, actual expenditures for overhead items are compared with the budget allowances (see Fig. 65).

The *plant-and-equipment budget* (i.e., the capital investment budget) allocates funds for the purchase of equipment and for plant modernization and expansion required to meet the immediate output goal (budgeted production) and the capacity needs for future business. Such systematic long-run budgeting enables the treasurer to accumulate from retained earnings (undistributed profits) and sale of securities funds which the firm can use to purchase property, construct new plants, or expand existing facilities when market prices are favorable.

SERVICE DEPARTMENTS' BUDGETS. The heads of auxiliary and service departments prepare their budgets primarily on the basis of the manufacturing budget. To prepare a plant maintenance, inspection, personnel, engineering and research, or other departmental expense budget, the department head considers both the services his department will perform to meet the projected volume of business and his special programs and projects; he then computes the budget allowance (cost) on the basis of his estimates and past costs or standard costs.

THE FINANCIAL BUDGET. The controller or treasurer prepares the financial budget from those drawn up by other departments. His budget (Fig. 66) which summarizes the anticipated receipts and payments for the period, shows the expected receipts for each month (from cash sales, accounts receivable, notes receivable, and other sources of income) and expected disbursements (computed from other budgets)

DEPARTMENTAL BUDGET						19___
Department _____ _____ Quarter Production Quota _____						
COST ELEMENTS	TOTAL		UNIT COST		PAST UNIT COST	DIFFERENCE
	ESTIMATE	ACTUAL	ESTIMATE	ACTUAL		
Direct Labor						
Indirect Labor						
Materials						
Supplies						
Other Overhead						
Totals						

Fig. 65. Departmental budget form.

by the week or month for payroll, procurement of material, and overhead charges.

When budgetary revisions are to be made or when a flexible budget is used, the controller carefully notes the changes in anticipated receipts and disbursements. On the basis of financial analysis he ascertains the current sources of funds, determines the need, if any, for additional funds and bank borrowing, and plans the allocation of working capital. His advance knowledge of any shortage of funds makes possible the timely modification of individual budgets without

---

MONTHLY CASH BUDGET

		JUNE 19	
__THIRD__ Quarter		RECEIPTS	DISBURSEMENTS
JUNE 1	Balance on hand	$ 110,050	
	Nonoperating income	2,060	
	Accounts Receivable (collections)	380,100	
	Materials		150,010
	Payroll		85,050
	Rent		800
	Insurance and Taxes		1,510
	Maintenance		1,830
	Utilities		2,000
	Factory Expense (misc.)		2,540
	Selling Expense		30,100
	Administrative Expense		40,500
			314,340
JUNE 30	Cash Balance		$177,870

Fig. 66. A simplified monthly cash budget.

---

impairment of the company over-all program. The controller's continual financial analysis promotes the co-ordination of the various budget plans and helps the budget committee and the president appraise the soundness of the budget program and business operations. For example, the controller may uncover and suggest a timely remedy for wasteful use of working capital caused by the accumulation of excess inventories, ill-planned production, excessive overtime, or slow collections of bills. From his analysis and the preparation of projected profit and loss statements and balance sheets, the controller can foretell the financial position of the company for the various intervals during the budget period.

Steps for Preparing the Budget and Achieving Control. The executive committee, or its subcommittee, is generally responsible for planning and overseeing the preparation of the budget. The president, as chairman of the budget committee, delegates to the budget officer, usually the controller or treasurer, the task of carrying out the budgeting procedure, which generally involves these steps: (1) a preliminary conference of the budget committee to outline policies and plans, (2) compilation of cost and other information and transmission of these data to departments, (3) preparation of budgets by department heads, (4) consolidation of budgets into final form, and (5) budgetary control through periodic appraisal of performance and corrective action when necessary.

PRELIMINARY CONFERENCE. The chief executive outlines to the budget committee the broad plans and policy decisions that will be incorporated in or that will influence the company budget. In establishing the main lines of progress, the committee must assess such primary factors as the phase of the business cycle and other economic prospects, including a forecast of major shifts in demand and changes in prices and wage rates; decisions covering changes in products; plans for plant modernization and expansion or contraction of capacity; and plans for substantial changes in outlays for research, advertising, and sales promotion. Next the committee estimates or establishes the sales and production quantities for the period. On the basis of anticipated sales volume, prices, and costs, it can predict the probable profit for the period.

COMPILATION AND PROVISION OF INFORMATION. The budget officer advises the department heads and provides them with information necessary for the preparation of the various budgets: volume or output quotas broken down by production divisions, present and anticipated costs, record of past performance, and any other data that may be requested.

PREPARATION OF DEPARTMENTAL BUDGETS. Each department head prepares his own budget on the basis of the company production program and the information supplied by the budget officer; sometimes, however, the budget officer prepares the tentative budgets and submits these to the respective executives for review and revision, when necessary. In any case, informal meetings between the budget officer and executives are generally necessary to iron out conflicting estimates and to co-ordinate the various budgets.

CONSOLIDATION INTO FINAL FORM. The budget officer consolidates the various budgets into the master budget (see Fig. 67) and prepares a projected balance sheet and profit and loss statement to show the anticipated financial position of the company at various intervals of

ANNUAL MASTER BUDGET

	Estimate	
	Minimum	Maximum
Sales Budget		
Product A sales	$4,000,000	$5,000,000
Product B sales	500,000	600,000
Product C sales	400,000	500,000
Total	$4,900,000	$6,100,000
Manufacturing Budget		
Product A cost	2,400,000	3,000,000
Product B cost	320,000	390,000
Product C cost	280,000	350,000
Total	$3,000,000	$3,740,000
Estimated Gross Profits	1,900,000	2,360,000
Marketing Budget		
Sales administration	100,000	110,000
Operation of sales districts	500,000	550,000
Advertising and promotion	200,000	250,000
Total	$ 800,000	$ 910,000
Administrative Budget		
Administrative expense	300,000	310,000
Estimated Net Profit	$ 800,000	$1,140,000
Financial Budget		
Taxes	100,000	180,000
Dividends	200,000	360,000
Reserve for expansion	300,000	300,000
Increase in surplus	200,000	300,000
Total	$ 800,000	$1,140,000
Plant and Equipment Budget		
Expansion and modernization	500,000	500,000
New stock issue	300,000	300,000
Balance from retained profits	$ 200,000	$ 200,000

Fig. 67. A master budget.

the budget period. He presents the final draft and a summary of the company budget to the committee for an appraisal of its balance and its realism. The president reconciles divergent judgments and, as the ultimate authority, approves the budget in its final form before it is transmitted to the various executives by the budget officer.

BUDGETARY CONTROL—CHECKING PERFORMANCE. To maintain control of business operations, management must follow the budget up— that is, it must compare actual performance with budget estimates. To achieve such control the budget officer periodically sends performance reports to the various executives. He and the executive concerned analyze deviations from the budget for corrective action. The budget officer consolidates and summarizes the various budget reports and, together with his analysis, submits the results monthly, or at shorter intervals, to the president and the budget committee. On the basis of the reports and consultation with the committee, the executive officer initiates measures to insure achievement of goals at the proper level of efficiency. By analyzing current results he gauges the trend of his business and, when necessary, revises the budget to guide and properly control the enterprise.[3]

BREAK–EVEN ANALYSIS

The *break-even chart* (Fig. 68) shows the relation of volume of production and sales to expense and income. It shows volume of production along the horizontal axis and it shows expense and income along the vertical axis. Management can see at a glance the volume of production at which the firm breaks even (in Fig. 68, for example, total receipts just cover total cost at 70,000 units) and it can see the amount of profit or loss at various volumes of sale.

Carefully prepared break-even charts summarize the firm's operations under various internal and external business conditions; they aid executives in their analysis of certain types of business problems and in choosing alternative managerial programs and forecasting operating results.

Construction of a Break-Even Chart. To prepare a simple break-even chart, the analyst plots sales receipts at various volumes of output —e.g., starting from the left-hand corner in Fig. 68, he plots receipts at 30,000, 60,000, and 90,000 units of output. He compiles cost data for operations at various volumes of output and breaks down expenses into fixed and variable categories. He plots fixed cost ($300,000 in Fig. 68) through the range of capacity and plots variable cost ($200,-000, $350,000, and $500,000) for the respective volumes of output. His chart shows that the firm operates at a loss until it reaches 70 per cent of capacity. Above this point it operates at a profit.

The chart in Fig. 68 illustrates the basic principles of break-even analysis. The chart, however, is valid for estimating profits and analyzing business for only a single set of assumptions because it is drawn up on the supposition that costs, selling prices, and product-mix are

[3] John A. Shubin, *Managerial and Industrial Economics* (New York: Ronald Press, 1961), Ch. 10.

constant and that plant size, production, technology, and efficiency remain unchanged for the time period under survey. In a period of a year or two it is often not uncommon for most of these factors to be reasonably constant for many firms.[4]

ESTIMATED ANNUAL INCOME AND EXPENSE

Volume in Units	30,000	60,000	90,000
Sales Receipts @ $10 Per Unit	$ 300,000	$ 600,000	$ 900,000
Fixed Costs	300,000	300,000	300,000
Variable Costs	200,000	350,000	500,000

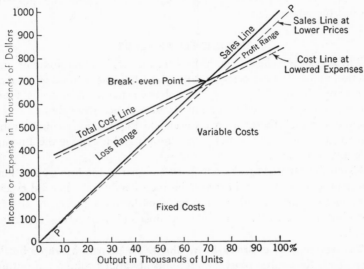

Fig. 68. A simplified break-even chart constructed from the estimated annual income and expense figures shown above the chart.

Procedure for Preparing a Chart. (1) If the firm is a multiplant enterprise, decide whether to prepare a company-wide chart or a chart for each branch; (2) select a suitable unit to measure output, and plot sales receipts (income line) on the basis of a carefully estimated product-mix and selling prices; (3) carefully compile and match costs with output; then plot fixed and variable costs at various volumes of output.

[4] Break-even charts are sometimes drawn up to cover a long period of years with no correction or adjustment for changes in prices, plant, technology, and efficiency. Such "general" charts are prepared from annual data and use sales volume in current dollars to measure output. The charts present only a rough gauge of business operations under given conditions.

Scope of Charting—Company-Wide or Branch Charts. Multiplant firms (e.g., rubber-tire producers and meat packers) whose branch establishments turn out completed products for regional markets often include constituent plants of varying degrees of newness and efficiency and of different labor and materials costs. The analyst in this case would find it difficult to prepare a useful, company-wide break-even chart because shifts in regional demand result in different total company cost figures, even though the over-all dollar sales volume is the same. For such firms he would prepare a chart for each branch or operational division. However, when constituent branches comprise different stages in the over-all process of producing completed goods (or, of course, if the company is a single-plant firm), the analyst can prepare a valid company-wide chart.

Measurement of Output and the Sales Line. For firms with a comparatively constant product-mix, the analyst has little difficulty in selecting a unit (e.g., a given quantity of a combination of items) to measure output on the horizontal axis of the chart. If the product-mix varies but the profit margin contributed by products is comparable, the analyst can overcome the problem of a changing product-mix by merely plotting output in terms of dollar sales volume. If the profit margins contributed by the products differ, however, the dollar sales method of measuring an output with a changing product-mix would not properly relate costs (particularly material and labor costs) to the output. In this case the analyst would express output in terms of a common unit of measure, such as a representative product model, tons, barrels, board-feet, or perhaps man-hours. He would then plot the sales receipts line on the basis of a carefully forecasted product-mix and prices.

The analyst can usually assume comparatively steady selling prices, since most imperfectly competitive enterprises employ cost-plus formulas for setting or adjusting prices. Moreover, changes in cost are usually accompanied (with some lag) by comparable shifts in selling prices. During periods of a general price decline, for example, the pressure for cost reduction is intensified, and the postponement or control of important outlays tends to compensate for uncontrollable changes in selling prices and for rigidities in certain factor prices (standby charges and wages set by union contracts).

Compilation of Costs and the Cost Line. To compile and plot total costs (segregated into fixed and variable categories on the chart) so as to indicate business operations at various volumes, the analyst accumulates data from profit and loss statements, accounting records,

343

and standard cost records, or from cost studies. (Cost studies, for instance, would have to be made for charts prepared for new plants, for expansion or modernization programs, or for other business programs calling for outlays.)

To show the correct relation between cost and output, the analyst carefully matches cost with the proper output. He avoids errors in cost computation that result from wide variations in the timing of large expenditures, particularly semi-investment types of expenditures—e.g., heavy outlays for research, maintenance, and promotion and advertising. He carefully matches such outlays to output by properly allocating the costs not only to current output but also to past and future output. In many cases he can minimize the problem of "matching" by using annual cost data. To assure valid presentation of data, the analyst likewise avoids excessive extrapolation and plots costs only for the anticipated range of production volume (e.g., the volume need not begin at zero).

The analyst finds that total costs frequently vary from the volume of output at an inconstant rate and that total-cost lines are not ordinarily straight. He finds this to be true because costs tend to increase at intermittent intervals with increases in output—e.g., the change in total cost resulting from the opening up of a department or the inauguration of a second shift.

Managerial Uses of the Chart.[5] Management can employ break-even charts to project the cost and revenue picture under various anticipated future conditions and for alternative business programs. Hence, management can use charts (1) to show the relative importance of different classes of costs, how they vary with volume of production, and how they may be controlled; (2) to show the impact of changes in sales volume on profits; (3) to predict the effect of price and cost changes on the break-even point; (4) to show the gain needed in sales volume (or productivity) to maintain profits when prices or costs change in a specific way—e.g., when prices decline but wages and the cost of materials do not; (5) to select the proper size plant or to predict the effect of changes in plant size or modernization of plant on the break-even point; (6) to appraise the promotional possibilities of a new venture or a merger; or, (7) to compare the profitability of two or more firms.

ANALYSIS OF COSTS. The relative importance of fixed costs deter-

[5] Break-even charts have been used by government agencies, investment analysts. and labor unions.

mines the profit and loss potentials of the firm. When fixed costs are comparatively small, both the profit potential and loss potential are proportionately small. When fixed costs are large, however, the firm enjoys substantial profits above the break-even point, but sustains large losses below the point. Such high investment (hence high fixed-cost) industries as steel, power, and railroads typically experience large profits or losses during sharp fluctuations associated with prosperity and depressions.

The total-cost line shows the extent to which costs increase with increases in volume. When a given cost item or cost class (e.g., marketing or administrative cost) is to be analyzed, it should be plotted last—i.e., placed on top just under the total-cost line. A planned reduction in the item can then be shown and its influence on the break-even point indicated.

ANALYSIS OF CHANGES IN PRICE AND SALES. To estimate the probabilities of total revenue at different selling prices and at different sales volumes, the analyst can draw a series of sales lines on the chart. Since its slope will reflect the selling price it represents, each line will cross the total-cost line at a different break-even point. In Fig. 68, for instance, sales line "pp" crosses at 77,000 units while the solid sales line crosses at 70,000 units. The break-even points for different selling prices indicate the increase or decrease in sales required to break even at the respective prices. The chart does not predict profits; it merely shows how a given price change will determine the volume at which the firm breaks even. Some firms, for example, may cut prices to attract business but do not achieve a comparable lowering of costs; other firms may be able to control costs as sales (or prices) decline.

CONTROL OF PLANT SIZE AND CAPACITY. Through break-even analysis management can estimate what amount of investment in plant capacity is economically justified for the projected volume of sales. The chart indicates overinvestment (the selection of too large a plant) by showing that the anticipated sales receipts just approach the break-even point or are at some point below and hence do not equal total cost. The proper size plant can then be determined by systematically cutting back investment in capacity (i.e., planning a smaller plant) and reducing the magnitude of fixed costs until anticipated sales volume is beyond the break-even point and the available extra capacity is sufficient to meet possible increases in sales in the years immediately ahead.

Similarly, if management plans to purchase a plant, to invest in expansion and in modernization, or to shut down or to re-open one of its plants, it can use break-even analysis to determine the profitability of such programs by comparing charts before and after the change.

Questions

1. What key methods can management employ to plan and control the enterprise as a whole?

2. What are the steps for designing a company budget system?

3. Explain how the preparation and application of a company budget give management a comprehensive picture of the business and serve as a device for over-all control.

4. What prerequisites (preparations) must be established before budgeting can be successful?

5. Why are flexible rather than fixed budgets used by most businesses?

6. Distinguish between the "step budget" method and the "formula" method for drawing up a flexible-type budget.

7. Explain how the individual budgets that make up the master budget are interrelated.

8. How is the length of a budget period determined?

9. Explain why the capital (plant and equipment) budget is usually prepared for a longer period than the operating budget.

10. What are the steps for preparing the company budget after the system has been set up?

11. What methods may be employed to minimize the "padding" of departmental budgets?

12. How is budgeting used to gauge and control departmental performance?

13. What are the procedural steps for preparing a break-even chart?

14. Explain how such data as the comparative balance sheet, fixed and variable cost classes, standard costs, and incremental costs may be used in the construction of break-even charts.

15. What are the difficulties in preparing a company-wide break-even chart (a) for a firm with geographically scattered branch plants producing completed goods for regional markets, and (b) for a firm with a constantly changing product-mix?

16. Contrast the problem of preparing a break-even chart for a multiple-product firm in a competitive field with that of preparing a chart for a monopoly firm manufacturing a single product.

17. What are five managerial uses of the break-even chart?

18. How will a decline in prices or an increase in wages affect the break-even point?

19. How do unions employ break-even charts in collective bargaining?

20. (a) How is the break-even chart used in selecting the proper size plant to be erected? (b) How is the chart used for determining the reduction in cost achieved by the shutting down of a branch plant of a multiple-plant firm which has been operating below its break-even point?

346

Selected Bibliography

Case Problems Books in Business Management

(Any of the case books listed can be used with Business Management—Efficiency Surveys and Systems.)

Folts, Franklin E., *Introduction to Industrial Management,* 5th ed. New York: McGraw-Hill Book Co., Inc., 1963.

Holden, Paul E., and Frank K. Shallenberger, *Selected Case Problems in Industrial Management,* 2nd ed. New York: Prentice-Hall, Inc., 1962.

Kelley, Pearce E., and Kenneth Lawyer, *Case Problems in Small Business Management.* New York: Prentice-Hall, Inc., 1952.

Smith, Albert George, *Policy Formulation and Administration.* Homewood, Ill.: Richard D. Irwin, Inc., 1951.

Terry, George R., *Case Problems in Business and Industrial Management.* Dubuque, Iowa: Wm. C. Brown Company Publishers, 1952.

Organization and Administration

Davis, Ralph C., *The Fundamentals of Top Management.* New York: Harper & Brothers, 1951.

Holden, Paul E., Lounsbury S. Fish, and Hubert L. Smith, *Top-Management Organization and Control.* New York: McGraw-Hill Book Co., Inc., 1951.

Marvin, Philip R., *Top-Management and Research.* Dayton, Ohio: Research Press, 1953.

Newman, W. H., *Administrative Action.* New York: Prentice-Hall, Inc., 1951.

Shubin, John A., *Managerial and Industrial Economics.* New York: Ronald Press, 1961.

Research and Product Engineering

Chase, Herbert, *Handbook on Designing for Quantity Production,* 2nd ed. New York: McGraw-Hill Book Co., Inc., 1950.

Larson, Gustave E., *Developing and Selling New Products.* Washington, D.C.: U.S. Dept. of Commerce, Office of Domestic Commerce, 1949.

Maynard, H. B. (ed.), *Industrial Engineering Handbook.* New York: McGraw-Hill Book Co., Inc., 1956.

Mees, C. E. Kenneth, and John A. Leermaker, *The Organization of Industrial Research.* New York: McGraw-Hill Book Co., Inc., 1950.

Paden, Donald W., and E. F. Lindquist, *Statistics of Economics and Business,* 2nd ed. New York: McGraw-Hill Book Co., Inc., 1956.

Phelps, D. M., *Planning the Product.* Homewood, Ill.: Richard D. Irwin, Inc., 1947.

Selected Bibliography

Work Simplification, Time Study, and Plant Layout

Harrington, Carl C. (ed.), *Materials Handling Manual*. New York: Conover-Mast Publications, Inc., 1952.

Materials Handling Institute, Inc., *Modern Methods of Materials Handling*. New York: Prentice-Hall, Inc., 1951.

Morrow, R. L., *Motion Economy and Work Measurement*, 2nd ed. New York: Ronald Press, 1957.

Niebel, B. W., *Motion and Time Study*, 3rd ed. Homewood, Ill.: Richard D. Irwin, Inc., 1962.

Shubin, John A., and Huxley Madeheim, *Plant Layout—Developing and Improving Manufacturing Plants*. New York: Prentice-Hall, Inc., 1951.

Quality Control and Inspection

Duncan, Acheson J., *Quality Control and Industrial Statistics*, rev. ed. Homewood, Ill.: Richard D. Irwin, Inc., 1959.

Juran, J. M. (ed.), *Quality Control Handbook*, 2nd ed. New York: McGraw-Hill Book Co., Inc., 1962.

Kennedy, Clifford W., *Quality Control Methods*. New York: Prentice-Hall, Inc., 1948.

Thompson, J. E., *Inspection Organization and Methods*. New York: McGraw-Hill Book Co., Inc., 1950.

Purchasing

Heinritz, Stuart F., *Purchasing*, 3rd ed. New York: Prentice-Hall, Inc., 1959.

Lewis, Howard T., *Procurement Principles and Cases*, rev. ed. Homewood, Ill.: Richard D. Irwin, Inc., 1952.

Westing, J. H., and I. V. Fine, *Industrial Purchasing*, 2nd ed. New York: John Wiley & Sons, Inc., 1961.

Production Planning and Control

Landy, Thomas M., *Production Planning and Control*. New York: McGraw-Hill Book Co., Inc., 1950.

Moore, Franklin G., *Production Control*, 2nd ed. New York: McGraw-Hill, 1959.

Marketing and Selling

Alexander, R. S., J. S. Cross, and R. M. Cunningham, *Industrial Marketing*, rev. ed. Homewood, Ill.: Richard D. Irwin, Inc., 1961.

Bakken, Henry H., *Theory of Markets and Marketing*. Madison, Wis.: Mimir Publishers, Inc., 1953.

Canfield, Bertrand R., *Sales Administration Principles and Problems*, 4th ed. New York: Prentice-Hall, Inc., 1961.

Converse, P. D., H. W. Huegy, and R. V. Mitchel, *The Elements of Marketing*, 6th ed. New York: Prentice-Hall, Inc., 1958.

Kleppner, Otto, *Advertising Procedure*, 4th ed. New York: Prentice-Hall, Inc., 1950.

Lewis, Charles W., *Essentials of Selling*, 2nd ed. New York: Prentice-Hall, Inc., 1952.

Industrial Relations and Compensation

Belcher, D. W., *Wage and Salary Administration*, 2nd ed. New York: Prentice-Hall, Inc., 1962.

Blake, R. P. (ed.), *Industrial Safety*, 2nd ed. New York: Prentice-Hall, 1953.

Dunlop, John T., and James J. Healy, *Collective Bargaining*, rev. ed. Homewood, Ill.: Richard D. Irwin, Inc., 1953.

Gardner, B. B., and D. Moore, *Human Relations in Industry*, 3rd ed. Homewood, Ill.: Richard D. Irwin, Inc., 1955.

Ghiselli, Edwin E., and Clarence W. Brown, *Personnel and Industrial Psychology*, 2nd ed. New York: McGraw-Hill Book Co., Inc., 1955.

Scott, W. D., R. C. Clothier, and W. R. Spriegel, *Personnel Management*, 6th ed. New York: McGraw-Hill Book Co., Inc., 1961.

Yoder, Dale, *Personnel Principles and Policies*, 2nd ed. New York: Prentice-Hall, Inc., 1959.

Office Management

Maze, C. L. (ed.), *Office Management—A Handbook*. New York: Ronald Press, 1947.

Wylie, Harry L., and Robert P. Brecht, *Office Organization and Management*, 3rd ed. New York: Prentice-Hall, Inc., 1953.

Business Finance, Budgeting, and Costs

Bonneville, J. H., and L. E. Dewey, *Organizing and Financing Business*, 6th ed. New York: Prentice-Hall, Inc., 1959.

Gerstenberg, Charles W., *Financial Organization and Management of Business*, 4th ed. New York: Prentice-Hall, Inc., 1959.

Heckert, J. B., *Business Budgeting and Control*, 2nd ed. New York: Ronald Press, 1955.

Prather, Charles L., *Financing Business Firms*, rev. ed. Homewood, Ill.: Richard D. Irwin, Inc., 1961.

Business Journals and Periodicals

Advanced Management	*Mill and Factory*
Dun's Review and Modern Industry	*Modern Management*
Factory Management and Maintenance	*Monthly Labor Review*
General Management Series	*Personnel*
Harvard Business Review	*Personnel Journal*
Journal of Business	*Purchasing*
Management Review	*Survey of Current Business*

Final Examination

(After you have completed all three parts, turn to p. 360 to check your answers)

1. True-False. Indicate your answer by placing T or F on the line at the right of the statement.

1. Scientific management evolved early in the Industrial Revolution. ___

2. The scientific managerial survey can be applied to all managerial problems. ___

3. An individual proprietorship ordinarily has a better credit standing than a partnership of the same size and financial circumstances. ___

4. An officer of a corporation who makes a contract for the firm is personally liable for the corporation's obligations under the contract. ___

5. A co-operative is a nonprofit organization that provides goods or services to its members at cost. ___

6. The economies of large-scale operation is the sole factor accounting for the growth of business combinations. ___

7. Mergers and holding companies are illegal in America. ___

8. Holding companies invariably achieve the economies inherent in vertical combinations. ___

9. Corporations can enlarge their capital holdings or expand capacity only through the sales of securities to investors. ___

10. The shorter the time cycle of production and the more rapid the turnover in the sales of goods, the smaller the need for working capital. ___

11. A firm can often closely estimate the amount of fixed and working capital that it needs to establish a branch plant. ___

12. Watered stock usually implies overcapitalization. ___

13. The line type of organization achieves specialization in labor as well as in management. ___

14. The primary strength of the line-and-staff type of organization is that it can achieve efficiency through specialization and control through clear-cut and undivided delegation of authority and responsibility. ___

350

15. The company organization structure should always be designed to fit the talents and personalities of the executives. ____

16. Policies should be formulated only after an organization structure has been set up and the firm established. ____

17. Policies, committees, and standard procedures are effective means for achieving co-ordinated business operation. ____

18. Determination of levels of authority is the basis for the organizational hierarchy. ____

19. The procedural steps for setting up an organization structure are applicable to large as well as small firms. ____

20. Because the magnitude of seasonal variations can not be gauged in advance, methods for adjusting to seasonal variations should not be considered until after the firm has been in operation for a time. ____

21. Interchangeability of parts among product models not only reduces investment in plant but also makes for continuous use of machinery. ____

22. Parts and standard supply items used in small quantities are usually cheaper to buy than to fabricate. ____

23. The first step in reducing business risk is to take out the widest possible business insurance coverage. ____

24. "Percentage of net sales receipts" is ordinarily a more accurate basis for measuring profitability than "rate of return on investment." ____

25. All location factors should receive equal consideration in selecting a location. ____

26. If various locations have comparable unit costs of production and distribution, the location requiring the least investment should ordinarily be chosen. ____

27. Decentralization of location is always the best policy for an expanding enterprise. ____

28. An "industrial district" usually offers the advantages of low property taxes. ____

29. American industry spends approximately the same amount of funds for pure research as it does for industrial research. ____

30. Trade associations conduct research that does not affect the relative competitive position of the member companies. ____

31. Since it is a result of chance and inspiration, the inventiveness of a scientist can not be directed by management toward particular fields of technological development. ____

32. It is not uncommon to find two or more forms of technological advance in a single inventive development. ____

33. The profitability of an invention can not be evaluated until commercial testing—the product produced and sold. ____

34. The engineering department should always have final authority for selecting products and models to be manufactured. ____

35. Products should be designed to achieve consumer acceptance irrespective of the cost of manufacture. ____

36. Responsibility for all routine product-design changes should be centralized in the engineering department. ____

37. Whereas product simplification eliminates uneconomical variety, diversification adds new products, styles, and sizes. ____

38. Although a product-simplification program reduces the need for fixed capital (machinery) it does not reduce the need for working capital. ____

39. The purchase of machinery for replacement often gives rise to "capital-savings" technology, which permits output of more goods per dollar invested. ____

40. For mass production, product-design specifications (blueprints, bills of materials) and projected volume of output determine the kind of equipment selected. ____

41. When alternative machines are suitable, the most economical machine is always selected on the basis of the "lowest initial investment." ____

42. "Retooling" is the provision of new jigs, fixtures, dies, and gauges for the output of a new model. ____

43. It is sometimes practical to adapt or design conveyors for pacing work, performance of operations, and temporary storage and inspection in transit. ____

44. The only justification for multistory factory buildings is the possible use of gravity handling of materials. ____

45. A single-story building is generally more adaptable than a multistory building for layout purposes and for ease of plant revision and expansion. ____

46. Good lighting achieves equal and uniform illumination of all work areas irrespective of the type of operations performed. ____

47. Repainting of plant and office interiors with a proper combination of colors can increase intensity of illumination and reduce glare, but can not improve "perceptive seeing." ____

48. When a plant needs steam for processing purposes, it is generally cheaper for the firm to produce power than to buy it. ____

49. The "load" factor of a plant is the ratio of average power to the peak power used during a given period. ____

50. Since they both deal with technical matters, plant engineering and product engineering should always be combined in one department. ____

51. Time standards and incentive wages are not suitable for any type of maintenance work. ____

52. Since machine failures can not be avoided, there is little that management can do to assure continuity of production. ____

53. Budgets are practical means for planning and controlling maintenance work. ____

54. An analyst should use cost data to direct his efforts to those phases of business where big improvements can be made. ____

55. Facilities and departments expensive to operate should be singled out for improvement before less costly activities are analyzed. ____

56. The flow process chart is a graphic tool useful only for the analysis of manufacturing processes. ____

57. An "operation analysis" is a disciplined procedure that subjects a machine or workplace to a detailed improvement study. ____

58. During operation analysis jigs and fixtures should be studied and improved before the adoption of more suitable raw material is considered. ____

59. A "motion study" of a work cycle should be made only after improvements based on operation analysis have been achieved. ____

60. Motion study raises employee productivity and reduces fatigue by selecting the fewest basic motions, achieving rhythm and automaticity, and improving working conditions through proper lighting, ventilation, and reduction of noise and vibration. ____

61. Micromotion study achieves its biggest improvements in repetitive manufacture where many operators do identical work. ____

62. Time study is useful only for wage-incentive purposes. ____

63. Time study is more applicable to repetitive than to job-order manufacture. ____

64. Work simplification should be completed and jobs standardized before the best results from time study for wage purposes can be expected. ____

65. The fastest worker performing the task should always be selected for the setting of a standard time. ____

66. In setting the standard time for a task, the analyst should include allowances for fatigue and unavoidable delay. ____

67. Under the right conditions and with ample data, time standards can be predetermined "synthetically" without actual clocking of tasks. ____

68. Production methods can best be improved only while taking time studies. ____

69. Nonrepetitive intermittent processes are common in oil refineries and cement plants. ____

70. It is best to select equipment in conjunction with the development of a plant layout plan. ____

71. The plant site and type of building should always be selected and acquired before a layout study is undertaken. ____

72. Process layouts are suited to job-order manufacture whereas product layouts are suited to repetitive manufacture. ____

73. In principle, process grouping of machinery and work stations achieves flexibility at the sacrifice of economical handling. ____

74. Operation analysis and motion study can often eliminate bottlenecks without need for purchase of machinery. ____

75. Product simplification, work simplification, plant layout, and good incentive-wage plans often substantially increase output capacity without need for investment in plant. ____

76. The inspection function should always be set up as an independent department under the manufacturing division. ____

77. High precision inspection can be successfully carried out only through the centralized (crib) plan. ____

78. Centralized inspection is more suitable for surgical equipment manufacture whereas floor inspection is more suitable for locomotive manufacture. ____

79. For economical production the percentage of rejects and scrap should always be kept at the absolute minimum. ____

80. The chief inspector should have primary jurisdiction over the setting of quality standards. ____

81. Statistical quality control techniques can minimize substandard work and inspection costs more easily for repetitive than for job-order production. ____

82. The purchasing agent should have the authority to decide "what," "where," and "when" to buy. ____

83. "Hand-to-mouth" purchasing should always be employed during the upswing period of the business cycle. ____

84. Under a "decentralized storekeeping" system several employees working out of one stockroom are responsible for the issue and control of all items. ____

85. Under the "classification system" stores items are arranged and placed in the stockroom in the order corresponding to the numeric or to the mnemonic method of identification. ____

86. The LIFO method takes the current cost (purchase price) of materials for the computation of the unit cost of the product. ____

87. The "ordering point" indicates the minimum quantity to which stock may fall without need for replenishment. ____

88. The taking of physical inventory is necessary under perpetual inventory systems. ____

89. A single "ideal" production-planning-and-control system can be designed to apply to all types of manufacture. ____

90. Routing is primarily concerned with the relative time at which production is to occur. _____

91. It is usually impossible to ascertain potential demand for a new product. _____

92. A firm's price-fixing power and market control do not guarantee profits, since monopolistic as well as competitive industry sustains losses from declining demand during recessions. _____

93. When firms consistently employ cost-plus pricing (i.e., always add the same markup), they ignore elasticity of demand and the influence of volume of production on unit costs. _____

94. If a firm has a good product that is priced right, the marketing outlets to be used become unimportant. _____

95. "Selective selling" can increase sales while lowering distribution costs. _____

96. Selling through middlemen gives a manufacturer quicker turnover on working capital than selling directly to consumers. _____

97. Large expenditures for advertising by all firms during a depression is one sure way of increasing consumer wants and creating market demand and thus re-establishing prosperity. _____

98. The growing mechanization of industry is decreasing the importance of personnel management. _____

99. Because of their confidential nature, personnel policy statements should not be distributed to employees. _____

100. Personnel departments in large-scale industry should take over foremen's responsibility for carrying out personnel policies and procedures. _____

101. The final choice of men for work in the factory should always be made by the personnel department. _____

102. Morale may vary widely without any change in wage levels. _____

103. To be effective, employee recreation and service programs must be initiated and operated solely by management. _____

104. "Accident prone" individuals are often unconsciously motivated toward mishaps. _____

105. Though an employer pays high wages, his labor costs per unit may be low because of high worker productivity. _____

106. Job evaluation studies deal with the occupation as well as with the employee holding the position. _____

107. Separate job evaluation studies should be conducted for salaried employees and wage employees. _____

108. A single wage survey should be conducted for both salaried and wage employees and results presented on one chart. _____

109. Unions ordinarily prefer payment on the basis of a "wage-rate range" rather than on the basis of a "flat wage rate." _____

355

110. "Key bargains" in labor-management agreements establishing wage patterns in leading industries contribute to uniformity of wage levels in allied industries. ____

111. Incentive-wage payment is suitable for work which is readily measurable, where a close causal relationship exists between effort and output, and when quality will not be affected or sacrificed. ____

112. Incentives are more applicable to direct than to indirect labor. ____

113. Incentive-wage plans are best suited to mass production where work is mechanically paced and precison products are manufactured. ____

114. The controller should have jurisdiction over both intra- and interdepartmental records and clerical activities. ____

115. Work simplification can not be applied to office work. ____

116. The company internal auditor examines the firm's accounts and financial statements in the interest of stockholders. ____

117. The credit manager should always maintain credit standards that keep bad debts at an absolute minimum. ____

118. Cost accounting should be used only for computing the unit cost of the product. ____

119. Cost accounting is applicable only to manufacturing. ____

120. The machine-hour cost method of distributing overhead should ordinarily be selected when investment in equipment is heavy and operating costs are high. ____

121. Variable costs are constant per unit of output. ____

122. The "principle of exceptions" can be applied when standard costs are used. ____

123. The computation of the unit cost of the product is ordinarily more difficult for job-order than for repetitive manufacture. ____

124. The master budget is a consolidation of separate budgets covering various departments and phases of the business. ____

125. Variable budgets are more useful than fixed budgets for most business enterprises. ____

126. The length of the budget period should always coincide with the period for which financial statements are made. ____

127. A firm which adopts a budget system should introduce it in all departments simultaneously. ____

128. The financial budget should be prepared before the sales and the manufacturing budgets are prepared. ____

129. Break-even charts are used to forecast the company sales volume and the trend in prices. ____

130. Break-even charts should always use "dollar volume of sales" to measure output. ____

II. Multiple Choice. On the line after each sentence place the letter representing the phrase which makes the statement correct.

131. The firm's internal organization structure often needs revision because of: (a) the death of a key executive, (b) nepotism, (c) excessive competition, (d) seasonal variations in demand, (e) the changing scope of business operation. ____

132. The responsibility of the foreman is to: (a) maintain the required finished inventory, (b) direct the work of operators and fulfill output schedules, (c) raise the quality of work, (d) control and compile costs. ____

133. The function of inspection is to: (a) improve quality standards, (b) check work against specifications, (c) salvage poor work, (d) raise employee workmanship. ____

134. The responsibility of the PPC department is to: (a) offset seasonal variations, (b) keep work in process at a minimum, (c) formulate production policy, (d) schedule output to fulfill sales needs, (e) avoid inventory losses. ____

135. The conference method is most suitable for training: (a) plant technicians, (b) clerical workers, (c) machine operators, (d) supervisors, (e) new sales personnel. ____

136. Total current assets less current liabilities is: (a) fixed capital, (b) net capital, (c) investment capital, (d) working capital, (e) idle surplus capital. ____

137. The Gantt chart is a control device for: (a) maintaining quality, (b) arranging floor plans, (c) machine-loading, (d) sales forecasting. ____

138. Personnel problems exist: (a) only in large firms, (b) in all firms regardless of size, (c) only in firms that have no personnel departments, (d) only in unionized firms. ____

139. Office routines are set up when work is: (a) difficult, (b) recurring, (c) monotonous, (d) interdepartmental. ____

140. Planning and scheduling office work require a knowledge of: (a) accounting, (b) statistical control methods, (c) job evaluation, (d) work measurement. ____

141. Long-range company budgeting is difficult because of: (a) changes in internal organization structure, (b) unanticipated union wage demands, (c) hampering government regulations, (d) inability to forecast costs and sales volume far in advance. ____

142. A company break-even chart is easy to prepare: (a) for single-plant firms, (b) when product-mix is comparatively steady, (c) when standard cost figures are comparatively accurate, (d) when input costs and selling prices are comparatively steady, (e) when all the foregoing conditions are present.

III. Matching. Identify each item by placing the appropriate letter on space at the left of the item.

143–148.

_____ Company policies
_____ Functionalized activities
_____ Staff men
_____ Standard procedures
_____ Committees
_____ Organization charts

a. promote co-ordinated team work
b. promote specialization
c. stipulate aims and objectives
d. promote executive effectiveness
e. show scope, lines, and levels of authority
f. achieve vertical combination
g. implement the "principle of exceptions"

149–155.

_____ Product simplification
_____ Plot plan
_____ Flow process chart
_____ Flow diagram
_____ Operation analysis
_____ Motion study
_____ Time study

a. break-even analysis
b. movement of items on floor plan
c. amount and variety of inventories
d. activities in manufacturing cycle
e. site utilization
f. work cycle
g. task standards
h. workplace and machine station

156–162.

_____ Job analysis
_____ Job specification
_____ Job evaluation
_____ Merit rating
_____ Wage survey
_____ Incentive wage
_____ Supplementary pay

a. wage rate differentials
b. prevailing occupation pay levels
c. shift differentials
d. compensation on basis of output
e. study of an occupation
f. job composition
g. pay increases and promotions
h. payroll and labor budget

163–168.

_____ Synthetic process
_____ Special-purpose facilities
_____ Balanced capacity
_____ Product diversification
_____ Job-order manufacture
_____ Tooling up

a. assembly-type production
b. mass production
c. model change
d. backlog
e. inventory valuation
f. elimination of bottlenecks
g. utilization of idle capacity

169–174.

_____ Materials control	a. sequence of machine operations
_____ Routing	b. production order follow-through
_____ Scheduling	c. work simplification
_____ Dispatching	d. progress of production
_____ Control boards	e. rush order and shortage
_____ Expediting	f. perpetual inventory
	g. work priority and output time

175–180.

_____ Secular trend affects	a. dividend policy
_____ Cyclical fluctuation affects	b. location policy and growth
_____ Seasonal variation affects	c. research policy
_____ Profit fluctuation affects	d. equipment replacement policy
_____ Technological change affects	e. product planning
_____ Consumer wants affect	f. working-capital policy
	g. public relations policy

ANSWERS TO FINAL EXAMINATION

1. F	36. T	71. F	106. F	141. (b)	(g)
2. T	37. T	72. T	107. T	142. (e)	(b)
3. F	38. F	73. T	108. F	143–148.	(d)
4. F	39. T	74. T	109. F	(c)	(e)
5. T	40. T	75. T	110. T	(b)	175–180.
6. F	41. F	76. F	111. T	(d)	(b)
7. F	42. T	77. F	112. T	(g)	(d)
8. F	43. T	78. T	113. F	(a)	(f)
9. F	44. F	79. F	114. F	(e)	(a)
10. T	45. T	80. F	115. F	149–155.	(c)
11. T	46. F	81. T	116. F	(c)	(e)
12. T	47. F	82. F	117. F	(e)	
13. F	48. T	83. F	118. F	(d)	
14. T	49. T	84. F	119. F	(b)	
15. F	50. F	85. T	120. T	(h)	
16. F	51. F	86. T	121. T	(f)	
17. T	52. F	87. T	122. T	(g)	
18. T	53. T	88. T	123. T	156–162.	
19. T	54. T	89. F	124. T	(e)	
20. F	55. T	90. F	125. T	(f)	
21. T	56. F	91. F	126. F	(a)	
22. T	57. T	92. T	127. F	(g)	
23. F	58. F	93. T	128. F	(b)	
24. F	59. T	94. F	129. F	(d)	
25. F	60. T	95. T	130. F	(c)	
26. T	61. T	96. T	131. (e)	163–168.	
27. F	62. F	97. F	132. (b)	(a)	
28. T	63. T	98. F	133. (b)	(b)	
29. F	64. T	99. F	134. (d)	(f)	
30. T	65. F	100. F	135. (d)	(g)	
31. F	66. T	101. F	136. (d)	(d)	
32. T	67. T	102. T	137. (c)	(c)	
33. F	68. F	103. F	138. (b)	169–174.	
34. F	69. F	104. T	139. (b)	(f)	
35. F	70. T	105. T	140. (d)	(a)	

Index

361

Index

17; trade associations, 19; trust, 18; vertical, 19

Business failures, 51, 56

Business functions: administrative, 5, 31, 331; departmental, 31–34; managerial, 5–6, 31

Business objectives. *See* Management decisions

Business promotion and planning: appraising profitability, 53–54; business adaptability, 58; business environment, 49–51, 56–57; continuous planning, 55–56; design of products, 51–52; economic analysis and forecast, 49–51; financing, 22–23, 53, 57; launching the firm, 55; objectives and scope of, 51; product and market analysis, 47–48; selecting processes and layout, 53; selecting size and location, 52; sources and reduction of risks, 56–59; survey procedure for, 46; time of entry, 50. *Also see* Management decisions

Business research and forecasting. *See* Economic analysis for business

Capacity, 52, 89, 146, 151, 156, 202, 212, 213, 214, 217, 221

Capital: defined, 21; intermediate, 22; long-term, 22; short-term, 22. *Also see* Investment

Capital stock, 24–25

Capital structure and corporate control. *See* Financing a business

Carriers, 180

Carrying charge, inventory, 185, 209

Cashier, 324

Charts. *See* Forms and charts

Classification and identification: classes of inventory, 185; mnemonic system, 186; numeric system, 186; in storeroom layout, 193; symbolization, 185–186

CIO, 256

Collective bargaining. *See* Labor relations

Combinations. *See* Business combinations

Committees: design and control of, 32, 38–39; for budgeting, 339; for research, 71; for standards, 82; for wage administration, 278

Commodity exchange, 175n

Communication, media of, 255

Company (corporation) organization: financing procedure, 22–26; holding company, 18–19; illustration of, 30–34; legal formation of, 15–16

Competition, 48–49, 71, 238–239

Conciliation, 257n

Construction of buildings, 99–100

Consultants, management, 5–6

Continuous process, 197

Control through reports and standards, 316–317

Controllership: breakdown of department, 32; divisions—accounting, 319–324, auditing, 323, budgeting, 324, cost accounting, 323, credit and collections, 324, general office, 317, tax, 323; financial statements, 319–323; functions of, 316; records and reports, 316–318; role of, in budgeting, 339–340; survey procedure for setting up, 315–317

Conversion, 56, 225n

"Conveyorization," 94

Co-operative, 14–15

Corporation. *See* Company organization

Cost-accounting control: breakdown charts, 90–91, 327; in break-even analysis, 341–345; for budgeting, 333–334; classification of costs, 326–327; cost studies—advertising, 252, equipment selection, 88, job-order estimates, 221–223, location, 65–66, lot-size computation, 209, methods analysis, 124, 325, parts (buying or making), 52–53, 204, power source, 107, pricing standard products, 240–241, process development, 77, product development, 72, 74, quantity to buy, 186–187, sales, 254, work routing, 207; decision-making costs, 329–330; defined, 324; inventory evaluation, 187–188; maintenance control, 119; manufacturing cost statement, 319–320; overhead distribution, 327–328; procedure for program, 325–328; standard costs, 328–329

Cost and financial control. *See* Budgets

Index

through research, 72–77; risk of, 56–57

Testing laboratory, 171–172

Therbligs, 128

Time study: allowances, 139–140; analysis during, 138; breakdown of cycle, 137; clocking, 138; computation of time, 139–140; in equipment selection, 89; introduction of, 135; leveling, 139; maintenance of times, 141; operation time study, 140; procedure for, 137; production time study, 141; stop watch, 135–136; synthetic time study, 141; types of, 137; purposes of, 134

Tolerances, 162–163

Tool control: equipment for, 193–194; symbolization, 185–186; system for, 191–192; tool-crib layout and system, 191–194; tooling up and retooling, 86, 190, 225n

Top management, 5–6, 27, 31, 35. *Also see* Management decisions

Trade associations, 19, 79

Trade-marks, 48n

Traffic management, 179–180

Training. *See* Employee Training

Transportation, 62, 177. *Also see* Materials handling

Treasurer, 31, 32, 337

Uniform cost accounting, 325

Utility company, 107

Variances, 329

Ventilation, 103

Vertical integration, 19–20

Wage and salary administration: and ability to pay, 295; and cost of living, 294–295; job evaluation methods, 279–286; job specifications, 281, 285; key jobs, 281n; maintenance of, 292; merit rating, 296–300; objectives and policies of, 277–278; occupation differentials, 279–280, 288; periodic wage adjustments, 293–296; prevailing wages, 286–288, 294; role of incentives, 291–292 (*also see* Wage incentives); setting wage levels, 286–

291; supplementary pay, 291; survey procedure for, 277, 279; union role in, 279, 290n, 294–305; wage survey, 286–289; wage-bargaining criteria, 294–296

Wage incentives: analysis for, 310–311; component elements, 302–303; day rate *vs.* incentives, 300–302; essentials for plan, 309–310; group plans, 307–308; for indirect labor, 302n; "lump-of-labor" attitude, 313; prerequisites for, 309; selection or design of, 311–312; survey procedures for, 308; types, 302–308; union attitude, 302

Wage rates in industry, 288–289

Wage system and problems. *See* Wage and salary administration

War, effects on business, 4n, 56, 79

Work simplification: benefits of, 123; cost guides to, 124; industrial engineering function, 122–123; in materials-handling survey, 93; methods-time measurement, 132; micromotion study, 132; motion study procedure (*see* Motion study); for office work, 318–319; operation analysis procedure, 126–127, 156; for plant layout, 153–157; preliminary studies, 124–125; priority in studies, 122; process analysis and charts, 125, 126, 147, 154; related to—job analysis, 280n, incentive wages, 309, time study, 134–135; scope of, 123, 125; survey procedure for, 123–129

Working capital: affected by—production planning, 196–197, purchasing, 174–177, simplification, 82, turnover, 24; borrowing, 22, 25–26; budgetary control of, 337–338; computing need for, 23

Working conditions: air conditioning and ventilation, 103–106; benefits resulting from motion study, 132; and climate, 63; employee services, 270–271; health and safety, 271–275; layout of service activities, 151–152; lighting effectiveness, 100–103; noise control, 106

Workmen's compensation laws, 272n